Patrick White

History of Clare and the Dalcassian Clans of Tipperary Limerick, and Galway

Patrick White

History of Clare and the Dalcassian Clans of Tipperary Limerick, and Galway

ISBN/EAN: 9783337326142

Printed in Europe, USA, Canada, Australia, Japan

Cover: Foto ©ninafisch / pixelio.de

More available books at **www.hansebooks.com**

HISTORY OF CLARE

AND THE

Dalcassian Clans

OF

TIPPERARY, LIMERICK, AND GALWAY

"na céada ran g-cat; na veigeanaca ar."
"THE FIRST INTO BATTLE, THE LAST OUT OF IT."

WITH AN ANCIENT AND A MODERN MAP

BY THE

VERY REV. P. WHITE, PP., VG.

DUBLIN
M. H. GILL & SON
50 UPPER O'CONNELL STREET
1893

TO

THE DESCENDANTS

OF THE

Dalcassian Clans

AT HOME AND ABROAD

THIS BOOK

IS RESPECTFULLY DEDICATED BY

THE AUTHOR.

PREFACE.

THIS work must not be criticised too severely. It was written under many disadvantages, and cannot be free of mistakes. The Author had solely in view to link together scattered records, and present an outline of the march of life in Thomond during all the past centuries. He felt, as many others must have felt, the need of something like this, and offers it more as a kind of elementary history for general readers than an attempt at erudite research.

His acknowledgments for valuable aid rendered during its composition are thankfully tendered to Mrs. Morgan John O'Connell of Ballylean, P. J. Ryan, Esq., M.R.I.A., Dublin; P. W. Joyce, Esq., LL.D., M.R.I.A., Dublin; and Mr. John O'Brien of Miltown-Malbay.

The Maps are enlarged from one edited by P. W. Joyce, Esq., LL.D., M.R.I.A., for Messrs. G. Philip & Sons.

CONTENTS.

CHAPTER I.

Extent — Population — Geographical Features — Natural Advantages—Scenery—Soil—Lakes—Minerals—Tuameens, near Tulla—Atlantic Ocean and Shannon—Environment—Moher Cliffs—Submergement at Milltown-Malbay—Kilkee—Bishop's Island—Loop Head—Carrigaholt Castle—Iniscatha—St. Senan's Island—Monasteries—Castles—Ennis and Quin Abbeys—Bunratty—Falls of Doonas, Killaloe — Kincora — Holy Island—Burren—Abbey of Corcomroe—Cell and Legend of St. Colman MacDuagh—Lisdoonvarna, ... 1

CHAPTER II.

Earliest known History—By whom peopled—Race of Eber—Mogha Nuadhat—Division of Ireland into Leathmogha and Leathcuin—Luighaidh Meann, descended from Ossian, drives the Firbolgs out of Clare—Tuadh Mhumhain—Thomond—North Munster—Will of Oilioll Oluim—Origin and Division of the Thomond Clans—Their present Descendants—Crimhthan, King of Munster, becomes King of Ireland—Is poisoned at Cratloe—Conal Eachluaith — Niall of the Nine Hostages — Exclusion of the Dalcassians from Sovereignty, ... 11

CHAPTER III.

FROM A.D. 432 TO 554.

Christianity introduced — St. Benignus, Nephew and Successor of St. Patrick, preaches in Thomond and Kerry — St. Patrick blesses Clare from Knoc Patrick, near Foynes—Baptises there People from Corcovaskin—Prophesies the Birth of St. Senan—Incidents in the Life of this Saint—His Labours—His Death and Burial—St. Ruadan, Abbot of Lorha, in East Thomond, curses the Ard-Righ and his Palace of Tara—Its Abandonment, 24

CHAPTER IV.

FROM 554 TO 800.

Dearth of Historical Records—Mode of election of Chief, Prince, and King—Their Privileges and Tributes—Boromean Tax—Its Abolition at the instance of St. Molaing of Ferns—Influence of Christianity on the Arts and Customs of the People—Learning fostered—Long Peace, ... 31

CHAPTER V.

FROM 800 TO 952.

Earthquake in West Clare—Danish Invasion—Cormac MacCuilenan—Flahertach, Abbot of Iniscatha—Both defeat Flann, the Ard-Righ, at Tullamore—Defeated near Carlow—Cormac surrenders the Crown of Munster to Lorcan, Prince of Thomond—His Death and Character—Callaghan, King of Cashel—Brian Boroimhe born—His father, Ceinnidigh, defeated and slain by Callaghan, 42

CHAPTER VI.

FROM 952 TO 1014.

Mahon, Brian's elder brother, becomes King of Munster—His Murder—Brian succeeds—Takes Vengeance on the Murderers—His Character—His Victories—Defeated at Nenagh by the Ard-Righ Malachy—Deposes Malachy—Wise Administration of the Kingdom—Clontarf—His Death, ... 49

CHAPTER VII.

FROM 1014 TO 1086.

Dissensions among the Victors—Brian's son Donogh procures the Murder of Teigue, his own Brother—He becomes King of Munster—Claims Supreme Rule—Parliament at Killaloe—Donogh flies to Rome with the Regalia of Ireland—Turlogh succeeds—His Exploits, ... 72

CHAPTER VIII.

FROM 1086 TO 1171.

Mortogh Mor, last Dalcassian Ard-Righ—His rival, Turlogh O'Connor of Connaught—His Defeats and Death—Conor, son of Diarmid, elected—Death of Ceallagh (St. Celsus)—Building of Cormac's Chapel at Cashel—Contests on Lough Derg and the Western Coast—Another Turlogh succeeds Conor—Diarmid MacMurrough

—St. Malachi—National Councils—O'Ruarck, Prince of Breffny—Expulsion of Diarmid, father-in-law of Turlogh — English Invasion, ... 88

CHAPTER IX.

FROM 1171 TO 1194.

Life in Thomond before the Norman Invasion—Battle of Thurles—Defeat of the Normans—Alleged Submission of Roderick, the Ard-Righ, to Henry II.—Capture of Limerick—Recovered and burned by Donal O'Brien—Defeat of the Eoghanachts—Battle of the Curlieu Mountains — Pursuit of the English—Second Defeat of Thurles – Death of Donalmor, ... 109

CHAPTER X.

FROM 1194 TO 1267.

Capture of Limerick—Surrender of Cork—English Garrison driven out of Munster—Dissension again—Donogh Cairbreac O'Brien allows the building of a Castle at Killaloe—The Clans resist and drive out the English — Donogh surrenders to King John—Permits again the erection of a Castle at Killaloe and Roscrea—Abandons Kincora for Clonroad — Rise of Ennis — O'Heney, Bishop of Killaloe, at the Fourth Council of Lateran—MacNamaras and O'Shaughnessys—Clare invaded—Donogh gives Hostages—Conor succeeds, and founds the Franciscan Monastery at Ennis in 1247—Drives out the English from all Thomond in 1257—Conference of Irish Princes at Caeluisce (Ballyshannon)—Another Invasion of Thomond — Defeat at Kilbarron, near Feacle—Battle at Suidene, in Burren—Defeat and Death of Conor-na-Suidene, ... 122

CHAPTER XI.

FROM 1267 TO 1343.

Clare Castle—Another Invasion of Clare—Brian Rua, the reigning Prince, deposed by his uncle MacNamara—He instals Turlogh, son of Teigne Caeluisce—Richard de Clare unites with Brian Rua—Builds the Castle of Bunratty — Murders Brian Rua—Consequences of the Murder — Intestine Conflicts — The *Cathreim Turlogha*—Battle of Dysart O'Dea, ... 130

CHAPTER XII.

FROM 1343 TO 1500.

Another Brian—The Black Death—Brian murdered by the "Clann Keogh" — Revenge — O'Briens and MacNamaras defeat the

English at Aenagh, on the Maigue—Ulic de Burgho defeated by the MacNamaras—Marries a daughter of the reigning Prince, and assumes the Irish title of MacWilliam Oughther — Submission to Richard II.—MacNamara builds Quin Abbey—Peace —MacMahon, attacked by Teigue O'Brien and the O'Malleys, defeats them—Teigue brings all Leinster and Munster to submission—Covets the dignity of Ard-Righ—Dies 1467—The Earl of Kildare, Lord-Deputy, invades Clare—Is defeated at Ballyhicky, near Quin, ... 141

CHAPTER XIII.

Internal Condition of Thomond at this period—Its Religion—Its Politics—The Manners and Customs of its People, . . 153

CHAPTER XIV.

FROM 1500 TO 1540.

Disastrous Battle of Cnoctuagh, near Galway—Reversed at Monabraher, near Limerick—O'Daly of Corcomroe—Battle of Knockaroe, near Strabane—Defeat at Camur on the Suir—Earl of Kildare after Capture of Maynooth takes refuge in Clare— Portcroissi, above Castleconnell — Lord Grey in Clare — Submission but no Occupation, ... 160

CHAPTER XV.

FROM 1540 TO 1559.

Henry VIII.—Surrender of O'Brien, MacNamara, O'Grady, and O'Shaughnessy for English Titles — Plunder of the Clans— Chiefs bribed by Gifts of Suppressed Religious Houses—Struggle to maintain Brehon Law—Battle of Spancil Hill, A.D. 1559, . 173

CHAPTER XVI.

FROM 1559 TO 1576.

Internal Conflicts—The Castles of Ballyalla and Ballycar captured by the Earl of Thomond and the English—Introduction of Clan Sheehy and Clan Sweeney—Subdivision of Clare between the Contending Parties—Execution at Tuaclea, near Lisdoonvarna— Morogh of Ara, the stripling, first Protestant Bishop of Killaloe— Malachy O'Molony, Cornelius O'Mulryan (Maol-Ryan), Catholic Bishops—First Assize at Ennis Monastery, A.D. 1570, . . 183

CHAPTER XVII.

FROM 1576 TO 1590.

Clare, annexed to Connaught in 1569, is reannexed to Munster in 1576—The Dalcassians for the first time consent to pay Tribute—How Clare and Tipperary became at last an English Possession—The last Tanist of Thomond—The Protestant Earl of Thomond cuts asunder the Allied Northern and Southern Catholics—Donogh of Ennistymon, ancestor of the Dromoland O'Briens, hanged at Limerick, A.D. 1582—Fate of Donogh Beg O'Brien—Tripartite Deed—MacNamara and other Chiefs refuse to sign—Stout Resistance of Mahon O'Brien of Cluanoon (ancestor of the Clare Mahons)—Owners of Castles in Clare at this period—Suppressed Abbeys, ... 192

CHAPTER XVIII.

FROM 1590 TO 1602.

The Earl of Thomond joins the English in an Attack on the Northern Princes—Driven back—Besieged in Armagh and Newry—O'Brien of Ballycorick hanged—Defeat at Ballyshannon—Uprising in Clare—O'Donnell's Raid in Clare—Sieges of Carrigaholt, Dunbeg, and Dunmore—Second Raid of O'Donnell, A.D. 1600—The Earl of Thomond reduces Clare to submission, ... 210

CHAPTER XIX.

FROM 1602 TO 1641.

Recusants—Priests flung overboard at sea after leaving Scattery (Iniscatha) Island—Parliament in Dublin A.D. 1613—Interesting State of Protestantism in Thomond, as described by Protestant Bishops—First Great Confiscation, ... 225

CHAPTER XX.

FROM 1641 TO 1646.

The Rising—Sieges of Ballyalla, Inchicronan, and Tromoroe—Swearing of Affidavits—Curious Incidents—Proposed Extermination of Catholics—John O'Malony of Killaloe surprised near Quin—Siege of Bunratty—Cardinal Rinuncini—His Description of Bunratty—Thomond freed once more of the Foreigners, . . 242

CHAPTER XXI.
FROM 1646 TO 1651.

Morogh na Thothaine—Cromwell—Ormond in Clare—Council of the Confederation takes refuge in Ennis—Ireton—Betrayal of the Irish Cause—Ludlow at Inchicronan—Surrender of Limerick—Mauria Rhua, ... 255

CHAPTER XXII.
FROM 1651 TO 1690.

Formation of the Irish Brigade—Second Great Confiscation—Expulsion of Priests—Destruction of Clare Castles—Families transported to Clare—Partial Recovery of Properties at the Restoration of the Monarchy—Bishops of Killaloe—Curious Lettings—Clare Representatives in King James' First Parliament—Burgesses of Ennis—Officers of King James—Battle of the Boyne—Athlone—Limerick—Sarsfield—Clare's Share in the Defence, ... 263

CHAPTER XXIII.
FROM 1690 TO 1703.

Second Siege of Limerick—Butchery on Thomond Bridge—Treaty of Limerick—Flight of the Wild Geese—Clare reduced to a Desert—The Third Great Confiscation—Plans for Plunder—Those who secured it—Sums paid for it—Origin of Titles of most of the Present Owners, ... 285

CHAPTER XXIV.
FROM 1703 TO 1770.

Working of the Penal Laws in Clare—Government Tools—Bishops in the Penal Times—Curious Elections—Cutting of Woods—Irish Brigade—Letter of Lord Clare—Thomond Marshal of France—Flag presented by Louis XVI.—Charles Lucas, . 297

CHAPTER XXV.
FROM 1770 TO 1801.

Condition of Clare—Dilapidation—Commerce impeded—Population increasing—Families from Neighbouring Counties—Public Spirit reviving—First Signs of Toleration—Building of Catholic Chapels—Clare Members of Parliament on the side of Liberty—Relief Acts—Nationalist Meeting at Ennis—Spanish Admiral O'Kuoney—Donogh Rua MacNamara—And. Magrath—Thomas Dermody—Other Clare Celebrities of the last century, 312

CHAPTER XXVI.

FROM 1801 TO 1828.

The false Lord Clare—The Forty-Shilling Freeholders—Influence of Napoleonic Wars on Clare—O'Connell—Clare Protestants in favour of Catholic Relief—O'Connell's Duel with D'Esterre—Major MacNamara—Famine of 1822—Tom Steele—"Head Pacificator of Ireland"—The O'Gorman Mahon—Amusing Incidents—Vesey Fitzgerald—Father Murphy of Corofin—Ennis besieged—Nomination Speeches—Droll Story against O'Connell—Obstruction Tactics of the Protestant Party—Declaration of the Poll—Clare killed with one blow Protestant Ascendancy and the Catholic Association, . . . 328

CHAPTER XXVII.

FROM 1828 TO 1851.

Bill of 1829 for Catholic Emancipation—Petty Restrictions—O'Connell at the Bar of the House claiming to sit as M.P. for Clare—O'Gorman Mahon succeeds him in '30—Unseated on Petition for Bribery—Quarrel with O'Connell—"Terry Alts"—Classical Schools—National System—Workhouses—Monster Meeting at Ballycoree—From Life to Death—The Famine—Drowning at Poulnasherry—The *Times* becomes a Balaam—Statistics of Evictions and Deaths—Letter of Very Rev. Dr. Kelly, P.P., V.G., Kilrush—Father Malachy Duggan, . . 342

CHAPTER XXVIII.

FROM 1851 TO 1893.

Effects of the Famine—William Smith O'Brien's Career—O'Gorman, O'Donnell, and Doyle—Proselytism in Clare—Springfield College leading on to Diocesan College—Contests on Independent Opposition Principles—Six-Mile Bridge Massacre—Narrow Escape at Tulla—Uncertain Tenure and Unrest—Distress in '63 and '64—Fenianism—Its Consequences—Amnesty—Home Rule—Farmers' Club and Land League in Clare—Parnell—Meetings at Ennis and Milltown-Malbay—Phases of the Land Struggle—An Irish Parliament at least within reach, . . 360

HISTORY OF CLARE.

CHAPTER I.

Extent — Population — Geographical Features — Natural Advantages—Scenery—Soil—Lakes—Minerals—Tuamcens, near Tulla—Atlantic Ocean and Shannon—Environment—Moher Cliffs—Submergement at Milltown-Malbay—Kilkee—Bishop's Island—Loop Head—Carrigaholt Castle—Iniscatha—St. Senan's Island—Monasteries—Castles—Ennis and Quin Abbeys—Bunratty—Falls of Doonas—Killaloe—Kincora—Holy Island—Burren—Abbey of Corcomroe—Cell and Legend of St. Colman MacDuagh—Lisdoonvarna.

THE County of Clare has an area of twelve hundred square miles, with about 130,000 inhabitants. Its greatest length from Killaloe to Leap Head—now improperly called Loop Head, as the old Irish name, Ceann Leime, or "Head of the Leap," testifies—is close on sixty Irish miles. Its breadth is very variable, but on an average about twenty Irish miles. It possesses every variety of soil, from the rich alluvial lands along the Shannon, to the barren peaty ranges on the west and north, and the rocky but fertile region of Burren on the north-west. Between its two ranges of hills—the Ogonnelloe, Broadford, and Truagh Hills on the east, and the Feakle, Glendree, and O'Dea Hills towards the north-west and west—lies the extensive undulating plain which may well be called the heart of Clare. Narrow on the north at Scarriff and Tomgraney, where it abuts on Lough Derg, and looks over towards Holy Island, it widens out gradually till it rests southwards on the whole extent of the Shannon between Limerick and Kildysart. It is for the most part excellent grazing, meadow, and tillage land, and is beautifully diversified. Lakes, fairly stocked with fish of various kinds, nestle between the numerous low hills, which are nearly all ornamentally planted. At about its centre, near Tulla, Quin, and Carahen, mines have been worked for lead and silver ore; but whether from lack of capital to work them thoroughly,—as I believe,—or that the finds have not been sufficiently productive, all effort in that direction has ceased.

Close to one of those abandoned mines, within about two miles of Tulla, on the Molony property at Kiltannon, is one of those freaks of nature which, if found say in England, Scotland, or Wales, would attract crowds of visitors, and mayhap inspire the poet's pen and the painter's pencil, but which is scarcely ever noticed or heard of. It is called "the Tuameens." A small stream coming down from the Glendree Hills has made itself a subterraneous passage for a considerable distance, till it emerges again and pursues its even course towards the Shannon. There are at intervals openings from above, overhung and festooned with honeysuckle and other beautiful undergrowth, through which the buried stream is easily reached. With some little difficulty, if the river be not swollen with late rains, the whole way underground may be traversed. It is with no little feeling of wonder and almost of awe that the eye travels over the dark winding river, having on both sides solid, massive lines of rock, apparently chiselled by the hand of man, but really chiselled by the slow yet ceaseless drip of water from above, and serving as buttresses for the splendid arches of limestone which bridge the sunken stream. Here, as at the better known Bridges of Ross, near Loop Head, nature looks not unlike art as it comes from the brain and hand of man.

This central plain was to Clare on a small scale what Lombardy was to Italy—the scene of almost perpetual conflict. Were there no written records testifying to this fact, the numerous castles scattered through every parish, still grim and defiant-looking even in their ruins, are only too eloquent on this subject. But it was not all war. The many abbeys and churches yet standing in all parts of Clare, though partly demolished and wholly desecrated, bear testimony to the strong faith and practical piety of its people in the past. In these pages, as we go along, the story of those old monuments will be told as fully as can be gathered from the most authentic sources.

Westwards to the Atlantic Ocean the country is very hilly, and for the greater part the land is poor and unproductive, except where patient industry has made it comparatively fruitful. Here the grouse and the snipe and the hare have a wide domain. Owing to the fierce Atlantic breezes, which will not permit, except in sheltered valleys, the growth of trees, the whole district looks bare and unattractive. To the lover of bold scenery—and who does not love it?—there is ample compensation for this wherever, and that is nearly everywhere, the sea or Shannon comes within view. From Black Head in its northern extremity, towering over Galway Bay, to Loop Head on the south, the broad Atlantic wages incessant war with frowning cliff and jutting headland. It stretches out, huge, vast, illimitable, compelling admiration in all its ever-changing moods; sometimes as placid as a lake, but nearly always tossing and fretting and moaning as if some great trouble stirred its inmost depths. Away to the north-west is the range of the Connemara Mountains,—fitting background for one of nature's finest panoramas,—with the Arran Islands lying nearer, calling to mind the olden days of Erin's Christian glory, when saint and sage fled the busy world for the calm and the silence of their sea-bound recesses. Nearer still are the majestic Moher cliffs, rising sheer up to the height of nearly a thousand feet, straight as an arrow, for miles in length over the heaving ocean; while in sharp contrast with them there stretches away southward the low, broken, rocky coast outline, called by the Spaniards aptly enough after the Armada disaster, Malbay. Its sunken aspect, between the precipitate Moher and Baltard cliffs on its north and south, dotted with numerous rough islets, strongly corroborates the statement in the *Annals* of the Four Masters, that, more than a thousand years ago, an earthquake occurred, burying the land then standing there, with over a thousand inhabitants, in the depths of the sea. The reef sometimes visible at very low tides outside the bay is called by the fishermen "the Monastery," or "St. Stephen's Church;" and some now living will tell you gravely, and with evident conviction of its truth, arising surely out of their vivid Celtic imagination, that they have seen distinctly down in the clear waters the tower of the church and the roofs of the houses of the engulfed town.

Pursuing our course still southwards, the coast-line all the way to Loop Head stands up again precipitate as a wall, sternly facing the onward rush of the Atlantic. Though not so high as Moher,—rarely exceeding three hundred and seldom dipping under one hundred feet,—it presents more variety, well repaying the visitor with pleasing combinations of pillared rock, lonely island, yawning cave, and wave-worn bridge. This frowning line of cliffs is broken at intervals by little bays, round one of which, anciently called Dough, is built the town of Kilkee, one of the most attractive of the many attractive seaside resorts round the coast of Ireland. Near here, lonely "Islaun an Aspuig," or Bishop's Island, stands up in stern grandeur from the sea. Being only a few hundred yards away from the mainland, two stone structures of the beehive kind can be plainly discerned. It is therefore certain that in the days of early Christian fervour, holy men retired here from the busy world to commune alone with God in the presence of His glorious works. The wearing away, by the ceaseless action of the ocean, of the means of communication with the mainland that must then have existed, has served a good purpose. It has warned off the thoughtless, perhaps sacrilegious, hand from these sacred buildings. Ever since, while looking over on them, the mind must travel back to that far-off age of Christian anchorites and hermits; and many doubtless have asked, and many more will yet ask, themselves the question, Who were the wiser—the hermits who struggled there for the inheritance of the saints, or the worldlings whom they left immersed in pursuit of the "goods that perisheth"?

From Kilkee, seventeen miles more of ever-changing cliff— the natural "Bridges of Ross" challenging special attention and admiration—lead to Loop Head, the most remote point of Clare. It is indeed a wild and lonely but truly majestic spot. In some minds it inspires terror; for most it possesses a pleasing fascination. Along the narrow headland, on both sides, are steep precipices frowning over the surging, mysterious sea-depths below. In the distance, far off over the Atlantic wave, the graceful outlines of the Connaught mountain ranges are clearly within view; while, on the other side, looking by contrast almost within arm's reach, though twenty miles of mingled sea and Shannon away, is the towering, imposing mass of the Brandon Hills. At the end of the headland, upon which a graceful lighthouse is reared, is the chasm that gives it its fanciful name. It is about forty feet across, but three hundred down to the surging mass below. Across it to the little island—Ceann Leime, or in English correctly, the "Head of the Leap"—the Fenian warrior was said to have leaped, bearing his pursued lady-love. Though now trodden only by the wild sea-birds, there are evidences of the hand of man in stonework on its summit, suggesting the less poetic thought that it might have been somehow reached for the purpose of concealing treasure in troubled times. An unsuccessful attempt was made some years ago to bridge the chasm. I fancy that here it was that one of our well-known Irish writers, Richard Dowling, caught the idea of a novel which brought him at a bound into fame, but the scene of which he lays at the better known Bishop's Island, near Kilkee.

Two sections of the cliff on the northern side of the peninsula are deserving of notice. The larger of the two is called the "Hull Rock," owing to its resemblance to the side of a ship. In both the surface is smooth and quite black, and shows, all along down till it is lost in the sea, a curve as regular and graceful as if it were the effect of design. What a poor thing was the famous Tarpeian Rock in ancient Rome compared with this terrific descent!

On the southern side of the peninsula there can be discerned still a few out of what had evidently been a circular group of stone cells, surrounding a narrow enclosure. They are of very curious construction; each one is narrow, low, curving slightly as it enters into the earth, and if ever used as a place of rest, could have been nothing better than the apartment of torture called in England "Little Ease." It is very hard to believe that even early Christian fervour, as archæologists tell us, adopted such a method of seclusion and mortification. A practical, hard-headed man of the modern world would rather regard them as safe depositories for smuggled goods.

Not far away from this relic of the distant past there is now a handsome Gothic church, containing another interesting relic, but of a very different kind. It is a miniature wooden chapel, set on wheels, which was placed on the sea-shore by the parish priest, the Rev. Father Meehan, when, after the famine years of the middle of the present century, a vigorous and persevering attempt was made to proselytise the people of this remote district. It was barely sufficient to shelter the priest saying Mass within, while the people assembled around in the open air in all weathers. From it for years he preached to them in their own Irish tongue. He called it "The Ark," not inaptly, as from his point of view it proved an ark of salvation to his beleaguered parishioners.

From Loop Head to Lough Derg, Clare has "the lordly Shenan, rolling like a sea," for its whole southern and eastern boundary. It confers enormous advantages on the county and its inhabitants, fertilising it as it flows, and is rich itself in its abounding wealth of choicest fish. It is navigable for ships of the heaviest burden all the way up to Limerick; and with its tributary, the river Fergus, offers facilities for exports and imports to nearly all parts of the country. Places of note, either as picturesquely-situated residences or of historic fame, abound on its bank for its whole length of nearly a hundred miles round Clare, from Loop Head to Holy Island, in Lough Derg.

Proceeding from its mouth upwards, the first to secure attention is Carrigaholt Castle, once the proud stronghold of the MacMahons, now dear to Irishmen as the fortress round which Lord Clare trained those Yellow Dragoons, whose exploits under his command in the wars of Europe have given some of the brightest pages to history, and form the subject of one of Davis's most spirited ballads. It is still in a good state of preservation, due in no small degree to the care taken of it by the Burton family, into whose possession it fell.

About eight miles farther up, close to the important town of Kilrush, lies the famed Island of St. Senan, now called

Scattery—a corruption for Innis Catha, "Island of Battles." It received this significant appellation from its having been so frequently assailed and plundered by the Danes during the eighth and succeeding centuries. Those marauders found little difficulty in plundering and murdering unarmed monks. Some will see the hand of Providence in the fact that the desecration of the holy place was well avenged on the plains of Clontarf by Brian and his Dalcassians. At the present day, the group of ruined churches nestling under the graceful round tower bear witness to the importance of this little island as a centre of piety and learning in the days before the Danish incursions, when Ireland was the university of Europe. One of these is called "St. Senan's Bed." It is held in the deepest veneration, being popularly regarded as his burial-place. No Catholic woman would think of placing foot upon it, in deference to the traditionary story of the Saint's exclusion of the softer sex from his holy isle. The present writer, while in charge of the island as parish priest of Kilrush, had the spot dug up where, if buried there, the Saint's remains should lie; and found portions of a skeleton, which, when submitted to competent authority without notifying any of the facts in reference to it, were declared to be the remains of a very old man, evidently in the earth for a great many centuries. He retains and zealously guards a small part of what he believes to be a very precious relic, but restored the rest to the hallowed ground. Farther up the river, at the estuary of the Fergus, is a group of islands, one of which is called Canon Island. The priory from which it takes its name was built for Canons Regular of St. Augustine, in the twelfth century, by Donal Mor O'Brien, King of Munster. The church, with a square tower, adds much, even in ruin, to the beauty of the scenery. It was seized on with all its property, and granted to Donogh, Earl of Thomond, in 1605, as a reward for his submission to the English invader.

A few miles away, on the banks of the Fergus at Ennis, another and a much more important edifice, the Abbey of Clonroad, was built for Franciscans by Donogh Cairbreac O'Brien in 1241; and enlarged and ornamented soon after by Mac-Con M'Namara, the founder of the still more beautiful

Abbey of Quin. Of these much will have to be said in the course of this history.

The land from the Fergus to Limerick is extremely fertile. A considerable portion of it has been rescued from the tidal waters of the river. Like Holland, it must still be protected from its encroachment by strong embankments; and like it, too, is well worth the cost and labour expended on it. The large district here called Tra-da-Righ, King's Strand, is noted for its sturdy race of inhabitants, mostly of MacNamara descent. At its extremity towards Limerick stands still the imposing, massive Castle of Bunratty, almost unscathed, spite of the many fierce conflicts it passed through. Farther on is the extensive ancient Wood of Cratloe, which, in days not very long ago, afforded secure shelter to the hunted outlaw. The highway robber, too, made it his haunt. The road from Ennis to Limerick lay through it. In the troubled days of the last century, travellers had need to look to their weapons of defence while passing through, and only too often looked to them in vain. The making of one's will was said to be not an unusual preparation for the journey. Its chief claim to historic interest lies in the fact that here Sarsfield and his brave companions rested for awhile in safety before entering Limerick, after the clever surprise and destruction of the English convoy at Ballyneety.

From Limerick, four miles away, to Killaloe,—a distance of twelve miles,—the Shannon, owing to shallows at both these points, ceases to be navigable, but communication is kept up by a canal running along the Clare side. About half way up are the celebrated Falls of Doonas. The banks on both sides are well planted; and views are had as lovely and picturesque as one could desire. Here, and at the rapids of Killaloe, the lovers of Izaak Walton's gentle art find full scope for enjoyment, as well in the charming scenery as in the bright treasures yielded up to their skill by the bounteous river. Nor is ecclesiastical or archæological taste left unprovided for. Castleconnell's battered castle, and, far more interesting still, St. Flannan's Cathedral and the two stone-roofed churches ascribed to St. Molua, who flourished in the sixth century, and still lives in the name Killaloe, are worth more than one visit.

About a mile above Killaloe is Kincora,—Ceann Corha,

"Head of the Weir," historic Kincora,—which will be heard of again and frequently in these pages. It is now called Balboru. One of the finest, if not the finest, of Irish earthen circular raths stands there still. The Clare tradition is that, when Brian Boru held state a mile away at his palace at Killaloe, gallowglasses lined the whole covered passage between the fort and the palace.

The river, hardly fifty yards across at this point, nor much wider down to Limerick, begins to widen out into the proportions of a noble lake—Lough Derg. At the Killaloe side it is "guarded and sentinelled" by lofty mountains on both sides, with well-wooded slopes and rugged summits. The view down the lake towards Killaloe cannot be easily forgotten.

On this lake, at the head of Scariff Bay, and close to where the counties of Clare and Galway meet, lies Holy Island. Like its southern sister, Iniscatha, it has a round tower and group of churches, with which the name of St. Camin is associated. It is much smaller than Iniscatha. Its remote position secured those who sought its calm and solitude from, except on rare occasions, Danish or other marauders. The Four Masters tell us that Brian Boroimhe was a special benefactor to this holy retreat; and that he built within view of it, near Tomgraney (Tuaim Greine, "Altar of the Sun"), at the head of the bay, another round tower, not a vestige of which now remains. The *Chronicum Scotorum* fixes the date of its erection at A.D. 965.

From Lough Derg to Galway Bay the northern aspect of Clare is wild and rugged, relieved only by the lonely but beautiful lake, Loughgraney. The land is mostly barren and uncultivated. An imaginary boundary line, running on the eastern side through heath and moorland, and on the western side over the mountains of Burren, separates it from Galway. These Burren Hills present a very strange appearance. They are composed of limestone ledges rising one over the other to the very top, making them look like so many well-planned fortifications. No grass or vegetation appears on the surface; but in the interstices of the rocks herbage of the most nutritious kind grows. The sheep fed on it are coveted and prized because of the sweetness and flavour of their mutton. Within these rock-bound fastnesses are many monuments of the past —mostly ecclesiastical, and in a few instances very unique. In a gloomy secluded valley, now bare but then thickly planted, St. Colman MacDuagh lived his lonely life of hermitage for years,[1] until his relative, Gauaire, King of Connaught, becoming aware of his sanctity, insisted on his coming forth to do God's work among the people. The round tower and seven churches of Kilmacduagh, only a few miles away, in Co. Galway, remain as monuments of the energy of the Saint and the munificence of the King.

. Another better-known relic of the pious past in this region is the Abbey of Corcomroe, called in ecclesiastical records *de petra fertili*, "of the fertile rock." It was built for Cistercians by that most indefatigable of church-builders, Donal Mor O'Brien, A.D. 1193. It was connected first with the Abbey of Inislannaght on the Suir in Co. Tipperary, but later on, strangely enough, with that of Furness in Lancashire. It had an offshoot some ten or twelve miles south at Kilshanny. Had the monks anything to say to the growth of the famous oyster-beds at Pouladoody and Redbank, in their immediate neighbourhood?

On the borders of this Arabia Petræa of Clare are the well-known though lately discovered Lisdoonvarna Spas. Sulphur, chalybeate, copper, and magnesia waters are here quite close to each other, springing as if almost from the same source, and proving that minerals abound below the surface. The sea and mountain breezes sweep over this favoured locality. It is now regarded as one of the most famous health-giving resorts in all Europe. In the writer's Philistine mind the Burren mutton is credited with no small share of the recuperatory powers of the place.

The county, which has, as the foregoing short sketch may suggest, peculiarities of its own, has also a history of its own. No matter how imperfectly presented, it ought to have interest for people of Clare blood at home and abroad.

---

[1] A curiously-marked rocky road leading to his cell gave occasion to the name "Pass of the Dishes." A banquet, prepared far off, was said to have been carried over it to the famishing Saint and monks who came to visit him.

CHAPTER II.

Earliest known History—By whom peopled—Race of Eber—Mogha Nuadhat—Division of Ireland into Leathmogha and Leathcuin—Luighaidh Meann, descended from Ossian, drives the Firbolgs out of Clare—Tuadh Mhumhain—Thomond—North Munster—Will of Oilioll Oluim—Origin and Division of the Thomond Clans—Their present Descendants—Crimhthan, King of Munster, becomes King of Ireland—Is poisoned at Cratloe—Conal Eachluaith—Niall of the Nine Hostages—Exclusion of the Dalcassians from Sovereignty.

THE history of Clare before the Milesian occupation is lost in obscurity; and for centuries even after that remarkable epoch, references to it in the national records are so few and so scattered as to give no reliable materials for a continuous narrative. Some reliance is placed on passages in Ptolemy, in which he is believed to refer to the inhabitants of this county and part of Galway, calling them Gangani. This opinion is strongly supported by the fact that in ancient Erin they were known as the Siol Gangani; and Camden and Dr. O'Connor trace their ancestry to the Concani, a people of Spain.[1] Eugene O'Curry, one of Clare's most illustrious sons, and of whom much will appear from time to time in these pages, notes it as a curious fact that all the ancient colonists of Ireland carry up their pedigrees to Magog, the second son of Japheth,[2] concerning whose descendants Holy Scripture is silent. From him also the Bactrian, Parthian, and other tribes claim descent.[3]

The Irish pedigrees were all collected into one book, called *Cin Dromsneacth*, or Book of Dromsneacth, written by Duagh Galach, King of Connaught, an Ollamh or Doctor in history and genealogy, who reigned just before the arrival of St. Patrick in 432. He must have used in this great work the

---

[1] Lewis' *Top. Dict.*   [2] Genesis x.
[3] O'Curry's *Man. Mat.* p. 205.

tribe-books then in existence, and have observed strictly the accuracy in his quotations, which ancient Irish law rigidly prescribed under severe penalties.[1] According to the law universally accepted over the whole island, every man in the tribe was eligible for the chieftaincy if it came to the turn of his family; and so the greatest care was taken in the principal families to keep a clear record of their descent, and this record was again checked by that of the public officer named for the purpose by the tribe or province.[2] This is the foundation upon which we have to build when bringing together the facts of Irish history; and, taking an impartial view of the question, it is a matter for serious inquiry whether any other nation except the Jewish, and not excepting the Greek or Roman,[3] can justly lay claim to anything more solid or more unassailable. It is beyond all rational doubt that a people called the Milesian did colonise Ireland at a very early period, having brought to complete subjection all whom they found in possession of the country. From this race the bulk of the Irish people are descended; and with their fate and fortunes, this, I fear, weak attempt at the history of my native county must be chiefly concerned.

It would be vain to try and find the exact date of the Milesian Conquest with anything approaching to historic certainty. Our annalists trace to Ugaini Mor, who flourished more than five centuries before the Christian era, all the principal families of Ulster, Leinster, and Connaught; so the invasion must have taken place at some period far more remote. After the successful struggle for the possession of the island, the two sons of Milesius, Eber and Eremon, divided it between themselves and their followers, each one ruling supreme in his own territory. This amicable arrangement did

---

[1] O'Curry's *Man. Mat.* p. 206.   [2] Saltair of Tara.
[3] Sir James Mackintosh, *History of England*, vol. i. chap. ii., writes: "The chronicles of Ireland written in the Irish language . . . enable the Irish nation to boast that they possess genuine history several centuries more ancient than any other European nation possesses in its present spoken language. . . . Indeed, no other nation possesses any monument of literature in its present spoken language which goes back within several centuries of these chronicles." He is here giving his unbiassed opinion of the authorities relied on by the Four Masters and other Irish historians.

not last. Brothers as they were, they quarrelled over their prize, and Eber being slain in the unnatural conflict, Eremon reigned over the whole kingdom. The family of Eber, however, was not extinct, and they in time recovered the possession and the sovereignty of the whole of Munster. To this family and their followers is traced the ancestry of the Milesian inhabitants of Clare. How they lived and fought and died in those truly dark ages is in all probability beyond the possibilities of historic research. Later on, we arrive at a period on which light at last begins to dawn. The events of this latter period were of a kind to impress themselves on the whole future of the Irish nation, and, occurring as they did within the Christian era, and not very long before the introduction of Christianity into Ireland, can be relied on as in substance fairly authentic.

About the year A.D. 150, a fierce struggle was carried on for the supreme rule between the famous Con of the Hundred Battles, the recognised King of Ireland, and Mogha Nuadhat (of the Silver Hand), King of Munster.[1] The former claimed as the representative of the line of Eremon, while the latter insisted on his right as head of the line of Eber. After much waste of life and destruction of property, a compromise was effected, by which the island was partitioned. The northern half was made subject to Con, while Mogha ruled over the southern. To this day, in the language of the people, this partition is recognised, the northern division being called Leathcuin, or Con's half, and the southern Leathmogha, or Mogha's half. A line of gravel hills extending from Dublin to Clarinbridge in the county of Galway, and called Eiscar Riada, formed the boundary.

It is evident that this treaty must have made a profound impression on the Irish mind, probably from the feeling of relief occasioned by it, as the recollection of it is so well and so universally preserved, whereas the arrangement itself lasted for little over a year. The blessing of peace was only just beginning to be felt when the old rivalry flamed out again.

[1] These events find a place in all authentic histories of Ireland. They are introduced here, as they have a direct bearing on the internal history of Clare.

In the battle of Moylena, fought in A.D. 167, Mogha was overthrown and slain, and Con resumed supreme authority. Oilioll Oluim, son of Mogha, became then King of Munster, and Con wisely secured his submission and friendship by giving him his daughter in marriage. Of this marriage eight sons were born, seven of whom were slain in the great battle of Magh Macruimhe, A.D. 195, in the county of Galway. Between the surviving son, named Cormac Cas, and Fiacha (the eldest son of Mogha's eldest son, Eoghan), the dying king divided his territory of Munster, giving to Fiacha the southern, to Cormac Cas the northern half. At this time the county of Clare was still in the possession of a tribe of the old Firbolg race. Cormac Cas[1] took to wife the daughter of the great poet, Oisin or Ossian, who was son of the celebrated warrior Finn MacCumhaill, and had by her a son, Mogh Corb, whose great-grandson, Luighaidh Meann, wrested from the Firbolgs the county of Clare, in which they had hitherto succeeded in holding sway. From him this territory thus added to his patrimony received the name of Tuadh Mhumhain, or North Munster, which, in modern times, is Anglicised into Thomond; and now begins whatever is most reliable in the history of the ancestors of its present inhabitants.

In all probability the Milesian invaders utterly extirpated or drove north into Connaught the Firbolg race, as we find very few among the people of Clare of that low-sized, thick form and swarthy complexion which tradition attributes to those Irish aborigines. It would be deeply interesting to take, so to speak, a good look at the Clare of that day—its people, their customs, their modes of life, their religion.

It is not unlikely that then the land, that now is stripped for far the greater part of all ornament, was extensively and thickly wooded. At an earlier period the whole island was known by the name of the "Wooded Island," and we have no reason to think that when the Milesians first took possession it had changed its aspect. I could point to places on our seaboard, where, under high-water mark, trees still stand rooted as they grew, no one can know how long ago, but where certainly no tree can now rear its head for miles around and

[1] O'Curry's *Man. Mat.* p. 209.

hope to live. Atmospheric changes in all probability account for much of this; but it is certain that since the Norman invasion it became the policy as well as the profit of those marauders to strip the country of the woods, which to the Irish, in their long and stubborn resistance, served as fortresses. We can, without much effort, picture to ourselves the beauty of this county in those early days, when the full and varied foliage of summer and autumn clothed the hills with majesty, making of it, with its Shannon and Atlantic surroundings, one of the most charming spots of earth for man to dwell in. Of its people it may in good truth be confidently asserted, that they were a "brave and hardy race" in every generation, noted, even in Ireland, for the most splendid soldierly qualities. In every battle in which they engaged, the tall, well-formed, vigorous Claremen made sure of being "first in the fray and last out of it;" and, as we go along in this history, we will find proofs without number that they have always held a foremost place in the sustained struggle for Irish liberty.

For many centuries before the introduction of Christianity, though frequently there was fierce internal conflict, public law was acknowledged and enforced. The decisions of the legislative assembly held at regular intervals in Tara, were known and respected in every part of Ireland. She alone of all the countries of Northern and Central Europe had learned to substitute law for mere force. She could boast in those early days of a civilised government and a homogeneous free people, enlightened in all the then known arts of peace, and possessed of literary culture. Their religion had one great blot. It sanctioned and required human sacrifice in time of war. But apart from this barbarity, which in all likelihood was practised rarely, and only in time of great popular excitement, it was of a more spiritual nature than the idolatrous worship practised in even the cultivated Greek and Roman nations. We hear nothing of the grossness conveyed in the character ascribed to Venus or Bacchus or Mercury or Jupiter. The Irish worshipped a Supreme Being called Crom. They took as his representative the sun; and, probably following their Eastern traditions, offered to this great luminary, and to fire in general, worship and sacrifice. They had two great religious festivals on the days answering to our 1st of May and 31st of October, the memory of which, curiously enough, in spite of the deeply Christian character of the people, carries with it yet some undefined superstitious respect. The centre for this worship in Clare in those far-off centuries was probably the place whose name still commemorates it—Ardsolus, "the High Light," between Quin and Newmarket. They had also their minor deities, patrons and protectors of poetry, art, and, above all, of war; and Clare could lay claim, in the person of her first Milesian chief, to a descendant of Ireland's greatest warrior, Finn MacCumhaill, and Ireland's greatest poet, Oisin, both objects of the nation's pagan worship. Persons and places devoted to these heathen practices were held in the highest respect. The Druids, who were not only priests, but also teachers of youth in science and poetry, enjoyed privileges unknown in other nations.

The chief Druid ranked next to the Ard-Righ, or "High King;" and a similar honour, together with liberal grants and rewards, was enjoyed by the Druids of the subordinate kings and princes. Next to these ranked the numerous petty chiefs with their warriors; while smiths and armourers formed a connecting link between them and the despised mechanics and tillers of the soil. This was but natural in a country peculiarly adapted for pasturage, and among a people who, though cultivating, for the time, in a high degree the arts of peace, were much addicted to war. To the women was left the task of grinding the corn and spinning wool, and providing generally for the necessities and comforts of home. There was but little commerce or communication with other nations,—though, on the one hand, it is certain that the merchants along the Mediterranean, as well as those of Spain and France, found markets for their wares even in Ultima Thule; while, on the other, adventurous Irish kings and warriors made their arms felt and dreaded among the peoples on the Continent. In the Clare, then, of the period about which I now write,—the dawn of the Christian era,—lived a strong and warlike people—knowing very little and caring less for luxury—clothed in their own homespun woollen garments, so well suited to their humid climate—passionately fond of poetry and music—strongly clannish in their traditions, while submissive in no small degree to the broader national will—the progenitors of generations who were destined from time to time to make distinctive marks on Irish and Continental history.

We must now retrace our steps in order to clear the way for a history of Clare as consecutive as the materials generally relied on will permit. Its claim to distinction rests in a great measure on the will of Oilioll Oluim. This monarch ordained that the sovereignty of Munster should be held alternately by the descendants of Eoghan and Cormac Cas. The posterity and dependents of Eoghan (called Eoghanachts), who was killed in the battle of Magh Macruimhe, A.D. 195, possessed all South Munster. Being the more numerous and more widely extended, whenever they could they disregarded the will of their ancestor, and consequently we find them possessed of the throne of Munster much more frequently than the descendants of Cormac Cas. These latter ruled in North Tipperary and Clare. From the time that Luighaidh Meann, the fourth in descent from Cormac Cas by his wife, the daughter of Oisin, and grand-daughter of Finn MacCumhaill,[1] wrested Clare from the Firbolgs, this county became the patrimony of the principal families claiming descent from Cormac Cas. To Luighaidh Meann[2] succeeded his son, Conal Eachluaith, or Conal of the Fleet Steeds. This Conal had a son called Cas, after his great ancestor, and to this Cas are traced back all the chief Clare families, called after him by the well-known and illustrious title Dalcassian,—the O'Briens, the MacNamaras, the MacMahons, the O'Deas, the O'Gradys, the O'Molonys, the MacClanchys, the MacInernys, the O'Quins, the O'Hehirs, etc. It is a fact that cannot be called in question, that, while over nearly all Europe changes, dynastic and popular, were frequently made, in Clare, and indeed in all Ireland, the possession of the soil remained and still remains in the hands of the descendants of those ancient colonists. No other European people, except the Greeks and Romans, can lay claim to such antiquity.

Oilioll Oluim, King of all Munster, died in A.D. 234, and was

[1] The visit of Finn MacCumhaill to Conan of Ceann Sliebhe (Mount Callan), in Clare, forms great part of the Ossianic legends.
[2] O'Curry's *Man. Mat.* p. 209.

succeeded by his grandson, Fiacha Muilleathan. His contemporary as King of all Ireland was Cormac, grandson of Con Ceatha.[1]

Between these kings, cousins by blood, an almost continual war raged, no less than nine battles being fought, as the Four Masters relate, in one year alone, A.D. 241. The most remarkable of these was that fought at Knocklong, in the county of Limerick, when Cormac suffered a severe defeat at the hands of the Munster men, and, having been pursued into Ossory, was compelled to deliver hostages in pledge of his undertaking to make reparation for the many injuries he had inflicted on Munster. The victorious Fiacha, having died, was succeeded on the throne of Munster, on the alternative plan, by Mogh Corb, son of Cormac Cas, of whom mention has been made above, while Cormac was succeeded on the throne of Ireland by Cairbre Liffeachair. Between these also the old unnatural hostility was maintained, till, in the year A.D. 284, and in the seventeenth year of his reign, Cairbre was killed at the battle of Gabhra, in Meath, where Mogh Corb and the Munster men again defeated the monarch of Ireland. While Mogh Corb continued his reign over Munster, the eldest son of Cairbre mounted his father's throne, and reigned for thirty-seven years, till he was slain by his nephews, the three Collas, sons of his brother Eoghy.

The eldest of these usurped the throne of Ireland, beginning his reign about A.D. 322, but in turn he and his brothers were defeated, A.D. 326, and banished into Scotland, with their followers, by Muireach Tireach, the son of Fiacha, whom they had foully slain. This monarch ruled for thirty years, till he fell in battle with Caelvah, the King of Ulster,[2] in 356, who, again, was slain by Eoghy Moyveon, son of Muireach. This king reigned over all Ireland for about eight years, and died at the Plain of Tara, A.D. 365, which was then and for the two subsequent centuries the seat of the national government. At this time Crimhthan (pronounced Criffaun), sixth in

---

[1] O'Curry's *Man. Mat.* p. 209.

[2] The royal palace of Emania, in Ulster, had been levelled to the ground by the three Collas, after their victory over his predecessor, Fergus Fogha, which led to the dismemberment of Ulster.

descent from Oilioll Oluim, through Eoghan Mor, was king of Munster; and, as a remarkable dynastic change occurred in the sovereignty, of the kind which will be described in the following chapter, and which led to important results in Irish history, I desire to state here, before proceeding with it, as a matter of deep interest to Clare and Tipperary people, the origin of the great clans whose history will be traced in these pages down to our own time.

For this purpose the authority of Eugene O'Curry may be relied on with great confidence. He was an erudite Irish scholar. He had access to the most approved Irish manuscripts, the contents of which, so obscure to nearly all, if not all, others of the present generation, he thoroughly mastered. His character for painstaking and truthful translation was never called in question. Here, then, is what he found in the ancient, carefully compiled and collated records.

Cas, the common ancestor of the Dalcassians, and who was the seventh in descent from Cormac Cas, the second son of Oilioll Oluim, had twelve sons. The eldest son, Blod, was the ancestor of the O'Briens, who, by right of birth, as well as by the force of their strong right hand,—*Lauve Laudher*,—held undisputed pre-eminence in Clare. Their chiefs were frequently kings of Munster, and sometimes monarchs of all Ireland. From Blod, through his two sons, Cairthinn Finn and Brenân Bân, descend also many other Clare families, namely, the MacMahons, the O'Malones and O'Molonys, the O'Currys, the O'Hurleys, the O'Riada (now Reidy), the O'Seasnain (now Sextons), the O'Hogans, and various others, spread through Tipperary and Limerick as well as Clare, such as the O'Mearas, the O'Sheehans, the O'Bolands, the MacInirys, the O'Fogartys, the O'Ryans, the O'Gleesons, etc.

From Caisin, the second son of Cas, descend the MacNamaras, who, in extent and wealth of territory, and in strength of numbers, ranked next to the O'Briens; the O'Gradys, the MacClanchys, the O'Deas, the MacInernys, the O'Meehans, etc. From Luighaidh, third son of Cas, descend the O'Liddys; from Aengus Cinnaitin, the O'Quins, the O'Hehirs, the O'Howards, etc.; from Aedh, the O'Heas, etc.; and from Dealbaith, the MacCoghlans, the O'Scullys, etc.

The descendants of the other sons of Cas cannot now be directly traced, probably because by intermarriages they were absorbed into the more numerous and more powerful neighbouring clans. This is of very little moment in the Thomond of to-day. Its people are literally one family, bonded together by the well-defined ties of ancient blood and historic descent. The transmission and survival of the old clan names amid all the changes of so many centuries puts this beyond all doubt. Even the intermixture of English blood and English names, which were, in not a few cases, assumed for prudential reasons after the last siege of Limerick, does not materially affect this view of our present condition. Let any one, rich or poor, of Clare descent but take the trouble to note the names of his progenitors, maternal as well as paternal, for three or four generations, and, using the knowledge thus acquired as a medium through which to glance back into the distant past, he will in all probability find himself in touch with all, or mostly all, the brave clans that figured in "letters of light" on the glorious field of Clontarf. "One in name and in fame are the sea-divided Gael." This is unquestionably true of the inhabitants of Clare, not divided, but encircled by sea and Shannon, and may well be regarded as accounting for their well-known strong and abiding spirit of Irish nationality.

On the death of Eoghy Moyveon,[1] monarch of Ireland, at the Palace of Tara in A.D. 365, his children—of whom Brian was the oldest—being too young to reign, their uncle, Crimhthan, King of Munster, and head of the house of Heber, ascended the throne. He was selected for this dignity as being the one naturally qualified to watch over, and bring up in a manner suitable to their high estate, the children of his brother-in-law, Eoghy. The latter had, in pagan fashion, a second wife, Carinna, daughter of the King of Britain, by whom he had a son, Niall, to whom eventually the throne fell; who, as Niall of the Nine Hostages, is famed in history as one of the most powerful monarchs of his age, and in whose family—the Hy Niall—the sceptre of Ireland was swayed for the succeeding six centuries. Crimhthan, ascend-

[1] Four Masters.

ing thus the throne of Ireland, had to vacate that of Munster. Acting on a principle not rare in either ancient or modern times, he placed his own relative, Conal Eachluaith, a descendant of Cormac Cas, on the throne of Munster. This was resented by the descendants of Eoghan Mor as an open violation of the will of their common ancestor, Oilioll Oluim; and though the Eoghanachts were far from blameless themselves in this respect, Conal magnanimously agreed to refer the matter to the arbitration of chiefs selected from both families. Thus an unnatural conflict was averted. Corc, of the race of Eoghan Mor, was declared the rightful possessor of the throne, and held it till 366, when he died, and was succeeded by Conal Eachluaith. Once more, then, the chosen chief of the Thomond clans ruled all Munster—his sense of justice and desire of avoiding bloodshed being rewarded by the restoration, after only about one year, of the crown.

In the meantime, Crimhthan was securing himself on the throne of all Ireland by a wise and vigorous policy. He diverted attention from the irregularity of his accession by raids on the peoples of the Continent. It is not unlikely that the natives of Britain, whose king was allied to the royal house of Ireland, gave him willing aid in those plundering expeditions. His reign is spoken of by Irish annalists as one of the most successful known to Irish history; and very probably this it was that aroused the jealousy and excited the impatience of his sister, the widow of Eoghy, and urged her to the commission of an enormous crime. In her passionate anxiety to see the reversion of the crown to her eldest son, Brian, she administered poison to her own brother, the ruling monarch. It is even recorded that, to avert his suspicion and make sure of his death, she herself partook freely, and of course with a fatal result, of the poisoned drink. His career was thus foully brought to a close while he was on a journey through Clare. He died in A.D. 379, near Cratloe, on the mountain called, from this event, Slieve-Oighe-an-Righ, "the Hill of the King's Death." The wicked design of the barbarous sister was, however, frustrated. The choice of the electorate fell not on her son, but on Niall, son of the second wife; and of her descendants, only two, long afterwards, enjoyed the sovereignty, and both brought much misfortune to Ireland.[1] From her son Brian, who had to be content with the crown of Connaught, were descended the unlucky monarch Turlogh Mor and his son Roderick O'Connor. With the death of Crimhthan and the accession of Niall, the connection of Clare with the sovereignty of Ireland ceases for the long period of about six hundred years, when once more a descendant of Oilioll Oluim, a prince of Thomond and King of Munster, far more renowned and more powerful than even Niall of the Hostages, assumed sway over the whole island.

The choice of Niall for the throne was due, probably, to an early display of warlike abilities. His subsequent career would warrant this belief, for his long reign of twenty-seven years was one of the glories of Irish history. Being the son of a British princess, he attacked with great vigour the Roman general Stilicho, who then held Britain in subjection. The poet Claudian gives a picture of his prowess. Speaking in the person of Britain, he uses for her these words: "By him (Stilicho) was I protected when the Scot moved all Ierne against me, and the sea foamed with her hostile oars;" and the same poet relates that the success of the Roman Legion under Stilicho, in resisting the incursions of the Irish under Niall, procured for them the honour of being recalled to defend Rome itself against the fierce onslaught of the Goths. It is not at all unlikely that Niall had in view, in his incursions into Britain, not only to aid his maternal relations against their oppressors, but also to give the encroaching Romans practical proof of the stubborn resistance they might expect if they attempted a conquest of his country. Nor did he confine his attentions to Britain, as we learn from the fact that his death took place in the British Channel. He was there assassinated—the annals do not say for what cause—by Eoghy, son of Enna Kinsellagh, in the year A.D. 405, and was succeeded by his nephew, Dathi, son of Fiacha.

[1] Four Masters.

This prince was animated by the same spirit of foreign adventure. Some may call it a spirit of plunder, but, before utterly condemning it as such, it must be borne in mind that Christian monarchs of our own enlightened nineteenth century are sometimes actuated by a similar policy. They seek to divert attention from home affairs by foreign war; and, when successful, are not above seizing the property as well as the territory of the vanquished. The records of this king's reign are very scanty, the most significant being the manner in which it came to a close. Like Niall, he fell far away from Ireland on one of his expeditions. He was killed by lightning at the foot of the Alps, A.D. 428. We are not told where Niall was interred; but it is stated that Dathi's warriors brought his body home and buried it in Rath Cruachan, where he began his reign as King of Connaught. His cousin Laoghaire, the eldest son of Niall, mounted the throne. He was the first of what came to be known as the Hy Niall race of monarchs. His reign was signalised by the introduction into Ireland of Christianity. This great event put an end to the martial expeditions of the Irish. The next time they invaded Britain and the continental nations, they sought and won success, not with the sword of the warrior, but with the Cross of the Crucified.

CHAPTER III.

FROM A.D. 432 TO 554.

Christianity introduced—St. Benignus, Nephew and Successor of St. Patrick, preaches in Thomond and Kerry—St. Patrick blesses Clare from Knoc Patrick, near Foynes—Baptises there people from Corcovaskin—Prophesies the Birth of St. Senan—Incidents in the Life of this Saint—His Labours—His Death and Burial—St. Ruadan, Abbot of Lorha, in East Thomond, curses the Ard-Righ and his Palace of Tara—Its Abandonment.

THOUGH this county was not at any time blessed by the presence of St. Patrick, his coming to Ireland effected such a radical change in the social and moral, as well as religious, condition of the whole of the people of the country, that the events attending it are not out of place within the narrow limits of a county history. He had been preceded in the effort to convert the nation by St. Palladius. For some reasons not explained, this holy man "did not," in the words of the Four Masters, "receive much respect in Ireland," so he had to depart, having failed to impress the people, and died on his return towards Rome—his ill-success hastening in all probability his demise. St. Patrick then offered to the Pope, St. Celestine, his services in attempting the difficult task of weaning the Irish from their ancient and comparatively enlightened pagan worship. He knew the language and customs of the people, having been for years a slave among them, probably brought over into bondage by Dathi after one of his foreign expeditions. The escaped slave panted to rescue from a worse form of slavery those at whose hands he had suffered so great a wrong. St. Celestine blessed his design. He was consecrated Bishop. And so St. Patrick, having received his mission from the successor of St. Peter, turned his face towards the "Wooded Island" of the West, and landed with some companions on our shores, A.D. 432, in the fourth year of the reign of Laoghaire, King of all Ireland.

As might be expected, he met with much opposition, his life being often in danger. The Druids and their fanatic followers could not be easily won over from their ancient superstitions. The preaching of Christianity meant to many among them the loss of valuable and dearly-prized privileges. It pleased God, however, to protect him from their machinations, and the spectacle, unique in the history of the world, is presented of a whole nation converted to the faith of Christ by the energy of one man, and without the loss of a single life. The time for the shedding of blood in defence of faith came much later on. At St. Patrick's arrival, Aengus of the Eoghanacht line was King of Munster, and embraced the Christian faith.

The conversion of the island was in no small degree facilitated by its singularly peaceful condition. Judging from all the accounts of the progress of St. Patrick, from end to end of the country, we can reasonably infer that no intestine war raged. As Christ came into the world, so did His apostle bring the knowledge of Him into Ireland, in a period of profound peace.

It is very likely that, as the Saint himself did not visit Thomond, some of his disciples preached the faith there;[1] the fact of their having done so being overshadowed by the much better known and more successful preaching of St. Senan some years after. While St. Patrick was preaching in the country of the Hy Figeinte,—the western portion of the present county of Limerick,—the people of Corcovaskin, on the Clare side of the Shannon opposite, crossed over to invite him to preach and baptize in their country. The chief and his people claimed descent from Conary I., King of Ireland, but became afterwards amalgamated with the more numerous and more powerful Dalcassian clans. Finding himself unable to accede to their request, he consoled them by foretelling the

[1] It is recorded in the Acts of St. Benignus, the successor of St. Patrick, that, while yet a priest, he preached in Clare and Kerry, as St. Patrick himself was unable to visit those places.

birth of one of their own race who would do for their country what he was doing for the rest of Ireland. Tradition asserts that, going to the top of the mountain, called after him to the present day, Knoc Patrick, overlooking the territory of Corcovaskin, he stretched his hands out towards Thomond, and solemnly blessed it and its inhabitants. His prophecy was fulfilled, in the birth, forty years later on, of St. Senan, A.D. 488. This date, Dr. Lanigan asserts, tallies best with the historical, as distinct from the legendary, accounts of the holy Saint's life.

The various authors who wrote of him agree in pointing out Magh-Lacha, within about three miles of Kilrush, as his birthplace. The lake in the district, called after him St. Senan's Lake, is held in great veneration. Every year crowds flock to it, performing pilgrimages in honour of the Saint, and seeking his intercession. His father's name was Ercan, his mother's Coemgilla. Very little that can be relied on is known of his early youth. The first noticeable incident was his being compelled to take arms under his chieftain in an attack upon the people of Corcomroe. But he made no use of those arms, feeling that the raid was unjust. The invaders were repulsed with great loss. Senan was taken prisoner, but God softened the hearts of his captors, and the peace-loving youth was set at liberty.

He now resolved to enter on a life of religion, and placed himself under the guidance, first of the Abbot Cassidan, and next of St. Naal (Natalis) of Kyle na Managh, in Ossory. I pass over various stories told of miraculous events in this part of his career. After some years with St. Naal, he was prevailed on to establish a monastery at or near Enniscorthy. The accounts given of his journey, soon after, to Rome, and of his intimacy with St. David of Wales, are not well founded. We next hear of his building a church at Inniscarra,—now the Great Island,—near Cork. Leaving this, as may well be inferred, in a flourishing condition, he turned his face towards his place of birth. He seems to have had a passionate desire for the establishment of monastic houses, and churches adjoining, in retired places suitable for contemplation, as on his way homewards he built again monasteries on the islands of

Inislunga and Inisluaidhe in the Shannon, two of the group of islands at the junction of the Fergus with the Shannon. As if to gird Corcovaskin with holy houses, he stretched out into the Atlantic, and, landing on Iniscuireach, now Mutton Island, within full view of Aran-na-Naoimh, he again laid the foundation of and constructed a house for holy retreat. At last, after having made provision in so many places for the adoption and pursuit of a life of religion by those—and in those days of fervent faith they were countless—who felt called to it, the time came for his final and most important undertaking. The desire to surround the holy man with, as it were, an atmosphere full of miracles, accounts for the numerous legends which the writers of his life revel in. They tell us that at this, the turning-point of his career, an angel of God brought him up into a mountain, probably Baltard, near Kilkee, which is not far distant from Iniscuireach, and, pointing out to him an island in the broad expanse of the Shannon, within view of his native Magh-Lacha, told him that this was to be the place of his burial, where he should await the resurrection; as also of many other Saints. In order that no crime should stain its soil, a sea-monster was allowed to hold sole possession of it till he for whom God intended it should arrive. The legend further tells how St. Senan banished it, driving it into Lough Doologh, near Slieve Callawn. The one fact that stands out from this mist of pious legend unquestioned and unquestionable, is that St. Senan did settle down in the Island of Iniscatha, and made there his resting-place, and a home for piety and learning in the revolving centuries. The group of churches still standing, with the graceful round tower, almost untouched by the hand of time, keeping watch and ward over them through all the ages, speak of no name but that of St. Senan. Such an impression did his work make on the people of Southern Clare, that to-day he is spoken of almost as familiarly as if he were yet a living reality among them. He is as vividly present to their minds as the Round Tower, the building of which they attribute to him, is to their eyes. They love to speak of the miracles wrought by him.[1] Some of these are

[1] St. Brigid of Feenish Island, at the mouth of the Fergus, is said to

almost exact copies of the miraculous events related in Holy Scripture, and may therefore be regarded as quite unauthentic. Indeed, I should not wish to pin my faith to most of the wonders attributed to him by tradition or the writers of his life. Underlying all of them is the manifest purpose of bringing into view the holy Saint's strong and efficacious faith in Christ. But that he did work miracles can hardly be doubted. We can in no other way rationally account for the strong current of tradition attributing them to him.

No credence can be placed on the tale told of the opposition he met with from the chief of the Hy Figcinte, who is said to resent St. Senan's occupation of his territory, unless, indeed, he objected to his episcopal jurisdiction on the other side, seeing that the island is on the Clare side of the Shannon, and most probably belonged to his own people of Corcovaskin. There is an air of truth in what is related of his ordaining that no female should land on the island. This was quite natural. Under his rule Iniscatha became simply a monastery, intended exclusively for men, like so many other establishments of the same kind in every age of the Church. Curiously enough, some writers, in their ignorance of Catholic spirit, regard this as evidence of harshness and a morose disposition in the holy Saint; while our own national poet, Moore, in his song on the subject, treats of it in the flippant manner not quite unnatural to his versatile genius.

We have no account of when or by whom he was raised to episcopal dignity. If what is told of his having given the veil to a daughter of the chief of Hy Figcinte while he was in Inislunga be true, it is likely that he had been a bishop for a considerable time before his arrival in Iniscatha. Whether this be so or not, it is certain that while there he exercised episcopal functions, making it the seat of a diocese which extended for miles on both sides of the Shannon as far as Limerick, and of which much will be heard later on in these pages. The two oratories still standing, defiant of time and storm, on Bishop's Island, near Kilkee, are supposed to have

have sent him a vestment, setting it afloat down the river in a basket. Hence the mistake about St. Brigid of Kildare sending one round by the sea.

been built by him. The name by which it is still spoken of among the people, "the Island of the Hungry or Fasting Bishop," renders this morally certain. In that remote period there must have been a passage from the mainland to the island, since worn away by the encroaching Atlantic; and it is very probable, considering the ascetic character of St. Senan, that he provided this place of occasional retreat for himself and his monks. There indeed was a locality suitable for silent communings with God in the presence of His wonderful works, and we can well conceive the holy man, with some chosen companion, so absorbed there in contemplation as to be unmindful of the needs of the frail body, becoming in good truth "a starving bishop." Like so many other Saints of God, he desired to live in continual mortification. He is said to have prayed earnestly that affliction of the flesh should never be wanting to him, and that his prayer was heard. Neither the exact date of his arrival on the island nor of his death can be ascertained; but the great fame attaching to it, for so many centuries, from his life and works there, is clear proof that his rule lasted over many years. The writers of his life regard it as very probable that he took possession of Iniscatha about 540, and died about 560. He took ill while on one of his visitations,[1] at a convent called Kyleschaille, on his way home,—very probably Kyle na Gaillagh, the remains of which may still be seen within a short distance of his monastery in the parish of Moyarta, now called after its principal village, Carrigaholt. It is not certain whether he died there or in Iniscatha, but there is no doubt about his being buried in the island of his choice—the place of rest, as it was the place of greater labour, marked out for him by Divine Providence. Thus passed away, after a life of good works, one of Clare's most illustrious sons. The people still regard with reverence not only the little church, St. Senan's Bed, whch encloses his remains, but the island with which, in preference to his other foundations, his name and his fame are indelibly associated.

About this time occurred two remarkable events, which,

[1] It is believed that it was to the little oratory at Ross Bay, still standing, where St. Cassidan gave him the religious habit.

though not strictly part of Clare history, yet, inasmuch as they took place within the kingdom of Thomond, deserve at least passing notice. In 562, according to the *Annals of Clonmacnoise*, St. Brendan of Birr, one of the shining lights of the infant Irish Church, " was seen to ascend to heaven in his chariot;" and St. Ruadan of Lorha excommunicated the monarch of Ireland. This king, Diarmid, openly professed paganism. He paid no attention to the rights and privileges of the Christian Church. He violated the sanctuary of the monastery at Lorha, by dragging thence Curnan, son of the King of Connaught, who took refuge there, and putting him to death. This barbarous invasion of the rights of his cloister, which was under the patronage of St. Columb-cille, so filled with a holy indignation the breast of the fiery Dalcassian abbot, that, like another St. Ambrose, proceeding to Tara, he reproached the monarch to his face, and pronounced a malediction on his palace. This excommunication had a lasting effect on the history of the country. The ancient royal residence of the Ard-Righ of Erinn was doomed. The Four Masters, under the year of the age of Christ 554, say, " The last feast of Tara was given by Diarmid, King of Erinn." After him no king dared to occupy the palace lying under such solemn ban. To this early abandonment and continued desertion for so many centuries of the once famous Hill of Tara, is most probably due the fact that not a trace remains of its ancient splendour. Oxen and sheep roam at will over the spot where, in the days when Ireland was almost if not the only civilised and cultured nation in all Europe north of Italy, kings and chiefs and Druids met periodically in the hospitable halls of the supreme monarch, to make laws and take counsel on the affairs of the nation. It is still further consecrated to Irish veneration, from the fact that there St. Patrick had appeared boldly before the august but naturally hostile assembly, bringing to them the first tidings of their and the world's redemption.

CHAPTER IV.

FROM 554 TO 800.

Dearth of Historical Records—Mode of election of Chief, Prince, and King —Their Privileges and Tributes—Boromean Tax—Its Abolition at the instance of St. Molaing of Ferns—Influence of Christianity on the Arts and Customs of the People—Learning fostered—Long Peace.

DURING the three subsequent centuries the history of Clare is involved in almost hopeless obscurity. As far as the present writer can ascertain, very little of it indeed is recorded in the MSS. of the Irish annalists.[1] Nor can they be blamed for this. The Dalcassian clans were thrown into the background, being greatly outnumbered by their rivals for power in Munster, the Eoghanachts. In open violation of the will of their common ancestor, the latter, being able to outvote the Dalcassians, held fast hold of the sovereignty of Munster. Owing to the prominence of South Munster, Thomond fell for the time into the shade, so much so that even the Four Masters, those diligent searchers into the mists of the past, have little to say for her. Following the same rule of "might against right," of which the world even in our enlightened age knows something, the northern Hy Niall usurped the sovereignty of the whole island. As a set-off against the dearth of local history, it will not be amiss, even at the risk of some repetition, to glance here at the system of selection of chiefs and kings recognised by Irish law which operated so unfavourably against the clans of Thomond, as well as at the general aspect of Irish society in the bright period between the introduction of Christianity and the invasions of the Danes.

[1] St. Colman, who, with the aid of his relative, Gauaire, King of Connaught, founded Kilmacduagh, A.D. 620, lived for the seven years preceding as a hermit in the gloomy wooded valley of Carron in Burren.

The succession to power and dignity in Erinn, in every grade, from that of chief of the clan up to the Ard-Righ himself, was regulated by a system, partly hereditary and partly elective. It is not quite clear that any method more just, or better calculated for the weal of the clan itself, or more ruinous to the general interest, ever existed in any other country, either in ancient or modern times. Every clan was a family, each member of which had well-defined rights to a portion of the clan territory, and had a vote for the selection of the chief. His office was to decide in all matters of dispute among his clansmen, in accordance with the interpretation of the common law of the land, as explained by the Brehon, or Judge, and to lead his clan in time of war. Stability of government was provided for, in the recognition of the claim of certain families in each clan or kingship, as being the first to be considered when an election was to take place. By an arrangement, somewhat like that which prevails in the relation of the President and Vice-President of the United States towards each other, the danger of disturbance on occasion of the death of the chief or king was averted. His successor was already selected by a vote of the whole people. And just as this wise provision secured the peaceful transmission of power, so the right on the people's part of selecting not the nearest of kin, but the most worthy of those nearest in blood to the chief or king, afforded a healthy stimulant to the display of wisdom in council and valour in battle among the aspirants to the coveted dignity, while it tended to save the commonwealth from the evils arising from incompetency in its leaders.

The same principle regulated the election of the provincial kings and the Ard-Righ of all Ireland, but with the difference that for these higher and more exalted positions the electors were not the people generally, but the chiefs and subordinate princes. On the day fixed for voting, the electors met in the open air at the rath or mound specially erected or set apart for this most important purpose. The one on which the kings of Thomond were acknowledged, as will be seen later on, still maintains its attitude of immovable repose about half way between the villages of Tulla and Quin. The elect, henceforth called the Tanist, or Righ Damna (or "making of a king"), having received from the chief or prince next in power the white straight wand typical of the purity and uprightness with which he should rule, took henceforth the place of honour and dignity and privilege next to the chief or sovereign. To use the modern phrase, he was recognised as heir-apparent to the throne.

The one flaw in the system, as there must be some weak spot in everything human, was the temptation, so pressing and so strong, on the elected to step as soon as possible into power, even if it had to be over the murdered remains of their predecessors. Yet with all this, though there had been deeds of violence in the struggle for the first place, they were few and far between, till the Danish invasion threw the country into a condition bordering on anarchy. Each monarch or king, or prince or chief, on accession to power, became entitled to certain well-defined privileges, and received fair warning against encroaching on the rights or privileges of others. These are all to be found in minute detail in that very ancient work, the *Psalter of Cashel*, and still more minutely in O'Curry's *Manners and Customs of the Ancient Irish*. The former compilation is attributed to St. Benignus, the nephew and pupil of St. Patrick, and his successor in the See of Armagh and Primacy of all Ireland. To allay the jealousy excited against him among the people of Munster, for whom he ministered, by reason of his apparent preference for the people of Connaught, to whose spiritual needs also he largely devoted himself, he composed this book, wherein the customs and claims of the princes of Munster receive special notice. It is highly probable that the work, now well known as the *Leabhar-na-g-ceart*, or *Book of Rights*, is a development and enlargement of that inserted by St. Benignus in his *Saltair Chaisil* or *Psalter of Cashel*. The original of the Psalter was literally and carefully preserved in various MSS. all along, but that portion of it dealing specially with the rights of the kings of Munster was, for an obvious reason, revised, and, so to speak, edited and continued, first under the direction of Cormac MacCuilenan, King of Munster and Archbishop of Cashel in the ninth century, and secondly by command of Brian Boru, monarch of Ireland in the eleventh century. Alas! most of those ancient MSS., so full of interest to students of Irish history, were destroyed or lost in the troubled period when Irish as a spoken language became banned by the Saxon usurper. Connell MacGeoghegan, in dedicating his translation of the *Annals of Clonmacnoise* to Terence Coghlan, dated April 20, 1627, laments their great loss in the following strain: " Kinge Bryen, seeing into what rudeness the kingdom was fallen, after setting himself in the quiet government thereof, and restored each one to his auncient patrimonye and repaired their churches and houses of religion, he caused open schools to be kept in the several parishes to instruct their youth, which by the said warres were growen rude and altogether illiterate. He assembled together all the nobilitie of the kingdom, as well spirituall as temporall, to Cashel in Munster, and caused them to compose a booke containing all the inhabitations, events, and septs, that lived in this land . . . which booke they caused to be called by the name of the Psalter of Cashel; signed it with his owne hand, together with the hands of the kings of the five provinces, and also with the hands of all the bishoppes and prelates of the kingdome; caused several copies thereof to be given to the kings of the provinces . . .

" Since which time there were many scepts in the kingdome that lived by itt, and whose profession was to chronicle and keep in memorie the state of the kingdome . . . and now . . . neglect their bookes and choose rather to putt their children to learn English than their own native . language, insomuch that some taylors do cutt with their scissars the leaves of the said bookes which were [once] held in greate account, and sleice them in long peeces to make measures of, so that the posterities are like to fall into grose ignorance of any things which happened before their time." [1]

The rights or privileges claimed by the kings and princes of Ireland were, in some instances, of a distinctly Christian origin. For instance, the King of Cashel—*i.e.* of all Munster—claimed from the territory of Corcovaskin " ten hundred oxen and ten

[1] *Book of Rights*, Introduction, p. 23.

hundred cows," and from Burren " a thousand cows and a thousand oxen, and a thousand rams and a thousand cloaks ; " but it is carefully noted that " it is not for inferiority (of race) that they pay these tributes, but for their territories and for the superiority of the right of Caiseal and for its having been blessed by Patrick."[1] It would appear from an examination into these nicely adjusted rights and prerogatives all over Ireland, that while the kings of Ireland and the provincial kings received large contributions in kind from the whole country over which they ruled, they in turn had to make grants and distribute favours to some of the minor princes and chiefs. For instance, the King or chief of Corcovaskin was entitled to receive from the King of Thomond " a drinking horn, two score steeds, and a king's or chief's apparel ; " and the chief of Corcomruah received from him " his choice ship on a day of voyage, two hundred cows, and his blessing with his daughter in marriage,"—a rather curious arrangement, but illustrative of the manner in which the clans and great families were, for their mutual advantage, kept in a state of dependence on each other. This policy of " give and take " established between them a strong bond of union for offensive and defensive operations. In this same chapter of the *Book of Rights* the following appears : " The first with him (the King of Caiseal or Thomond) into another country belongs to the King of Dal Chais ; " which, of course, means that in the wars of the King of the province of Munster, the place of honour as well as danger, the leading of the van, belonged to the Dalcassian clans. In modern times they were said to be always " the first into the fight and the last out of it." Here we have in this ancient record proof indisputable of the fact that they were regarded from time immemorial as remarkable for valour among the bravest people on the face of the earth.

The Clare of to-day may well be proud of such an inheritance. As this county will be found, later on, to be identified with the most glorious pages of Irish history during the reign over all Ireland of its most illustrious son, Brian Boroimhe, it may be well here to quote from the *Book of Rights* the law

[1] *Book of Rights.*

relating to such an event. "Here follows concerning the laws of the right of Caiseal and of the tributes and rents given to it and by it, and of the stipends to the King of Mumhane (Munster), and the other kings of Eire by the King of Caiseal when it is the seat of the monarchy.

"Caiseal is derived from 'Cais-il,' *i.e.* a stone on which they used to lay down pledges; or 'Cis-ail,' *i.e.* 'the payment of the tribute,' from the tribute given to it by the men of Eire. Sidh-dhruim ('fairy hill') was the name of the place at first." Then follows the description of the appearance of an angel on the hill to swineherds, who foretold the coming of St. Patrick, and blessed the hill and the place. "The figure which appeared there was Victor, the angel of Patrick, prophesying that the grandeur and supremacy of Eire would be perpetually in that place. Accordingly, that town is a metropolis to Patrick, and a chief city of the King of Eire. And the tribute and service of the men of Eire are always due the king of that place *i.e.* the King of Caiseal, through the blessing of Patrick the son of Alplainn. Now, here are the stipends of the kings from the King of Caiseal, if he be King (monarch) of Eire, and his visitation and refection among them on that account."[1] It is curious to find this prophecy of supremacy gravely attributed to an angel, in presence of the well-known fact that the supremacy of Eire had not for many centuries rested in the King of Cashel or Munster. The only explanation I can find for this notable incongruity is in the supposition that in the time of Brian Boroimhe the story was invented, with a view to establish the right all along of the supremacy of Cashel by virtue of the blessing of St. Patrick; and now, when the supposed right had become a fact, the stipends and tributes to the subordinate princes were decreed in order to secure their allegiance. A monarch so vigorous and so successful as Brian Boroimhe may well be credited with a desire to retain, for the throne of Munster, the supremacy of all Ireland, which he had won for it with his good sword; and what better means could be devised than, first, to invest it with a kind of Divine right by reason

[1] *Book of Rights*, p. 31.

of the blessing of St. Patrick, and then prop it up by paying for the support of some of the provincial kings and petty princes? That such a policy was inaugurated in his reign is not at all unlikely. We find wise provision made in the *Book of Rights* for carrying it out; for, while the monarch in Cashel was bound to share with some of the kings and princes the tributes he received from most of the territories of Erinn, he exacted from them in return, not only their support in war, but also the maintenance of his army for certain well-defined periods, while on his way to punish, or to seize the property of, refractory tributaries. For instance, "one hundred drinking-horns, one hundred swords, one hundred steeds, and one hundred tunics (are given) from him to the King of Cruachan (Connaught); and refection from the King of Cruachan to him for two quarters of a year, and to accompany him into Tir-Chonaile."[1] Here is evidence of an arrangement with the King of Connaught to overawe and keep in subjection the sturdy northern men. But it would require a succession of monarchs in Cashel, brave and skilful as Brian, to effect such a purpose, and such a succession was not forthcoming. The whole island was subjected to obligations of a like kind, with a view clearly to the establishment of a strong central authority. It would be well for Ireland if it had proved successful.

The scheme had, however, a fatal blot. It proceeded on the *divide et impera* principle, which is sure to foster and develop deadly enmities, ready to burst out into flame when the strong controlling power itself grew weak. We shall find only too many evidences of this in the history of the succeeding centuries. The "prohibitions" were, in a great measure, directed against the continuance of pagan practices, and so bestowed a Christian character on what was in its origin a druidical code of laws. Even in Christian times there was no relaxation of the unfair and unjust imposition on Leinster of what was called the Boromean tax. The origin of it is traced to the monarch Tuathal, who recovered possession of the throne, from which, for

[1] *Book of Rights*, p. 31.

some time, a successful revolt of the Firbolgs hurled him. In their revolt they had the active and continued aid of the King of Leinster, for which he and his successors were in this wise punished. Not only were the tributes in kind to a large extent exacted, but, what was far more humiliating, they were obliged to provide one hundred and fifty male and female servants to attend at the Palace of Tara. It was manifest that vigorous resistance to so odious an impost might be expected, and so the monarch very wisely ordained that a third of the tribute belonged to Ulster, a third to Connaught, and the other third should be divided between the queen of the monarch and the King of Munster. In this way he secured the co-operation of the provincial kings in giving effect to the exactions. Nevertheless, resisted it was again and again. In fact, it was one of the principal causes of all the bloodshed which stained the soil of Ireland for many centuries.

In the year 595, Aodh, the monarch of Erinn, himself fell in the attempt to enforce the payment of the tribute; and this was but one of many other disastrous events which followed. An end was at last put to it in a manner which shows how deeply the teaching of Christianity entered into the hearts of the people and their rulers. About the year 684 A.D., Fionactha, monarch of Ireland, marched into Leinster to seize the usual tribute—fifteen thousand head of cattle—and insist on the fulfilment of the other conditions. He was met by St. Molaing, Bishop of Ferns, who remonstrated with him on the injustice of the impost so successfully, that then and there it was for ever (except on special occasions as a punishment for some transgression) abolished, just as St. Columb-cille, more than a century before, had procured the freedom from tribute of the Irish colony in Scotland. The period to which this chapter is devoted, for the purpose of a general sketch, was unquestionably the most glorious in Irish history.

The acceptance of Christianity put an end, in a great degree, to the ravages of war. The fervour with which it was embraced was unexampled in any country on the globe. The Irish, as a nation, turned their attention almost exclusively to the carrying out of the Christian ideal, and the promotion of learning, science, and art. The whole island was covered with religious houses, ecclesiastical seminaries, and hermitages, the ruins of some of which exist almost untouched by the hand of time to the present day. The oratory of St. Flannan at Killaloe, the beautiful little church in the island close to it, and the beehive structures of St. Senan on the Bishop's Island near Kilkee, may be mentioned as among the numerous buildings, of a similar kind, and for a like holy purpose, which are to be found yet standing in every county of Ireland, attesting the longing for the higher virtues which animated our forefathers. To this period must be attributed, in all probability,—though, strange to say, the known Irish annalists are silent on the subject,—the erection of the round towers which add such grace to Irish scenery, and those other buildings, like Cormac's Chapel on the Rock of Cashel, which, for beauty of design and chasteness of execution, have hardly ever since been equalled. The unknown artists and their employers worked for God alone. They would not have the merit of their work marred by the vainglory of its publication. The unrivalled beauty of the illuminated MSS. of those far-away ages—the work, too, for the most part of unknown hands—is another proof of the high state of perfection to which art bounded under Christian influence.

But what most deserves notice is the generosity with which learning, sacred and profane, was fostered, while all northern and western Europe, including Britain, was little, if anything, beyond the stage of barbarism. While Charlemagne himself was barely able to affix his signature to public documents, the schools of Erinn were crowded with the youth of the country; and those of the other nations anxious for learning, had to bend their steps to the remote but illustrious isle of the West. No doubt the preaching of Irish Saints on the Continent contributed to this influx of foreign students; and it is a striking fact that, as if to encourage this egress of apostolic preachers and ingress of foreigners seeking enlightenment, all the great schools were built either on the sea or the rivers giving easy access to it. Lismore on the Blackwater,

Taghmon on the Slaney, Beg-Erin in Wexford Harbour, Bangor and Armagh on the Belfast Lough, Mungret and Clonmacnoise on the Shannon, and Aran-na-Naoimh on the Atlantic Ocean, were among the most noted of these; and such generous provision was made by the Irish princes for the support of education, that no distinction was made between those who could and those who could not pay for it. The rich, of course, did pay, as well they might, for a boon so rare and of such priceless value; but to the deserving poor both education and sustenance while seeking it were as free as the air of heaven. No costly buildings were raised for this purpose, nor expensive living indulged in. In all probability, the students themselves, as they came, and as the necessity for it arose, helped to put up structures of the simplest and easiest kind, just sufficient, and no more, for the end in view. They were satisfied with the plainest fare and the scantiest lodging, while they imbibed learning from masters who set them the same example. Under such easy conditions, thousands of young students could be, and actually were, effectively taught, with little cost as compared with modern methods, and with the greatest care, under the vigilant eyes and unceasing watchfulness of their religious instructors. The priests chanted matins with their pupils at early dawn, offered with them the Holy Sacrifice, shared with them their modest meals, joined them in their hours of recreation, but devoted far the greater part of the day to literary, scientific, and religious instruction. No thought was there for many succeeding centuries of separating religious from secular instruction. They went hand in hand, blessing the givers and the receivers alike. A great zeal for the spread of the faith was enkindled. Fired with it, very many holy men of the Irish race crossed the seas into Britain, France, Germany, Switzerland, and even into Italy, spreading the light of the gospel, establishing schools and monasteries, spending their whole lives ungrudgingly, some of them securing the martyr's crown, in bringing to those peoples, as yet lying in darkness, the blessings of Christian civilisation.

The names of St. Columb-cille, St. Aidan, St. Rumold, St. Killean, St. Gall, St. Columbanus, St. Fiacre, St. Dympna,

St. Feargal, or Virgilus, etc., are still venerated in those countries, as well as in the land of their birth. To the latter, who became Bishop of Salzburg, are attributed some of the hymns now in use in the Roman Breviary, as well as a knowledge of the sphericity of the earth. He was the first to propound to an unbelieving age this new and startling doctrine. A controversy on this strange subject was maintained with vigour for some time between him and St. Boniface in Germany. His eminence in such and kindred knowledge procured for him the title of "The Geometer." For a considerable period, too, a difference of opinion more serious, more prolonged, and more exciting, prevailed in the Irish Church at home, on the question of the proper day for the celebration of the Easter. It was not, of course, a vital dogma of faith, only a matter of discipline; and though for a while the anxiety of the Irish to retain the usage introduced by St. Patrick brought them into conflict with the rest of the Church, which had, after his time, adopted the more correct Alexandrian computation, yet the feeling of loyalty to the Chair of Peter inculcated by the Irish apostle set the question at rest. The Irish Church became one on this point of discipline with the Church Universal. The names of the Saints who shed a bright lustre on those first three centuries of Christianity in Ireland need not be recorded here. They are on every one's lips. They succeeded in welding, as it were into one, Catholic faith and Irish character, thus preparing the country for the fierce struggles it had to undergo, and out of which it came victorious in the succeeding ages.

It is easy to understand how, under all these healing and civilising influences, old rivalries and animosities softened down. That worst of all curses, intestine war, almost entirely disappeared. Upon a country thus lapped, almost continuously for three centuries, in Christian peace, came that terrible avalanche of paganism and barbarity—the Danish invasion. It supplied, as the sequel will show, only too much material for history.

After this rapid survey of the general conditions of the country, we turn to events occurring in Clare, or with which the county had intimate connection.

CHAPTER V.

FROM 800 TO 952.

Earthquake in West Clare—Danish Invasion—Cormac MacCuilenan—Flahertach, Abbot of Iniscatha—Both defeat Flann, the Ard-Righ, at Tullamore—Defeated near Carlow—Cormac surrenders the crown of Munster to Lorcan, Prince of Thomond—His Death and Character—Callaghan, King of Cashel—Brian Boroimhe born—His father, Ceinnidigh, defeated and slain by Callaghan.

THE Four Masters, under the year A.D. 799, *recte* 804, give the following description of a terrible convulsion of nature along the west coast of Clare: "There happened great wind, thunder, and lightning, on the day before the festival of St. Patrick in this year, so that one thousand and ten persons were killed in the territory of Corca - Bhaiscinn, and the sea divided the island of Fitha into three parts." This island is now called Iniscuireach, or Mutton Island. The other Irish annalists all bear the same testimony, differing only in the year,—a proof that they quoted from different but very ancient MSS., now unhappily lost. For instance, here is how the *Ann. Clon.* write of it: "A.D. 801.—There was such horrible great thunder the next day before St. Patrick's day, that it put asunder a thousand and ten men between Corca-Bascynn and the land about it; the sea divided an island there in three parts, the seas and sand thereof did cover the earth near it." The annalists all agree upon the day, as is natural, it being a remarkable one—the eve of St. Patrick—and upon the number lost; but it is not unlikely that the "ten" affixed to the "thousand" means idiomatically some considerable but indefinite addition to the multitude surely destroyed. It is quite clear that this was much more than a mere thunderstorm. The "dividing of the island into three parts" implies disturbance by an earthquake; and thus well-authenticated history gives support to the tradition handed down among the people of West Clare, that in one of those awful convulsions of nature the whole coast-line was changed. The land lying between Baltard and Hag's Head, with all its inhabitants, was engulfed in the ocean; leaving only Iniscuireach, with its neighbouring little rocky islands, visible, and making navigation along the submerged sunken reefs so difficult and so dangerous. Though the account of this disastrous event marks the first notable glimpse—after a long interval, thanks to the destruction by Dane and Saxon of Irish records—into Clare life, yet, before the present chapter closes, we will find the country of the Dal-Cas leaping out into the light of authentic history, taking henceforth a foremost and a justly famous part in Irish affairs.

During this century the Danes began their organised incursions into Ireland. It is stated, but it has not been clearly established, that their first inroad was along the Shannon, making their way up even into Lough Derg. If so, they passed close to a place which became afterwards, to their nation, a name of terror—Kincora. In the year 830 they first plundered Armagh, and this city of the See of St. Patrick must have afforded tempting loot to those pagan marauders, for we read that three times within one month they seized its spoils. The Irish evidently were completely taken by surprise, never imagining that a place so holy could be so ruthlessly and so sacrilegiously assailed. Besides, they had no standing army or navy; and enemies like the Danes hovering about the coast could choose at their leisure the time and place for attack most suitable to them, and had always their ships to retreat to when they had reason to fear their being outnumbered or overpowered. So, during the years following, from year to year we find in the Four Masters a dismal record of the incursions of these northern barbarians into all parts of the kingdom. Wherever they had reason to expect that objects of value were to be found, there they fixed their hungry eyes, and, watching a favourable opportunity, pounced like hawks upon their prey. Churches and monasteries were unmercifully and repeatedly plundered; and sometimes men of note were carried away as hostages, and also with a view to their afterwards securing a good reward for their ransom. The Danes gratified at once, in these ravages, their rapacious instincts and their hate of the Christian religion.

Nor were they alone guilty of such sacrilege. We find Feidlim, son of Crimhthan, of the race of the Eoghanachts, King of Munster, imitating their barbarous example. In the year 831, and again in 832, he ravaged and burnt to the very door of the church the property of the monastery of Clonmacnoise.[1] This sacrilege was well and justly avenged by Cathal, King of Connaught, who defeated, with much slaughter, Feidlim and the Munster forces in two battles—the first in 834, the second in 836. It is more than probable that the Thomond clans had no share either in the sacrilege or its punishment, as the continued usurpation of the throne of Munster by the Eoghanachts caused constant feuds between them and the Dalcassians. The first approach to a right understanding between the two great Munster families was made by Cormac MacCuilenan, Archbishop of Cashel and King of Munster. This prince ascended the throne in the year 895. Though already charged with the solemn duties of an archbishop, the burden and cares of the crown of Munster devolved on him. His reign was a very memorable one. As might be expected, he was a great patron of learning and a strenuous upholder of Church rights; but the unseemly spectacle was presented of a bishop of the Prince of Peace driven frequently into the field of battle. He may have tried to avoid it, but could not. We have proof that it was forced on him. In the year 901, Muireach, son of the King of Leinster, led an attack on the Munstermen, but was defeated and slain. In the same year, and probably by concert, Flann, the monarch of Ireland, who had signalised the first year of his reign in 877 by an assault on the province of Munster, plundering "from Boraimhe to Corcagh," *i.e.* from Killaloe to Cork,[2] made another successful raid on the dominions of King Cormac, plundering "from Gobhran to

[1] Four Masters, *Ann. Clon.*   [2] *Ibid.*

Luimneach."[1] But Cormac, ecclesiastic as he was, being a prince of more than ordinary vigour, determined to avenge this unprovoked insult. He conciliated the Dalcassians by a promise, which he afterwards honourably fulfilled, of restoring to their prince the right to the throne of Munster, of which they were so long wrongfully deprived. Flahertach, his kinsman, the warlike Abbot of Iniscatha, rallied them to the standard of the King-Bishop of Cashel. With the united clans of all Munster, Cormac marched to give battle to the monarch Flann. The latter had with him the united forces of Leathcuin, *i.e.* the northern half of Ireland. The opposing forces met at Magh-Lena, near the present town of Tullamore, and here the Eoghanachts and Dalcassians paid off old scores, by defeating, with great loss, the monarch and his army. Cormac and Flahertach did not rest content with this victory. They turned their arms against the southern Hy Nialls and Connaughtmen, who had in all probability taken sides with the monarch Flann, and, defeating these also, "they carried away the hostages of Connaught in their great fleets on the Shannon; and the islands of Loch Ribh were plundered by them."[2]

These events deserve special notice in this history, as they brought for the first time for centuries into bold prominence the strength and valour of the Dalcassian race, and gave promise of the greater prominence which they were soon afterward to acquire. Elated by these successes, some of the Munster princes, and notably Flahertach, the restless Abbot of Iniscatha, urged Cormac to revive the long-abandoned claim for tribute from Leinster. The son of the King of Leinster had indeed invaded Munster three years before, but paid for his rashness the penalty of his life. Cormac felt that this could be no justification for such an arrogant claim. Against his will he was dragged, however, into the assertion of it; and it was perhaps this sense of the injustice of the demand that filled him with a foreboding of disaster. Before venturing on the unlucky expedition, he made presents of gold and silver and altar vessels to the religious establishments at Ardfinnan, Lismore, Cork, Cashel, Armagh, and

[1] Four Masters.   [2] *Ibid.*

Iniscatha. Having a presentiment—some say a Divine forewarning—of defeat and death, he called to his side Lorcan, prince of the Dalcassians, and, presenting him to the Eoghanacht chiefs, declared him as his successor in obedience to the will of their common ancestor, Oilioll Oluim. The latter looked with disfavour on this arrangement, being determined to retain the right of succession to the throne of Cashel among themselves, and did retain it till superior force, as we shall soon see, compelled them to yield. Having thus in so far relieved his conscience in this matter, Cormac, after a vain attempt to turn aside the Munster chiefs from this adventure, marched with them into Leinster. This was the signal for a coalition between the Ard-Righ Flann and the King of Connaught, both of whom he had chastised so severely, with the King of Leinster. Their united forces outnumbered four times Cormac's army, and inflicted on him a severe defeat.[1] He himself, with many of the Munster princes, and no less than six thousand of their followers, was slain.

Thus fell by the sword one of Ireland's greatest sons, in a cause in which his heart was not. He was not only a wise and powerful prince and bishop, administering with firmness and skill both temporal and spiritual affairs, but he was also a man of profound learning, as the *Cormac Glossary* and the *Psalter of Cashel*, part of which was probably written by him, testify. Pity that such a fate befel such a man. He lived long enough, however, to turn to good account in his country's cause the splendid abilities with which he was endowed, and to deserve being ranked among the most illustrious of our Irish kings.

The Abbot of Iniscatha, Flahertach, who, though living in the Dalcassian territory, was a prince of the Eoghanacht line, being the son of Inmhainor, King of Cashel, Cormac's predecessor, was made prisoner in this fatal battle by Carbhall, King of Leinster. The latter prince dying within a year, Flahertach was restored to liberty, and, churchman as he was, being full of ambition, succeeded, in spite of the will of

---

[1] Keating calls it the "Cath Beallagh Mumghna," battle of Ballymore, near Carlow.

Cormac, in getting himself recognised as King of Cashel. It would appear that Lorcan and the Dalcassians were unable to assert their right to the succession, and had once again to submit to the old injustice. Might for some time longer prevailed over right. It is not unlikely that conscience smote Flahertach for this usurpation, as we find in the Four Masters that "in 920 he went upon his pilgrimages; and Lorcan, son of Conlingan, assumed the kingdom of Cashel."

How long he held the throne is uncertain. In five years afterwards an event occurred destined to change the whole current of Irish history. In 925 was born Brian, surnamed Boroimhe, son of Ceinnidigh, son of Lorcan, "twenty-four years before Maelseachlain, monarch of Ireland, whom he deposed."[1] The date of Lorcan's death is not given; nor can it be ascertained whether Ceinnidigh, Brian's father, made any effort to succeed him on the throne. If he did, he failed, as the Four Masters under the year 934 record the plundering of Cluain-Mic-Nois, first "by the foreigners of Ath-Cliath," *i.e.* by the Danes of Dublin, and afterwards, alas! "by Ceallaghan Caiseal and the men of Munster." In the very same year this sacrilegious act was avenged on the Danes. Donnchadh, son of Flann, the King of Ireland, attacked them in their principal stronghold, burning Ath-Cliath (Dublin) to the ground; nor was retribution on Callaghan and his Munster men very long deferred. This king deserves to be regarded as one of the worst and most ignoble in Irish history. We find him again, three years later on, devastating and plundering the territory of Meath in the congenial company of the Danes, who had established themselves in his own territory at Luimineach (Limerick), sparing not even the churches or monasteries, and carrying away the abbots as prisoners.[2]

We may hope that the Dalcassian clans had no share in the sacrilegious raids of their ancient rivals. It is certain that no special mention is made of their participation in the unholy work, as might be expected, if they actually engaged in it. Callaghan suffered his first defeat at the hands of the Ard-Righ Donnchadh in the following year, and had to

[1] Four Masters. [2] *Ibid.*

deliver hostages for his future good behaviour. This did not last long. He soon turned his arms against the Leinster tribes, in revenge for their having submitted to his rival, and made great slaughter of them. The latter, uniting all their forces, in turn attacked Callaghan, and defeated him with great loss. This defeat was completed, when, in the same year, Muircartagh, King of Ulster, swooped down on Leinster and Munster, taking captive and bringing with him into bondage, among others, the two provincial kings, Lorcan and Callaghan. In this he acted for Donnchadh, the Ard-Righ of Ireland, having his forces under his command; and on his return delivering up to him his prisoners, the most formidable of whom was his old enemy Callaghan, "that unruly king of Munster, that partaked with the Danes."[1] Muireartagh was so famed for his exploits that the Four Masters styled him "the Hector of the West of Europe." He fell as such a prince would like to fall, in battle with the enemies of his religion and his country, at Ardee, in Louth, on the 26th March of the year following, A.D. 941, or 943 according to the revised correct computation.[2] Two noteworthy events in Clare history took place the following year. Flahertach, Abbot of Iniscatha, and for a time King of Munster, died; and Ceinnidigh, prince of Thomond and father of Brian, was defeated in battle at Magh-Duin, by Callaghan of Cashel.

[1] *Ann. Clon.*   [2] *Annals of Ulster.*

CHAPTER VI.

FROM 952 TO 1014.

Mahon, Brian's elder brother, becomes King of Munster—His Murder—Brian succeeds—Takes Vengeance on the Murderers—His Character—His Victories—Defeated at Nenagh by the Ard-Righ Malachy—Deposes Malachy—Wise Administration of the Kingdom—Clontarf—His Death.

WE have now arrived at the period when Clare and all Thomond, emerging from the obscurity of the past, began to take a leading part in the affairs of the nation. The Danes had established themselves in Limerick, and ravaged at will the rich territories of Tradaree and Corcovaskin.[1] The two sons of Ceinnidigh, Prince of Thomond, Mahon and Brian, undertook the defence of their territory, and then began a series of struggles which culminated in the battle of Clontarf. A very interesting and detailed account of them, though bombastic and exaggerated, is to be found in a work, attributed to MacLiag, poet and historian of the Dalcassians in Brian's reign, called *Cogadh Gaedhal 'se Gallaibh*, carefully translated and annotated by H. Todd, T.C.D.

The first attempts to dislodge or cripple the Danes were not successful. Mahon was compelled to enter into terms with them, but Brian's proud spirit did not permit him to yield even in appearance. He, with his own followers among the Dal Cas, taking refuge in the woods of Cratloe and Tradaree, maintained for years a guerilla warfare with the foreigners.[2] He was so weakened by the constant struggle, that at last, the historian states, he was reduced to fifteen men, yet still he kept up the fight.

[1] *Cogadh Gaedhal 'se Gallaibh.*
[2] They had come from Norway and Denmark. The Norwegians were called by Irish writers, White Gentiles; the Danes, Black Gentiles.

Meantime, Mahon's ambition was in another direction. Leaving for awhile the Danes to Brian, he prepared to assert his claim to the throne of Munster. At the death of Callaghan's son Donogh, he appeared in such force at Cashel that the Eoghanachts had to submit and acknowledge him king, A.D. 964. But it was only in appearance. Maelmuidh (Molloy), their acknowledged prince, was soon in open revolt. He easily secured the co-operation of the Danes of Limerick under Ivar and Donovan, whose territory lay along the Shannon on the south. Mahon and Brian at once summoned all the Dalcassian clans to their side. They pushed straight into the heart of the Eoghanacht country; and, finding their foes encamped at Sulcoit,—now called Solihead, near the town of Tipperary,—forced on a battle. From sunrise to mid-day it raged with great fury on both sides, till at last the united forces began to give way. The Dalcassians directed their attack chiefly on the Danes, pursuing them to Limerick, which they carried by storm. The Danes who were not slain in the battle or the pursuit were captured and brought to the place now called Singland,—anciently Saingel,—where "every one that was fit for war was put to death, and every one that was fit for a slave was enslaved."[1] Such was the savage nature of war in those days. This important battle was fought A.D. 968.

Mahon took hostages from Molloy and Donovan, and for six years was the acknowledged King of Munster.

Ivar, who, with some of the Danes, had escaped to the coasts of Britain, collecting a large force, returned and took possession of Iniscatha and the islands at the mouth of the Fergus. He entered into a conspiracy with Molloy and Donovan to entrap and assassinate Mahon. He was invited to the house of Donovan at Bruree, in the county of Limerick, and went there under a safe-conduct ratified by the bishop and clergy. From thence he was induced to proceed into Molloy's country, and was treacherously murdered at the hill now known as Sliabh Riach, on the borders of Cork and Limerick, within a few miles of Fermoy.

The plot was so far successful, but it led to the ruin of the

[1] *Cogadh Gaedhal 'se Gallaibh.*

three chief conspirators, for it paved the way to the throne of Munster for Mahon's more vigorous brother Brian, whose whole soul was bent on avenging the murder. The accession of Brian to the throne marks the most remarkable epoch—excepting only the arrival of St. Patrick—in the annals of ancient Ireland. The whole country may be regarded as having been one vast battlefield. Blood flowed freely through the length and breadth of the land. The peace that settled down on the people after the introduction of Christianity had been rudely interrupted by the incursions of the northern barbarians. Those marauders, hovering in their ships round the coast, chose, as already stated, the times and places most favourable for attack, and, though often repulsed, only too often, nevertheless, succeeded in carrying away booty; and, worse still, planted their feet firmly in some of the maritime cities and towns. Their advent was the signal for the revival of the old spirit of internecine struggle among the petty kings and princes. Old jealousies were stirred up. The *divide et impera* policy of later invaders was brought into play, and the spectacle had been not infrequently witnessed, for more than a hundred years preceding, of Irish kings and princes making war, not only on each other, but even on holy places, with the aid of the foreign pagans.

It can well be conceived how learning and religion must have suffered amid such deplorable intestine disorders. The cloister was no longer a safe retreat for those who desired to renounce the world for the service of God; and the hot passion of war left little time or thought for the pursuit of science or learning. But with Brian's elevation to the throne of Cashel of the Kings, the hope of a brighter future began to dawn on the scene of turmoil and slaughter. It was the glorious destiny of this the most illustrious of the Clare Dalcassians, that for him was reserved the freeing, not only of his own principality of Thomond and kingdom of Munster, but of the whole island, from the hated yoke of the Dane; and the substitution of law and order for the chaos into which the country was plunged. In the very year when the Danes imposed their rule on the Saxons and Britons, the Irish, under

Brian, utterly and finally defeated and routed them. But I am anticipating.

Having secured himself on the throne from which so many of his Dalcassian predecessors were unjustly excluded, Brian's first thought was to rescue the holy sanctuary of St. Senan from the hands of the Danes. In 975 he seized on Iniscatha, and doubtless made short work of its Danish usurpers, for we find the Four Masters speak of it as a "violation." In their monastical view of things, any attack, followed by bloodshed, upon a religious retreat was regarded as a violation; but possibly, with the rest of their countrymen, they found it an easy task to condone such a vigorous display of religious patriotism. Following up this success, he attacked the Danes of Limerick, and slew Ivar, their king, and his two sons. Harold, another of his sons, having been elected in his stead, with the aid of Brian's inveterate enemy, Donovan of Hy Figeinte, assumed sway in Limerick. The victorious Brian would not brook such insolence in his kingdom of Munster. He made an incursion first into Donovan's territory, overcoming and slaying him; and then, attacking Harold, made a great slaughter of his people, including himself; and returned home loaded with immense spoils, in the second year after the murder of Mahon.[1]

In the Dublin copy of the *Annals of Innisfallen* the above events are thus curtly described, and given under the year 977: "Brian, son of Kennedy, marched at the head of an army to Hy Figeinte, where he was met by Donovan, chief of that territory, aided by Auliff, King of the Danes of Munster. Brian gave them battle, wherein Auliff and the Danes and Donovan and his Irish forces were all cut off."

The work his heart was most set on remained yet to be accomplished. Having thus punished the subordinates in the treacherous murder of his brother, his next effort was directed against the arch-conspirator, Maelmuidh himself. In making war on him, he had not only to avenge the death of Mahon, but also to assert the Dalcassian claim to the throne of Munster. Gathering round him the clans with whom he had marched so often to victory, he proceeded into the country of

[1] *Cogadh Gaedhal 'se Gallaibh.*

the Eugenians. Maelmuidh met him at the head of his own forces, and as many of the Danes as he could muster after their many defeats. The battle was fought at a place called by the Four Masters, Beallach-Leachta. The battlefield is differently named by the other annalists, and the date given is not the same. This is clear proof—and the remark applies to most of the events recorded in the annals of ancient Ireland—that various but independent sources of information existed, differing, as might be expected, in details, but all testifying to the substantial accuracy of the fact recorded.

In the present instance they all agree in describing the victory of Brian and his Dalcassians as complete and final over Maelmuidh and his Eugenians and their foreign allies; twelve hundred men fell on their side. Maelmuidh himself was slain by the hand of Morogh, son of Brian, who, though probably little more than a stripling, had the proud satisfaction of avenging his uncle's murder. The result of this decisive battle, as between the rival claimants to the throne of Munster, was that the whole course of Munster history was reversed. The Eugenians, who had for so many centuries held sway with the strong hand, were so crushed and broken that they never again made any notable effort to recover their lost prestige. Brian, the head of the Dalcassian clans, was at once recognised as not only King of Munster, but, so prominent had his victorious career made him, of Leathmogha, or the southern half of Ireland. It needs no effort of imagination to picture the scenes of rejoicing which must have been witnessed from end to end of Clare, but especially in the royal palace of Kincora, on the return of Brian and his victorious troops. Many other victories were on previous occasions celebrated, but this one outshone and crowned them all. It restored to the Thomond clans the rights of which they had been for so long and so unjustly deprived. Their rivals in South Munster had hitherto ignored their claims to alternate rule, founded on the undisputed will of their common ancestor, Oilioll Oluim. A keen sense of injury rankled in the breasts of this proud race from generation to generation. The day eagerly longed for to assert their hereditary rights had at length arrived. Their chosen prince was pre-eminently gifted with that warlike genius, that fertility of resource, that talent for combination, which alone was required to give full effect to Dalcassian daring and bravery. Under such a leader success in any undertaking was assured, and the decisive victory of Beallach-Leachta brought into every household in Thomond the proud conviction that the brand of inferiority was removed—that henceforth power and authority in the broad domain of Munster and Leinster belonged to the Dalcassian race.

Little time, however, was given to rejoicing. Soon after, he turned his arms against the Prince of Ossory. It may be that the latter had aided his enemies in the late struggle, or that he had refused to acknowledge Brian's authority; but, whatever the cause, the Dalcassians were marched into Ossory, and, over-running that country, returned with much booty, and brought the Prince Gilla Phadruig with them prisoner. On his return, Brian found that, taking advantage of his absence, Maelseachlain, who had lately assumed the sovereignty of Ireland, jealous very probably of the growing power and influence of Brian, entered into and ravaged the principality of Thomond. This unjustifiable attack was aggravated by an insult of a very marked and offensive character.

From time immemorial it was the custom, when the election of each succeeding chief of the Dalcassians took place, to have a solemn inauguration of his authority, in presence of the representatives of all the clans, at the place called Magh-Adhair,[1] about half-way between Tulla and Quin. The selection was invariably made from the O'Briens, the most numerous and powerful of the clans, and ratified by having the wand of dignity and office handed over by the chief of the MacNamaras, the next in rank and power, at the great tree of Magh-Adhair. The indignation of Brian and his Dalcassians was intense when they learned that not only

---

[1] A notable event took place at Magh-Adhair in the reign of Lorcan, Brian's grandfather. In an invasion of Thomond by Flann, the Ard-Righ, he occupied this fort, and, in contempt, sat down playing chess on it with one of his nobles. An account of this insult was soon conveyed to the Dalcassian clans. Hastening from all sides, they bore down on the king, and kept up a desultory fight for three days, compelling him to retreat with considerable loss.—*Book of Munster*, Vallencey's Collection, vol. i. p. 450.

was their country ravaged, but that this tree—the emblem, in a sense, of elective authority in Thomond—was, in a spirit of wanton insult, torn up by the roots, cut into pieces, and carried off to be used in roofing the monarch's palace. Brian lost no time in seeking ample satisfaction for the wrongs he and his people suffered. He entered the Ard-Righ's territory with an army, but contented himself on this occasion with devastating that portion of it now called Westmeath. Later on in this history, it will appear that it was an unlucky hour for Maelseachlain, when, in the exuberance of youthful ardour and lately-acquired power, he determined to measure swords with the aspiring chief of the Dal Cas.

A period of peace succeeded. For some considerable time Brian reigned undisturbed over the southern half of Ireland. Even the Ard-Righ seemed unwilling to provoke any further the hostility of Brian and the well-tried warriors of Thomond. During this interval he turned his attention to the internal administration of his kingdom. It is only reasonable to assume that a prince endowed with such a vigorous intellect applied himself energetically to the much-needed task of restoring order in the distracted land. He could scarcely have neglected doing for his own kingdom that which he afterwards accomplished with such marked success for the whole nation. The first interruption to this unwonted tranquillity was an incursion, made A.D. 987, by the men of Munster against the people of Connaught. They were defeated, and with great loss, deservedly, for they pressed into their service against their fellow-countrymen the common enemy, the Danes. It was the first serious reverse they endured, owing, no doubt, in some measure to the fact that Brian himself was not there to lead. The command was given to Dunlaing, who must have been a brother's son, or near relation of Brian, as he is called by the Four Masters "the royal heir, *i.e.* Tanist of Munster," and who paid with his life for the unprovoked assault. In the same battle fell also his opponent, the Righ Damna, or Tanist of Connaught.

Brian had not forgotten or forgiven the attack of Maelseachlain on his territory. That inauspicious event marked the beginning of what proved to be a lifelong duel between the two most powerful of the Irish princes, and prolific of ruin and misery to their subjects. Finding the Ard-Righ engaged in warfare with Connaught, Brian once more, A.D. 995, led his troops into Westmeath, and, though the Four Masters state that "they did not take a cow or a person, but went off from thence by secret flight," the account given in the *Annals of Clonmacnoise* seems far more probable, as being written in the invaded territory. It is as follows: "During the time the Ard-Righ was in Connaught, Bryan Borowe with his Munster men came to Meath and there wasted and destroyed all places until he came to Lough Innell, where the king's house was; insomuch that they left not cow, beast, or man that they could meet withal, untaken, ravished, and taken away." In return for this, Maelseachlain marched his troops into Munster, and, meeting the Munster forces at a place called Carn-Fordroma (not now recognised), inflicted on them a severe defeat.[1] Not to speak of wounded or captured, six hundred of the Munster army were killed, including Donal, Brian's uncle, who very probably had command, as no mention is made of Brian's presence at the fight. (A few years before, A.D. 993, Brian had advanced in a fleet of boats up the Shannon, to the extremity of Lough Righ, and there took satisfaction for the defeat the Munster men suffered at the hands of the Connaught men. He returned with much booty from Leitrim and Cavan.)

The victory of Maelseachlain at Carn-Fordroma was followed by a kind of truce, which lasted many years. Both sides seemed weary of the struggle. Brian had to submit to the authority of the Ard-Righ, and when war broke out again he was not this time the aggressor. Whatever gave occasion to it, Maelseachlain in the year 994 again invaded Munster, and, being met by Brian and his army at Aenach-Thete, now called Nenagh, defeated him with great loss. At this period of his rule Maelseachlain exhibited great vigour. Again and again he had made the Danes feel the weight of his arm, but was unable to hold them in permanent subjection, much less to drive them from the kingdom. Maelseachlain and Brian, forgetting for a while their domestic feuds in a spirit of

[1] Four Masters.

patriotism, which brought joy to the whole nation, united their forces, and in 997 marched to attack the foreigners in their greatest stronghold. They seized Ath-Cliath (Dublin), and carried off the greater part of the wealth of the Danes, as well as hostages for their future good behaviour. Having, as they perhaps thought, thoroughly subdued the Danish spirit, they parted company; for we find in the *Annals of Ulster* that in that same year the Ard-Righ made an incursion into Connaught; while Brian, on his return through Leinster, once more subjected to his yoke the stubborn people of that province, renewing the claim to that ancient tribute, by reason of which he got the surname of Boroimhe, or "Cow-tribute."

It would appear that the Danes, receiving probably reinforcements from abroad, became soon again troublesome. They made war on Leinster, taking its king, Donal, captive, and preyed upon the whole province. To curb and keep in check the rising power of the foreigners, Maelseachlain—whom we shall henceforward call by the name better known in modern history, Malachy—and Brian reunited their forces and marched towards Dublin. The Danes, emerging from their fortresses, encountered the Irish forces at Glenmama, now Dunlavin, in the county of Wicklow, and there suffered a severe defeat. They were pursued into Dublin, which was again captured, and for a whole week Malachy and Brian ravaged the town, taking from the Danish invaders the plunder they had carried away from the sacking of Clonard, Kells, and so many other religious establishments. There was again rejoicing in the halls of Kincora, and through the length and breadth of Thomond, at this second return of Brian and his Dalcassians, within so short a time, laden with gold and silver and carrying many prisoners.

The truce between Malachy and Brian was soon at an end. The year following, A.D. 999, Brian made manifest his determination to wrest the crown of Ireland from Malachy. This first attempt proved a failure, though made at the head of a numerous host. Collecting under his standard the forces of Leinster, Ossory, and South Connaught, and bringing with him also the vanquished Danes, who were only too glad to assist in widening the breach between their victorious enemies, he proceeded towards Tara. The Danes, who were mostly cavalry, pushing forward to be first in the plundering of that rich territory, were cleverly led into an ambush by Malachy, surrounded and cut to pieces almost to a man. This energetic movement of the Ard-Righ checked the ardour of Brian, and made him abandon for the present his pretence to the sovereignty of all Ireland. He broke up his army and "returned back without battle, without plundering, without burning. This was the first turning of Brian and the Connaught men against Malachy."[1]

Once more, A.D. 1001, he renewed his ambitious project of deposing Malachy and reigning in his stead. Marching at the head of an army composed of Munster, Leinster, and Danish troops, he proceeded towards Athlone, thus cutting in two the forces of Malachy and the men of Connaught, who had returned to their allegiance to the Ard-Righ. Malachy, overawed by the superior strength and activity of Brian, resigned the crown in his favour, and thus, for the first time in six hundred years, since the death of Crimhthan, supreme rule passed over into the hands of a prince of the Dalcassian line. It was no easy task to overthrow a dynasty as firmly established as any in all Christendom at that time, and Brian's success, if not evidence of his sense of justice, is certainly one of many proofs he gave that he was, to use a modern phrase, "a born leader of men." Malachy gets the credit from some of the annalists of yielding to his rival for the public good. What gives colour to this view of his submission, is the fact that not only did he not interfere with Brian's admittedly able and successful administration of the kingdom by attempting to reassert his ancestral rights, but that he at once ranged himself and his forces under Brian's banner.

Taking hostages soon after from the princes of Connaught, Brian, accompanied by Malachy, proceeded to the conquest of Ulster; but, meeting the northern army at Dundalk, determined to offer a stubborn resistance, he withdrew for the time, to prevent, say the chroniclers, the effusion of Irish blood.

[1] Four Masters.

Later on, he received the submission of the northern princes without bloodshed, which may be attributed, as the sequel will show, more to their being then unprepared for war than to the renown of his arms.

From the day he was acknowledged Ard-Righ, he devoted his energies to the internal administration of affairs, and with such success that the whole kingdom was blessed with such peace and plenty as it hardly ever enjoyed before or since. According to the Four Masters, he was then in the seventy-sixth year of his age; but the date of his birth, A.D. 941, given in the *Annals of Ulster*, seems more likely, as he would then be in his sixty-first year,—Malachy, whom he deposed, being about fifty-three. He set to work building or beautifying churches,—Killaloe, Iniscaltra, and Tuamgreine, in his own native Clare, being specially mentioned,—establishing monasteries, and administering justice with such a firm hand that during the rest of his reign violence of every kind almost disappeared from the land. In Moore's melody, "Rich and Rare," we have a poetical description of the state of the country in that blessed and happy interval. As far as can be gleaned from history, Brian's was among the most successful and the most prosperous reigns in all Christendom for centuries before and after. The unceasing incursions of the northern barbarians, as well as the constant wars between the Britons and Franks, kept these countries in turmoil and disorder, from which, for a time at least, the Irish nation was comparatively free, owing to the firmness with which Brian maintained his ascendancy.

The first local event of importance in Clare after the accession of Brian to supreme sway was the death of Concovar, chief of Corca Moyruadh. This territory is now recognised as the plain stretching along both sides of the river from Ennis towards Galway and on to the sea. Concovar, who was slain A.D 1002 in a petty quarrel with a Connaught clan, must have been a chief of more than ordinary note, for from him the O'Connors of West Clare took their surname. In the following year, 1003, Brian, supported by Malachy, marched through Connaught, with the object of proceeding round the whole coast of Ireland to assert his authority, but the men of the North stoutly resisted any encroachment on their territory. They met the monarch with such a show of resistance at Ballysadare, on the borders of Co. Sligo, that the latter turned back his forces, probably because he saw they were greatly outnumbered. This reverse did not turn Brian aside from his purpose of subjugating the whole of the North. About a year after he renewed the attack, but in a different direction. Proceeding through Meath, he marched northwards to Armagh, where he spent a week, and left upon the altar twenty ounces of gold,—a sum more than equivalent to ten times the amount in our time. Continuing his progress, he entered the territory of Dalriada, from which he returned after receiving hostages. But the Four Masters, evidently anxious to laud the independent spirit of the O'Neills and O'Donnells, quote, in a manner quite unusual with them, as if for greater authority, from the *Book of Clonmacnoise* and the *Book of the Island of Saints in Lough Righ*, to prove that Brian again failed to overcome the hardy clans of the north-west. The *Annals of Ulster*, however, which cannot be regarded as unduly biassed against the Ulster princes in favour of Brian, record his complete success in the second enterprise. Under the year 1005 they describe the triumphant progress of the monarch through the whole North, including by name Tirconnell and Tirowen. He then divided his army, the Leinster men going directly south to their own territory, the Danish contingent proceeding by sea to Dublin, while the men of Munster and Ossory retraced their steps homeward through Malachy's friendly territory. Thus, after many reverses, his perseverance and indomitable energy placed him at last on the highest pinnacle to which he could aspire. He returned to his palace of Kincora the acknowledged Ard-Righ of the Irish nation. The palace, looking down on the noble Shannon from the height on which now the village of Killaloe is built, became the centre of all authority in the island, and the Dalcassian clans secured hard-won precedence among the men of Erinn.

The years following afford proofs of the truth that "uneasy lies the head that wears a crown." Domestic troubles came thick upon him. First, his brother Marcan, "head of the clergy of Munster," which must mean Archbishop of Cashel, died. Then came the loss of his wife, the daughter of the King of Connaught, followed two years later on by the death of his son Donal. Nor was he free from other troubles. Though supreme monarch, the turbulent spirit of some of the subject princes left him little time for rest. In the year 1010 he once more led an army into Ulster, and, reducing the men of the North to submission, brought back with him their hostages to Thomond. Though history is silent on the subject, we can easily picture to ourselves the unhappy fate of some, at least, of those hostages, seeing that in the very next year we find Brian again turning his arms against, and bringing back with him "in obedience to Kincora," no less a personage than the prince himself of Tirconnell. His son Morogh was detached, after this success, with the bulk of the army, comprising the men of Munster, Leinster, Meath, and part of the North, to strike terror into, and reduce to thorough submission, the still defiant clans of the extreme North. With such a force victory was certain; and soon after they followed Brian southwards, bringing with them three hundred prisoners and a great prey of cattle.

Two years afterwards this same Morogh led an army into Ossory. What occasioned this invasion is not stated. Probably it was again to recover the tribute which caused so much bloodshed in the past; but be it what it may, the punishment inflicted on the unfortunate inhabitants was very severe. The whole country as far as Glendalogh and Kilmainham was plundered, and Morogh carried back with him "great spoils and innumerable prisoners." From this forward, not only from Ossory, but from all Ireland, tribute flowed regularly to Kincora. Keating, translating from an ancient MS., styled *Boroimhe Baile na Righ*, gives the following: "From Connaught annually on the 1st of November 800 cows and 800 hogs. From Tyrconnell 500 cloaks or mantles and 500 cows. From Tyrowen 60 hogs and 60 loads of iron. The Clan Ruraighe of Ulster were bound to furnish 150 cows and 150 hogs. The people of the Oriels 160 cows. From Leinster 300 beeves, 60 hogs, and 60 loads of iron. From the Danes of Dublin 150 pipes or hogsheads of wine; and 365 pipes of red wine every year from the Danes of Limerick." The tribute from Munster is not stated; probably it was mostly, if not altogether, service in time of war.

Brian was now far advanced in years, and might naturally be supposed to long for rest and the quiet enjoyment of his throne. But a great achievement, and one which singled him out as one of the most powerful and most successful princes of his age, was still in store for him. Having created a nation out of a number of petty and conflicting principalities, he conceived the bold project of crushing the foreign power that had been taking deep root in the country during the preceding two centuries. Those pagan marauders, swooping down in their ships from the bleak countries of Northern Europe, carried into every nation they attacked the terror of their arms. Their first object was plunder, but, flushed by success, they soon aimed at permanent dominion. They completely subjugated the English nation, establishing firmly there a Danish dynasty. In Ireland the resistance offered to their frequent attacks was so stubborn that they could plant themselves only in the neighbourhood of harbours, where their ships afforded them support in time of attack or refuge in case of defeat. Their coming, though disastrous in the extreme to the country, was not an unmixed evil. Communication with other nations was made more easy, and commercial enterprise became largely developed. Hence, in Dublin, Waterford, Limerick, and other places similarly situated, they were so far tolerated that intermarriages between them and the Irish were of not infrequent occurrence. Brian himself married the divorced wife of a Dane, and, as we have seen, made use at the outset of his career of the Danish arms in the furtherance of his ambitious projects. Nevertheless, they were still "ferocious," made frequent war on Irish chieftains, and mercilessly plundered religious houses.

The opportunity now presented itself to decide once and for ever whether they were to be any longer masters in Ireland. Hitherto the jealousies and intestine quarrels of the Irish princes made any combined resistance to the invaders impossible. Now, however, that Brian had secured such sway as no Irish king had hardly ever before enjoyed, the patriotic purpose to rid Ireland of the foreign yoke took possession of his heart. It is not at all unlikely that the recent insolent activity of the Danes against Brian's authority had much to say to this determination. They had not only joined the Leinster king, Maelmorha, in his resistance to the payment of the tribute, but, moved probably by a desire to weaken Brian's prestige, had collected a fleet and attacked and burned Cork, the principal seaport in Brian's own hereditary kingdom of Munster. Here, however, they met with severe chastisement. Before they could effect their retreat, the people of South Munster, under the leadership of Cathal, a local chief, attacked them, slaying great numbers; among these being the son of Sitric, lord of the foreigners, who was a nephew of the King of Leinster. Many other notable men among the Danes and their Leinster allies were slain or captured.

In the preceding years Brian had been gradually strengthening and fortifying his own kingdom of Munster. All the annalists describe the works in which he engaged. He constructed roads and built bridges, to enable him to concentrate his forces, whether for attack or defence. He fortified more strongly than ever his own palace of Kincora, and built fortresses likewise in Roscrea, Cahir, Bruree, Limerick, and various other places, some of which cannot now be recognised in the Irish names given. Nor were the needs of religion overlooked. Churches and monasteries claimed much of his attention. He enlarged and beautified many of these; special mention being made of Killaloe, Iniscaltra, and Tuamgreine, where he built also a *Cloctheac*, or round tower.[1] This may throw some light on the

---

[1] "It is Brian also that gave distinctive surnames to the men of Ireland, by which every tribe of them is known. It is by him, likewise, the church of Cill Dalua and the church of Inis Cealtra were erected, and the steeple of Tuaim Greine was renewed."—Keating quoting MacLiag. The present church of Killaloe, built by Donal Mor, at the close of the twelfth century, replaced it.

vexed question of the origin of those graceful structures, even though no trace of this one now remains. He wisely decreed that families and clans should henceforth adopt surnames in order to facilitate the transmission of property, and to give greater clearness and sequence to Irish history. It is probable enough that, encouraged by him, his example was followed by the other princes, thus providing for the better internal administration as well as for the greater security of the whole kingdom.

He now resolved to precipitate a decisive struggle with the Danish power. His first step was in marching an army towards the borders of Leinster, and fixing a camp at a place called Slieve Mairge, to serve both as a threat and a check to the enemy. He then repeated the exploit of his son Morogh, as related above, traversing the plains of Leinster to Glendalogh, pushing on to the very walls of Dublin, and returned with great booty. Neither were his opponents idle. Fearing to attack Brian himself, they went northwards to strike at his trusty ally Malachy, and, probably taking him by surprise, plundered the country and the churches, taking off with them "many captives and countless cattle."[1]

Both sides were now thoroughly exasperated, and each determined at any risk to put an end as soon as possible, in one great battle, to this desultory but ruinous conflict. The Danes summoned to their aid "the foreigners of the west of Europe," among whom were a thousand men clad in "coats of mail."[2] They had as their allies the troops of the King of Leinster, aided by his subordinate princes, notably the brave O'Tooles and O'Byrnes. Brian's army was composed mainly of his own brave and well-trained Clare and Tipperary Dalcassians, upon whom, as we shall presently see, fell the brunt of the fighting and the greater part of the loss. With them fought the clans of Munster and South Connaught. The Irish, too, who had colonised Scotland, sent a contingent to aid their brethren against the common enemy; but the most deserving of credit on the Irish side was Malachy with his Meath men. This prince, forgetting the injustice done him,

[1] Four Masters.   [2] *Ibid.*

in his zeal for the public good, so far from holding aloof while the battle was proceeding, as some writers most unjustly and without any show of authority allege, contributed largely to the greatness of the victory. He, "by dint of battling bravery and striking," say the Four Masters, completed the overthrow of the enemy even after so many of the Dalcassian and other chiefs had been slain. History does not furnish a brighter example of unselfish patriotism than is found in the relations of Malachy with Brian, during the twelve years from the day of his deposition to his restoration after the death of Brian at Clontarf.

The particulars of the great battle cannot be given with any certainty. The fact of its being fought at Clontarf, under the walls of the Danish stronghold, is proof enough that Brian forced the fighting. Like all the battles of the period, it partook in a great measure of the character of a hand-to-hand fight. Even bows and arrows were then unknown. Cold steel alone, the battle-axe, pike, and sword, decided the issue — "bravery and striking," as the Four Masters pithily put it. The numbers engaged on both sides are not given in any of the Irish or Danish accounts of the battle; but as the Danes suffered a loss, according to the least computation, of four thousand, including the thousand in armour to a man, and three thousand fell of the Leinster forces, it is clear that more than twenty thousand on each side must have entered on the struggle. Though called the "battle of Clontarf," and notwithstanding the common belief that all the fighting took place along the shore of Dublin Bay, between what is now called the Crescent, near Annesley Bridge, and Conquer Hill at Dollymount, it is very probable that much, if not most, of the battle raged much nearer, and on the site now occupied by North Dublin itself.

This may be inferred from the description given in what is regarded as one of the most ancient and reliable of our Irish annals, the *Wars of the Gaedhal with the Gaill*. In page 181, the writer, who is believed to have been a contemporary, if not MacLiag, Brian's historian,—or if not a contemporary, one who must have lived, as the whole tone and method of the narration implies, while the stirring scenes of the great battle were still fresh in men's minds,—says, "And it was attested by the foreigners, men and women, who were watching from the battlements of Ath-Cliath, that as they beheld they used to see flashes of fire from them on all sides," probably the sun-flashes from the helmets and weapons of the combatants. And again, the King of the Danes of Dublin says to his wife, who was a daughter of Brian, "Well do the foreigners reap the field; many is the sheaf they turn over;" to which the Dalcassian woman retorted, "It will be at the end of the day that will be seen." From these extracts it would appear that friends and foes could be distinguished by those anxiously watching from the walls, which could hardly be the case if they were so far off from the Dublin of that day as has been generally surmised.

Later on, when it became evident that victory declared for Brian, as the Danes were seen flying to the sea, his daughter taunted her husband for his boasting in the early part of the day. "It appears to me that the foreigners have gained their inheritance." "What meanest thou, O woman?" said he. "The foreigners are going into the sea—their natural inheritance. I wonder is it heat that is upon them?" she asked; for which, it is told, he dealt her a rude blow.[1] It may be added that some of the earlier writers do not call it the battle of Cluain Tairibh. The *Neala Saga*, a Danish narrative, calls it "The Battle of Brian," and the history already quoted speaks of it as the "Battle of the Fishing Weir of Clontarf," which was situated on the Tolka, near Ballybough Bridge, and therefore nearer to Dublin than to the present Clontarf. But it little matters where exactly the great battle raged. The fortunes of the day may have brought the thick of the fight now nearer to Clontarf, now nearer to Dublin, thus covering the whole ground in dispute. The Danes, or "foreigners of the West of Europe," as the Four Masters call them, for their army had been recruited not only from the shores of the Baltic, but also from England, the islands round Scotland, and the territories along the German Ocean over which they had established their supremacy, were under the command of two formidable warriors,

[1] *Cogadh Gaedhal 'se Gallaibh.*

Brodar and Sigurd of the Isles. With them also were the Leinster tribes, dragged probably against their will into this unnatural contest by their king, Maelmorha, who could not brook Brian's supremacy, or it may very probably be because of his renewing and exacting from them the Boroimhe tribute. Having learned that Brian had sent a detachment under his son Donogh to forage in Leinster, they resolved, at a council of war held on Holy Thursday, to surprise Brian's army before the return of Donogh. They at once drew out of Dublin as many as could be spared from the garrison, and sent their ships along the coast to bring together all their available forces, "both the foreigners of Ath-Cliath and the Leinster men, and they formed seven great battalions."[1]

Brian, having learned from his scouts that an attack in great force was contemplated, did not wait for it in camp. He marched out, leaving a sufficient force to watch the city, and, selecting his ground, took up a position directly in the line of the Danish advance. During the march, the Dalcassian clans, with probably Malachy and his Meathmen, and the Celts of Scotland under Donal, Steward of Mar, being the flower of Brian's army, were under the command of Morogh—the king himself being too old to take part in the struggle. Marching with these were the Eoghanachts, led on by their respective chiefs, supported by the men of the present county of Waterford and the southern portion of Tipperary, under Mothla, chief of the Deisi. The Connaughtmen brought up the rear, under the command of their chiefs, O'Kelly and O'Heyne.

A somewhat similar order was observed in the opposing army —the foreign Danes, including the thousand men in armour, marching in front under the leadership of Brodar—the Danes of Ireland advancing under the command of Dubhgall, son of Aulaff, their king, and in the rear were the men of Leinster, led on by their king, Maelmorha. Late in the evening of Holy Thursday, April 22, A.D. 1014, the two armies sighted each other; but, darkness coming on, the dread conflict had to be postponed till the following morning. It is probable, though neither the Danish nor the Irish annalists say anything on

[1] *Cogadh Gaedhal 'se Gallaibh.*

the subject, that the interval was availed of on both sides to form into regular order of battle. It is certain that Morogh and Brodar, with their contingents, were opposed to each other,—Morogh on the left wing of the Irish army, next the sea and the Danish fortress, consequently the post of danger and honour; and Brodar commanding the corresponding right wing of the Danish advance. In the Irish centre were the troops of Connaught, under the command of their princes, O'Kelly and O'Heyne, to whom were opposed the men of Leinster, under Maelmorha, the rear on both sides having advanced during the night; and on the Irish right fought the Eoghanacht clans, supported by Mothla, prince of the Deisi, and Donal, Steward of Mar, with whom fought, on the Danish left, the Danes of Ireland, under the command of Sitric and Dubhgall, son of Aulaff, King of Dublin.

The dawn of the following eventful day, Good Friday, April 23, 1014, found the two armies within striking distance of each other, and then commenced in right earnest one of those conflicts which try the mettle of nations as well as men, and mark a turning-point in history. Every man of both armies, rising from the ground on which he lay, saw in the dim early light his armed foe to his face, and, in self-defence, had at once to strike, without so much as a thought of food or drink. They were, if not all, almost all trained soldiers, inured to battle, either the vanquishers or the vanquished in many a well-contested battle. War was their usual occupation, and this accounts for the stubborn, deadly struggle maintained on either side from dark to dark. No raw levies or hastily-formed battalions could have been equal to such a fearful strain. Even in the famous battles of Crecy and Agincourt, fought much later on, when the fatal art of war had acquired more method, panic soon decided the issue, leaving little else to the victors but pursuit and slaughter. All that long day at Clontarf there was no thought of retreat on either side. Man fought with man, steel encountered steel; ay, even, as in the case of young Turlogh, grandson of Brian, when the hand, wearied and tired and powerless from slaughter, refused to do its fell work, the death-grip was held till the rising waters of the incoming tide quenched the lives of both combatants for ever.

History affords but few examples of such a well-contested battle, or of such obstinate, it may well be called desperate, valour on both sides. The long incessant fight of twelve hours gives colour to the tradition recording the manner of Morogh's death. It is related that, having flung to the earth a Danish chief, Anrud, whom he encountered late in the day, while bending over him, trying to drive with his chest the sword his swollen hand could not grasp through his prostrate foe, the latter, seizing his opportunity, slew him with a quick upward thrust of his dagger.

So waged the fight all that memorable day, no quarter sought or given by Dane or Celt, till, at the approach of night, the foreigners began to give way all along the line. Irish valour was triumphant. The foe that found such easy prey on the Saxon race bit the dust before Brian's battled array. Even with the knowledge that they had their ships and their fortresses close at hand, they were not able to hold the field. But just before the final rout the most tragic event of that tragic day occurred. Brodar,[1] with some of his Danes, being hard pressed, took refuge in the wood of Tomar skirting the battlefield, and near which was pitched the tent of the aged Irish monarch. His bodyguard, dreading danger no longer, pushed forward to feast their eyes on the flight of the enemy. Brodar, from his hiding-place, saw his advantage, and, rushing forth, struck down the defenceless old king, who was on his knees in prayer,[2] calling those with him to witness that his hand it was that smote to death the monarch of Erinn. But his boasting was soon at an end. The Dalcassian bodyguard of Brian, returning soon to their charge, saw with horror the lifeless remains of their loved chief, and, pursuing his slayer, they in their indignation slowly disembowelled him.[3]

Darkness was settling down on that field of carnage, under cover of which the Danes and their Irish allies retreated, leaving Brian's army in undisputed possession of the battleground.

What joy and what sorrow in the Irish camp that night!

[1] *Neala Saga*—the Danish Chronicle.
[2] Marianus Scotus, O'Flaherty's *Ogygia*, p. 380.   [3] *Neala Saga.*

Victory, indeed, was theirs,—one of the most notable victories of that age,—but at what a cost! Neither the Irish nor the Danish writers offer any conjecture as to the numbers who fell on the Irish side. The Danes who fled could not pretend to count the slain, and the Irish annalists, while giving the numbers of the enemy killed, are silent as to the total losses on their own side. At the lowest computation, about five thousand of the "foreigners" left their bones on the plains of Clontarf, among these the thousand in mail, who were cut down to a man, the weight of their armour in all probability rendering escape from their unencumbered victors impossible.

Their Leinster allies lost three thousand more—a total of eight thousand slain on one side, showing the determined and desperate character of a conflict where "bravery and striking" alone, unaided by any of the later inventions for killing, had to decide the issue. Among these were Maelmorha, King of Leinster, from whose son Bran the Ui Broin or O'Byrnes of Leinster take their surname; MacTuathal Brogarvan, Tanist of Offaly, ancestor of the O'Tooles, and many other chiefs of note who followed the standard of Maelmorha, together with Brodar, Sigurd or Sitric, Dubhgall, and many others of the formidable Danish leaders.[1] The loss of chiefs on the Irish side was still greater, including Morogh, Brian's son, Turlogh his grandson, Conaing his nephew; Mothla, chief of the Deisi; Eogha, chief of the Clann Scannlan of Kerry, Niall O'Quin of Inchiquin, and Cuduligh—these three being Brian's chief companions, or noblemen of the bed-chamber;[2] Donal of Corcovaskin; O'Kelly and O'Heyne of Connaught; Donal, Steward of Mar; with many others of nearly equal note. But, most lamented of all, Brian himself fell in the hour of his greatest achievement, in the moment when victory crowned the fiercest struggle of his long and chequered career.[3] The chance blow of a defeated and flying Dane

---

[1] Four Masters.   [2] *Ann. Clonmacnoise.*

[3] His sceptre and harp are still in existence. The sceptre was presented to the Museum of the Royal Dublin Society by the Marchioness of Thomond, after the death of her husband without issue in 1857. The harp is now in the Museum of Trinity College. It had been presented by Donogh, Brian's son, to the Pope, with the regalia of Ireland. It was given to Henry VIII. when that dutiful son of the Church received the title of

struck down to the earth, in his hoary old age, the man whose genius and force of character and soldierly qualities welded the discordant elements of Irish life into a force that successfully resisted and crushed for all time in Erinn the formidable foe whose iron hand smote down and kept in subjection the other peoples of Northern Europe.

Defender of the Faith. He gave it to the first Lord Clanrickard. From that family it passed to the MacMahons of Clenagh, near Newmarket-on-Fergus, now represented by John O'Connell of Longfield and Kildysart, grand-nephew of the Liberator, and from them to the Right Hon. M. Conyngham in 1782. He gave it in charge to Trinity College, where it is jealously preserved.—*Collectanea in Rebus Hibernicis.*

CHAPTER VII.

FROM 1014 TO 1086.

Dissensions among the Victors—Brian's son Donogh procures the Murder of Teigue, his own Brother—He becomes King of Munster—Claims Supreme Rule—Parliament at Killaloe—Donogh flies to Rome with the Regalia of Ireland—Turlogh succeeds—His Exploits.

THE fall of Brian, with his son and grandson, all three together, in that glorious but fatal field, threw the whole kingdom once more into a state of anarchy. Had they survived, the whole current of Irish history might have taken a direction very different from that which it afterwards pursued. Supreme power would certainly rest with them. No Irish prince would be likely to measure his strength with the victors of Clontarf. The prestige acquired by such a splendid achievement could not but make more than ever potent for good the already acknowledged administrative capacity of the old monarch; and this, supported by such vigour and bravery as Morogh and his son Turlogh displayed in the battlefield, might well have secured to their house the allegiance of the whole nation. Under a strong central authority, time would cement together by degrees the elements of Irish society, and such a nation in those days would have been safe from the invasion which afterwards brought on Ireland prolonged and acute misery. But for this view of what might have happened after Clontarf, much as the Irish mind may love to dwell on it, there is only conjecture.

Still it is not to be supposed that the victory was entirely barren of good results. One great object was achieved—the Danish power was finally broken, and all fear of a permanent occupation of the country by these Northern barbarians disappeared. The conversion of some of them to Christianity had little if any effect on the general character of the invaders.

They remained to the end plunderers and devastators, attacking churches as freely as lay property, wherever they could, and in their incursions sparing neither age nor sex. Those of them who settled in the cities did indeed open up the great highway of the sea, by which commerce, to a degree unknown before, was greatly facilitated, but this advantage, substantial as it was, was, all things considered, but poor compensation for the ruin they wrought during two centuries on the face of the whole country. The Dalcassian victory destroyed for ever their power for evil in the country. Some of them were allowed to remain in the interests of trade and commerce, but after Clontarf they are hardly to be heard of any more in Irish history.

In the Four Masters [1] we find the following record: "Maelmuire" (which signifies servant of Mary), "son of Eochaidh, successor of Patrick, proceeded with the seniors and relics to Aord-Choluim-Chilli; and they carried from thence the body of Brian, King of Ireland, and the body of Murchadh, his son, and the head of Conaing and the head of Mothla. Maelmuire and his clergy waked the bodies with great honour and veneration; and they were interred in Ardmacha in a new tomb." We can well picture to ourselves the gloom and grief, struggling with pride, that settled down on the people of Thomond, when it became known that they were not to have the sad satisfaction of receiving the hero's remains. But they belonged to Ireland more than to Thomond, and it was becoming that Erinn's Primatial See should be their shrine, and St. Patrick's successor their custodian.

Henceforward in the pages of this narrative, events of a very different character, sad to say, will have to be recorded for the most part. Dissension sprung up at once, not only among the rival clans, but even among the Dalcassians themselves. Immediately after the quotation given above, from the Four Masters, relating the mode and place of Brian's and Morogh's burial, we read the following: "A battle between the two sons of Brian, *i.e.* Dounchadh and Tadgh. Dounchadh was defeated, and Ruaideri Ma Donnagain, Lord of Aradh, and

[1] O'Donovan's translation, which, with his learned notes, is largely availed of through this work.

many others along with him fell in the battle." Thus the disappearance of Brian and Morogh from the scene began only too soon, in the very year of their great triumph, to foreshadow disaster. But before this acute crisis among the Dalcassians themselves was reached, they had to encounter, in their weakened condition, two grave and threatening dangers. Malachy, who had acted with such magnanimity throughout, was, immediately after the battle of Clontarf, acknowledged King of Ireland once more. The death of Brian, who had wrested the throne from him, cleared the way to his restoration. The Dalcassian princes, even if so inclined, were not in a position, after their enormous losses, to dispute his right. They were more concerned with resisting the claims advanced on the spot by Cian, representing the Eoghanachts, to the throne of Munster. He appealed to the well-known will of their common ancestor, Oilioll Oluim, regulating an alternate succession between the Eoghanacht and Dalcassian chiefs; but the latter alleged, as well they could, that the Eoghanachts had again and again violated the compact, and should not demand its revival. They would maintain, they declared, by force of arms, if driven to it, the rights won only by force of arms by their great father; and promptly refused to yield up hostages to Cian as a surrender of those rights. Fortunately for the decimated Dalcassians, as well as in the interests of peace, there was dissension among the Eoghanacht chiefs. Donal, son of Duvdavoren, viewed with jealousy the attempt of Cian, who had married Saibh, Brian's daughter, to seat himself on the throne of Munster. The design of Cian becoming known to him, he resolved to defeat it. Withdrawing his contingent from the Eoghanacht force, his rival found himself unable, single-handed, to cope with the Dalcassian troops, and prudently turned southwards from the borders of Kildare towards his own country.

Another and an equally dangerous foe presented himself to the Thomond troops, on their way back. The people of Ossory, under their chief, MacGiolla Phadruig, through whose country the Thomond troops were marching home, seized the opportunity for revenge offered them by the weakness of their hereditary enemy. They swarmed down on them with such determination, and in such numbers, as threatened to annihilate them. This treacherous and cowardly attack at such a time aroused the indignation of the Dalcassians to such a pitch, that even the wounded insisted on being allowed to share in the fight. At their urgent request, stakes from a neighbouring wood were fixed in the ground, on which they might support their weakened frames, keeping their right hand free to strike. Near each wounded man was posted a soldier to shield and succour him, and in this unexampled manner they presented an undaunted front to the foe. This extraordinary order of battle so impressed their enemies, that they dared not risk an encounter with such enthusiastic valour, and retreated, leaving the way open for the remnant of Brian's army to proceed to their own country. The memory of this strange incident, so creditable to the spirit of the Dalcassian wounded warriors, is still preserved in the name of the place where it occurred—Gorthnaclea, *i.e.* " field of stakes," a townland in the barony of Upper Ossory in the Queen's County. Moore has immortalised it in his beautiful song, " Remember the glories of Brian the Brave," but his version of it there is not historically correct. "The moss of the valley " did not " grow red with their blood." They could not conquer, for the reason that the enemy did not close in the fight. Yet the poet's version is not unreasonably extravagant. The heroic spirit, ready to conquer or die, was certainly displayed there, and sheds a parting gleam of glory on the victors of Clontarf.

Though the Danes, after their long struggle to establish their rule in Ireland, as they had in England and some neighbouring nations, were finally crushed at Clontarf, yet it cannot be called a victory for Ireland. The death of Brian and Morogh and Turlogh in the same fatal hour, left the kingdom without any authoritative representative of that strong centralised authority which it was the whole aim of Brian's life to establish. The country literally fell to pieces once more. Malachy, indeed, was recognised as monarch. He had clearly the best right to supreme authority. Most of the chiefs and territorial princes looked with great jealousy on the Dalcassian ascendancy, and welcomed back to power the dethroned monarch. But nevertheless his prestige was gone. He had acknowledged and submitted to defeat, and that could never be forgotten by a people so proud and warlike as the Irish. He could not exercise the strong personal authority which Brian had won and maintained with his good sword. The old rivalries and family pretensions, no longer firmly kept in check, as in Brian's time, broke out afresh, and nowhere with more virulence and with more deplorable results than among the victorious Dalcassians themselves. The right of the throne of Munster, won for his house by Brian, was, after the Eugenian prince's vain protest, for some time undisputed; but which of his surviving sons was to succeed? It is probable that Teigue, the eldest living, was the elect of the Thomond clans. He was able to defeat in a battle the attempt of his ambitious brother Donogh, who had married Driella, sister of Harold, afterwards King of England, to oust him from the throne.[1] In this unnatural struggle much of the best blood on both sides of the Shannon was shamefully wasted; nor did it cease till, as a climax, the horrid crime of fratricide was perpetrated. But this did not take place for some years, during which Donogh was compelled to yield a sullen submission, as the energies of both, and all the forces they could command, were needed to repel the attacks which probably their own well-known internal dissensions invited.

The first came from their old rivals, the Eoghanachts. Donal, the son of Duvdavoren, who had befriended the Dalcassians on their return from Clontarf, now sought to reduce them to submission. He marched an army to Limerick, but was there met by Teigue and Donogh with their forces, and completely routed. He himself, "and numbers along with him, fell."[2]

In this year, 1015, the Four Masters note the death of "Meanma, son of the Lord of Ui Caisin," the chief of the clan, which soon after assumed the distinctive title of MacNamara. They record also a marauding expedition, headed by Mael-Foghartach, into Thomond. Great spoils were captured.

[1] Four Masters.   [2] Ibid.

A hastily-organised pursuit of the plunderers by Teigue and Morogh was unsuccessful, some of the leading chiefs being slain in the attempt to recover the spoil. But next year, A.D. 1016, even worse misfortune was in store for the harrassed and weakened Dalcassians. The clans of Connaught, finding the men who had reduced them to submission beset on every side, swooped down on them, and plundered and demolished Kincora and Killaloe.[1] The men of Thomond retaliated, pushing their way as far as the islands on Lough Righ, in which, doubtless for greater safety, much of the wealth of the province had been stored, and with which the Dalcassians returned triumphant. In this year died a man of great eminence, MacLiag, the chief poet of Ireland, and bosom friend of Brian Boroimhe, whose achievements, and, alas! whose tragic death too, had been the theme of his song.

For some years following peace reigned in Thomond. The Dalcassians, having made it clear that they could not be attacked with impunity, were allowed to recuperate after the heavy losses they had sustained. It was varied by one curious incident, recorded by the Four Masters, round which a mystery hangs. They give it in the following words, as occurring in the year A.D. 1019: "The son of Carnach, son of Aedh of the Ui Caisin" (*i.e.* the clan MacNamara), "attacked Donogh, son of Brian, and gave him a stroke of a sword in his head and across the arm, so that he struck off his right palm. The son of Brian afterwards escaped, and the son of Carnach was slain." This reads like a personal quarrel, resulting probably from some wrong done by Donogh, which brought death to the son of Carnach, and left Donogh maimed for life. But this was no stay to his ambitious designs. He longed to recover the dignity and authority won for the Dalcassian race by his father, and soon after the opportunity presented itself.

In two years, A.D. 1028, Malachy died, forty-three years after his being acknowledged Ard-Righ of Erinn. His death left the throne vacant, but one great obstacle to its possession presented itself to Donogh. His brother Teigue was acknowledged by the clans of Thomond as the heir to Brian's dignity.

---

[1] Four Masters.

He resolved to remove him from his path, and, forgetting the close tie of blood, and all law, human and Divine, he procured his assassination by the people of Ely O'Carroll. History does not tell how the foul deed was accomplished, or what price was paid for it. It lacked little, if anything, of the baseness of the crime of Richard III. much later on, and in a so-called more civilised age.

Another event followed close on this, which had no slight effect on the fortunes of Donogh. The Eugenian prince, Dungal, who ruled in Cashel during the temporary retirement of the Dalcassians, died in 1026, so that the provincial as well as the national throne offered itself to his grasp. The interval of two years since the murder of his brother sufficed to soften down somewhat the indignation naturally enkindled against him, so he determined to drown the remembrance of it in a bold effort to recover again the Dalcassian supremacy. Rallying around him the survivors of those who fought so often victoriously under the banner of his great father, as well as the many others who were fired to deeds of valour by the story of his triumphs, he marched straight into Meath, now bereft of its monarch, and, meeting with little opposition, pursued his way to Dublin, A.D. 1027, then back through Leinster and Ossory, bringing with him from all these places hostages in token of their submission. He was now beyond dispute King of Leathmogha, the southern half of Ireland.[1] But he was not allowed to pursue undisturbed his career of conquest. Flahertach, representing the Hy Nialls of the North, descended into Meath, and reduced it to submission; while the Ossorians, perhaps emboldened by this diversion, showing signs of revolt, were once more attacked by Donogh, whom this time they succeeded in defeating with great loss. This severe check reduced him for a while to inactivity, which was all the more galling, as he began to perceive a design on the part of Turlogh, the son of his murdered brother, to assert his right to the sovereignty.

It would be strange if he had not cause for such a

---

[1] His mother, Gormlaith, died in 1030. She had married first Aulaff, King of the Danes, next Brian, and finally Malachy. She was daughter of the King of Leinster, full of ambition, and void of morality.

suspicion. As we will find later on, this young man had inherited much of the fire of his grandsire, and it is no matter for wonder that he cherished within him an eager desire to avenge his father's death, and, at the same time, to assert his claim to the throne of Munster, and even of all Ireland. The first notable evidence of his ambitious views was an attack made on O'Dongan, chief of Ara-tire, the country lying along the eastern bank of the Shannon, in the principality of Thomond, who paid with his life his devotion to Donogh. It is probable that this onslaught was made while the latter was on an expedition against Art O'Ruarck, Prince of Breffney, as both events are recorded by the Four Masters as occurring in the same year, A.D. 1031. O'Ruarck had been carrying all before him along the course of the Shannon, overawing Connaught and threatening Thomond. Donogh wisely resolved not to wait for the attack on his own territory, so, pushing rapidly forward, he met O'Ruarck on the very day when he had plundered Clonfert, and defeated him with great loss of men and vessels.

This victory more than counterbalanced the defeat which he had sustained a short time before in Ossory; for, having been nearly all along acknowledged King of Leathmogha, or the southern half of Ireland, it secured him, as occurring in Leathcuin, or the northern half, that preponderance which gave, according to ancient custom, a claim to the dignity of Ard-Righ, or monarch of all Ireland. But it was only in name. The day for a strong ruling King of Ireland passed away with the disastrous victory of Clontarf.

For some years the clans of Thomond under Donogh were engaged in a desultory warfare with the men of Leinster, led by Diarmid, son of Donogh, surnamed Maelnamo, king of that province. It is not easy to discover what led to this long-continued struggle, for Diarmid was married to Dervorghal, daughter to Donogh. In the course of this struggle Diarmid slew Teigue, chief of the Clan Cuilean, next in rank under Donogh; but his death was dearly purchased. The Dalcassians pushed on and burnt Ferns, the Leinster capital, killing, among many others, Donal, the brother of Diarmid. Nevertheless Diarmid held his own, and established the house of

MacMurrough on the throne of Leinster in succession to the family of O'Byrne, who had previously ruled that province.

It may have been during one of those excursions against Diarmid that an event occurred which is thus described by the Four Masters under A.D. 1044: "Cluain-mic-nois was plundered by the Munstermen in the absence of Donogh, son of Brian. Donogh afterwards gave satisfaction to the Church, to wit, perfect freedom (of the Church) to God and to Ciaran to the day of Judgment, and forty cows to be given by him immediately; and he gave a curse to any Munsterman that should ever inflict any injury upon the clergy of Ciaran." From this it may be inferred that the Dalcassian chief felt himself accountable, and made amends for the misdeeds of his Munster subjects. Perhaps, too, he considered the murder of his brother quite enough to answer for without provoking in addition the just anger of the holy recluses at Clonmacnoise.

In the following year, 1045, we find noted the death of "Donal Ua Ceatfadha, head of Dalcas, and of the dignity of Munster," *i.e.* Archbishop of the province.

The condition of Ireland at this period was deplorable in the extreme. Confusion reigned everywhere, or if there was anything like firm rule, it was under the sway of the Dalcassian prince. He was strong enough to demand and receive the hostages of Ossory and Leinster in the year 1049. In the following year an event of more than usual interest and importance took place, which showed that Donogh was regarded as the Ard-Righ of Ireland. O'Donovan, translating from the Four Masters, gives the account of it in the following words: "Much inclement weather happened in the land of Ireland, which carried away corn, milk, fruit, and fish from the people, so that there grew up dishonesty among all, that no protection extended to church or fortress, gossipred or mutual oath, until the clergy and laity of Munster with their chieftains assembled under Donogh, son of Brian, *i.e.* the son of the king of Ireland, at Killaloe, where they enacted a law and a restraint upon every injustice, whether great or small. God gave peace and favourable weather in consequence of this law."

The peace which followed was not of long duration, as might well be expected where so many conflicting elements lay close together. This time Donogh and the men of Thomond, in conjunction with Conor O'Mealaghlin, his half-brother, were the aggressors. Viewing with jealousy the growing power of Diarmid, King of Leinster, they made an incursion into his territory, not hesitating to violate in their unholy fury the great church of Lusk. Those who took refuge there were carried away captives.[1] A just retribution awaited Donogh. Diarmid, gathering together a strong force, first had his revenge of the son of Malachy by ravaging Meath, and then, turning southwards, plundered all Thomond, destroying Dun-tri-liag, near Corbally, in the county of Limerick, a fortress first erected by Cormac Cas, the great ancestor of the Dalcassians, and restored and strengthened by Brian Boroimhe. At this time Donogh was in South Munster, and, as misfortunes seldom come alone, Aedh O'Connor, espousing the cause of Turlogh, penetrated into West Thomond (Clare) down to the Shannon, carrying away great spoil from Tradaree and Corcovaskin. At this period, Tuaimfinlough, near Newmarket, must have been a place of note, as the Four Masters make special mention of its having been plundered.

Clare now became the theatre of a fierce civil war between the adherents of the aspiring Turlogh and the troops of King Donogh. His son, Morogh of the Short Shield, was sent with a strong force to dislodge Turlogh from the northern part of the country, where he had been, with the aid of the Connaught prince, entrenching himself; but, after a sharp struggle, he was forced to retreat, four hundred men and fifteen chieftains[2] being left dead on the field. Donogh endeavoured to buy off the hostility of Aedh O'Connor and his support to his rival Turlogh, by tendering him some measure of submission; but in vain, as we find the Connaughtmen the year following capturing and demolishing the king's fortress of Kincora, plundering and burning the adjacent town of Killaloe, and desecrating its holy well. This was in good truth a period of disaster for the people of Thomond. The King of Leinster advanced once more, and completely broke the power of Donogh, defeating his army with great slaughter in a battle near the present town of

[1] Four Masters. [2] *Ibid.*

Tipperary. After this he made easy prey of the whole country as far as the Shannon, including the city of Limerick, penetrating as far as Brandon Head, and taking hostages from the petty chieftains who hitherto owed allegiance to the Dalcassian prince. These, with full authority over South Munster, he left in the hands of his foster-son,[1] Turlogh, whose claim he all along supported against his own father-in-law, Donogh. The latter, after the return of Diarmid to Leinster, made, with his son Morogh, a last despairing effort to reassert his authority; but, being defeated by Turlogh, he gave up the struggle, hemmed in as he was on all sides by Turlogh's supporters.

Recognising the hand of Providence chastising him for his unnatural crime of fratricide, he proceeded to Rome to do penance for his sin and seek absolution, bringing with him, it is stated, the regalia of Ireland to lay at the feet of the successor of St. Peter. The Four Masters say emphatically " he was deposed," which implies of course a regular legal procedure, and that he died " under the victory of penance in the Monastery of St. Stephen the first Martyr." How eloquent of the close union with St. Peter's See in this bygone age!

For some years following peace reigned in Thomond. A remarkable proof of this is found in the fact that, in the year 1068, Maelisa, *i.e.* servant of Jesus, Archbishop of Armagh and successor of St. Patrick, made a visitation of all Munster, and received large offerings of money and other valuables. The first interruption to it came on the summoning of Turlogh by his foster-father and constant ally, Diarmid, to aid him in an attack on the prince of Connaught. Aedh O'Connor pretended to fly before the numerous army they had arrayed against him, until, having lured them into an ambuscade which he had with great ability set for them, he fell upon them by surprise. A panic ensued, and the invaders were defeated with great loss, including O'Connor, Lord of Kerry. Morogh, the son of Donogh, made a vain attempt to wrest the power from his cousin Turlogh, but soon after was killed in a raid into Meath.

[1] One of many proofs of the hold fosterage had on Irish life.

The death in battle of Diarmid, King of Leinster, and O'Connor, King of Connaught, the two most powerful of the Irish princes, cleared the way for Turlogh to claim the sovereignty of all Ireland. He had now no rival to the throne of Leathmogha, or the southern half of Ireland, and the Dalcassian prince only wanted the submission of Connaught or Ulster to have his claim to the dignity of Ard-Righ acknowledged. A very strange incident is recorded of him, both in the *Annals of Clonmacnoise* and of the Four Masters. I give it in the quaint language of the former:— "A.D. 1070" (*recti* 1073) "Terlagh *alias* Terence O'Bryen, son of Prince Teig MacBryen, succeeded as king next after King Dermott, and reigned full twenty-five years. Conor O'Mealaghlyn, King of Meath and Leath-Koyn, was treacherously and filthily slain by his own nephew, Murrogh MacFynn. Meath was wasted and destroyed between them. Clonard and Kells, with their churches, were burned within a month. King Terence O'Bryen did violently take out of the church of Clonmacnoise the head of Conor O'Mealaghlyn, King of Meath, that was buried therein, and conveyed it to Thomond. A mouse came out of the head and went under the king's mantle, and immediately the king for fear fell sick of a sore disease, by the miracles of St. Keyran, that his hair fell off, and he was like to die until he restored the said head again, with certain gold which was taken on Good Friday, and sent back the day of resurrection next ensuing." This Conor had espoused the cause of Donogh, his stepbrother.

Turlogh now took his first step towards securing the dignity of Ard-Righ. He marched an army into the southern part of Leathcuin, and, meeting with little opposition, returned to Thomond with great spoil. With the object of overwhelming the whole North, he collected in the year following, A.D. 1075, a great army of "Meathmen, Connaughtmen, the foreigners, the Leinstermen, the O'Sraighi, and the Munstermen."[1] His demand for hostages in token of submission was met with a fierce resistance by the Northern princes, who utterly defeated him in a battle at Ard-Mongron, near Ardee, in the county of Louth.[2] He was more successful on his

[1] Four Masters.   [2] *Ibid.*

march into Connaught. The king, Rory O'Connor, made willing submission, thus giving him the title he so longed for; but as the North held out, he was only Ard-Righ "with opposition." The people of Thomond, and indeed of all Ireland, were paying dearly then, and at all times, for this empty title.

One can well understand and commiserate the sufferings of the clans during all this horrid continuous system of plunder and warfare. The warriors themselves no doubt felt that fierce joy in conflict natural to a warlike race; but their families were scarcely ever free from the keen pangs of suspense. They had only too often to look their last on the husband or the son or the brother going away to die in a cause entirely unworthy of such sacrifice. If they sometimes shared the spoils of victory, they as often endured the ravages consequent on defeat. Only a race that multiply like the Irish could survive such a constant strain.

Nor were the other nations of Europe much, if at all, better off. Petty and internecine warfare was their normal condition too during the same centuries. Even later on, and in more settled times, and under more favourable conditions, we know what took place in the neighbouring country during the hundred and sixty years preceding the end of the Wars of the Roses. Out of eleven kings who came to the throne, six were deposed, and five died from violence. The nobles of England and Scotland and Wales were in each other's throats as often, or nearly as often, as the Irish chiefs, during all these centuries, and for centuries after. One may philosophise, and say that in those days, when there was no New World to suggest and encourage emigration, the "race for life" made—by a kind of paradox—war a necessity. If anywhere this theory could be advanced, it applies in a very special way to Ireland. The country was too small, too sternly circumscribed, for an ever-increasing population; and its people, it must be said, did not inherit that spirit of trade and commerce which could alone have liberated their well-known energy of character. War, horrid war, became at the same time their passion and their unholy industry. It came readiest to the hand of a people, not only in a remarkable degree constitutionally brave, but spurred on to it constantly by the cherished records of their clannish historians and the glowing eulogiums of their poets. Is it too much to say that the nation deserved, at the hands of a just God, the calamities inflicted on it by the English invasion? After this short digression, which suits just as well any other period and any other prince, we return to the career of the Dalcassians and their aspiring chief.

With the submission of Connaught the scale was turned, and Turlogh secured the requisite preponderance; but it was necessary to maintain it. For some reasons not given, he turned his arms first against the territory of Hy Kinsella, in Leinster, bringing away its chief in fetters; and next, Rory O'Connor, who had perhaps repented of his submission, banishing him from Connaught, and bringing back with him the spoils of the royal palace. He allowed his troops little rest, for we find him in the following year, 1080, at the gates of Dublin. It is to be presumed, though it is not stated, that he reduced the city to submission as his next record, and in the same year was the surrender of the King of Meath. "The men of Maelseachlain came into his house," say the Four Masters, "with the staff of Jesus, and with the successor of Patrick and the clergy of Munster." This can mean no other than his solemn inauguration as Ard-Righ of Ireland.

There was now another short interval of repose, within which died two men of note, Macraith, successor of Cronan of Ros-Cre, and Teigue O'Brian (probably grandson of Brian), successor of Flannan of Cill-Dalua.[1]

In 1084 the dogs of war were again let loose. The Connaughtmen swooped down on West Thomond (Clare), burning Killaloe, Moynoe, and Tuaimgreine. We can gather that in those early days these were places of great note, for they were frequently made the objective points of the Connaught invasions. This attack on his paternal domain was made in the absence of Turlogh and his Dalcassians, who were at the time engaged in Meath.

This year of strife closed with a bloody battle fought near Leixlip, "on the fourth of the calends of November," between the people east and west of the Upper Shannon

[1] Four Masters.

on the one side, and the Southerns, under the command of Mortogh, son of Turlogh, on the other. Four thousand were left dead on the field, including some of the most powerful of the chiefs. According to the *Annals of Ulster*, victory lay on the side of Mortogh, who brought with him, and posted up on the gate of Limerick, the head of his principal opponent, Donogh O'Ruarck. One other achievement of Turlogh, now well advanced in years, is recorded. He went himself in person to avenge the plundering, in his absence, of Killaloe, Tuaimgreine, and Moynoe, by the Connaught clans. "Morogh, son of Dubh, chief of all Muinter-Eolais (Leitrim), was taken prisoner by Turlogh O'Brian, and all Muinter-Eolais was plundered by him."[1] With this parting gleam of victory on his brow, the old Dalcassian chief, in the seventy-seventh year of his age and the thirty-second year of his reign, having never fully recovered the shock of the incident connecting him with the violation of the Clonmacnoise sanctuary, passed away peaceably at Kincora, A.D. 1086.

The Clare of to-day may well look back with pride on the career of one of her sons, who, imitating the vigour and piety of his illustrious grandfather, secured from Pope Gregory VII. a recognition of his supreme authority, and was spoken of by Lanfranc, Archbishop of Canterbury, in the following terms, in a letter[2] addressed to "The Magnificent Turlogh, King of Ireland:" "God was mercifully disposed towards the people of Ireland in giving him royal power over that land;" and bearing witness to his well-known character "for pious humility, severe justice, and discreet equity." This letter was one of the many evidences that the Danish Church in Ireland, of which he complains to its monarch for certain abuses that disfigured it, was under the direct jurisdiction of the Prelate of Canterbury. The Four Masters, as translated by O'Donovan, describe the manner of his death in the following pathetic and instructive words: "He died after long suffering, and after intense penance for his sins, and after taking the body of Christ and His blood; and Teigue O'Brian and his son died in

[1] Four Masters.   [2] Ussher, *Vet. Epist. Hibern. Syll.*

the same month. In commemoration of the death of Turlogh was said—

> Eighty years without falsehood,
> And a thousand of great extent,
> And six years from the death of the dear Son of God
> To the death of the modest Turlogh.
> The night of Tuesday, on the pridie of the Ides of July,
> Before the festival of pure Jacob of pure mind,
> On the twenty-second died the
> Mighty Supreme King Turlogh."

CHAPTER VIII.

FROM 1086 TO 1171.

Mortogh Mor, last Dalcassian Ard-Righ—His rival, Turlogh O'Connor of
Connaught—His Defeats and Death—Conor, son of Diarmid,
elected—Death of Ceallagh (St. Celsus)—Building of Cormac's
Chapel at Cashel—Contests on Lough Derg and the Western Coast—
Another Turlogh succeeds Conor—Diarmid MacMurrough—St.
Malachi—National Councils—O'Ruarck, Prince of Breffny—Expulsion of Diarmid, father-in-law of Turlogh—English Invasion.

TURLOGH'S son Mortogh was elected to succeed him as prince of Thomond, and was installed by the chief of the Clan Cuilean (MacNamara) at the royal rath of Magh-Adhair, near Tulla. He was recognised also by the Eoghanachts as King of Munster; for we find him, the year after his father's death, at the head of the army of Munster, doing battle with Donal, King of Leinster, for the supremacy of Leathmogha, the southern half of Ireland. In this battle the Dalcassian prince defeated his rival with great slaughter, in his own territory near Dublin.

The following year, however, was one of disaster for him. Rory O'Connor, his brother-in-law, anticipated attack by occupying in force an island at the northern side of Lough Derg, barring the passage up the Shannon. In an attempt to dislodge him from this position, the Dalcassians suffered a defeat with considerable loss. No better fortune awaited them later on, when, sailing round by the Atlantic, an attack was made on Connaught from the sea. They were again repulsed, and Rory, taking advantage of the confusion consequent on those defeats, marched into Corcomroe, devastating all before him, but losing three of his chieftains, who were intercepted and slain. There followed a still greater collapse. Donal MacLaughlin, of the Northern dynasty, claiming the throne of Ireland, overawed O'Connor, taking hostages from him in token of submission. Both together then advanced by the eastern side of the Shannon on Limerick, and, laying it in ruins, plundered the rich plain to the south as far as Emly and Bruree. On their return they crossed the Shannon at Limerick, bringing with them the head of O'Ruarck, which had been exposed at Singland near that city; and, after "breaking down and demolishing" Kincora itself, returned in triumph with great spoil, and not fewer than eight score Dalcassian and Danish hostages. A time of woe indeed in proud Thomond. But the Dalcassian spirit was not subdued. A race less warlike might, for a time at least, succumb to such a series of defeats. In the very next year they tried to recover their lost prestige by an attack on Connaught. Ascending in their vessels, they plundered the islands in Lough Righ, sparing the holy sanctuary of Clonmacnoise. Here they again met with a repulse, and in their retreat found themselves confronted by Rory O'Connor, who had in the meantime taken possession of two islands which offered an advantageous position for intercepting their return homeward. Driven back towards Athlone, they were watched by Donal O'Mealaghlin, King of Meath, and had to surrender to him their vessels for a safe-conduct through his territory. With these vessels, O'Mealaghlin and O'Connor, who were acting in concert, swooped down directly on their baffled foes, and carried away great plunder from East Thomond (Tipperary).

The Dalcassians, being now exhausted, had to abandon for some time all hope of placing one of their race on the throne of Ireland. In the year following, a friendly meeting was arranged, at which the supremacy of the Northern Hy Niall was acknowledged by the Kings of Meath, Connaught, and Munster. Some encounters took place, in A.D. 1091, between the men of Munster and those of Connaught and Meath, wherein the former were usually defeated. It may be that this was due, in no small measure, to the fact that Mortogh did not command the undivided support of the Dalcassians. The sons of his elder brother contested his right to rule, and must have had a considerable following, as he found it necessary to effect some kind of compromise with them. It did not last long. The King of Connaught, who favoured their pretensions in order to weaken Mortogh, was encouraged by them to swoop down on West Thomond, where they committed great devastation, having taken Mortogh completely by surprise. For this he made them pay dearly the following year, A.D. 1093. Attacking Connaught with great force, he made O'Connor prisoner, and swept the country clear of his clan. They retreated into Tirowen.

The next year found the Northerns and Southerns once more at war for supremacy in Ireland. The Southerns, finding themselves overmatched, withdrew without engaging; but as soon as the Northern prince retired into his own territory, Mortogh wreaked vengeance on his allies, the King of Meath and the Danes of Dublin, whom he reduced to submission. He next turned his arms against the O'Connors, who had returned from Tirowen into their own country, but without success. A great pestilence, which took away some of the principal men of the kingdom, among whom is named "the priest of Cill da Lua,"[1] put an end for some time to the weary and melancholy shedding of blood. At a National Council held this year—the successor of St. Patrick presiding —a rigid fast and abstinence was proclaimed and put in force, as a continuance of the pestilence was greatly feared. "Many alms and offerings were made to God, many lands were granted to churches and clergymen by kings and chieftains; and the men of Ireland were saved for that time from the fire of vengeance."[2]

During the lull Mortogh and the Dalcassians built up again the fortress at Kincora which the Northerns had some years before demolished.

An incident recorded in the year A.D. 1096 is no way creditable to Mortogh. He delivered up a chieftain, MacCoirten, to his enemies, the O'Learys, on receiving from them eight hostages, one hundred cows, and thirty ounces of gold; a bribe of no little value in those days, but a poor compensation for so dishonourable a transaction.

The year ensuing found Mortogh again at the gates of the

[1] Four Masters. [2] *Ibid.*

North; this time with the men of Meath and some of the Connaughtmen swelling the Southern army. The Northerns, whose former allies were now in the ranks of the enemy, offered a stubborn resistance. A temporary truce was entered into—"God and the successor of St. Patrick made peace between them."[1] During this interval died, in his seventy-sixth year, Donal, Bishop of Killaloe, one of the Dal-Cas, and of such renown that the Four Masters call him "a noble bishop, head of the wisdom and piety of the Gael, fountain of the charity of the West of Europe, a doctor of both orders, Roman and Irish." It is clear from this that learning, and piety, and virtue, and intimate communion with Rome, were not unknown in the Clare of that stormy period.

When domestic troubles, occasioned by the death of his mother and wife within a few months, had somewhat softened down, the old lifelong passion revived. Mortogh summoned to his side all the South of Ireland, and, with his new allies of Meath and Connaught, marched to the North, once more to assert his claim to supreme sovereignty. Again the crozier of Armagh barred his progress, and a year's peace was agreed on. Before hostilities were renewed, there occurred the death of Donogh, chief of the O'Hehirs, MacConmara, son of Donal, Lord of Hy Cashen, another MacCraith, successor of Ciaran, and Cronan of Tuaimgreine.

The next attempt of the Dalcassian prince to subdue the fierce spirit of the Northerns was made in the opposite direction, towards Assaroe, the present Ballyshannon, as if to evade the interference of "the successor of St. Patrick;" but again he had to retire with loss. In order to counteract his lost prestige, he then summoned to Cashel the leaders, ecclesiastical and civil, of the people, and made solemnly a grant for ever of Cashel of the Kings, free of all kinds of charge, to the religious of Ireland. Come whence they might, as long as anything was there, every religious could claim part ownership.

It may be that this act of religious generosity revived the drooping Dalcassian spirit. Consequent on it, another assault was made on the stronghold of the North, and this time with

[1] Four Masters.

complete success. Following in the footsteps of his great-grandfather, Brian Boroimhe, Mortogh made a triumphant circuit of the whole island, meeting with hardly any opposition, so overpowering was the force he commanded, and bringing back with him the very stones of the royal stronghold of Aileach, as a reply to the demolition, some years before, by the Ulster prince, of the Dalcassian fortress of Kincora. After this "circuitous hosting," he returned in triumph to Kincora, and supreme rule in Ireland rested once more on the Clare side of the Shannon.

The next event of importance was the invasion of Ireland by the Danes, under their king Magnus, in the year A.D. 1102. Mortogh summoned all Ireland to resist the old enemy, and marched straight to Dublin. Instead of war there was matrimony. Probably the Danish king saw little hope of final success, and so contented himself with securing for his son in marriage a daughter of the Irish king, "with many jewels and gifts."[1]

Meanwhile a civil war broke out in the North between the Cinel-Eoghain on the west and the Ulidians on the east. For reasons not assigned, but which may be guessed at after remembering the unending hostility between the Dalcassians and the Cinel-Eoghain, Mortogh, with all the forces he could collect, marched to the aid of the Ulidians. Donal, at the head of the former, adopted the Fabian tactics with great success. A diversion was made by Mortogh against the people of Dalriada (Down), who took sides with the Cinel-Eoghain, in which he suffered defeat, with the loss of his nephew Donogh, O'Connor Kerry, and many other men of note. This reverse encouraged Donal to assume the offensive. Pushing on towards Armagh, before Mortogh's army could recover confidence, he inflicted on them a severe defeat. There was hardly a princely family of the South that had not to bewail its loss. Among the slain were Mortogh, the King of Leinster, Giolla Phadruig of Ossory, O'Murray, Lord of Kerry, Thorston, with other Danish commanders, and, strange to relate, an Amazon, heading the Ui Cuinsellagh or O'Cavannaghs. The Northern princes returned in triumph,

[1] Four Masters.

bringing with them "valuable jewels and much wealth, together with the royal tent and standard."[1]

For some time after this great disaster, Mortogh felt himself so crippled that he ventured on only a few expeditions. In one of these he deposed Donogh, King of Meath, dividing it between the two sons of its former prince, Donal O'Mealaghlin, and then, turning towards Ath-Cliath, made war on the Danish king, Donal O'Loghlin; but peace was made through the exertions of St. Patrick's successor, the Bishop of Armagh. He next deposed Rory O'Connor, inaugurating his brother Turlogh in his place. These attacks on those who had been so lately in arms with him, would lead one to believe that he suspected them of treachery or desertion on the fatal day of his defeat near Armagh.

The annalists record in the year 1107 a fierce storm, first of snow for a whole day and night, followed by thunder and lightning, during which both Cashel and Kincora were burned, and vast quantities of mead and beer were rendered useless. This last entry shows how minutely and accurately the march of events was described.

A synod, attended by fifty bishops, three hundred priests, three thousand ecclesiastical students, was held, A.D. 1111, at Uisneach, in West Meath. The successor of St. Patrick, Ceallagh, was present; but, for probably territorial reasons, Gilbert, Bishop of Limerick, presided. The main object in view was to reconstruct the Irish ecclesiastical edifice; defining the jurisdiction of the bishops, of whom in future there were to be only twenty-four; and, following the political division, giving one Archbishop, Armagh, to Leathcuin (the North), and another, Cashel, to Leathmogha (the South); in which arrangement it is easy to discover the direct Hy Niall and Dalcassian influence. What a clear proof of the disturbed state of society in that period, is afforded in the fact that the same Mortogh O'Brien, Ard-Righ of Ireland, who, on the side of the laics, was the chief personage in the Irish Synod, is found soon after, in the very same year, instigating, as the Four Masters testify, his own clansmen, the Dal-Cas, to an attack on the peaceful brotherhood of Clonmacnoise.

[1] Four Masters.

Within two years the dogs of war were again let loose. Donal MacLaughlin, chafing under the indignity put upon him and his principality by the triumphant progress through it of the Dalcassian chief, collected all his tributaries and marched towards the south. His rival was not asleep, as we may gather from the fact that the expedition returned without striking a blow, the Archbishop of Armagh, Ceallagh, having effected a year's truce between the contending parties.

Dissensions cropped up soon after between the Northern princes, of which Mortogh availed, by marching an army against the old enemy, the Hy Nialls. Again the successor of St. Patrick interposed, and bloodshed was avoided. But only for a short time. The same forces in the same year once more confronted each other, for a full month, in the county of Meath. Once more religious influence prevailed in the person of the Archbishop of Armagh. Peace for a year sent both armies homeward.

The year following, A.D. 1114, was an eventful one. Mortogh was so prostrated by disease that he could no longer rule, and Diarmid, his brother, without regular election, assumed the reins of government. He did not long enjoy the position. In the next year, 1115, Mortogh, having recovered, deposed Diarmid, and once again ruled the kingdom. Some petty chiefs of Leinster, who had recklessly revolted, were very soon reduced to submission—their churches, alas! as well as their other property, being brought to ruin. The explanation is simple enough. The defeated sought refuge in the holy places, but a rough and victorious soldiery care little for sanctuary.

The illness of Mortogh, from which he never fully recovered, invited attack. Turlogh O'Connor, with the men of Connaught, penetrated as far as Limerick, along the east side of the Shannon, carrying off much plunder. This success encouraged a direct attack on the royal fortress of Kincora, in the year following, A.D. 1116. The fortress, together with the earthen outworks, a mile northwards on the Shannon, erected by Brian Boroimhe, then and still called by his name, Beal Boroimhe, was captured and destroyed, but the booty seized on was restored, strangely enough, "in honour of God and Flannan." Here we have strong testimony to the veneration in which the patron of the diocese of Killaloe, who was consecrated at Rome so early as 639, was held.[1] Diarmid, who had been reconciled to his sick brother, led the men of Munster into Galway, and slew all they could find, the others flying, leaving after them "their provisions, their horses, their arms, and their armour."[2]

In the year following, 1117, the Connaught prince retaliated, fighting his way farther into the Dalcassian territory than ever invader did before, and inflicting a severe defeat at Lachen, in the present parish of Kilmihil, on Turlogh, son of Diarmid, and nephew of the dying Ard-Righ. This was followed up by invasion of East Thomond, where again fortune forsook the Munster forces. These reverses, following thick and fast on the Dalcassian monarch in his declining years, quenched out all hope of any further successful assertion, by force of arms, of his claim to supreme sovereignty. He was the last of the Dalcassian line who attained this dignity.

The cup was not yet full. Diarmid, who is called King of Munster and of all Leathmogha, during the retirement of Mortogh, died at Cork. Turlogh O'Connor seized on the opportunity, marched down to Glanmore unopposed, and cut across the power of Munster by establishing the MacCarthys as rulers of Desmond. Returning, he crossed the Shannon at Limerick, and once more razed Kincora to the ground— "hurling it," the Four Masters say, "both stone and wood into the Shannon." Alas! in that evil day for the departed glories of the Dal-Cas. It was now time for Mortogh to disappear from a scene of such disaster. He had persistently aimed all his life, in spite of many a defeat, at supreme rule, following in the footsteps of his great ancestor, and only secured it, to see it after a little while slipping for ever from his grasp. He died, "after the victory of reign and penance," as the annalists pathetically put it, in March 1119, and was interred in the church of Killaloe.[3]

[1] Ware's *Bishops*, Harris edition, p 590.   [2] Four Masters.
[3] A tomb was built over his remains in 1123, the beautiful doorway of which, a relic of an older church, may yet be seen.

Mortogh's eldest son, Donal, was at this time a monk in the monastery of Lismore, after having ruled, by their own choice, for some years previously the Danes of Dublin and their dependencies. The choice of successor fell on Conor, son of Diarmid, who was proclaimed in the following year King of Munster, while his brother Turlogh was elected for the principality of West Thomond.

Within the next few years various incursions were made by Turlogh O'Connor into Thomond, and beyond it, carrying his arms as far as Cork and Tralee, with the view of preventing a union among the Southern princes, which might lead to a renewal of the claim to the throne of Ireland. He placed a fleet of a hundred and ninety vessels on Lough Derg as a permanent menace to the people of Thomond. Conor was not slow in accepting the challenge. He sailed up the Shannon from Kincora, and in A.D. 1127, the strange spectacle was witnessed of a naval battle on Lough Derg. The Connaughtmen were victorious. It may be taken for granted that the vessels on both sides were small, and chiefly managed with oars.

The command of the Shannon enabled Turlogh to strike when and where he liked at his Munster rivals, and contributed in no small degree to their downfall. He made it quite enough for them to defend their own territory, without a thought of the throne of Ireland; and we can well imagine the disturbed state of the peoples east and west of the Shannon, with such enemies driven in like a wedge between them. One may easily believe that plunder, followed by retaliation where possible, was the order of the day.

At the age of fifty, in the prime of his life, A.D. 1129, died Ceallagh (St. Celsus), Archbishop of Armagh, who had so often stood between contending forces and saved much bloodshed, through the influence of his high authority and great personal sanctity. He was seized with his last illness while on a visitation, or perhaps to bring about a peace, in Munster, and was buried by his own request at Lismore.

In 1138, Conor, King of Munster, collecting an army, proceeded into Leinster, and, taking the hostages of that province, asserted his authority as King of Leathmogha. He then pressed northwards into Meath, which was under the rule of Turlogh O'Connor as King of Ireland. A skirmish took place between the cavalry on both sides, in which the Connaught force was defeated, with the loss of one of the O'Connor princes and their chief poet, but nothing more came of this expedition. The Dal-Cas did not press their advantage for want of sufficient force, as well as from a wholesome dread of the well-proven prowess of Turlogh O'Connor. But in another direction, and from an unexpected quarter, attack was made upon Connaught. The vessels which had been defeated on Lough Derg sailed out with large reinforcements through the mouth of the Shannon, and, turning northwards, inflicted heavy loss on the Connaught seaboard, making great slaughter of the people, including some notable chieftains. This success was followed up, A.D. 1133, by a combined attack on the part of Conor O'Brien and Cormac MacCarthy against the common enemy, resulting in the destruction of some forts in the heart of the O'Connor territory and the seizing of great booty. Both sides were tired of the prolonged struggle, and, at the instance of the clergy of Munster and Connaught, peace was proclaimed.

This blessed interval of peace was availed of for a noble purpose, and one which is sufficient history for the year 1134. Cormac, Prince-Bishop of Cashel, erected that beautiful structure called after him, Cormac's Chapel, which was of sufficient importance, according to the Four Masters, to be consecrated by a synod of the clergy, and which stands to the present day, along with the numerous exquisitely illuminated manuscripts, and the elaborate filigree-work in so many gold ornaments, as unassailable proof that Irish art had in these branches hardly a rival in those remote ages.

During this armistice between Munster and Connaught, the old rivalry between the Eugenians and the Dal Cas sprang up afresh. At a battle in the present county of Tipperary, the Dalcassians, though victorious, lost heavily. Among the slain were O'Loughlin, Prince of Burren, and Cumara, *i.e.* "dog of the sea," chief of the Hy Caisin, whose name was adopted by the powerful clan MacNamara. The Danes of Waterford, with the people of the Deisi, espoused the cause of the MacCarthys, upon which Conor O'Brien marched on Water-

7

ford, aided by Diarmid MacMurrough, whose sinister influence on Irish history will appear later on, and took away their hostages in token of submission. So bitter grew the animosity between the two great Southern families, that, after an attack by Cormac of Cashel on the city of Limerick, he, though a bishop, was foully assassinated in his own palace by Turlogh, Prince of Thomond, who became later on King of Munster, aided by the two sons of O'Connor Kerry. In order to secure the permanent co-operation of MacMurrough against the Eugenians, Conor O'Brien surrendered the Dalcassian claim to supremacy by giving hostages to the Leinster king. Being thus safe on that side, the Dalcassians and their allies turned their attention to the Danes of Dublin, from whom they bore away hostages; and, proceeding into Connaught, inflicted chastisement on their old enemy. With this gleam of victory, so dearly bought, on his arms, Conor passed away at Killaloe, A.D. 1142, and was succeeded by his brother Turlogh, who had been till then ruler of the principality of Thomond. His only son Mortogh succeeded him in Thomond, while his brother Teigue Gle, who, aided by Turlogh O'Connor, made a vain attempt to seize his crown some years before, had to remain content with the subordinate rank of Prince of Ormond. This seems to have been the order followed then as well as at other periods. The elect of the Dalcassian clans first ruled in West Thomond (Clare), succeeding next to the throne of all Munster, and then striving with might and main for supremacy in Leathmogha, and finally for the throne of Ireland.

For some years there was comparative quiet in Thomond. The success of Conor in Connaught, as related above, checked the hitherto victorious career of Turlogh O'Connor. The new King of Munster, jealous of his cousin Conor, son of Donal of Lismore, and grandson of Mortogh Mor, banished him into Connaught. Thereupon O'Connor, gathering together a large force from his own province, with the troops of Meath, Breffny, and Leinster, marched against Munster, east of the Shannon, but was foiled, and had to return, bringing with him, however, hostages from Leinster. The Dalcassian king now began to make himself felt. He advanced into Leinster, probably with a view to counteract the action of his brother in the surrender to Diarmid MacMurrough, and committed great havoc there, bringing back with him much spoil. In an incursion into Kerry, his next in command, the chief of the Hy Caisin, or the Clan MacNamara, slew Donogh O'Connor, lord of that territory. These successes emboldened O'Brien. He entered Connaught, A.D. 1143, but did little more than destroy the coronation fort and tree of the O'Connors, which insult was soon after dearly paid for. In the meantime, both parties being exhausted, a kind of peace was patched up between them by the clergy in an interview at Tirglas in Upper Ormond. This lasted only for a short time, as, soon after, an attack was made by the Munster king against Meath, by way of Slieve Bloom, which was successfully resisted by a powerful coalition under the leadership of O'Ruarck, of Breffny, Turlogh O'Connor, O'Mealaghlin, and MacCarthy, the Eugenian rival of the Dalcassians, having with them Conor O'Brien, who had been some time before expelled from Munster by Turlogh. This may have been a feint to draw off O'Connor, for we find the Munster army immediately after in Connaught; whence, after slaying the chief of the O'Flaherties, they brought away as prisoner O'Kelly, chief of Hy Many.

Though it did not, as far as can be known, affect the condition of Thomond in any special degree, it may be well here to note that a Synod was held, A.D. 1148, at St. Patrick's Island, near Skerries, Co. Dublin, under the presidency of the celebrated Malachy O'Morgair, successor of St. Patrick. Fifteen bishops, attended by two hundred priests, were present. Laws for the better guidance of laity and clergy were made, and the primate St. Malachy proceeded to Rome, by direction of the Synod, to have those regulations confirmed. This disposes of the silly attempt made by some to degrade the Irish into a mere provincial Church, having no connection with Rome, the centre of unity, till the arrival of the English. This was his second visit to Rome. On the first occasion he had received the pallium from the hands of Innocent II. Staying for some time at the famous monastery of Clara Vallensis, to study its rules, with a view to introduce them into Ireland, he formed a fast friendship with St. Bernard, who afterwards wrote his life. This second journey was fatal to him. While making a sojourn with St. Bernard, he took ill and died, in the fifty-fourth year of his life, leaving behind him a world-wide reputation for learning, zeal, and sanctity.

Further and clearer evidence of the close relations between Ireland and Rome, is found in the visit, three years later, A.D. 1151, of Cardinal Papar, to impose the pallium and confirm the dignity of Archbishop on each of the four prelates of Armagh, Dublin, Cashel, and Tuam. He also ratified, in the Pope's name, the decrees of the National Council held in 1145, under St. Malachy, and presided at another held in Drogheda, where all the archbishops and bishops, and not less than three thousand clergy, secular and regular, were present. Severe penalties were here declared against prevailing abuses, and regulations made for the due administration of the sacraments. Could it be possible that the English Pope, who is said to have deputed Henry II. to reform the morals (bless the mark!) of the Irish, was ignorant of the holding of these National Councils only twenty years before?

In 1157, a great misfortune fell upon Turlogh and the Dalcassians while they were on an incursion into South Munster. Teigue Gle, Turlogh's brother, for the second time formed an alliance with Turlogh O'Connor, giving him hostages in token of submission. These were joined by the King of Meath and Diarmid MacMurrough, both of whom Turlogh had a short time before attacked. This powerful coalition, supported by the MacCarthys, whose territory had been ravaged by Turlogh, intercepted him on his return, at a place called Moinmore, in the parish of Emly. A bloody battle, in which the Dalcassians were greatly outnumbered, but which they contested with all the old energy, was fought with great loss on both sides. It was a complete victory for the allies. The Dalcassians must have been nearly annihilated, not less than seven thousand of them, according to the *Book of Lecan*, being left dead on the field. Turlogh himself escaped, with only the remnant of one battalion [1] out of the three which

---

[1] A battalion usually consisted of three thousand men.

he formed into line of battle, and fled, with what jewels and gold [1] he could carry, into the North of Ireland, from the vengeance which he knew awaited him if he fell into the hands of the victors. It was indeed a day of woe for Thomond. There was hardly a family that had not to bewail its own loss. Among those who fell, the ancient authority above quoted gives the names of chiefs of the O'Briens, the O'Kennedys, the O'Deas, the O'Shannons, the O'Quins, the O'Gradys, the O'Hogans, the Lynches, the O'Neills of Dalcassian origin, the O'Hehirs, the O'Hearns, or Aherns, etc. We find no mention of the MacNamaras, though next in power to the O'Briens, probably because they were exempt from this service, owing to their having a short time previously overcome unaided O'Connor Kerry; nor of the MacMahons, who, living in the extreme west, were farther removed from the direct O'Brien influence.[2] Turlogh O'Connor was now undisputed lord of Munster, which his son Rory, the future monarch of Ireland, plundered of much booty. Turlogh restored something like order by making Teigue Gle, Prince of Thomond; Dermod MacCarthy, Prince of Desmond; and another Turlogh, grandson of Conor-na-Cathrac, Prince of Ormond. Soon after, the old enmity between the Eugenians, now headed by the MacCarthys, and the Dalcassians, revived to such a degree, that a civil war raged, bringing ruin and devastation over all Munster. Church and State suffered alike; and such was the dearth of provisions, that many died of hunger, and many more fled the country, and sought refuge in the North. Possibly they ranged themselves once more under the banner of the King Turlogh, who fled to the protection of the Northern princes after the disastrous Dalcassian defeat at Moinmore.

Flattered by the submission to him of the descendant of Brian Boroimhe, Mortogh MacLaughlin, the head of the Hy Nialls, determined to strike a blow for the sovereignty of the whole kingdom. He began by restoring first Turlogh to the throne of Munster. Marching a strong force southwards, he

[1] " Ten score ounces, sixty beautiful jewels, and Brian's drinking horn."—Four Masters.

[2] This clan ranked in importance next to the MacNamaras.

entered Westmeath before O'Connor, who summoned the Munstermen to his aid, crossing the Shannon at Athlone, could intercept him. The Northern prince, acting with consummate skill and energy, held the Connaught king in check with part of his army; while with the greater part, consisting of two battalions of the flower of his troops, he rushed so quickly on the advancing Southerns, that, taking them by surprise, he defeated them near Tullamore with much slaughter, and dispersed them. Returning victorious to his own camp, he prepared for an assault on the Connaught forces. Learning that they were in two divisions at different points, he pounced upon that commanded by Rory, Turlogh's son, and, defeating him with ease, compelled Turlogh to fly with his own division back across the Shannon. Many of the Connaught chiefs, including a grandson of Turlogh, fell in this battle. Mortogh entered Munster without further opposition, after receiving the hostages of O'Mealaghlin, King of Meath, and established Turlogh once more as ruler in Thomond and Ormond. The unhappy Teigue, whose plotting had wrought so much woe on the Dalcassian clans, flying before one brother whom he had wronged, fell into the hands of another and a younger brother, Dermod, who rendered any further attempt to create disturbance on his part impossible, by cruelly putting out his eyes, of which he died the following year, 1154. The Four Masters relate, in this same year, the burning of Killaloe, Roscrea, Emly, Lorha, and Durrow, but do not say by whom. Probably it was the work of the Prince of Desmond, after the return of the Northern army, and before Turlogh O'Brien had fully recovered power, as there is a record the same year of a prey taken from the Dalcassians by the people of Desmond. The Dalcassians quickly retaliated, seizing and bringing back much booty. They were, however, between two fires. Turlogh O'Connor, sailing down the Shannon through Lough Derg, compelled Turlogh, weakened as he must have been, to make submission. This was his last success, for he died soon after, leaving his son Rory in quiet possession of his kingdom.

Turlogh O'Brien, having good reason to dread another invasion from Connaught, with which he could not hope to cope successfully in his shattered condition, made submission to Rory, leaving twelve of the Dal-Cas as hostages. The Northern prince, recognising in Rory a formidable rival, determined once more to assert his supremacy. With his usual vigour he made a forced march through friendly Meath into Leinster, demanding and obtaining hostages from Dermod MacMurrough. He next marched through Ossory into South Munster, compelling submission as he went. He then turned upon Thomond, whose prince, Turlogh, had behaved towards him with so much ingratitude in recognising Rory as Ard-Righ, and, overrunning the whole country east of the Shannon, laid siege to Limerick, where Turlogh had taken refuge. The Danes, who mostly inhabited the city, did not dare to resist, and Mortogh, entering the town, from which Turlogh escaped only with his life, dictated terms once more to all Munster. He left Dermod MacCarthy, who had given him hostages, in possession of South Munster, and made Conor, son of Donal of Lismore, Prince of Thomond. Meanwhile Turlogh fled to Connaught, putting himself and his cause into the hands of his former enemies. No sooner had the Northern prince returned to his own territory, after having secured the dignity of Ard-Righ, than Rory marched an army into Munster, restoring Turlogh in Thomond, and taking hostages from MacCarthy, or rather a promise of them if Mortogh MacLaughlin did not come within a specified time to defend them.

It is not out of place to note here the holding of another National Council in 1157 at Drogheda, seventeen bishops and a large number of priests being present. The successor of St. Patrick solemnly consecrated the Abbey of Mellifont. Many of the princes of the kingdom were present with rich gifts, and the occasion was utilised, among other things, to solemnly depose O'Mealaghlin, King of Meath, who had treacherously murdered O'Quinlivan[1] of the race of Laoghaire— a prince, say all the annalists, of great worth—and this in the teeth of a most binding treaty of peace between them, ratified by both ecclesiastical and civil power. It is gratifying to find,

---

[1] The Quinlivans of Clare are an offshoot of this clan, which claimed descent from the first Christian King of Erinn.

amid the warring elements of the period, such a strong sense of justice prevailing.

Through the intervention of the clergy, and under their protection, Conor and his son, having made submission to Turlogh, returned to their native Thomond. To prevent the possibility of their ever again renewing their rivalry with him, and forgetting all the ties of blood and the solemn promise of protection given them, this cruel prince had their eyes put out. The civil wars of Ireland as well as of other countries in those days were only too often stained by such like savage practices. Wicked the crime was beyond all doubt, but it had the effect of restoring for some years internal peace to the distracted country, as there was no one now to dispute Turlogh's authority. He could safely turn his attention to his enemy in South Munster, whom he defeated in two battles, A.D. 1161, wherein were slain the son of Cormac MacCarthy, Prince of Desmond, and the chiefs of the two powerful clans, the O'Donohues and the O'Keefes. Notwithstanding these successes, it may well be assumed that during those years he ruled with a stern hand, loved neither by his own family nor by the people; for as soon as his son Mortogh came of age, he took up arms against him, and banished him from Thomond. This unnatural rebellion seemed permitted by Providence in punishment of Turlogh's faithless and barbarous treatment of his kinsmen. Following upon the death of the Ard-Righ Mortogh MacLaughlin,[1] Rory O'Connor, King of Connaught, took the first step towards succeeding to this dignity. He marched an army into Leinster and Munster, and, receiving the submission of the princes of Leathmogha, left them undisturbed in possession of their territories. With this shadow upon the Dalcassian line, which had for so long ruled in Leathmogha, and in exile, Turlogh O'Brien ended his stormy career A.D. 1167, leaving his son Mortogh undisputed ruler in Thomond.

The most notable event in his short reign was his, as above stated, marching with the Dalcassians, under the banner of O'Connor, through the North, to procure its sub-

---

[1] He was slain in battle in 1166 by Donogh O'Carroll, having committed a crime similar to that of Turlogh O'Brien.

mission. The rebellion of this prince against his own father —wicked as he certainly was—had a tragic ending. He was slain the following year by his cousin Conor, grandson of Conor-na-Cathrac, and sub-chief of that portion of Thomond lying east of the Shannon. Vengeance for this crime was taken, under direction of Rory O'Connor, who was stepbrother to Mortogh, by his grand-uncle, Dermod Fionn, and O'Phelan, chief of the Deisi, who slew Conor, and thus cleared the way to the throne of Munster for Donal, Mortogh's brother, now chief of the Dalcassian line, and known afterwards as Donalmor, or Donal the Great. He took to wife a daughter of Dermod MacMurrough, and this alliance brought upon him the shame of aiding and abetting the invasion of Ireland by the Normans.

Between Dermod MacMurrough and O'Ruarck, Prince of Breffny, a long and bitter feud existed. The wife of the latter had eloped with MacMurrough nearly twenty years before. Though a money compensation was made,—one hundred ounces of gold,—and though the unhappy woman had soon after atoned for the scandal by retiring to a life of penance in a convent, the gross insult rankled all along in the mind of O'Ruarck. Collecting an army, he overran Leinster, compelling MacMurrough to fly into England. This perfidious prince sought assistance from King Henry II., who was only too ready to grasp at any excuse for meddling in the affairs of a country upon which he had already fixed a covetous eye. At first he gave but little help,—only sixty men in armour crossed over into Leinster,—so that when Rory O'Connor advanced to repel this invasion, "thinking nothing of the Fleming," as the Four Masters erroneously describe them, he was content to accept the submission of MacMurrough on receiving his only son as a hostage for his future good behaviour. It is probable that all this time no thought of a permanent occupation by the Normans entered into MacMurrough's mind. This would imply the handing over of his son—the sole hope of his house—to what he well knew would be certain death. In all likelihood the astute English king concealed from him his ultimate designs till he had been completely in his power.

Soon his eyes were opened, for in May 1169, Robert Fitz-Stephens and Maurice FitzGerald, both sons by different fathers of Nesta, the cast-off mistress of Henry I., landed at the creek of Bannow, with thirty knights, sixty men in coats of mail, and three hundred archers. These were followed by Richard de Clare, Earl of Pembroke, called Strongbow, who landed on the 23rd of August at Downdonnell, near Waterford, with a well-appointed army of one thousand men and two hundred knights in armour.[1] Here, indeed, was the thin end of the wedge with a vengeance. This formidable body of desperate adventurers, trained and disciplined in the wars of Henry, and armed in a manner far superior to the Irish, set at once to the task of conquest with fierce courage and untiring energy. Strongbow took in marriage Eva, the daughter of MacMurrough, and so in a manner put himself in the place of the unhappy hostage, who had to pay with his life for the perfidy of his father. With their united forces they first stormed Wexford, which made the first day a bold resistance, but surrendered the second day—the people being reminded by some clerics that after all MacMurrough was their lawful king. They next seized Waterford, and then proceeded to Dublin with their joint forces, numbering probably not less than ten thousand men. The city, inhabited chiefly by Danes, offered a stout resistance. At this time the celebrated St. Laurence O'Toole, son of the Prince of Imayle, was Archbishop of Dublin. His sister had been the wife of Dermod, and mother of Eva, the wife of Strongbow. When the citizens fully realised the impossibility of successfully resisting the large force around their walls with such means for attack as the Normans brought with them, asking for a truce, they selected St. Laurence, the near relation of both Dermod and Strongbow, to make for them what they hoped would prove honourable terms of peace. While St. Laurence was in the camp of the besiegers, a base advantage was taken; for Miles de Cogan, with a select body, assaulted the city, and, taking its defenders by surprise, easily captured it. The Danish commander, Asculph, fled, and St. Laurence returned to find the city a scene of pillage and

---

[1] *Hibernia Expugnata*, lib. i. cap. 16; Harris' *Hibernica*, p. 23.

slaughter. Rory O'Connor, with O'Ruarck, marched to oppose them, but, finding the Leinster troops and their English allies safely entrenched within the walls of Dublin, they did not attempt an attack, and returned without effecting anything. As soon as they were out of sight, MacMurrough and the English moved northwards, pillaging the country, burning Kells, Slane, Clonard, and many other towns, and scattering religious communities. In his patriotic striving against the invaders, Rory was greatly impeded by the hostile attitude of Donal O'Brien, who in his absence rescued the Dalcassian hostages previously surrendered in token of submission to him. To punish him for his defection, Rory sailed down the Shannon and carried the sword and torch into Thomond. The O'Kellys repeatedly plundered Ormond, while the troops of West Connaught made inroads on the whole country, from the Bay of Galway to the Shannon. In the Hy Cashin territory they met with such stubborn resistance [1] from the hastily summoned MacNamaras, O'Gradys, O'Lyddys, and their kindred clans, the O'Molonys, the MacInernys, the Magraths, etc., that they had to retire hastily, leaving some of the principal chiefs dead after them, but burning the bridge at Killaloe, and so crippling for a while the Dalcassian forces. Having thus checked any attempt on the part of Donal to advance in support of his father-in-law, MacMurrough, Rory O'Connor, once more aided by O'Carroll and O'Ruarck, marched upon Dublin. Leaving a detachment of his army watching the city, he took the greater part with him to destroy the growing crops, with the view of cutting off the supplies of the besieged; but these sallied out, and, taking them completely by surprise, put to utter rout the troops left near Dublin, and compelled the others, under Rory, to retire for the second time. The year A.D. 1171, Dermod Mac-Murrough died from—the annalists say—a loathsome disease. He had brought upon himself the malediction of his own people, and left to history a name that is a reproach to Ireland. Giraldus Cambrensis describes him as a man of great frame and stature, fierce and brave in war, but tyrannical in conduct, "hated by all and loved by none." Following

[1] Four Masters.

the feudal law, Strongbow, as the husband of his daughter, claimed the sovereignty of Leinster, and thus the house of Dermod, the betrayer of his country's freedom, disappeared in gloom and dishonour.

Meanwhile, Henry II. viewed with a jealous eye the success of his subordinates, more particularly when he learned that Strongbow assumed a regal title. He issued a proclamation forbidding any others of his subjects to cross the Irish Sea; whereupon Strongbow, now fully alive to the danger of his position between the hostile Irish on the one side and his angry liege lord on the other, determined at once to make abject submission. He returned to the feet of Henry and surrendered to him his conquests. He was, after some show of displeasure, received into favour, and allowed to accompany him in the expedition already organising by Henry for the conquest of Ireland.

CHAPTER IX.

FROM 1171 TO 1194.

Life in Thomond before the Norman Invasion—Battle of Thurles—Defeat of the Normans—Alleged Submission of Roderick, the Ard-Righ, to Henry II.—Capture of Limerick—Recovered and burned by Donal O'Brien—Defeat of the Eoghanachts—Battle of the Curlieu Mountains—Pursuit of the English—Second Defeat of Thurles—Death of Donalmor.

THE Norman invasion turned the current of Irish history into an entirely new channel. For greater clearness in the narration of its subsequent events, I will henceforth use for West Thomond its comparatively modern name, Clare. At this notable turning-point in its history, it will be interesting to pause for a while, and try to take a look into its inner life —into the social and religious condition of its people before the Norman intruder crossed their path. What must give a zest to this inquiry is the admitted fact that, though a change came in the name of the county, and though undoubtedly there was an infusion of new blood, yet the people of the Clare of to-day are, for far the greater part, the direct descendants of the clans who held its wooded hills and fertile valleys for more than two thousand years before the Norman or any other invader secured a foothold west of the Shannon. The old names still survive and crowd the land—the O'Briens, the MacNamaras, the MacMahons, the O'Loughlins, the O'Molonys, the MacInernys, the O'Currys, the O'Slatteries, the O'Maddigans, the Magraths, the O'Deas, the O'Gradys, the O'Reidys, the O'Hehirs, the MacClancys, the O'Quins, the O'Hallorans, the O'Neills (Dalcassian, not Northern), the O'Liddys, the O'Kennedys, the O'Mechans, the O'Malones, etc.; and even of the names which, like the present writer's, appear English in their origin, many were assumed for protection's sake, as will appear later on, by Clare families living within reach of their victorious and relentless enemies, when their last hope died out with the surrender of Limerick. No people in Europe, hardly even the Greeks, can trace from so ancient a period such pure and lineal descent. Of their early condition, as far as can be gathered from authentic history, something has been already told in a previous chapter. But in approaching its study, whether then or in the period before the Norman invasion now about being glanced at, a great difficulty besets us. Beyond all doubt the Irish were a lettered, cultivated nation, and all along records were carefully kept, especially in the religious houses after the introduction of Christianity. But, alas! the destroying hand of the ruthless Dane carried fire as well as the sword into the haunts of learning and piety through nearly the whole island during two centuries of constant warfare; and it needs no great effort of imagination to realise the enormous loss that Irish literature must have suffered from such havoc. Then, when the country was only recovering from the evils introduced by one horde of barbarous invaders, another, scarcely less barbarous, rushed in. Again the pen had to be laid aside for the sword; and in the frequent ransacking of towns and cities and monasteries, many ancient manuscripts must have perished. But the evil was aggravated and intensified later on. Not satisfied with seizing the lands and goods of the Irish, a fanatic attempt was made by Protestant England, and persevered in for many generations with what Edmund Burke fitly called "hellish ingenuity," to uproot and utterly destroy every trace of Ireland's ancient faith and national literature. Yet in spite of all this, here and there among some of the old families, or in the more remote religious houses, or on the shelves of European libraries, where they were placed by Irish missionaries or Irish exiles, some of the ancient records escaped the general destruction, and from these sources, scant as they certainly are, the manners and customs and religious movements of the people may be gleaned. Even the English enemy contributes in some degree to the task of picturing for our days the general features of the Ireland of the pre-Norman period; and what was true of Ireland generally applies to Clare in particular.

No sooner was the Danish power broken, than the old love of learning and religion revived. As already related, council after council was held, at one of which a cardinal, representing the Holy Father, appeared, for the purpose of checking the licentiousness so natural to the disturbed state of society; and it is well worthy of note, as showing the relative position of the two countries, that in the Council of Armagh, 1171, a decree was passed restoring to liberty all the Saxons who were then held in bondage in Ireland. A generous Christian impulse, stirred up, indeed, by fear of God's anger for so unholy a traffic, proved more effective and more thorough in the cause of human freedom than the halting legislation of this enlightened century, with which the name of Wilberforce is inseparably and so honourably connected. May not the inference be drawn from this fact alone, that the people were settling down, in spite of the petty civil warfare kept on here and there, to the ways of Christian peace. To those foreign slaves, and the subdued native Firbolg tribes, was usually committed the task of cultivating the land and practising handicraft of all kinds, save that of smith, or armour-maker, or bell-founder, which crafts were held as of note and honour. The clansmen were too proud to engage in other handiwork. In time of peace they were much given to the exchange of hospitalities. The Danes of Limerick supplied Clare with wines and other luxuries at a good profit, in exchange for the wool, hides, tallow, etc., in which the county abounded. Oak and other choice timber formed also a valuable export. It was with Irish oak, traditionally said to be of East Clare growth, that the Abbey of Westminster was roofed. The broad expanse of the Shannon afforded great facilities for imports and exports; so we never hear complaints in the old annals of much want in those days. Sports and pastimes, and the pleasures of the chase, were of course among such a people keenly enjoyed; and, to while away the hours after banqueting was over, they had the glorious music of the harp, the eager contest over that mimic battlefield, the chessboard, and the thrilling stories of the Bards recounting the brave deeds of their ancestors. But, best of all, if we except the subject race, who were but few in number, there was that manly spirit of independence kept alive by the equality of clanship, and the never-forgotten descent from a common ancestor. Such a state of society, while encouraging and intensifying family and kindred affection, had indeed its one great ruinous defect. It promoted those internal rivalries and dissensions which laid eventually the nation open to attack from an organised external foe; and made such attack, for want, not of courage or love of country, but of combination, sure of ultimate success. Nor was the necessity of preparing for war forgotten in those intervals of peace. The "gallowglasses," answering to the paid soldiers of modern times, remaining always under arms, few indeed in number, but well trained, fairly provided with means of offence or defence, formed a nucleus round which the lighter and far more numerous "kern" could gather in time of war. These were armed with spears, pikes, slings, and *skians* or short swords, and carried light shields or bucklers. They allowed the hair to grow down over the shoulders, plaiting and strengthening it in such a way as to afford some protection to the head and neck. In this shape it was called the "Coulin," with which Moore's beautiful melody has made us familiar. In battle they rushed in on the enemy with great speed, trying to break the ranks to make an opening for the heavy-armed "gallowglasses." When war was over they were disbanded, but were always liable to service at the call of their chief or prince.

It is not probable that learning was much cared for among the many, where intestine warfare was so very frequent. Only in the religious houses was any serious attention paid to it. In the ancient annals, those, for instance, of Innisfallen, commenced about A.D. 1000, and those of Boyle, covering the period of time from A.D. 420 to A.D. 1245, both carried on by the monks of those abbeys, there is interpersed a considerable share of Latin; and there can be no doubt that classics and science were taught in the monasteries of Iniscatha and Holy Island, as well as in those other well-known seats of learning throughout all Ireland. There was, undoubtedly, great laxity of morals everywhere, which called forth later on the scathing censure of St. Bernard. The Church was grievously oppressed by the petty princes and chiefs, who sometimes seized the revenues of parishes and bishoprics, and were called priests and bishops, while in fact they were mere laymen, getting the spiritual work done for them by clerics. This abuse was checked at the Council of Clonfert, A.D. 1170, held by commission from Pope Alexander III., at which, "for example," say the *Annals of Clonmacnoise*, "they deprived seven such intruders;" but, apparently by a compromise, ordained that holy orders should be given to their sons. Such did the Norman invasion find the people of Clare, brave to a fault, cultivating more the ways of war than of peace, hospitable, possessing the advantages of such learning as was known at that period, proud of their ancient descent, and maintaining a local independence, which, freeing them from any central authority, and bringing them into frequent conflict with others of the petty principalities, weakened them all alike, and made their subjugation to foreign yoke only a question of time.

Henry II., having collected an army of about four thousand men, sailed from Milford Haven in a fleet of two hundred and forty small vessels, and landed near Waterford on the 18th October 1171. That city was at once delivered up to him by Strongbow. The news of his arrival soon spread, causing a general panic. It was known that not only were his forces equipped in a manner immeasurably superior to the Irish gallowglasses and kern, but that he was also armed, as he alleged, with a Bull from the Pope. He lost no time in the endeavour to establish his authority. He marched first to Lismore, and thence on to Cashel, both of which places surrendered without a blow. At Cashel a synod was held, presided over by the Bishop of Lismore, who had received from the Pope the appointment of Legate. The alleged Bull from the Pope was produced, and Henry made a bid for clerical support by ostentatiously encouraging their claim to immunity from cesses and blood-tax. Some of the provincial princes made, without waiting for attack, an inglorious submission. Among these, as might be expected from his connection with the MacMurrough family, was Donal O'Brien. Taking with him a considerable escort of Dalcassian troops, he proceeded towards Waterford, and went through the empty form of handing over to Henry, as his liege lord, the city of Limerick, with a promise of paying tribute. How that promise was kept history doth not tell, but certain it is that, on his return to Kincora, things went on in Thomond as before; pretty much as if there were no Saxon invader in existence. This having come to the knowledge of Strongbow, after the departure of Henry, who had been summoned by the Pope to account for the murder of St. Thomas à Becket, he marched an army of Normans and Danes into Munster to assert the king's authority. It is best to tell the result in the very words of the old annalists. We find the following, at the year A.D. 1174, in the *Annals of Innisfallen*: "A great army was led by the Earl of Strigul to plunder Munster; and he sent messengers to Dublin, desiring all the Galls left there to join him; and a battalion of knights, officers, and soldiers well armed, came to him, and they all marched to Durlas O'Fogarty (Thurles). But Donal Mor O'Brien there defeated the earl and the knights, and slew four of the knights and seven hundred of their men. When that news came to the hearing of the men of Waterford, they killed the two hundred that were guarding the town. Then the earl went on an island that was near the town, and remained there for a month; and then went back again to Dublin."

The account, in the Four Masters, of this battle differs from the above only in this, that they say that Roderick, the Ard-Righ, with his Connaught battalions, fought side by side with the Dalcassians, and that seventeen hundred—probably a mistake—of the English were slain.

Alas that such vigour was not followed up! Had it been, the English invader could have been easily driven from the country; and, following upon their expulsion, the establishment, for the common defence, of a central government in Ireland would assuredly have maintained its independence. But a policy of this kind was perhaps impossible, when so many petty kings and princes claimed independent jurisdiction; so the Dalcassians returned, satisfied with the glory of having been the first to inflict, with their Connaught allies, a serious defeat on the common enemy.

Strongbow was now thoroughly alarmed. He at once summoned to his aid Raymond le Gros and his contingent of the Normans who had retired into Wales, and sent him with a strong force against O'Brien. They proceeded to Limerick, and, finding the garrison over-confident, as they had broken down the bridges, they, with great intrepidity, headed by Raymond, in whom they had boundless confidence, dashed across a fordable part of the river, near where King John's castle now stands. The defenders, thrown into a state of utter disorder and consternation at the boldness of the attack, fled, leaving the city in the hands of its assailants. It may be that Donal suspected treachery, for immediately after he seized at Castleconnell, in their own house, two of his own family, Dermot and Turlogh O'Brien, putting out cruelly their eyes,[1] from which Dermot died soon after, and slaying their guest O'Connor, son of the Prince of Corcomroe.[2]

In the meantime, Rory O'Connor had sent ambassadors direct to Henry at Windsor, where a very curious kind of treaty was entered into, as given in Rymer, vol. i. It was stipulated that Henry was to be recognised as supreme lord of Ireland, Rory holding under him, according to the ancient Brehon law, and the provincial kings also retaining their independence, but all paying tribute to Henry, and leaving him in undisturbed possession of Dublin, Meath, the rest of Leinster, and the territory stretching from Waterford to Dungarvan.

The first exercise of this authority, supposed to be delegated by Henry to Rory, was the marching of an army by the latter into Thomond to punish Donal for the crimes above narrated. He laid waste Clare, compelling Donal to fly, with as many of the Dal-Cas as he could rally, first to Limerick; whence, failing to recover that city, he pursued his course

---

[1] Four Masters.

[2] This territory, in the north-west of Clare, was so called from Core Moruagh, great-grandson of Rory Mor, King of Ireland about A.M. 3845, and from whom the O'Connors and O'Loughlins are said by the old Irish genealogists to be descended.

towards Cashel. Here he found himself face to face with Raymond, supported by the men of Ossory, who were incensed against Donal, not only in memory of the old enmity, but because the son of their prince had been recently slain by Donal. The Dalcassians fought with the greatest determination, but were finally defeated, and Donal was compelled to make his submission to Raymond.

Soon after, and while both were in Limerick, news came of the death of Strongbow. Raymond hastened at once to Dublin, having given over the charge of Limerick to Donal as liege of Henry. No sooner was Raymond outside the walls, than O'Brien, renouncing his dependence, set the city on fire, that it might no longer be a nest for foreigners.

In the absence of the invaders, the wretched old quarrel between the Dal-Cais and the Eoghanachts broke out afresh. In 1178 the former proceeded southwards in great force, laying waste the whole country, and driving the inhabitants, notably the O'Donovans and O'Collins, before them into the mountains of Kerry and the recesses of South Cork. The *Annals of Innisfallen* give an epitome of this disastrous civil war in the following words: " A.D. 1178. There was a very great war between the O'Briens and the MacCarthys, so that they desolated the entire country, from Limerick to Cork, and from the plain of Derrymore to Brandon Hill; and the greater part of the race of Eoghan fled to the woods of Ivaha, south of the river Lee, and others to Kerry and Thomond. On this occasion the Hy Conaill Gabhra and the Hy Donovan fled southwards to the Mangerton mountains." The Four Masters bear similar testimony. It is curious to note that some of them took refuge even in the territory of the enemy; from whom are descended, in all probability, the MacCarthys, the O'Collins, and the O'Donovans, who are at this day settled down in considerable numbers through all Clare.

It would be interesting to note at this turning-point in Clare history the localities occupied by the principal clans. This can be done with the greater accuracy since they began to be known by certain family names, though the old prized title of Dalcassian belonged then and ever since to all alike. The O'Briens, as the dominant clan, had secured lands in many parts of the county, the principal being the territory round the palace of Kincora, the greatest part of the barony of Inchiquin, part of Tradaree, and the district along the Atlantic,[1] from Dunbeg, by Milltown-Malbay to Ennistymon. The MacNamaras, whose chief was hereditary Lord Marshal of Thomond, owned nearly all the eastern part of the county, from Tulla and Broadford on the north, out of which they drove the O'Kennedys, down nearly to the Shannon. In the days of their power their chiefs were styled respectively Princes of East and West Clancuilean. The O'Deas owned the country called from them Dysart O'Dea, while between them and the O'Brien lands at Kilfarboy, and the O'Gormans and O'Donnells of Clonderalaw, through the present parishes of Inagh, Kilnamona, Kilmaley, and Clouna, near Ennistymon, were fixed the MacClanchys, hereditary lords justices of Thomond, the O'Hehirs, and the MacBruidins or Brodys, hereditary historians of Thomond. The O'Quins had the beautiful, though not extensive, territory around Corofin, while all the rest of north-west Clare, out to the ocean, belonged chiefly to the O'Loughlins and the O'Connors. The O'Hallorans owned the country south-west of Tulla towards Ennis, while the O'Molonys had the district north of it to the borders of Galway. Between these and the O'Briens at Kincora, along the Bay of Scariff, south and south-west of it, were the O'Liddys, the O'Gradys, the MacInernys, the O'Malones, and others of less note, because lesser in number, but of the same origin and inheritors of the same soul-stirring traditions. The names are all here still; the people bearing them cling yet to the lands owned by their forefathers since long before the Christian era; but the chiefs of those clans, where are they? The few who claim to represent them—most of them having long since disappeared, or being known only by tradition—are now, and have been for two centuries, wedded to the English interest and to the English faith. How they have come to assume this most unnatural position will appear later on.

It will not be out of place to note here the death, in

---

[1] The remains of their castles, in those and other places in that district, are still to be found.

A.D. 1180, of St. Laurence O'Toole, at Eu, in Normandy, inasmuch as he was maternally of Dalcassian descent. Ireland lost in him, at a most critical time, one of the noblest of her sons. Few men in history have left a brighter record of pure patriotism allied to unsullied holiness of life.

In A.D. 1182, say the Four Masters, " Brian, son of Turlogh O'Brien, was treacherously slain by Randal MacNamara Beg."

Henry did not long observe the conditions agreed to in the treaty of Windsor. He coolly partitioned the country among his barons, assigning Thomond first to FitzHerbert, who declined the dangerous gift, and next to Philip de Brassa. The latter, called by the Four Masters " De Unserra," or of Worcester, marched towards Limerick; but, finding the Dalcassians up in arms against his pretensions, he thought it useless to try to take Limerick, which had been burned, as related above, lest it might afford shelter to the invader. He too recoiled from the task of reducing the stubborn Dalcassians to submission.

With the year 1184 we find the English policy of "divide and conquer" commenced. In that year one of the O'Briens, Dermot, son of Turlogh, was instigated by the English to make an attack on Art O'Mealaghlin, Prince of Meath, in which the latter was treacherously slain; but his death was soon after avenged by his successor, who defeated Dermot with considerable loss.

In this year died Kenfador O'Grady, abbot of the then famous monastery of Tuaimgreine.

John, son of Henry II., sailed for Ireland in 1185, with a fleet of sixty ships, to assume, in his father's name, the reins of government. He met with no opposition in the province of Leinster; but in his attempt to establish himself in Thomond he and his army were put to flight, after great slaughter, by the Dalcassians under Donal O'Brien.[1] Yet this same victorious Dalcassian army is found allied with the English later on in the same year. A war having broken out between the claimants to the throne of Connaught, the Normans seized on the opportunity to secure a

[1] Four Masters.

footing in that province. It was only too easy for them to induce O'Brien to share in the plunder of that distracted country; but he soon had reason to repent of this alliance. The O'Connor princes made a truce with the English, and in conjunction with them marched into the Dalcassian territory. One contingent, under Cathal, grandson of Roderick, "burned Killaloe, as well churches as houses, and carried off all the jewels and riches of the inhabitants;"[1] while another, under the command of Conor, his father, made a successful raid on other parts of Thomond. How blind to their true interests those Irish princes were! Within a few months the Normans succeeded in driving them into a ruinous war with each other, fighting now on the one side and now on the other, plundering and weakening both alike. It was but the head of the chapter. The same policy was tried, and with nearly always the same success, all through to the end.

In the year 1188 died Edwina, daughter of O'Quin, and Queen of Munster. Of the chief of this clan the following description appears in O'Heerin's topographical poem :—

> "To O'Quin of the good heart belongs
> The extensive Muinter-Jfernan ;
> The fertile district of this splendid man
> Is at the festive Corofin."

A vigorous attempt was made by the English, following up the success narrated above, to subdue the whole West under John de Courcey, and in great force they crossed the Shannon. Their design was so manifest, that, in the alarm created by it, the Irish princes forgot for the time their petty jealousies and late hostilities. The Dalcassians and Connaughtmen, uniting, fell upon them in the Curlieu mountains, defeating them with great slaughter, and very nearly cutting off their retreat. It was probably on this occasion that Donal O'Brien made the qualified submission, of which the Four Masters write, to Conor Moinmoy, who had deposed his father, Roderick O'Connor. O'Brien "went to his house," thereby acknowledging his superior authority; but in refusing the tempting subsidy of "sixty cows from

[1] Four Masters.

every cantred of Connaught, and ten articles ornamented with gold" offered to him, and accepting only a precious goblet which had belonged to his grandfather, he plainly intimated that his was not an unreserved submission.

The Dalcassians, returning in triumph to their homes after this important victory, were left undisturbed for the next four years. During this period they doubtless restored the towns and churches which had been reduced to ruins by the allied English and Connaughtmen, a short time before the decisive victory of the Curlieu mountains. The Normans, however, only took breathing time to recruit their ranks, with the fixed purpose of returning to the assault. In 1192 they gathered together all their forces scattered through Leinster, and, entering East Thomond, the present Tipperary, committed great depredations. They then boldly pushed across the Shannon at Killaloe, turning southwards along the plain by the river, with the view of striking into the heart of Clare; but here the Dalcassians opposed their further progress, and obliged them to retreat after much slaughter. They followed up their advantages, pursuing the flying English till, coming up with the main body near Thurles, the scene of their former victory, they once more utterly defeated their formidable foes. They dared not pursue them further, knowing well that their old enemies, the Irish of Leinster, would be sure to rally to the side of the Normans. Had the former seized the golden opportunity, and, uniting their forces with the triumphant Dalcassians, fallen upon the common foe, he might have been expelled the kingdom. After such a lesson, the invasion, in all likelihood, would have come to an end, and the country been spared the long agony it afterwards suffered. But the inherited clan animosities barred the way once more to the unity of action so essential for the national welfare. The Dalcassians had to remain content with ridding their own territory of the foreign enemy; and, recrossing the Shannon, disbanded, giving themselves up once more, for a brief space, to the unaccustomed enjoyments of peace. In two years after Donal died. Notwithstanding his occasional coquetting with the invaders of Ireland, the vigour with which he maintained the independence of his Dalcassian principality and his claims to be acknowledged King of Munster, if not of all Ireland, gave him some right to his title, in Irish history, of Donalmor, or Donal the Great. His son Mortogh was chosen to succeed him in the manner prescribed by the Brehon law.

Towards the end of his reign he built the present church of Killaloe, and the Cathedral of St. Mary in Limerick. The two beautiful structures—one close to the church of Killaloe, now used for Protestant worship, and the other in the little island opposite—are evidently of much more ancient origin, and are attributed to either St. Flannan or St. Molua. The splendid doorway yet to be seen in St. Flannan's Church, bearing eloquent testimony to ancient Irish artistic skill, was taken from an older edifice—probably that built by Brian Boroimhe.

CHAPTER X.

FROM 1194 TO 1267.

Capture of Limerick—Surrender of Cork—English Garrison driven out of Munster—Dissension again—Donogh Cairbreac O'Brien allows the building of a Castle at Killaloe—The Clans resist and drive out the English—Donogh surrenders to King John—Permits again the erection of a Castle at Killaloe and Roscrea—Abandons Kincora for Clonroad—Rise of Ennis—O'Heney, Bishop of Killaloe, at the Fourth Council of Lateran—MacNamaras and O'Shaughnessys—Clare invaded—Donogh gives Hostages—Conor succeeds, and founds the Franciscan Monastery at Ennis in 1247—Drives out the English from all Thomond in 1257—Conference of Irish Princes at Caeluisce (Ballyshannon)—Another Invasion of Thomond—Defeat at Kilbarron, near Feacle—Battle at Suidene, in Burren—Defeat and Death of Conor-na-Suidene.

THE marriage of Donal's only daughter, Moira or Mary, with Cathal Crovdearg (the Red-handed) O'Connor, illegitimate brother of King Roderick, but whose ability and force of character secured him the succession to the throne in spite of his spurious birth, became the occasion of an alliance between the Dalcassians and the O'Connors, which led to important results. Marching southwards,[1] their forces were swelled by the adhesion of the Desmonians, under Donal MacCarthy. They first laid siege to Limerick, from which they drove the English, who had lately got hold of it, with great loss. They then proceeded to Cork. The English there capitulated, on condition of being allowed to depart unmolested, which MacCarthy gladly acceded to, as it saved the city from burning. They then turned their arms against other English garrisons, driving them everywhere before them, till the common enemy had not so much as a foothold in the Southern province.

[1] Four Masters and *Annals of Innisfallen*.

This alliance did not last long. The old jealousies revived. The Dalcassians listened to the insidious advice of William de Burgho, designed to cripple the growing power of the Desmonians. In A.D. 1200 they again marched southwards, not as before against the foreigners, but in company with them, to attack their own flesh and blood. Under the leadership of three of the brothers of the reigning prince, they, with the English under De Burgho, traversed the whole country down to Cork, undoing their previous patriotic work, and slaying, among others, Auliff Mor O'Donovan, Prince of Carberry, and MacCostelloe, chief of his clan.[1] Finally a peace was made between the Dalcassians and the Desmonians through the intervention of Mahon O'Heney, the Pope's Legate, and the Bishops of Munster, but the policy of De Burgho was triumphant in the end. The English recovered lost ground by setting the Irish against each other. Would that this were the last instance of the kind to be recorded! But, alas! with an infatuation which speaks badly for their intelligence, the Irish princes, almost without exception, allowed themselves to be duped in like manner, time after time, till their own and their common country's ruin was accomplished.

The English connection brought infamy of a deeper dye still on the Dalcassians. Along with them, and under the same leaders, they, in the year 1202, not only plundered but polluted the Abbey of Boyle. It is only fair to add that this latter phase of the seizure of the holy place was the work of the English alone; for in the *Annals of Kilronan*, which give a full account of the dastardly outrage, it is said to have been the work of "the archers of the army." Cathal Carach O'Connor, who had deposed his own father, Roderick, and against whom the expedition was planned, was slain, with other Connaught chiefs of note, leaving the way to the throne clear for Cathal Crovdearg O'Connor, brother-in-law to the Dalcassian princes.

The return of the Dalcassians to their own territory was but the prelude to fierce internal dissensions. The blindness of Mortogh unfitted him for the sovereignty in Thomond. The claim of the next brother, Conor Roe, was disputed by

[1] *Annals of Innisfallen.*

the next to him, Donogh Cairbreac, but unsuccessfully. Conor ruled only for a short time. He was slain by Mortogh, his own brother, according to the Four Masters and *Annals of Clanmacnoise*. This prince was soon after treacherously seized by the English of Limerick,[1] at the instigation of Donogh Cairbreac, and probably put to death, as we hear no more of him in Clare history. The beautiful doorway set in St. Flannan's Cathedral, at Killaloe, marks, it is said, his tomb. Donogh Cairbreac was henceforth acknowledged Prince of Thomond.

An attempt was made by the English, in 1207, to erect a castle at Killaloe. This concession may have been promised by Donogh in return for their support; but the Dalcassian spirit was not yet broken. The clans fiercely resented this intrusion into Clare, and the English had to retreat after considerable loss.[2]

A son of his uncle Brian, whose eyes had been put out by Donalmor, now laid claim to East Thomond, over which his father had ruled. With great vigour he seized upon the castles of Birr Lorha and Kennety. About this time, A.D. 1210, King John landed in Ireland with a large army. To secure his support against his cousin Mortogh, Donogh hastened to pay him homage, and on payment by him of a fine of one thousand marks, and a yearly tribute of one hundred pounds, was acknowledged by John as King of Thomond, to the exclusion of any other claimant whatsoever.[3] Another and a more galling condition had to be complied with—the erection of two castles by the English, one at Roscrea and the other at Killaloe. His rival Mortogh could not hold out against the combination; but Donogh paid dearly for the advantage he had secured. The English had not only a strong fortress overawing East Thomond, but another for the first time in West Thomond (Clare), and close by Kincora too, the ancient royal residence of the Dalcassian kings. Donogh did not relish the neighbourhood of the Saxon intruders. He changed his residence to Clonroad, in

---

[1] *Historical Memoirs of the O'Briens.*
[2] *Annals of Clonmacnoise.*
[3] Leland quoting Rymer.

the centre of the county, and so may be regarded in some measure as the founder of its present capital, Ennis.

The following appears in the Four Masters, 1215: "Conor (Cornelius) O'Heney, Bishop of Killaloe, died on his return from the Fourth General Council of Lateran." The year after, 1216, an Englishman, Robert Travers, was appointed to succeed him. For some time the two other sees of Roscrea and Iniscatha had been united to Killaloe, and have so continued ever since. This bishop built a house under the protection of the castle lately erected there by Geoffry de Marisco (Marche), but it is clear that the people did not accept his services. He had to resign, or was deprived some years after, and no other Englishman, one excepted, filled the see ever since.[1] In this important particular, at least, the people insisted on the continuance of their ancient privilege.

No events of importance enough to be recorded occurred in Clare for some years. The English contented themselves with the nominal subjection of Donogh in the name of the various clans. There was no renewal of the old feuds with the Desmonians. The MacNamaras, or Clan Cuilean, and the O'Shaughnessys, whose territory lay along the north of Clare, fought among themselves, A.D. 1223, for some cause not assigned. The chief of the O'Shaughnessys was slain, in spite of a compact entered into between those clans, and ratified by an oath on the crozier of St. Colman of Kilmacduagh.

After the death of Roderick and Cathal Crovdearg, A.D. 1224, a civil war of a desolating character broke out between the O'Connors. The succession to the throne was fiercely disputed. The claim of Hugh, son of Cathal, was supported by his uncle Donogh O'Brien and the Dalcassians, while O'Neill not only gave aid, but came into Connaught to inaugurate Turlogh, the son of Roderick. The Dalcassians, advancing rapidly with Hugh's Connaught supporters and the English who encouraged the feud, compelled O'Neill to withdraw, bringing with him the sons of Roderick.[2] They took much spoil, and in an attack upon the Termon, or sanctuary, of St. Caelainri, the English contingent suffered

[1] Ware, by Harris, vol. i. p. 521.   [2] *Annals of Kilronan.*

heavy loss, with such vigour was the holy place defended. The Dalcassians took no part, it would appear, in this attempted outrage.

A few years later on, A.D. 1235, the greater part of Clare was mercilessly plundered. The English of Connaught were joined by the Irish there, who had suffered from the Dalcassian invasion, and made an unexpected onslaught through the northern boundary of the county. Felim, son of Cathal Crovdearg, got intimation of this movement, and hastened to the relief of the Dalcassians. A battle was fought, in which the Dalcassians suffered heavy loss through the bad leadership of Donogh O'Brien. The English and their allies were victorious. Both infantry and cavalry were clad in armour, and, though probably much inferior in numbers, were able to resist successfully the impetuous assault of the light-armed Irish. The men of Connaught retreated to their own country, and on the next day Donogh O'Brien made terms with the English, giving them hostages. This was the first regular engagement on the soil of Clare since the English invasion. It was followed by a temporary peace. Clare was at rest during the remaining years of the life of Donogh O'Brien. He died A.D. 1242, and was succeeded by his eldest son, Conor.

It does not appear that the English followed up their success. For a long time after this they made no permanent settlement in the county, except at Killaloe. The lull from the fatigues and terrors of war was availed of for a purpose, at all times dear to the Irish heart. It has been already stated that since the intrusion of the English so near Kincora, that celebrated palace was deserted, and Clonroad, near Ennis, became the residence of the Prince of Thomond. The first noteworthy act in the reign of Conor was the erection near his palace of that monastery for Franciscan friars, which even now, in its ruin and decay, gives clear evidence of the generous spirit of its founder, and of the architectural skill of the Clare builders of that so-called benighted period. The exact date of its foundation was, according to the Four Masters, the year 1247. It became at once the recognised centre of learning for the county, and for centuries after, till the torch of the Reformers reduced it to ruins. Clonroad was one of the most renowned of the Irish schools. But of this more, later on.

The first call to arms made on Conor O'Brien and his Dalcassians, was from Henry III. of England in A.D. 1252. That monarch was at war with the King of Scotland. He summoned to his aid some of the Irish princes, among whom was the King of Thomond,[1] but before it could be known whether the Dalcassians would so far acknowledge fealty to him, the war ceased. The probability is, they would not, as within a very few years we find them once more up in arms against the foreigners. They fell upon the English of Thomond East and West, A.D. 1257,[2] and slew a great number. These successes emboldened the other Irish princes to unite for the defence of their common country. A meeting was arranged to be held at Cael Uisce (Narrow Water), near Belleek. The Northern and Connaught princes took counsel here with Teigue, son of Conor O'Brien. The Four Masters say that all present freely acknowledged O'Neill as Ard-Righ in the face of the common enemy. The other princes certainly made submission by delivering up hostages,[3] but as no mention is made of hostages being left by O'Brien, it is not clear that his consent was obtained. He might have refused as a descendant of the Dalcassian kings of Ireland, or he may have pleaded want of authority, in the absence of his father, to entertain such a serious question. If we may credit Magrath, historian of the Dalcassians, in his work, *Cathreim Turlogh*, the former was his motive. He describes the Dalcassian prince as claiming superiority by sending to O'Neill one hundred steeds as wages of war, and O'Neill replying by returning them, with two hundred more harnessed, and with golden bits, to O'Brien, which were also sent back. Great doubt rests on the narrative, from the fact that the other and more reliable historians make no mention of it. From this interview Teigue brought away the surname of Caeluisce. This promising prince died before his father, A.D. 1259, and his brother, Brian Rua, was acknowledged as Roy-damna, or heir-presumptive.

---

[1] Rymer, p. 426.   [2] Four Masters.
[3] *Annals of Ulster, of Clonmacnoise,* and of the Four Masters.

The disunion among the Irish princes soon became known. The English of South Munster took advantage of it. Marching hastily, under command of MacMaurice Fitzgerald, they crossed the Shannon, and, keeping northwards to effect a junction with those of Connaught, they pushed their way towards the centre of Clare. The Dalcassian clans, hastily summoned together by Conor O'Brien, intercepted them at Kilbarron, in the parish of Feakle, and, falling upon them with all the energy of men defending their threatened homesteads, put them to flight with great loss. Among the slain the Four Masters note specially the intruded parish priest, or parson, of Ardrahan. The priest who takes the sword deserves above all others to die by the sword. In return for this attack, the Dalcassians, led on by Brian Rua O'Brien, seized and demolished, after killing every man of the garrison, the castle erected by the English at Castleconnell.

With the disappearance of the enemy, internal discord began unhappily to prevail. The clans of Ormond (North Tipperary) and North-east Clare, refusing to pay tribute, were brought to submission by Conor O'Brien, at the head of the O'Briens, MacNamaras, and other clans of central Clare; but when advancing into Burren with a smaller force against the O'Loughlins and O'Connors, the O'Deas and O'Hehirs, he was met and defeated[1] with great loss at the wood of Suidene, in the parish of Drumcreehy. He himself, his son and daughter, and her son, O'Grady, and an O'Loughlin who took part with him, and many others of note, were slain. In the victorious camp was a section of the O'Briens, headed by his cousin Dermot, who, as the son of the elder brother of Conor, laid claim to the chieftaincy. His claim was rejected however, by the greater part of the Dalcassian clans, and being soon after killed by them for the part he took against Conor, Brian Rua became without further opposition prince of Thomond. Conor, who is known from the place of his death, Conor-na-Suidene, had married the daughter of the chief of the MacNamaras, and no little of his success in arms was due to the support of this powerful clan with whom he was so closely allied.

[1] Four Masters. O'Donohue's *Memoirs*.

His grandfather, Donalmor, had built and endowed the Abbey of Corcomroe in 1194, and here Conor received burial befitting his rank at the hands of the monks. It is touching to learn that the victors in the fight made no objection, though the abbey was in the heart of their territory. His tomb, with a reclining figure in stone, has escaped the ravages as well of time as of the ruthless foreign invader.

CHAPTER XI.

FROM 1267 TO 1343.

Clare Castle—Another Invasion of Clare—Brian Rua, the reigning Prince, deposed by his uncle MacNamara—He instals Turlogh, son of Teigue Caeluisce—Richard de Clare unites with Brian Rua—Builds the Castle of Bunratty—Murders Brian Rua—Consequences of the Murder — Intestine Conflicts — The *Cathreim Turlogha* — Battle of Dysert O'Dea.

FOLLOWING the ancient custom, no sooner was Brian installed King of Thomond at Magh-Adhair than he took up arms, not against his fellow-countrymen, as was only too often the case, but against the English enemy. He sent a contingent to the aid of his relatives, the O'Connors; but his son Turlogh, who was in command, allowed himself to be surprised by William de Burgho, and was slain. He himself " turned against the English, and committed great depredations on them; and the castle of Clar Athada Chorada was taken by him," say the Four Masters. This is the first intimation given of a settlement of the English in that quarter. It must have been the result of a mutual arrangement, as the castle lay so close to the residence of O'Brien at Clonroad. It was built on the little island in the Fergus, where the barracks of Clare Castle now stand. This castle it was—Clar Atha, "the Boarded Ford"—that gave the name Clare to West Thomond; though some, by a natural mistake, attribute it to Earl Clare, who was sent soon after to make a conquest of Thomond. Brian Rua cleared the county of its invaders. For six years it enjoyed an unwonted peace, but in 1273 an irruption was made into it by the English under the command of Maurice FitzGerald. The force commanded by FitzGerald was so considerable in numbers and armament, that he secured, without striking a blow, the submission of Brian. The latter made a show of surrender, giving hostages to FitzGerald, with which he seems to have been content, as he withdrew his forces and made no permanent settlement. This submission it was probably that gave such a shake to the authority of Brian as prepared the way for another claimant to the principality of Thomond.

Teigue Caeluisce, the elder brother of Brian, had a son Turlogh, who was fostered among the clan O'Dea. He put in no appearance, being yet young, at the installation of his uncle Brian. Though the chief of the MacNamaras officiated at that ceremony for his nephew Brian, later on, when Turlogh came of age, he, with the O'Deas, espoused the cause of the latter. Under the command of Sioda MacNamara and Loghlen O'Dea, their clans, with the O'Quins, marched upon Clonroad, and compelled Brian to fly across the Shannon. Turlogh was proclaimed in his stead.

While these events were occurring in Thomond, the Earl de Clare was on his way towards it, with the view of making effective, if he could, the grant of the county made to him by King Edward. The struggle between Turlogh and Brian Rua gave him the desired opportunity. He espoused the cause of the banished Brian, and procured from him, as the reward of his support, the beautiful and fertile strip of land along the Shannon named Tradarce,—" Strand of the King,"—which seems to have been the special appanage of the reigning prince. Collecting their respective forces, they proceeded to Clonroad, of which Brian took possession once more—Turlogh being then in the western parts of the county, soliciting the aid of the MacMahons, O'Gormans, and others, for the struggle that he knew was impending. The O'Kellys of Hy Many also came to his assistance; and at the head of a powerful force, consisting of the above-named, along with the MacNamaras, the O'Loughlins, the O'Deas, the O'Hehirs, and the O'Quins, he inflicted a severe defeat on Brian Rua and his allies, at a place called Magh-Gresain. They fled into the castle of Bunratty, which had been built by De Clare to secure his late acquisitions. Fearing perhaps that Brian Rua might strive to retain possession of the place, the English perpetrated an act of cruel treachery, which is thus described by the Four Masters: "Brian Rua O'Brien, Lord of Thomond, was treacherously taken by the son of the Earl of Clare, and afterwards drawn between horses; and this after both had entered into gossipred with each other, and taken vows by bells and relics to retain mutual friendship."[1]

Turlogh was now reinstated in Clonroad, and made no hindrance to, but rather encouraged, the vengeance that was taken upon De Clare by the sons of the murdered Brian.[2] In the following year, 1278, collecting their scattered forces, they surprised De Clare and his followers at Quin. The latter took refuge, after a short but bloody struggle, in the parish church dedicated to St. Finghin, but the church was burned over them by the enraged Dalcassians. A few only escaped to Bunratty, among whom was Thomas de Clare himself.[3] Turlogh followed up the advantage gained by his cousin. For awhile they forgot their rivalry and turned their united strength against the common enemy, driving them, with the exception of the small garrison which held the castle of Bunratty, out of Clare. They pursued the retreating English as far as the Slieve Bloom Mountains,[4] and only desisted when De Clare acknowledged the sovereignty of O'Brien in Thomond, and made compensation for the foul murder of Brian Rua.

Now that the English were subdued, the danger of civil war for the throne of Thomond became imminent. It was averted, however, by an arrangement between the rival claimants, by which Turlogh ruled in the eastern half of Clare, while the western half fell to Donogh, Brian's eldest

---

[1] See also the *Annals of Innisfallen, Clonmacnoise,* and the *Cathreim Turlogha*. In the remonstrance of O'Neill to Pope John XXII., it is further added that, as the most sacred of all pledges of union, they had both partaken of the same Host in the Holy Communion.

[2] It is worth noticing here that the O'Briens living at Aran Islands received yearly, from the merchants of Galway, twelve tuns of wine in return for protecting the harbour and trade from all pirates and privateers, by maintaining a suitable maritime force.—Hardman's *Hist. of Galway,* pp. 51, 52.

[3] *Annals of Innisfallen, Clonmacnoise,* and Four Masters.

[4] *Cathreim Turlogha.*

son. It is evident this could not last long. Within a short time the contest was renewed with varying fortune, till, in an engagement close to the Fergus, Donogh's horse was forced into the river by a chief of the O'Loughlins, and he himself drowned. Turlogh was allowed to reign without molestation over all Thomond to the end of his life, and displayed much vigour.

Following the example set him by the Normans, he built a castle on the peninsula on which Ennis now stands. It was the first of the kind built by the Irish, who had a foolish code of honour which excluded any fighting not done in the open and without the protection of armour. It is little wonder that the Normans, though in much smaller numbers, were so often more than a match for them.

Turlogh, having disposed of his rivals, turned his attention to the English, who were allowed by Brian to settle down in Tradaree. They were troublesome neighbours, notwithstanding the promise of submission made by them at Slieve Bloom. He pressed sorely upon them; and in a battle, fought A.D. 1287, defeated them with great loss,[1] including among the slain Thomas de Clare, Sir Richard de Exeter, Fitzmaurice, Sir Richard Taafe, and many others of note. In fact, he left them no secure foothold outside the castle of Bunratty.

For nearly twenty years peace reigned in Clare. It was time that the Dalcassian clans should lay down their arms and devote themselves to more profitable pursuits. Under the year 1300 the Four Masters note the death of "Congulough O'Loughlin, Bishop of Corcomroe, a man of learning, hospitality, and piety." At that time what is now called Burren was known as East Corcomroe; hence the abbey built in 1194 by Donalmor O'Brien, with the consent of the O'Loughlins, in the heart of their territory, still retains the name of Corcomroe. West Corcomroe was the patrimony of the kindred clan O'Connor.

In 1304 Turlogh crossed the Shannon with a powerful force. The clans of Ormond or East Thomond made him willing submission as king, by right both of descent and

[1] O'Donohue's *Memoirs, Cathreim Turlogha.*

election, over all Thomond. He demolished a Norman castle erected there while war was raging in West Thomond, and on his return compelled Richard de Clare, whose castle of Bunratty he besieged, to acknowledge his supreme authority. In thanksgiving for his long-continued success, he made grants to, and enlarged, the Abbey of Clonroad, which had been built and endowed as a seat of learning and religion by Conor, called, from the place of his death, na Suidene, in 1247. He died the same year, 1306, at Clonroad, and was buried in the abbey, close to the tomb of his cousin and chief supporter, Cumeadh Mor MacNamara, whose death occurred shortly before. By the Four Masters, in noticing his decease, he is called "a man the most illustrious, most pious, most humanely charitable, most prosperous, and most expert at arms that was in Ireland in his time."

The death of Turlogh was the signal for a renewal of turmoil in Clare. His eldest son, Donogh, was at once elected and inaugurated at Magh-Adhair; but the supporters of the family of Brian Rua were not idle. There were among them, besides a large section of the O'Briens, the clans inhabiting nearly all the north-east of Clare and North Ormond; the O'Gradys, the O'Kennedys, the O'Hogans, the O'Shinahans, the O'Lonergans, etc. Donogh could count with certainty on his relatives the MacNamaras, who were at the head of the Clan Cuilean families, the O'Liddys, the MacInernys, the O'Hallorans, the O'Slatterys, the O'Meehans, the O'Kearneys, etc., together with his father's fosterers (and probably his own), the O'Deas, with their kindred clans, the O'Hehirs and O'Quins. The Western clans, MacMahons, O'Loughlins, and O'Connors, kept out of the wretched and ruinous struggle. The Normans, who had enmities among themselves, took sides in it: De Burgho supporting Donogh, the reigning prince; and his father's enemy, De Clare, aiding his rival Dermod, grandson of Brian Rua.

Dermod's brother Conor was slain "treacherously by the black English,"[1] and Dermod himself suffered a reverse in the first attempt made to unseat Donogh. He returned to the conflict next year, 1311, this time with success, slaying

[1] Four Masters.

Donogh MacNamara, Donal O'Grady, and a considerable number of Donogh's supporters, but with heavy loss to himself. He compelled the O'Gradys henceforward to keep in line with their neighbouring clans — his supporters. Following up this advantage, with the aid of Richard de Clare, he again defeated Donogh in a battle at Bunratty, slaying six hundred of his opponents, and taking prisoner William de Burgho, who fought in Donogh's army. They then pushed on to Clonroad and took possession of it. Dermod's success was rendered complete by the death of Donogh, who was treacherously murdered by one of his relatives, Morrogh O'Brien, great-grandson of Donal Connachtagh. His brother Mortogh fled into Connaught, leaving Dermod in undisputed possession, but he did not long enjoy it. He died that same year, and Mortogh was chosen by the clans to succeed him.

Nor was he long without rivals. Donogh and Donal Bawn, the grandsons of Brian Rua, came on the scene with a large following, but they were badly defeated at the battle of Tully O'Dea—now Dysert—by Mortogh, who had the aid not only of his own Thomond forces, but of the O'Kellys, O'Maddens, and the English under William de Burgho. The latter had been previously released in exchange for two of the O'Briens, sons of Donogh, who had been seized by MacNamara, and carried off to De Burgho's friendly castle of Loughrea. They, however, rallied their forces under the walls of Bunratty Castle, and, being joined there by De Clare and his strong English contingent, turned upon Mortogh, whose Connaught supporters by this time probably had returned, and defeated him, compelling him to fly for the second time from Thomond. Donogh was now solemnly inaugurated at Magh-Adhair.[1]

Mortogh's friends were not idle. They contrived to have a meeting called in 1314 of the chiefs of the Thomond clans, at which, once more, a compromise was effected. Mortogh was acknowledged prince of the eastern half of Clare; but this did not satisfy him. Calling to his aid his Connaught supporters, he compelled, in turn, Donogh and Brian to fly. Thus we see the people of Clare constantly at civil war in behalf of those ambitious rivals.

[1] *Annals of Innisfallen.*

There was now another disturbing element added to the troubled sea of Irish life. The year after his great victory at Bannockburn, Robert Bruce sent his brother Edward at the head of an army into Ireland.[1] Donogh O'Brien went to him, offering him his and his adherents' services. Bruce marched as far as Castleconnell unopposed, but, learning that Mortogh was prepared with a large force to dispute with him the crossing of the Shannon, he withdrew. Donogh now turned into Connaught, and we find him, and those who still followed his fortunes, engaged the following year on the side of Felim O'Connor, at the disastrous battle of Athenry. The English were, as usual, clad in armour, and their crossbowmen did fearful havoc among the Irish. The defeat was a crushing one for the O'Connors and other Connaught clans, ten thousand of whom, it is said,—but it must be an exaggeration,—and most of their chieftains, were left dead on the field. Donogh was one of the few men of note who outlived that bloody fight, and, returning to Clare, kindled there once more the torch of civil war. He had all along the support of Richard de Clare. The latter sought for him the aid of the English of Dublin, but failed, as Mortogh had, in opposing the advance of Bruce, secured their good will.

While Mortogh was away in Dublin, Donogh was collecting an army, and this time made the Abbey of Corcomroe the base of his operations. Dermod, Mortogh's brother, marched

[1] In reply to the complaint made by the English king that Bruce had been allowed by the Irish princes to usurp the authority granted to his house by Adrian IV., Donal O'Neill, on their behalf, addressed the well-known Remonstrance to John XXII. In it he recounted the evil deeds of the English in Ireland—among these the barbarous murder of Brian Rua O'Brien by Thomas de Clare. He showed how, not only the soldiers, but the clerics sent from England, usurped, when they could, the rights and property of the native Irish. Having proved that their coming to Ireland, so far from forwarding the interests of religion as was pretended, introduced instead all kinds of disorder, he declared, in most eloquent terms, their determination to struggle to the last against their cruel invaders. This brought from the Pope an appeal to Edward III. for a total change of policy in the direction of the recommendations contained in the Bull of Adrian, which we well know went unheeded. At the same time he fulminated censures against all who aided Bruce in what he regarded as an unjust invasion of Ireland.

hastily to attack them. In the battle which ensued, Donogh was defeated and slain, A.D. 1317, with most of his family, but not before great havoc was made in Dermod's army also. It is stated by Magrath, who was then living, that the chief of the O'Connors of Corcomroe turned treacherously on Donogh, and slew him with his own hand. Brian Bawn alone survived to carry on the claims of his family to the principality of Thomond. On the other side the MacNamaras suffered most. Twenty-one men of note among them fell in the fight, says the contemporary historian,[1] along with chiefs of the O'Molonys and the O'Hallorans. The Abbey of Corcomroe contains the remains of the opposing chiefs who bit the dust in this bitterly fought contest. In giving them decent burial within the sacred enclosure, Dermod displayed more generosity than most of the victors in those stormy days of almost constant strife.

Brian Bawn fled into East Thomond. He, and those of his supporters who still adhered to him, were gladly supported by O'Carroll of Ely. This prince was defending his territory from the inroads of the English under William de Burgho and Edmond Butler. Mortogh O'Brien joined his forces with the latter, with the hope of capturing or slaying Brian, his only remaining rival to the throne; but they were defeated with considerable loss, Mortogh narrowly escaping with his life.[2] Both now returned to Clare, where the old struggle was renewed with fresh vigour. Brian's victory gave heart to his former supporters, many of whom flocked to his standard once more. Richard de Clare again espoused his cause, and determined to make a bold effort to recover the prestige lost at the defeat of Corcomroe. At the head of all the English he could muster, together with the Irish under Brian, a march was made into the O'Dea country. Here they were met at a deep stream, near Dysert, by their opponents, on the 10th of May 1318, and a vigorous battle ensued. Early in the fight De Clare's impetuosity led him into an ambush cleverly laid for him by Conor O'Dea. Pretending to retreat, he drew him across the stream. Here De Clare and those who followed him were cut off by a rush of the Irish concealed in the

---

[1] *Cathreim Turlogha.*   [2] Four Masters. Clyn's *Annals.*

woods, and slain to a man; O'Dea singled out and slew De Clare. His son also fell before the spirited onslaught of the O'Connors under their chief, Felim. A panic ensued among the English, who fled precipitately, but not before many of the leading knights, and a great number of their followers, were slain.[1] Among Brian's supporters the most notable who fell were the two sons of Mahon of Inchiquin,—grandson of Donal Connachtagh,—who had accepted, in defiance of Irish tanistry, letters patent from De Clare, making him lord, but in name only, of all West Clare. This important battle, the second fought on the same ground,—Tullagh O'Dea, *i.e.* the O'Dea Hills, stretching between Magowna and the Abbey of Dysert,—utterly extinguished the De Clare family and authority, and compelled Brian Bawn once more to fly. The historians of the Pale, Grace and Pembroke, assert that the body of the elder De Clare, Richard, was cut into pieces, so fierce was the resentment of the Dalcassians against him in particular for the murder of their prince. His widow, first burning the castle of Bunratty to the ground, fled the county with all the valuables she and her retainers could carry.

Brian Bawn and Mahon of Inchiquin retired to East Thomond, where Mortogh wisely aided them and their followers in acquiring a territory (O'Brien Ara[2]), which their posterity held and ruled for the succeeding centuries. Mortogh was now undisputed Prince of Thomond; and so weakened and disheartened were the English, that for more than a century they not only gave up all attempts to conquer Thomond, but were barely able to hold the strong places within the Pale.

The last, however, was not heard of the ambitious and daring Brian Bawn. His chief supporter, Mahon, was killed in an encounter with the MacNamaras two years after. This clan, always warlike and powerful, rose into greater distinction than ever, having acquired all the territory towards the Shannon occupied by the English and the supporters of Brian Bawn. Their territory was henceforward a well-defined

---

[1] Clyn's *Annals*. Grace's *Annals*.

[2] The country along the east bank of the Shannon, in Thomond, including parts of Tipperary and Limerick, was called Ara-Tire.

principality, stretching from the Lower Fergus and the line of the Glandaree Hills, eastwards by Tulla, and on to Broadford and Doonas, down to the Lower Shannon, Bunratty excepted, and was called East and West Clancuilean. Where and how they slew Mahon O'Brien is not recorded. His death at their hands is merely noted by the Four Masters under the year 1320.

Brian's first achievement was a victory over the English of Connaught, who pushed down into his newly-acquired posession, A.D. 1322.[1] He then directed his energy to extending and consolidating his possessions eastwards towards the boundaries of the Pale. Here again he came into conflict with his old enemies, the English of Connaught, under William de Burgho. He attacked and burned their castle of Atthassol on the Suir, and dealt destruction on the whole territory round. William de Burgho called to his aid his old allies, the O'Briens, MacNamaras, and other clans of East Clare, as well as the O'Connors of Connaught. To resist this forminable attack, Brian solicited and secured the co-operation of Maurice FitzGerald, Earl of Desmond, who was at open enmity with De Burgho, each aiming at superiority among the English in Ireland. The battle was fought near Thurles, A.D. 1328, and resulted in a victory for Brian. Conor O'Brien, Righ-damna of Thomond, together with other chiefs on the Irish and English side, fell. Victory must have declared itself early in the fight for Brian, as only about eighty of his men in all were slain. Mortogh, eager to recover his prestige and avenge the death of his son, returned to the fight in the same year. The Four Masters have the following entry, under the year A.D. 1328 : " Another army was led by Mortogh O'Brien and the Clann-Cuilean (the MacNamaras), against Brian ; but Mortogh was defeated and Conor O'Brien ; Donnoll of the Donnolls, the son of Cumara MacNamara, with many others, were slain." For years after, no one cared to risk an encounter with such a formidable antagonist; neither did he, though active in other directions, make any attempt to recross the Shannon till the death of Mortogh.

[1] Four Masters.

The MacNamaras, having made themselves so prominent in supporting, on every occasion, the claims to the supremacy in Thomond of their relative Mortogh, became a mark for the special enmity of his enemies. In the year 1343, "a great army, both of English and Irish,[1] was led by the Connacians into Munster against MacNamara; and they took hostages from him, and obtained sway over him. A part of this army burned a church, in which were one hundred and eighty persons and two priests along with them; and not one of them escaped the conflagration." This may be regarded as Divine retribution for the burning of the Church of St. Finghin at Quin, with the English within it, some years before. This onslaught on the common enemy may have contributed to the conclusion of a treaty of peace between Brian Bawn and William de Burgho, son of the Earl of Ulster. It was entered into in A.D. 1337, Brian restoring the castle taken from De Burgho, but receiving for it the former rent.[2] With the exception of this raid upon the MacNamaras, there appears to have been peace in Clare for full sixteen years after the defeat at Thurles. The troubled but successful career of Mortogh ended, after a reign of over thirty years, in A.D. 1343.

[1] Four Masters.   [2] *Ibid.*

CHAPTER XII.

FROM 1343 TO 1500.

Another Brian—The Black Death—Brian murdered by the "Clann Keogh"—Revenge—O'Briens and MacNamaras defeat the English at Aenagh, on the Maigne—Ulic de Burgho defeated by the Mac-Namaras—Marries a daughter of the reigning Prince, and assumes the Irish title of MacWilliam Oughther—Submission to Richard II.—MacNamara builds Quin Abbey—Peace—MacMahon, attacked by Teigue O'Brien and the O'Malleys, defeats them—Teigue brings all Leinster and Munster to submission—Covets the dignity of Ard-Righ—Dies 1467—The Earl of Kildare, Lord-Deputy, invades Clare—Is defeated at Ballyhicky, near Quin.

As soon as Brian heard of the death of Mortogh, he made all haste to Clare. In the meantime, Dermod had "assumed the lordship."[1] On the arrival, however, of Brian, with doubtless a strong force, his well-known energy of character, and the prestige of his many successes on the other side of the Shannon, bore down all opposition. The MacNamaras, his old enemies, had been, as already related, humbled. He had made peace with De Burgho. Without these, Dermod could not count upon a force sufficient to cope with Brian, so without a blow he relinquished the supremacy. Brian began now a peaceful reign over all Thomond. On neither side of the Shannon did he meet with any opposition. He had the good sense to keep on good terms with the clans who had, in the early part of his life, been his and his family's bitter and successful opponents. Clare enjoyed internal rest. Even the awful plague called the Black Death, which had ravaged Europe, and which was brought by the English into Ireland in 1348, left it untouched. Those parts of Ireland where the English[2] held their ground were reduced to the most

---

[1] Four Masters.   [2] Clyn's *Annals*. Stowe's *Chronicles*.

extreme misery, whole districts being almost depopulated by this fearful scourge.

This was too good to last long. In 1350, Brian was surprised, probably while insisting on his rights as sovereign in their country, by the Clan Keogh on the east of the Shannon, and treacherously slain.[1] This crime was immediately avenged by Turlogh Oge O'Brien, Brian's grandson, who slew fifteen of the most guilty, and, besides, despoiled the whole clan of their cattle and lands.

During the reign of Dermod, who succeeded Brian, nothing of note occurred in Clare.

Dying without issue, he was succeeded, according to the Four Masters, by his nephew Mahon, surnamed Moinmoy. This reign witnessed some internal dissensions, during which Donogh MacNamara, "the best son of a chieftain in Leath Mogha in his time," say the Four Masters, and the eldest son of the chief of Corcovaskin, were slain by the O'Briens, for which the MacNamaras had their revenge in killing Teigue, grandson of Turlogh O'Brien, some years later on. Mahon gave the English such trouble that they were glad to come to terms with him, by the payment each year of a considerable sum of money. It was called the "Black Rent."

Within a few years, two learned men, Gilla na naemh O'Conway,[2] chief professor of music in Thomond, and Gilla na naemh O'Davoren, chief Brehon or Judge in Thomond, died. There passed away also, A.D. 1365, O'Connor, Prince of Corcomroe, called the Hospitable, who with his own hand slew the younger De Clare at the battle of Dysert O'Dea, and thereby contributed so much to the rout of the English from Thomond. The death also of Donal MacNamara is recorded, A.D. 1368. In the following year, Mahon died in his own fortress at Clonroad, and "Brian O'Brien assumed," say the Four Masters, "the lordship of Thomond." This means probably a forcible seizure, as we will find his uncle Turlogh soon after disputing his claim.

No sooner was Brian in power than he gave proof of warlike vigour. At the head of his own troops, and supported by the Clan Cuilean, he crossed the Shannon, and gave battle

---

[1] Four Masters.   [2] *Ibid.*

on the 1st of July to the English of Munster, at Aenagh on the Maigne, near the great monastery founded in 1151 by Turlogh O'Brien, in the county of Limerick. The latter suffered a severe defeat. Garret, Earl of Desmond, John FitzNicholas, Sir Thomas FitzJohn, and many other nobles, were taken prisoners by the O'Briens and MacNamaras,[1] while their army was routed after great slaughter. They then turned upon the city of Limerick, and, taking it by assault, having burned part of it, compelled the English garrison to surrender. Sioda Cam MacNamara, " son of the daughter of O'Dwyre," assumed the wardenship of the town, but the English who were in the town acted treacherously towards him, and killed him.[2]

Civil war again broke out in Clare. The English, under the command of Richard de Burgho, espoused the cause of the banished Turlogh, Brian's uncle, and, coming in great force, compelled Brian to fly. They then invaded the territory of the MacNamaras, whose prince, Loughlin Laudher (the Strong), not being taken by surprise, like Brian, was able to make a stout resistance. Under the able leadership of his youngest son, Hugh, this warlike clan utterly defeated De Burgho, A.D. 1377, with great loss, among the slain being some of the Connaught chiefs who ranged themselves under the English banner. This success prepared the way for the return to power of Brian Catha an Aenagh, who was married to MacNamara's daughter. This prince wisely made terms with De Burgho, giving him his daughter in marriage, and thus detached him from the cause of his rival, Turlogh Mael.

The year after, Hugh MacNamara, son of Loughlin Laudher by his second wife, daughter of O'Daly of Corcomroe, slew his step-brother Teigue. This shocking crime, not unusual in that rude age, was probably prompted by his ambitious craving for the chieftaincy of the Clan Cuilean, and led to bitter enmity in after years between them and the O'Briens, whose ruling prince was married to Teigue's sister.

The fusion of the old English settlers with the native Irish had become at this early period a very noticeable feature of

---

[1] Grace's *Annals*. Four Masters.   [2] Four Masters.

Irish history. They were already beginning to adopt the dress and language, and customs and laws, of the native race among whom they lived. This one fact is a sufficient reply to the sneers of some English and other foreign writers, when describing or rather caricaturing the Irish of that day. The great Norman families who kept the despised Saxon in abject slavery, and who rarely intermarried with them, would not, it is fair to presume, abandon their own customs, and live like the Irish, if these were so rude as they were pictured. It was a tribute as great to their social, genial, and cultured excellence, as that paid in the past by the Romans to the Greeks, or by the Lorraine and Alsatian Germans of our own time to the French. It was with no little chagrin and indignation that the English began to speak of them as *Hiberniores Hibernesis ipsis*. As an instance of this, we find the Burkes aiding the Dalcassians, A.D. 1380, in exacting the tribute imposed on the English of Munster.[1] But clear proof was given soon after, in 1411, when Ulic de Burgho, who had married the Dalcassian princess, openly renounced the English connection, and had himself elected in the Irish manner as chief of his clan, assuming the title of MacWilliam Oughther, or Upper; while another of the same family, Edmond, assumed that of MacWilliam Eighther, or Lower.

Some time before this, A.D. 1394, Richard II. of England, having suffered reverses in his continental wars, determined to make a show of his authority in Ireland. He collected a fleet of two hundred vessels, and landed at Waterford with a force of no less than four thousand men-at-arms and thirty thousand archers. This was the largest army ever before launched against the Irish, and they prudently, and for want of cohesion among themselves, made signs of submission. The Munster and Ulster kings, O'Brien and O'Neill, "went into the house of the English king."[2] The same was said, but it was not true, of O'Connor. Rival princes of the name ruled then East and West Connaught, and so some minor chieftain was said to have personated the Connaught king. Art MacMurrough, who became so famous afterwards, put himself also in the power of the English king, for which he had to

---

[1] *Book of Lecan.*   [2] Four Masters.

pay the penalty of leaving hostages to secure his release. O'Brien and O'Neill, and even chiefs of lesser note, were received with great distinction. A description, evidently highly coloured, of the festivities and other transactions on this occasion—the strange dress and customs of the Irish guests being specially dwelt on—is to be found in the Chronicles of Froissart. He must have taken on trust what he heard from some Norman, and therefore hostile narrator. Much stress is laid on the knighting after the Norman fashion of the four Irish kings. They submitted to it, but with bad grace, as they declared that at seven years of age an Irish prince formally undertook the profession of arms. After this mock pageant, O'Brien and his Dalcassian bodyguard returned home, and things went on in Clare just as though Richard with his powerful army had never landed in Ireland. Peace reigned there till Brian's death, A.D. 1399, when, his sons by his wife Slaine MacNamara being too young to rule, his brother Conor was elected to succeed him.

At the year 1402 the Four Masters give the building for the Franciscan friars of the beautiful Abbey of Quin, by "Sioda Cam MacNamara, lord of Clan-Cuilean, who ordained that it should be the burial-place of himself and his tribe." Its ruins are there still, speaking eloquently of the splendour of the gift, and the excellence of Clare architecture of that period. No better answer can be given to the silly theory of Mr. Marcus Keane, that the "towers and temples of Ireland" could not be of Christian origin, than to point to the exquisitely finished workmanship of the towers and cloisters and chapels of Quin Abbey. It was all unquestionably the work of Irish hands, under the direction of a generous Irish prince, and in a county within which, as yet, nothing foreign had taken root. Probably it was only commenced in that year, and proceeded with in the subsequent years till 1433, when it was completed and occupied by the friars of the strict observance, as the latter is the date of the Bull of Eugenius IV. sanctioning the foundation, addressed to "Delecto filio nobili viro Mac son mac na-Mara Duci de Clandcullyan.[1] It may be assumed that it was for the

[1] Wadding, vol. x. p. 526.

furtherance of this great work Mahon MacNamara was proceeding to Rome, as his death while on the journey is recorded at the year 1404.[1] In the year 1407 died Sioda Cam MacNamara, the munificent founder of the abbey.

The building of such a noble structure affords clear proof that during those years the Clare clans were at rest. The English had quite enough on their own hands to engage them. Henry of Lancaster had deposed the weak and vacillating Richard II., and thus gave rise to the long internal struggle known as the Wars of the Roses.

An entry in the Four Masters at 1408 enables us to get a glimpse of the social life of the time. The sons of the chieftains of the O'Loughlins and the O'Shaughnessys were on a visit, it would appear, at Clonroad, enjoying the hospitality of Conor, Prince of Thomond. While engaged on the green at some athletic sports, probably fencing with sword or battle-axe, young O'Shaughnessy was accidentally slain by O'Loughlin. It does not appear that any bad feeling grew out of the fatality.

The following year the old feud between the descendants of Brian Rua and the reigning family broke out afresh. In an engagement which took place between them, Conor O'Brien was defeated and compelled to fly into Connaught, leaving as prisoners, among others, in his kinsman's hands, a son of the Earl of Desmond, who had been fostered at Clonroad,[2] and his own brother Dermot. This attack upon Conor must have been a surprise organised on the other side of the Shannon, where the descendants of Brian Rua had settled down. It certainly was not sustained; for soon after he returned to Clonroad and ruled there undisturbed to the end of his life. One great calamity, however, fell upon him. His son Donal, Tanist of Thomond, was slain in some petty quarrel by the chief of the Barrys, called Barrymore, A.D. 1411.[3] Five years after, his cousin, Cumeadh MacNamara, heir to the principality of Clancuilean, died. During those years Clare enjoyed unwonted tranquillity. So far from striving to subdue the

---

[1] Four Masters.
[2] The Four Masters call him by mistake a son of the Earl of Kildare.
[3] Four Masters.

hardy Dalcassians, the English for the greater part of this century were compelled to pay to the Thomond princes the tribute called by them in their chagrin the "Black Rent" (*dubh cios*). Neither did civil war stain the soil of Clare. From the restoration of Conor and for many years after his death there was profound peace. It is probable that the blessed interval was availed of for the erection not only of Quin Abbéy, but of many of the other churches and religious houses, the ruins of which, as monuments of the zeal of the Reformation period, are still scattered through Clare. Learning also was encouraged and patronised, as may be inferred from the account given by the Four Masters of the death in 1425 of "Magrath Ollav of Thomond in poetry." He is there described as "a prosperous and wealthy man." After an unusually long and prosperous career, Conor died, A.D. 1426; and immediately after, his nephew Teigue, the son of Brian Catha an Aenagh, was elected without opposition and installed as Prince of Thomond.

This event caused no disturbance in the even current of affairs. In the extreme west of the county a very cruel act was perpetrated; but it was in a family broil. Turlogh MacMahon, " Lord of Corca Baiscinn, was killed at an advanced age in a nocturnal assault by his own kinsmen."[1] As if to compensate for this, we have it given in the same record, that MacNamara, chief of Clan Cuilean, who died two years after, A.D. 1428, was "a charitable and truly hospitable man, who had suppressed robbery and theft; and established peace and tranquillity in his territory." His successor, Mealaghlin MacNamara, did not long survive him. He died in 1432. His successor, Maccon MacNamara, evidently the "Mac Son" of the Bull of Eugenius quoted above, lived only to witness the completion of the abbey. The Four Masters give his death at the end of 1433. In the same pages, at the year 1437, we find recorded the drowning of Geannan MacCurtin, "intended Ollav of Thomond in history.' There was not in Leth-Mogha" (the southern half of Ireland) "in his time a better material of a historian than he." This family gave, in nearly all the years following, up to a recent period, men of

---

[1] Four Masters.

note in Clare as preservers of the old traditions of the country in the Irish language. The last of the line was a teacher in the parish of Kilfarboy, who died only a few years ago. The frequent entries in the pages of the Four Masters recording the decease of Ollavs—*i.e.* doctors in history, law, and poetry—afford sufficient proof of the estimation in which learning was held even in the most troubled periods of Irish history.

Teigue O'Brien and Sioda Cam MacNamara died, A.D. 1444. Of the latter the Four Masters add that "he was the chief protector of the men of Ireland." This is explained by contemporary annalists, who speak of him as renowned for hospitality.

The first interruption to the peace which Clare had for so many years enjoyed was due once more to rivalry among the O'Briens. Teigue had been for some years before his death deposed by his brother Mahon. Their younger brother, Turlogh, who had married a daughter of Clanrickard, strove in turn to replace him, and with the powerful aid of his father-in-law succeeded,[1] but only after a fierce and protracted struggle, in which all Thomond was involved. He ruled till his death, 1459—in which year also Cumara MacNamara was treacherously slain.[2] He was succeeded, but only for a short period, by Donogh, the son of the deposed Mahon.

During those two years nothing more noteworthy is recorded of Clare in our annals, than the rigorous requirement of the tribute called *dubh cios* from the English of Thomond. This was but a fair and equitable charge for the use of the Dalcassian tribe-land which they had obtained, and out of which they could have been easily driven in this their period of weakness. Donogh had but one son, Brian, surnamed "of the Fleet," who acquired a bad pre-eminence by slaying his near kinsman, Turlogh, Bishop of Killaloe.[3] What led to this sacrilegious crime is not recorded. It is probable that in consequence of it he had to fly the country, as his name does not turn up afterwards in Clare history.

Teigue, the eldest son of Turlogh, surnamed an Chomhaid, from the townland adjoining the lake of Inchiquin, on which

---

[1] Four Masters. [2] *Ibid.*
[3] Ware's *Bishops*, by Harris, p. 594.

he built his residence, was acknowledged King of Thomond. He had a peaceful rule of six years, being troubled by no rival, and having the support of his mother's people, the Burkes of Clanrickard. He met, however, one serious check, A.D. 1460. Having some cause of quarrel with the MacMahons of Corcovaskin, he endeavoured to take them by surprise. His sons, probably with the aid of their relatives the Burkes, secured the co-operation of the O'Malleys with a view to an attack from the sea. Their approach along the coast and round Loop Head towards Carrigaholt could not escape observation. The MacMahons made ready for the attack, and, falling upon them in the first moment of their landing, compelled them to retreat precipitately to their vessels, slaying many, among whom were three chiefs of the O'Malleys. Donal O'Brien was taken prisoner. His brother Mahon was drowned before he could reach his ship.[1] This sharp lesson had the effect of securing the MacMahons the peaceable possession of their own country.

The most remarkable event of this reign was the revival of the Dalcassian claim to the throne of all Ireland. Teigue, making peace with the MacMahons, who in all probability had restored unharmed their prisoner Donal, summoned to his standard all the clans of Thomond. This appeal stirred up their ancestral pride, and met with a hearty response. He "marched with a great army across the Shannon in the summer of this year," A.D. 1466,[2] first southwards through Desmond, compelling the submission as well of the native chiefs as of the Earl of Desmond and the English; then eastwards through the old battleground of Ossory and Leinster, meeting with similar success. He returned through the city of Limerick, imposing upon the inhabitants, mostly of Danish and English descent, a yearly tribute of sixty marks. The approach of winter, a season so unfavourable to warlike pursuits in Ireland, compelled a cessation of hostilities. The Dalcassians were now once more supreme in Leathmogha. To secure, according to Irish Brehon law, the coveted dignity of supreme authority, it would be necessary to bring to submission one at least of the ruling princes of Leathcuin.

[1] Four Masters. *Annals* of D. F.   [2] Four Masters.

After their signal success through the South, had they marched directly North, they might without much difficulty have attained this object. Clans are not easily kept together when the love of home and the pride of being received as victors animate them. Perhaps, too, they hoped to recruit through the winter, so as to enable them to make that conquering circuit through the whole North, by which Brian Boroimhe established their rule. If such a vision they had, it soon vanished. Teigue, the animating spirit of this ambitious design, died soon after his return, and with him, as events soon proved, the last hope of an Irish Ard-Righ in Erinn. His brother Conor, nicknamed na Srona ("of the Nose"), was chosen to succeed him in A.D. 1467.

He was but barely recognised chief of the Dal-Cas, when he was called on by his relative, the MacWilliam of Clanrickard, to join him in a war against the O'Kellys of Hy Many, who had the support of the rival MacWilliam Eighther and the O'Donnells. The opposing forces met at Cros-magh-croin, now, Crosmacroin, near the city of Galway. A son of MacWilliam Oughther, two sons of O'Kelly, some of the leading O'Donnells, together with a large number on both sides, fell in this unnatural conflict; but victory remained with the Dalcassian and MacWilliam Oughther.[1] This only begat more strife. The O'Donnells mustered a strong force two years after, and, with the aid of MacWilliam Eighther, invaded and plundered the territory of MacWilliam Oughther. "MacWilliam (*i.e.* Ulick), however, drew and gathered to his assistance the sons of O'Brien (*i.e.*) Gilla-Duv, the son of Teigue, and Mortogh Garv, the son of Teigue, and a body of Dalcassian chieftains along with them."[2] The hastily summoned cavalry fell with great vigour on the Northern army retreating with its booty, but were twice repulsed, the last time with considerable loss, including a son of O'Connor of Corcomroe, at a place called Glanog, in the barony of Clare-Galway. O'Connor himself was slain in two years after, A.D. 1471, at Lahinch, by his own nephews. The Four Masters also give, at the year 1474, an occurrence little creditable to the O'Briens. Teigue, the son of Conor, the

---

[1] *Annals* of the Four Masters. *Annals* of D. F.   [2] Four Masters.

ruling prince, had a dispute with his cousin Dermot, who is called the son of Bishop O'Brien, about some land. It ended in the slaying of Teigue. Dermot was immediately taken prisoner and hanged by the enraged father.

This tragic occurrence was followed by peace in Clare for a period of more than twenty years. Within that time, at the end of 1482, died two of the chiefs of the MacClanchys, who were hereditary Brehons or judges of Thomond. In the beginning of the following year, Mahon O'Griffy, Bishop of Killaloe, was buried in the Abbey of the Canons Regular of St. Augustine, in the island at the mouth of the Fergus, called after them Canon Island, and the ruins of which to the present day lend such a picturesque effect to that broad expanse of the Shannon. At this period, Nicholas O'Grady, upon whom, in recognition of his eminent qualities, the freedom of the city of Limerick was conferred, presided as abbot at Tomgraney. There is mention made also of Donnell MacGorman of Ibricken, as "the richest man in Ireland in live stock,"[1] which shows how settled was the condition of Clare as regards the possession of property. But as yet there was not sufficient protection for life, as we read in the Four Masters that "Cumara MacNamara was exultingly slain by the sons of Donogh MacNamara" in A.D. 1486. In the same year died "Raighnault, daughter of John MacNamara, wife of Turlogh, son of Teigue O'Brien, lord of East Thomond,"[2] and in the year following, "Hugh, son of Philip Roe Mac-Namara, a brave and warlike man."[3] In the west of the county the MacMahons were engaged in an internal struggle, fomented by two rival claimants to the chieftaincy.[4] But the most important event of the dying century in Clare was the inroad made upon the Dalcassians by the Lord-Deputy, the Earl of Kildare, in revenge for their support of the illegitimate claimant to the earldom of Ormond, the rightful heir having married his sister. He marched an army across

---

[1] Four Masters.   [2] *Ibid.*
[3] And brother of Slaine MacNamara, who was wife of the MacWilliam Oughther.
[4] A famine decimated the whole country in 1497, so dreadful that in many places the dead were left unburied.

the Shannon through Limerick, surprised and seized the castle of Ballycullen, in the MacNamara country, and, leaving there a garrison, pushed on towards the O'Brien fortress at Clonroad. Conor-na-Srona hastily summoned together the Dalcassian clans to repel this invasion of their territory. The opposing forces met a little beyond Quin, near the castle of Ballyhicky, and there, after a hotly-contested battle, the English and their allies were put to rout. They fled across the Shannon in great confusion. Kildare had the mortification to be obliged to abandon the MacNamara castle, which he had so lately occupied. So once more Clare soil was rid of the foreigner. An attempt made two years later on by Kildare and Ormond to retrieve this disaster, was promptly met by the Dalcassians, who soon took the offensive, penetrated into Ormond, and at Moyaliff inflicted on them another severe defeat.

CHAPTER XIII.

Internal Condition of Thomond at this period—Its Religion—Its Politics—The Manners and Customs of its People.

THE sixteenth century was destined to witness a complete revolution in the religious and political life of Europe. The history of every country is full of the startling incidents of the new birth. Change in almost everything became the order of the day—much of it for good, but much of it also for evil. Our little remote Clare did not escape. For the first time in over one thousand years since the Dalcassian conquest, its right to self-government was seriously called into question. It is a curious fact, and not perhaps clearly known or appreciated by many of its own people, that for more than three hundred years after Henry II. had received the mock submission of the King of Munster, no English law ran or was at all recognised in Thomond. It will be interesting to take a look once again into its inner life at this eventful period, as far as the scant records remaining after pillage and plunder permit it.

On the religious aspect little need be said. The faith as preached by St. Senan, St. Benignus, St. Flannan, and St. Molua, remained all along unchanged. The ruins of hermitages, monasteries, convents, and churches scattered all over the county, from Bishop's Island and Iniscatha to Killaloe, and from Corcomroe to Canons' Island, all plainly devoted to Catholic uses and worship, leave no room for rational doubt on that subject. The very stones speak out. They tell us from first to last of hermit, and priest, and nun, and abbot, and bishop, and altar, and purgatory, till not one distinctive dogma of Catholic faith as it is now known is left unattested. Be they right or be they wrong, the hard facts are still there, pointing to undisturbed continuity. Only in one particular is there found a want of harmony. The term "abbot's son," or "bishop's son," occasionally turns up in the ancient manuscripts, and is faithfully given by such undoubted supporters of ecclesiastical celibacy as the Four Masters. But the explanation is not far to find. Undoubtedly there were some through all those troubled times who were unfaithful to their vows, and whose rank in their clans afforded them a kind of impunity. Rome was far off in those days, and communications with her were few and far between, except for the purpose of appointment to Church dignities. Other causes, however, contributed in a far greater degree to this anomaly in a country like Ireland, where chastity was assuredly held in such high esteem. Church emoluments were tempting baits, and many looked for them late in life. For instance, the Bishop O'Brien, whose son slew his cousin in 1474, as already related, was consecrated, as Maziere Brady testifies in his valuable work [1] in 1482, eight years afterwards. His son, then, was born to him long before, and probably in lawful wedlock, before he entered on the ecclesiastical state. But apart from that, a great abuse had crept in under cover of the confusion caused by the Danish irruptions. Members of the ruling families seized on the Church revenues, and usurped therefrom the title of bishop or abbot, while only laics, but providing, of course, and maintaining ecclesiastics chiefly from the religious bodies to discharge the religious functions. Not to speak of other numerous authorities to whom appeal can be made in support of this fact, Fr. Malone, in his learned *Church History of Ireland*, chap. iii., quotes extracts from two authors, "far as the poles asunder," but whose testimony is therefore placed beyond reach of doubt—St. Bernard and Gerald Barry. They are well worth reproducing as all-sufficient for the purpose. The holy Saint in his *Life of St. Malachy*, chap. vii., writes: "Well, from about the year 920 down for two hundred years, there were in the See of Armagh eight married men bishops, *but not in orders*, before Archbishop Celsus; and the practice deserved death." Gerald Barry, in his *Itinerarium*, says: "Many churches through

---

[1] *Episcopal Succession*, vol. ii. p. 116.

Ireland *have a lay abbot*. This arose from a wicked custom. . . . They leave only the offerings to the clergy, and cause themselves to be unduly called abbots. They impudently possessed themselves of the Church lands, which they leave to their children."[1] Looking to what has happened since, especially after the English occupation, on a much larger scale, and with no pretence of supplying the religious requirements, one may well say with Solomon, " There is nothing new under the sun." Save this innovation, no religious difference, certainly no doctrinal difference, no clashing of sects, disturbed the even tenor of religious life in Thomond for more than a thousand years since St. Patrick's mantle fell on St. Senan. If St. Cummian, whose learning illuminated the first half of the seventh century, and whom Dr. Lanigan believes to be identical with Cumin Fadha,[2] son of Fiachna, King of West Munster, could appear and address once more, in the beginning of the sixteenth century, the descendants of his kinsmen of Thomond, his language and his doctrines would be alike intelligible to them.

The clans, too, held their ground. Centuries came and went, leaving the great Dalcassian families all along in possession of their ancient territories. The Danes did not go inland. Plundering Iniscatha and holding Limerick contented them. Beyond a hazy tradition, originating probably in the name itself,—the Danes being sometimes called Laughlins,—there is no authentic proof that they settled down in and colonised Burren, and were the ancestors of the O'Loughlin clan. Surely the crags and rocks of that district could have little charm for those fierce freebooters of the sea. Neither did the English, Saxon, or Norman take any foothold. With the exception of the De Clare incident, which ended so disastrously for the invaders, no serious attempt was made by them, for four full centuries, to bring the war-loving Dalcassians under subjection. During all this time, notwithstanding the boasted conquest of Ireland in 1172, England might as well have been at the Antipodes as far as her influence upon Clare life is to be

---

[1] *Church History of Ireland*, by Fr. Malone, chap. iii.
[2] *Ecc. Hist. of Ireland*, vol. ii. chap. xv. p. 398.

taken into account. The clans made war or peace as it suited them. The description given by Gerald Barry[1] of the weapons they used in war in his day, probably applies to the period under review, for firearms were as yet practically unknown.

"They use three kinds of arms," he writes: "short spears and two javelins; also large battle-axes of fine polished steel, which they borrowed from the Norwegians and Ostmen. They use the battle-axe with one hand only, extending the thumb on the handle which directs the blow; from which neither the helmet can defend the head, nor the iron coat of mail the rest of the body. Whereupon it happened even in our own time that the entire hip of a soldier, though exceeding well environed with iron, was cut off by one blow of a battle-axe; on one side of the horse the hip together with the thigh; on the other side the body fell lifeless to the ground. They also used, with great promptitude, large stones when other weapons failed them, which proved very fatal to the enemy in battle." They slew their enemy, seized their property when they could, and hanged their prisoners without so much as a thought that their right to do so could be called into question. The word -savage or barbarous may seem, at first sight, the best suited to describe such a state of society. It was certainly the very antithesis to the modern idea of centralised government. But was it, after all, necessarily savage or barbarous? Exactly the same state of things, though of course on a much larger scale, existed for centuries in Italy. Every petty state in the peninsula was independent, and much given to war; yet it was during this reign of apparent anarchy that Italy reached the zenith of its fame as a civilised nation. The poets, the painters, the sculptors, the masters of music of that period, have crowned Italy with everlasting glory. Disunion then does not necessarily imply barbarism. So in Thomond too, though at a long distance, it is just as certain that there was a vigorous and wholesome public life. A savage, or uncivilised, or indigent people would never think of building up those strong and, for the

---

[1] *Itinerarium*, Book iii. chap. x.

time, admirably constructed castles, the ruins of which, may still be found in almost every parish. It may be easily taken for granted that the interior of these formidable dwellings was not altogether unworthy of the exterior; and that within them were enjoyed, from generation to generation, the comforts and some of the luxuries of life. One thing is quite certain, poetry and music of a kind rarely surpassed found their home among the Irish clans. The bard with harp[1] in hand has been regarded as a symbol of Ireland. That does not allow of the supposition that, even with all the turmoil, the people were uncultured. Nor was there a total want of the elegance of life. Some years ago, when the railway between Ennis and Limerick was being constructed, the workmen came upon a buried treasure. It consisted of a considerable quantity of gold ornaments exquisitely wrought, some of which were purchased for and are preserved in the Museums of Trinity College and the Royal Irish Academy. Mr. Wakeman, M.R.I.A., assured me that the artistic value of the whole was not less than £20,000. He believed the workmanship to date from before the Christian era. Much more of a similar kind hurriedly

[1] The harp of Brian Boroimhe is still to be seen in the Museum of Trinity College. Its history is full of interest. Brian's son Donogh, having murdered his brother Teigue, A.D. 1128, was deposed and fled to Rome to crave absolution for his crime, carrying with him his father's crown and harp, which he presented to the Pope. This act of submission was availed of in the alleged Bull of Adrian as a proof of his right to cede Ireland to Henry II. The harp was sent, with the title of Defender of the Faith, to Henry VIII. He presented it to the first Earl of Clanrickard. On the marriage of a Lady Eleanor De Burgh to Turlogh MacMahon of Clenagh, it formed part of the dowry, and hung for about a century in the halls of Clenagh. Donogh MacMahon and his eldest son had to fly to Austria in the early penal times. His second son, Henry, stayed at home and married an O'Brien of Arra. About 1750, Donogh's grandson Stanislaus returned, and, on having possession of Clenagh from his uncle's son, gave him the harp. It passed then by intermarriage to a MacNamara, by whose son, A.D. 1782, it was given to the Hon. William Conyngham, and deposited by him as a national monument in the collection at Trinity College. Mrs. Morgan John O'Connell of Ballyleen Lodge, whose son represents the MacMahons of Clenagh in the female line (the male line being extinct), has given me these details from family papers in her possession.

hidden away from the covetous eye of the English invader must still be, in all probability, in the soil of Thomond. This, taken in connection with the fact that the silks[1] and wines of Spain and France found their way regularly up the Shannon and along the coast of Clare, leads easily to the conviction that the Dalcassian clans knew not a little of the ways of civilised life.

But what of the poorer class, who had no castles to live in? It must be confessed that very little can be with certainty known of their mode of life. The whole fabric of society underwent since a resetting; and the troubles and vicissitudes of the following century have left few traces of their ways and manners. Rough and rude they must have been in the days when, even in the English court, the maids of honour attendant on the queen had fixed rations of beef and beer in good measure served out to them daily; and when Henry, anxious to pay special honour to Irish chieftains making submission, received them " in the Queen's closet at Greenwich," which for the occasion " was richly hanged with cloth of Arras and well strawed with rushes."[2] When such customs prevailed in courts, we may well look for simplicity in the homes of Dalcassian peasants. Fare and dress alike were of the homeliest kind, though substantial, as might be expected among a pastoral people. Fencing, hurling, and feats of strength and agility, constituted chief part of their out-door amusements; while, when evening fell, we can well picture to ourselves those sturdy clansmen gathered into the great hall of the chieftain's castle, discussing the topics of the day, enjoying the sweet music of their native land, and listen-

---

[1] The following, though from the hand evidently of an enemy, is worth giving, as it affords a glimpse of the habits of the period. It is in a letter, among the State Papers, written, A.D. 1537, by R. Cowley to Cromwell, advising "that no silk or saffron be set upon shirts; for especially against High Feasts at Christmas and Easter there is no Irishman of war—horseman, kernagh, nor gallowglass—for the most part but will steal rob out of churches or elsewhere to go gay at a feast; yea, and bestoweth for saffron and silk to one shirt many times five marks, so that more robbery and felony is against such feasts committed as all the year following."

[2] Letter of Henry VIII. in State Papers.

ing to stories of "the brave days of old" from the lips of their bards and seanachies. They had, too, their disputes, and then these castle halls became courts of justice. A MacCurtin or an O'Brody would be heard with respect, while reading out records of which he had hereditary charge, defining the rights of every member of the clan, and a MacClanchy sitting as Brehon would deliver judgment from which there was no appeal.

The standing of the clansmen up to the period under consideration was one of singular and striking independence. The poorest man was of the same blood with his chief, or prince, or king, and had an equal right to a share of the clan property. For this he paid no fixed rent as we understand it now. He was bound, however, to contribute a portion, adequate to his status, towards the general expenses, as well as to render military service when called on. This done,— and Brehon law was there to regulate it,—he was free as air. Touch him, and the whole clan was touched. "Spend me but defend me" is but a pithy way of expressing the relations that existed between each member and the whole body, with their elected chief at their head. This system must have been at times oppressive. It left, indeed, but little room for what is called progress, as it imposed a check on individual energy and the accumulation of personal property. But it had for compensation that it grew up out of the instincts and with the free will of the people. It was communism, consecrated by the usage of a hundred generations of freemen. Under it the splendours and glories of modern civilised life were impossible.

Neither did it admit of the degrading poverty and abject misery that festers away too often under the very shadow of the modern palace.

CHAPTER XIV.

FROM 1500 TO 1540.

Disastrous Battle of Cnoctuagh, near Galway—Reversed at Monabraher, near Limerick—O'Daly of Corcomroe—Battle of Knockaroe, near Strabane—Defeat at Camun on the Suir—Earl of Kildare after Capture of Maynooth takes refuge in Clare—Portcroissi, above Castleconnell—Lord Grey in Clare—Submission but no Occupation.

THE sixteenth century, as above stated, witnessed more changes, religious and political, over the face of Europe, and through the whole world, than any other since the spread of Christianity. During its progress, the ancient constitution of Thomond gave way, and foreign-made laws began to take the place of the laws and customs which had held their ground for more than twenty centuries. The train was laid in the first years of the century for this organic change by the disastrous defeat of the Dalcassians and their allies at the battle of Cnoctuagh, near the city of Galway. The name signifies the hill of axes, and was so called from the number of axes which were found there after the stubborn and bloody contest.

Turlogh O'Brien inaugurated his reign over Thomond, after the old barbaric fashion, by a raid into the county of Limerick in 1501. The O'Briens and O'Loughlins of Burren were induced by a chief of the O'Flahertys, who had a quarrel with his clan, to invade their territory.[1] They advanced as far as Killery Bay, where they were met by the O'Flahertys. The latter were defeated with considerable loss; but, summoning to their aid all in the country who could bear arms, they pursued the victors, and, falling on them unexpectedly, put them to flight. The leaders on the Dalcassian side, including O'Flaherty, trying to rally their forces, were with many others

[1] Four Masters, A.D. 1503.

slain, and so the unprovoked aggression turned out a miserable failure.

Worse still was in store for the people of Clare in the near future. MacWilliam of Clanrickard, the uncle of Turlogh O'Brien, fell upon his neighbours, the O'Kellys of Hy Many, and seized three of their castles. Thereupon O'Kelly appealed for aid to the Lord Justice Kildare, who had a private quarrel with Clanrickard. The latter was married to a daughter of Kildare, whom he treated with great cruelty. The Lord Justice was also allied to the O'Donnells, and was able to call to his standard nearly all the Northern chiefs, except the O'Neills. The Four Masters, A.D. 1504, give the following account of this unnatural and fatal conflict:—

"A great army was mustered by the Lord Justice, Garrett the son of Thomas, Earl of Kildare. He was joined first by the chieftains of Leath-Chuin, namely, O'Donnell, *i.e.* Hugh Roe and his son; then by the principal chieftains of Kenel-Connell and a party of Connacians, namely, O'Connor Roe, *i.e.* Hugh, the son of Felim Finn, and MacDermot, Lord of Moylurg. There came also, in the same muster, (all) the chiefs of Ulster, except O'Neill, namely, Art, the son of Hugh O'Neill, Tanist of Kenel-Owen; Donnell, the son of Magennis; MacMahon and O'Hanlon; also O'Rielly and O'Farrell, *i.e.* the Bishop; O'Connor Faly; the O'Kellys; the Clan William[1] Burke; and the forces of almost all Leath-Chuin. These forces marched without stopping till they arrived in Clanrickard. MacWilliam of Clanrickard mustered a great army to give them battle, namely, Turlogh, son of Teigue O'Brien, Lord of Thomond, and his kinsmen, with their forces the Sil-Aedha;[2] and Mulrony O'Carroll, Lord of Ely, with all the clans and chieftains, joined by the chieftains of Ormond and Ara.[3] MacWilliam and O'Brien, with their forces, then came to a

---

[1] The Burkes of Mayo, who were in almost perpetual conflict with the Galway Burkes.

[2] The descendants of Aedh or Hugh, another of the names by which the then powerful sept of MacNamara was then known.

[3] These were principally the O'Briens, O'Kennedys, O'Hogans, O'Fogartys, O'Mearas, O'Sheehans, etc. The citizens of Limerick seem, up to this period and for some time after, to have taken no part in these clan conflicts.

brave conclusion not to yield submission or hostages to their enemies, but to come to a battle with them exactly at Cnoc-Tuagh.[1] A fierce battle was fought between them, such as was not known in latter times. Far away from the combating troops were heard the violent onset of the martial chiefs, the vehement efforts of the champions, the charge of the royal heroes, the noise of the lords, and the clamour of the troops when endangered, the shouts and exultations of the youths, the sound made by fall of brave men, and the triumphing of the nobles over the plebeians. The battle was at length gained against MacWilliam, O'Brien, and the chiefs of Leath-Mogha; and a great slaughter was made of them; and among the slain was Murrough Mac-I-Brien Ara, together with many others of the nobles. And of the nine battalions in solid battle array, there survived only one broken battalion. A countless number of the Lord Justice's forces were also slain, though they routed the others before them." From this enumeration and description, which is also found in the *Annals of Ulster*, it is manifest that the Southern army, which was drawn from Thomond alone, was greatly outnumbered. They must have fought with desperate valour; whereas Ware, a careful authority, says: "The fight was sharply contested for some hours with equal loss on both sides; at last the victory fell on Kildare's side." He computes the Southern loss at two thousand.[2] The victors did not dare to pursue the vanquished, nor even to stir from the battle-field, till, by O'Donnell's advice, time should be given to their shattered and scattered battalions to reform. No English fell in this encounter. The few present did some execution with their crossbows from the distance. They were content, and

---

[1] A hill eight miles north-east of Galway, now called Knockdoe. The tradition in the locality is that the battle raged between the summit of the hill, occupied probably by the Southern army acting on the defensive, and the neighbouring townland of Turloghmore. The exact date of the battle was, according to Ware's *Annals*, August 19, 1504.

[2] The *Book of Howth* says nine thousand. This was probably an exaggeration; but when it is borne in mind that an Irish battalion numbered usually three thousand men, and that only one out of the nine engaged escaped without much loss, the calculation may not be far under the mark.

doubtless glad, to see the Irish slaughter each other. Again, as on so many previous and subsequent occasions, the policy of *divide et impera* prevailed. Kildare felt himself now in the position of Strongbow. The private enterprise of each, proving successful, paved the way for the further aggrandisement of the English crown.

It is easy to conceive what grief and terror was felt through the hills and valleys of Clare and Tipperary when the dreadful loss, both of life and prestige, began to be realized. To this was superadded the fear of invasion. In the panic which ensued, it might well be expected; and if any considerable force marched southward, it is not likely that much effectual resistance could be offered. Perhaps if Kildare had with him a sufficient body of English and Anglo-Irish troops, he might have followed up his success; but he had not. The Northern chiefs were presumably unwilling to engage in any further hostilities for Kildare's or the English advantage, so the Dalcassians were left for some years unmolested. That the time given to the clans to recuperate was well availed of, was proven soon after in the well-contested field of Monabraher.

The news of the success of Kildare was well received by the young king, Henry VIII., who in 1508 ascended the throne of England. He could desire nothing better than that the Irish should be kept slaying each other, while his representative came away with the *éclat* of victory. He renewed his authority as Lord Justice of Ireland.

Kildare now determined to afford evidence of his activity. He summoned to his standard the Anglo-Irish of Meath, Leinster, and South Munster, and such of the native Irish as were well affected to him. James, Earl of Desmond, head of the Southern Geraldines, together with the chiefs of the MacCarthys, brought their followers to his aid; while even O'Donnell, allied to him by marriage, marched down from the far North. Kildare proceeded first towards the county of Cork, meeting with little opposition. He took some castles, built another, and then entered the city of Limerick. In the meantime, the Dalcassian chiefs, anticipating attack, mustered their forces on the banks of the Shannon. There is no mention made of any of the Western clans, but probably the

O'Deas, the O'Hehirs, and the O'Quins joined their forces with their immediate neighbours, the O'Briens. The Sil-Aedha were present in great force. Of these the MacNamaras were the more numerous and more powerful, but were well supported by their kinsmen, the MacInernys, the O'Gradys, the O'Slatterys, the O'Liddys, the O'Hallorans, the O'Meehans, the O'Hartigans, the O'Molonys, etc. Clanrickard brought his whole strength to the aid of the Dalcassians, who had lately suffered such ·loss. The remembrance of the bloody field of Cnoctuagh stung the proud Dalcassian spirit to the quick. The opportunity of avenging it was now eagerly availed of. Kildare was well aware of the movements of his opponents. He marched to the wooden bridge at Port-croissi,[1] above Castleconnell, connecting East and West Thomond, and destroyed it. His object evidently was to give himself time to strike first at the clans of East Thomond, and crush them before aid from Clare could arrive. His plan was foiled by the energy and activity of the Dalcassians and their allies. Fording the Shannon near Killaloe, they made a rapid march, and encamped late in the evening so close to the invaders that "they used to hear one another's voices during the night."[2] Early in the morning Kildare withdrew his forces towards Limerick, probably with a view to select for himself the field of battle. Turlogh O'Brien hotly pursued, and, coming up to the retreating foe, forced on the fight. Kildare wheeled round at a place called Monabraher, i.e. "the Friar's Bog," in the parish of Killeedy, near the city of Limerick, placing the English and Irish of Munster in the van, the rear being occupied by the English of Dublin and Meath, supported by O'Donnell's force, which had just arrived. The battle was a fiercely-contested one, lasting the whole day,[3] night only separating the combatants. Victory was on the side of the Clare and Connaught clans. Ware, while admitting that the forces of the Lord Justice suffered more heavily, says that the victory was dearly bought. The Four Masters assert

---

[1] Four Masters. Ware's *Annals*. This bridge was thrown across the Shannon, A.D. 1507, by the united efforts of Turlogh O'Brien, Prince of Thomond, his brother Donal, and the Bishops of Killaloe and Kilfenara.

[2] Four Masters, A.D. 1510. [3] Ware's *Annals*.

that "the English army escaped by flight," owing their safety from perhaps utter annihilation to the "bravery and prowess of O'Donnell in leading off the rear." One thing is quite certain—Kildare never attempted to measure swords again with the Clare and Connaught allies, and in so far the victory of Cnoctuagh lost its effect. Incursions were made by him, and, after his death, A.D. 1513, by his son Gerald, who was made Lord Justice, into bordering territories, but Thomond and the Clanrickard country were left unassailed.

For some years, while tumult surrounded her borders, Clare enjoyed the blessings of peace. An entry in the Four Masters reminds us that learning was encouraged and flourished. O'Daly of Corcomroe is described as "a professor of poetry, who kept a house of general hospitality." We may take it that the term "professor of poetry" conveyed the same idea that professor of Belles Lettres does in modern times. This distinction was hereditary in the O'Daly clan, as was that of Brehon or Judge among the MacClanchys, and history and pedigree, so important in tribe life, among the MacCurtins and the O'Brodys. Another O'Daly, Donalmor, has left behind him in the same locality the tradition of great learning and accomplishments. His monument is shown near Kinvara. The former takes his long rest in the old abbey of Corcomroe. The payments made for their services to the professors of music, poetry, and languages, as well as to the hereditary Brehons and historian, were usually "in kind"—*i.e.* in goods, not in money—and with lavish hand. This accounts for the "hospitality" with which they are usually credited. How the teachers of those days and their patrons would look askance at the exact political economy of modern State systems!

In A.D. 1516, some serious cause of quarrel arose between the sons of the Earl of Desmond. John, the younger brother, who was married to More O'Brien, a near relative of the ruling Prince of Thomond, held as his portion the strong fortress at Lough Gur, near Bruff, in the county of Limerick. So grave was the task of attacking him in this stronghold, that James, the heir to the earldom, called to his aid, not only his own relatives, the White Knight, the Knight of

Kerry, and the Knight of Glynn, with their followers, but also the whole strength of the MacCarthy and O'Connor Kerry clans. John FitzGerald, after making all possible provision for a successful defence of his castle, went with all haste to claim assistance from his wife's people, the Dal-Cas. They promptly took up his quarrel and marched with him, being reinforced by some of the Butlers, to raise the siege. It is proof of the respect in which the fighting qualities of the Dalcassians was held, that the formidable English and Irish force withdrew at their approach, without waiting to strike a blow,[1] and took flight from the beleaguered fort. The Dalcassians returned in triumph to Clare, leaving John FitzGerald in quiet possession of his patrimony.

Another expedition of a similar character was undertaken by them a few years later on, A.D. 1523, but ended in failure. The O'Neills and O'Donnells being at war with each other, the former, who held aloof from the other Northern clans at the battle of Cnoctuagh, claimed in return for this the support of the Thomond prince and Clanrickard. These hastened northward to their aid. O'Donnell was made aware of their approach, and at once determined, though with an inferior force, to strike at O'Neill's army before the junction could be effected. O'Neill had pitched his camp on the hill Cnoc Buie, now Knocavoe, looking down over the town of Strabane. O'Donnell stormed the hill by night with great daring and vigour. O'Neill, though surprised, made a stout resistance, but was defeated with a loss of about nine hundred men,[2] and fled, leaving behind him all his military stores and provisions. Flushed with his success, O'Donnell turned round to face his Southern foes. They were at this time besieging the town of Sligo, but when they heard of the rapid approach of the victorious O'Donnells, a very unusual panic seized them. Under cover of the sending of messengers to sue for peace, they raised the siege and retreated precipitately, never halting till they put the Curlieu mountains between them and O'Donnell. He had now full satisfaction for his and his allies' defeat at Monabraher. The O'Briens,[3]

---

[1] Four Masters. [2] *Ibid.*

[3] Among whom was Turlogh O'Brien, Bishop of Killaloe, about whom

O'Carrolls, and O'Kennedys composed the main portion, if not all, of the Thomond contingent. No other names are mentioned in connection with it. Probably it was few in number, and this would account for a retreat so unlike what might be expected from the Dalcassian prince.

At this time, Pierce Roe Butler, Lord of Ormond, had supplanted his enemy, the Earl of Kildare, in the favour of Henry VIII., and was appointed by him Lord Justice of Ireland. To signalise his accession to power, he made war on Thomond; but before he had advanced into the eastern part of that territory, he was met by Teigue O'Brien, son of the prince, who had been in the hands of the O'Donnells, but honourably restored to liberty, and who burned to recover the lost Dalcassian prestige. The opposing forces met about two miles north of Cashel, at the ford of Camur on the river Suir. The Dalcassians, having lost their chief Teigue,[1] " killed by the shot of a ball " (the first notice of the use of firearms in the *Annals*), retreated in good order, bringing with them the body of their prince to be interred in the Abbey of Clonroad.[2] How few of the many who daily pass by the lone ruin at the head of Church Street in Ennis, give a thought to the succession of bold and brave O'Brien and MacNamara chiefs of bygone times, who for centuries kept at bay the English invader, and who sleep their long last sleep under its crumbling walls!

The Lord Justice[3] did not follow up his victory, if victory it were. For some years after, Thomond east and west of the Shannon was left unmolested. It is stated[4] that, so well and other bishops of his family something will have to be said in the following chapter.

[1] "The man of all men of his age most dreaded by his enemies." —Four Masters.

[2] *Memoirs of the O'Briens*, by O'Donohue, p. 160.

[3] This same Lord Justice pressed hard also upon FitzPatrick of Ossory. The latter took a roundabout and ineffective way of resisting him. He sent a messenger to the English court, who contrived to meet Henry as he was entering the church, and thus addressed him: "Stand, Sir King! My master sent me hither, and ordered me to say that if you will not chastise Peter the Red, he will himself make war upon you." —Leland, vol. ii. p. 133.

[4] *Memoirs of the O'Briens*, p. 160.

known was the stubborn vigour of the late Thomond prince, his influence had weight as against Henry in the councils of Francis I. of France. After a long and successful reign of twenty-nine years, he was laid with his fathers at Clonroad, A.D. 1528. He had by his wife Raignault, daughter of his kinsman, John MacNamara, Prince of Clan Cuilean, many sons, one of whom, the brave and warlike Teigue, had been slain in battle. The eldest, Conor, was chosen to succeed him. During his reign, which may be said to be uneventful as far as Clare was concerned, the power of the English crown came to be more directly felt in Ireland. Hitherto the great Norman families, of whom the FitzGeralds were the most powerful, while practically as independent as the native Irish princes, making war or peace at will, did not dare to cut themselves adrift from the English connection.

Henry VIII., finding himself comparatively free, after the battle of Pavia, from continental complications, turned himself to Ireland. Before making any attempt to subdue the native princes, he deemed it necessary to crush the Geraldine power. The great Earl of Kildare, to whom he had once more confided the Lord Justiceship, made his position one of danger to the English interest by the many alliances he formed with the Irish. Not satisfied with his relationship to O'Donnell, he further strengthened himself in the North, by giving his sister in marriage to the Prince of Cinel-Owen, Con Bacagh O'Neill. Another sister was married to MacCarthy Roe in the South. By intermarriage he had secured the goodwill also of his old enemies, the Butlers of Ossory. O'Carroll of Ely and O'Connor Faly were married to two of his daughters; whilst his cousin, sister to the Earl of Desmond, was the second wife of the Prince of Thomond. It is not to be wondered at that the English king looked with an eye of jealousy on a subject so closely and so powerfully allied with the Irish enemy. He took the bold step of summoning him to London. To disobey would mean rebellion. Leaving the reins of power in the hands of his son, the hot-headed Silken Thomas, he presented himself at the English court, and was forthwith committed to the Tower. To complete his ruin, the false rumour of his execution was set afloat, with a view to drive his son to desperation. Expecting nothing from the justice or mercy of Henry, Silken Thomas raised at once the standard of revolt, and invited to his side all who were desirous of shaking off the English yoke. For the purpose of a county history it will not be necessary to enter into the details of the struggle. Suffice it to say that the alleged treacherous surrender by his foster-brother, certainly the capture, of the castle of Maynooth disconcerted all the plans of Silken Thomas. His Irish relations were not wise enough to see that the opportunity now offered for a bold and manly stand against foreign dominion. Henry, on the other hand, acted with great vigour. He sent into Ireland, with all the forces he could hastily collect, Lord Leonard Grey and Sir William Skeffington, who followed up with great ability the stroke dealt to Silken Thomas by the seizure of his chief stronghold, the castle of Maynooth. The aid he expected failing him, he fled into Clare, bringing with him all he could carry of his valuables, and there he and his retinue of gentlemen of his own family were hospitably entertained for full six months. The fact that he felt safe there from the pursuit of the English commanders, shows how thoroughly independent was the Thomond of that day. His surrender, later on, to the very man—Lord Grey—who tempted[1] him into rebellion, his conveyance to London, his miserable captivity in the Tower, and his execution along with his five uncles, are all well known to readers of general Irish history. It is a curious fact that while in prison he contrived to write a letter to his servant Rothe, enclosing another to O'Brien, both of which fell into the hands of the English, as they are now to be found among the State Papers, vol. ii. p. 402, describing, in most pathetic terms, his utterly destitute condition, and asking twenty pounds on the strength of the plate left after him at the castle of Clonroad.

With the destruction of the Geraldines, all chance of cohesion between the Irish princes disappeared. Henry could now bring all his power to bear from time to time on each one of them singly. He began with Conor O'Brien, Prince of Thomond, but as yet only in a tentative manner.

[1] State Papers, vol. ii. p. 273.

The sole surviving Kildare, a stepbrother of Silken Thomas, only twelve years old, was sheltered in the castle of Clonroad. Henry demanded his surrender. The description of the manner in which this demand was met, as appearing in a letter of the Irish Council to Cromwell, dated August 22, 1536, is worth quoting *verbatim*.[1] "And as to O'Brent, notwithstanding his letter, and promises of subjection to the King's highness, we could neither get him to condescend to any conformitie according to the same, ne yet to deliver the erle of Kildare's second son with divers traditours of the servantes of the said erle and Thomas FitzGerald, and retaining them as it wear under his protection, both therein and otherwise in his communication and deeds, usith himself after that sorte as he think it not to be his duty to recognise the King's Majesty." From which it plainly appears, as well as from a most abject letter of Conor O'Brien to Henry VIII., that, while retaining some little of the spirit of independence, the Thomond prince hoped by soft words and empty promises to keep the English king at arm's length. Vain hope! The time for that had passed as well for him as for the other short-sighted Irish princes.

If he really entertained such a hope, he was soon undeceived. His eldest son, Donogh, who had married a daughter of the Earl of Ossory, was already plotting to secure the English interest in his own favour. Through his brother-in-law, Lord Butler, as appears in a letter from Parry to Cromwell, he urged an attack upon the castle of Carrigoguinnell, near Limerick, promising to support the attack. The Lord Justice Grey marched on the castle and took it, A.D. 1536, without loss, as Donogh had arranged to have it treacherously surrendered. The Lord Justice did not venture into Clare, but before returning destroyed once more the bridge over the Shannon, uniting East and West Thomond.[2] Lord Grey

---

[1] State Papers, vol. iii. p. 287.

[2] In the State Papers is a most graphic account of the assault upon the bridge, which had a strong castle built out into the water at each end for the purpose of defence. Donogh O'Brien led the English by a secret way, expecting to surprise the defenders, but in this they failed. It was taken only after hard fighting.

attacked on his way back another ally of Kildare, the O'Connor Faly. Here too he had the aid of domestic treachery,[1] in the person of Cathal Rua, O'Connor's brother. Having demolished O'Connor's castles and plundered his territory, the Lord Justice went into winter quarters, feeling sure that much had been done to serve the cause of his master in Ireland, in paving the way for further conquest.

The progress made towards the subjugation of the Dalcassians did not by any means satisfy Henry. O'Donnell, the most powerful of the Northern princes, had at last, as well as O'Neill, professed allegiance to the English king, when, as the Four Masters apologetically explain, "he saw that the Irish would not yield superiority to any one among themselves, but that friends and blood relations contended against one another." Thomond was still holding out stubbornly; so the opening of the spring of 1537 found the English forces again on the march towards that territory. The Lord Justice had little difficulty in securing the submission of the Ormond chiefs. The castles of Aglish and Birr were surrendered without a blow by the O'Molloys and O'Carrolls;[2] nor did the O'Kennedys, O'Mearas, MacIbrians Ara, or any others east of the Shannon, offer any effective resistance. He reached Limerick in June. This city, inhabited mostly by people of Danish and English blood, freely opened its gates to the representative of the English king. Its mayor—one of the Dalcassian O'Seasnans, but who had adopted the English mode of life, with his name anglicised into Sexton—and the corporation not only swore allegiance to Henry, but also renounced the authority of the Pope, and acknowledged the supremacy of the English king in Church matters. It is falsely asserted that the Bishop of Limerick joined in the recantation. John O'Quin, who then ruled the see, gave too many proofs before and after of his constancy in the Catholic faith, to give any colour to the charge. As a matter of fact, he was compelled to fly later on, and the apostate William Casey was intruded into the see. Though Conor O'Brien presented himself at Limerick, evidently to ward off invasion of his territory, it is not asserted that he swore

---

[1] Four Masters.   [2] *Memoirs of the O'Briens* by O'Donohue, p. 175.

allegiance, either temporal or spiritual. Morogh the Tanist, who held out stoutly, was supported evidently by the MacNamaras, as their castle of Bailecuilean, called in the State Papers Ballycongle, was soon after attacked and captured by the Lord Justice. Conor compromised, by surrendering to the English his rights over Coonagh, east of the Shannon; and, being probably in collusion with Morogh, made, by taking the field against him, such show of willingness to weaken Dalcassian resistance as to secure good terms for the time, and stave off the evil day of absolute submission. The letter of the Lord Deputy [1] and Council to Henry, explaining, and in a manner apologising for, the conditions entered into with the Thomond prince, would warrant this belief. To punish Morogh, Lord Grey pushed on to his fortress of Clare Castle. Here, as at Bailecuilean, the garrison made little or no resistance when they saw cannon—the new and to them terrible engine of war—levelled against the fortifications. With this display of force the Lord Deputy was for the time satisfied. His line of march towards Galway lay along the level stretch of the country through which the railway now runs. The O'Deas and O'Quins, being subordinate to Conor O'Brien, offered no opposition. Nevertheless, they watched with jealous eye the first encroachment on their territory since, about three hundred years before, De Clare and his force had been cut to pieces there. He pushed [2] on immediately, without leaving English garrisons in the captured castles. Conor O'Brien's castle of Clonroad, though so near, was left untouched. That had been probably part of the arrangement entered into between him and Lord Grey at Limerick. So it came to pass that he retained the ancient style and dignity of Prince of Thomond till his death, two years after, A.D. 1539. But the thin end of the wedge was driven in; and we shall have to see how henceforward it was slowly but inexorably driven home.

[1] State Papers, vol. iii. p. 176.
[2] Letters of Lords in Council to Henry VIII., under safeguard of O'Brien State Papers.

CHAPTER XV.

FROM 1540 TO 1559.

Henry VIII. — Surrender of O'Brien, MacNamara, O'Grady, and O'Shaughnessy for English Titles — Plunder of the Clans — Chiefs bribed by Gifts of Suppressed Religious Houses—Struggle to maintain Brehon Law—Battle of Spancil Hill, A.D. 1559.

In their letter to Henry VIII., the Lords in Council, "Sentleger, Jas. Ormond and Ossory, Wilm. Brabazon, John Travers, Thomas Cusacke," made much of the surrender by the Dalcassian prince of his territory of Coonagh, east of the Shannon. After detailing the tribute imposed upon each of his subordinate chiefs in Ormond,—thus in their view substituting allegiance to the English king for the immemorial submission to the elect of the clans,—they conclude with this significant sentence: "And we think the said O'Brien would hardlie have been brought to this pass, or to put in his pledge as he now hathe done, without open ware, but only that he saw that O'Neill had done the like, whiche was and is a spectacle to him and all other Irishmen." From this it appears plain that the Dalcassian principality was effectually cut in two. The chiefs east of the Shannon had all made submission, and on the accession of the Tanist Morogh, immediately after Conor's death in 1539, he found his sway acknowledged only in Clare. The grave question he had to put to himself and to his subordinate chiefs at the outset, was how long, or if at all, he could hold out, even there, behind the broad and rapid river, against the slow but sure advance of English power. It will be remembered that he was no party to the partial surrender of the late Prince Conor, and we will find him, for some time at least, maintaining the same bold attitude.

A new and disturbing element had been lately introduced into the public life of Ireland. At a Parliament so-called, but consisting merely of the creatures of Henry, held in Dublin on the 1st of May 1537, the King of England was declared henceforth head of the Church, all appeals to Rome forbidden, and officials of every degree bound to take the oath of supremacy. The penalty for opposition to this new departure was death on the charge of high treason. The "black rent," payable by English settlers to the Irish chiefs, was abolished, and fosterage with them again rigidly prohibited. The abbeys and convents were appropriated, with all their possessions, for the king's service. This last iniquitous provision had a far-reaching effect. It enabled the king to bribe with those rich gifts many of the Irish princes into subjection. The view taken of these enactments by the Irish is best understood from the picture given by the Four Masters, writing in the following century. Here are their words:—

"A heresy and a new error sprang up in England through pride, vain glory, avarice, and lust, and through many strange sciences; so that the men of England went into opposition to the Pope and to Rome. They at the same time adopted various opinions, and among others the old law of Moses in imitation of the Jewish people, and they styled the king the chief head of the Church in his own kingdom. New laws and statutes were enacted by the king and Parliament according to their own will. They destroyed the orders to whom it was permitted to have worldly possessions, namely, the monks, canons, nuns, brethren of the cross; and the four poor orders, that is, the order of the minors, the preachers, the Carmelites, and the Augustinians, and the lordships and livings of all these were taken possession of for the king. They broke down the monasteries and sold their roofs and bells. . . . They also appointed archbishops and sub-bishops for themselves; and though great was the persecution of the Roman emperors against the Church, scarcely had there ever come so great a persecution from Rome as this."

These strange enactments stirred up, as well might be expected, active opposition. The Northern princes, O'Neill and O'Donnell, united their forces, and, marching into the Pale, took and plundered the towns of Navan and Ardee,[1] but were pursued and defeated at Betahoe, on the confines of Meath and Monaghan, by a hastily summoned but large army of the English, under the command of the Deputy, Lord Grey. In the following year, 1540, Morogh O'Brien and the Dal-Cas made common cause with the defeated Northerns and O'Connor of Offaly. They all met together at Fore, in Westmeath, with a view to operate against the English. The Lord Justice Brereton, who succeeded Lord Grey, being made aware of this combination, marched an army of eight thousand men, with a train of artillery, with all despatch into Meath,[2] and with this formidable force so awed the Irish princes that they retreated each into his own territory, without striking a blow. This collapse paved the way for the final surrender of Dalcassian independence. It became evident that they could not hold out singly against English attack much longer, and so the policy of averting it by timely submission was at last reluctantly adopted.

The Lord Deputy Anthony St. Leger held a Parliament at Limerick in February 1542, with a view to arrange the terms of surrender. As soon as Henry was made aware of this peaceful surrender, he himself, in a letter to the Lord Deputy and Council,[3] had suggested that the ancient dignity of Prince of Thomond should merge into an English title of nobility. This was a bitter pill to Irish pride, but there was no help for it. Besides, it came to Morogh O'Brien gilt with the gift of "certain abbeyes lately suppressed," and the acknowledgment of ownership of property belonging of right to the clans. Others of the more powerful neighbouring chiefs, notably MacNamara and O'Grady, had also to be conciliated, and so at this Parliament arrangements were entered into [4] which were soon after completed in the king's palace of Greenwich. The policy of bribing the chiefs with the

[1] Four Masters.   [2] *Memoirs of the O'Briens* by O'Donohue.
[3] State Papers, No. 361, vol. iii. p. 368.
[4] Among others, the payment of one hundred pounds, a large sum in those days, to defray expenses of their journey. They were to be free, too, of all charges at court, and for the elaborate ceremony of installation.

plunder of the clans was inaugurated on that 15th day of February, A.D. 1542, in the city of Limerick.

The following is the heading of State Paper, vol. iii. pp. 388 to 473: "Sunday the 1st day of July,[1] at the Kinges mannor of Greenwich, in the 35th yere of the raign of owr Soveraign Lord King Henry the Eighth, was the creation of two Earles and a Baron of Ireland, whose names were these: the first, Morogh O'Brien, created Earle of Tomond; the second, William Burgh, created Earle of Clanrickard; the third, Donogh O'Brien, created Baron of Ybreckan, in the maner and forme following." Then follows a minute description of the ceremony, made as imposing as possible in order to "totally confyrme thym in good cyvilitie and order with the Kinges princely magnificence," and "after the King's Majestie was come into his closet to heare high masse." This king was far too good a one, of too delicate a conscience, to disturb the immemorial rights of the clansmen of Clare, without the appearance at least of religious sanction!

In the same third volume of State Papers, p. 476, there is a record of the king's letter to the Irish Council, declaring that "we have made the lord of Upper Ossory, MacNamarrow,"—such was geography in those days!—" O'Shaghnes and Denis O'Grady, knights," etc., with an injunction to them to "make out several patentes of all such landes as they now have in possession to them, and to their heires masles lawfully begotten." There was the further inducement to O'Shaughnessy, whether as the neighbour of the Anglo-Irish Clanrickard, or as one too remote to be easily come at, cannot be well known, that he was to have a bishopric or some other spiritual dignity for his kinsman "Malachy Donohoe, and the bishopric of Kilmacduagh for his son William Shaftnes or O'Shaughnessy." These were to be, of course, appointments made by the king without any reference to Rome.

It is to be inferred that the MacNamara felt sorely disappointed. He had applied through Lord Deputy and Council for the title of Baron of Clancuilean. In their letter of the 14th of May to the king, he is styled "an Yrish capttayn, Sheda MacNe Marro, bordering upon the sayde

[1] A.D. 1543.

O'Brien's landes, and lorde of Cloncullen in Thomond," and much pressure is brought to bear on the king to grant his request, on the grounds that "the saide MacNamarro ys a man whose ancestors have in those parties always borne a great swynge," etc. Having secured the O'Briens, the king could afford to deal as he wished with the MacNamara. The inferior title of knight he bestowed on him, not being much relished, was lost sight of in the stormy period that ensued during the conflict for the establishment of English instead of the old Brehon law in the county.

In the same letter also application was made on behalf of "the said O'Brien's servaunte, called Doctor Nelan, for a grant of a house of Observant Friers, called Enys, sytuate beyond the Shannon, within the precyncte of the same O'Brien country not yet dissolved, . . . after the suppression thereof, . . . which in our judgments he hath well deserved." The ravens were already beginning to put in their ghoulish appearance.

During these negotiations there was no sign from the other Dalcassian chiefs or their clans. It cannot be supposed that they looked on all this with indifference. In the submission of those lying nearest to the English power they read their own fate. It was the "writing on the wall." They might stave off the evil day, but they must have realised that it was near at hand.

To secure the submission of the chiefs, the same system of bribing them with Church property, which had been already so successful, was to be carried on. The following is found in a letter from the King to the Lord Deputy: "And for the better alluring those of the remote parts, we shall not much stick to let them have some of the religious houses which shall be suppressed in their countries," etc. (State Papers, vol. iii. p. 334).

It is curious to note that in the conferring of titles on the O'Briens, Henry acknowledged to some extent the Brehon law. Morogh was Prince of Thomond, but his nephew Donogh had been selected as his successor, according to the law of Tanistry. Hence, when naming Morogh Earl of Thomond, and Donogh Baron of Inchiquin, it was specially stipulated that on the death of Morogh the greater dignity should not descend to his son, but to the Tanist Donogh. This cunning device had the desired effect. There was about it an air of justice against which neither, in view of their ancient laws, could complain. Time was thus given to assimilate as far as possible the old system with the new while the recognised chiefs of the Dalcassian race still survived; and in keeping with the well-known English policy, a new element of disunion was successfully introduced. Here, as elsewhere through Ireland, the path of English supremacy was made smooth by the fostering of local rivalries.

The return of the newly-made English lords and knights was followed by a temporary lull. The full import of the ceremony near London took long to be understood. It meant a complete upheaval, though by slow degrees, of all the old institutions, religious and secular. A king instead of the Pope, and an English earl instead of an Irish prince, began to loom up before the wondering, almost incredulous gaze of the Dalcassian clansmen. They could not easily realise the fact that under the new system they were to be no longer, as in the past, independent owners of their hereditary lands, but only serfs of the chief who accepted an English title to the country over which their choice had made him a ruler. While Morogh lived, little, if anything, was done to give effect to this great radical change. The English made no inroad into Clare. The Brehon law alone still ran there. They were satisfied for the time with the submission of the most powerful of the chieftains to English authority. The death of Morogh in 1551[1] gave the signal for the beginning of a long and bitter and bloody conflict, the last of which is not yet seen.

Donogh O'Brien, Tanist of Thomond, who had been created Baron of Ibricken by Henry VIII., succeeded his uncle as prince of the Dalcassians.

The title of Earl of Thomond descending to him by the patent of Henry VIII. was to be only a life title. He, however, made such a complete submission to Edward VI., who had succeeded to the throne of England, that the latter con-

[1] Four Masters.

firmed him in the title, and made it hereditary. When it became known that his acceptance of the English title of Earl of Thomond involved the exclusion of all other members of the family from their rights according to the law of Tanistry, they flew at once to arms against him. Donogh wisely secured the support of the powerful Clan O'Dea. One of these, Cornelius, a member probably of the chieftain's family, had been named by Henry in 1546 Bishop of Killaloe, but was never acknowledged in Rome. His more than doubtful position was somewhat strengthened by Donogh, inasmuch as he procured for him and his son a grant of the castle and lands of Dysert. It is not known with certainty which side the MacNamaras took, but it may be assumed that they fought against Donogh for their old Clare rights.

In the first conflict between the contending parties, A.D. 1542, his cousin Mahon was slain. This was but the beginning of the family feud. In the following year, his brothers Donal and Turlogh made a nocturnal attack upon him at Clonroad. He escaped with his life into the tower, of which there is no trace now; but "they burned and plundered the town, and slew many persons."[1] In a few weeks after, on the eve of Passion Sunday, Donogh died, and immediately Donal was chosen to succeed him, according to the Brehon law.

Donal determined at once to strike a blow for Dalcassian superiority. Collecting the clans, who were doubtless elated at this revival, short-lived though it might be, of their ancient claims, he marched across the Shannon into Leinster, and afterwards took hostages from O'Carroll, Prince of Ely. The English were then posted at Leix, since called Maryborough, after the queen, Mary, who had just ascended the throne. To these he turned his attention, but after a parley the Dalcassians returned without striking a blow. They were hardly at home when word came that a son of the late Earl of Clanrickard, who was asserting in his own case the same elective rights for which they were contending, was besieged by his brother, the declared earl, in his castle of Benmore, near Loughcrea. Marching rapidly towards the castle, they compelled the besiegers to withdraw.[2]

[1] Four Masters.   [2] *Ibid.*

In the meantime, Conor, the son of Donogh, was not idle. He applied for aid to the Lord Deputy in support of his claim to the earldom, but could get none, owing to the state of uncertainty consequent on the accession of Mary. After his father's death he had to retire, with his few followers, to a castle called Dun-Michil, or Dun-Mulvihil, now Doon, in the parish of Inchicronan, on the borders of Galway. Here he felt comparatively safe, under the protection of his cousin, the Earl of Clanrickard. The protection afforded him by the latter was in a great measure the cause why Donal took arms against him; and now, when he had been beaten off, the attempt was made to seize Conor in his castle of Doon. Fortunately for him, another cousin, the Earl of Ormond, divined the object of Donal's march into Galway, and, coming up in good time with a considerable force, compelled Donal to raise the siege. The Dalcassians, however, would not return empty-handed. They made an incursion into the Clanrickard country, and brought away with them great booty.

The Lord Deputy St. Leger having fallen into disgrace at the English court, was recalled, and Thomas, Earl of Sussex, was sent to replace him. The vigour with which Donal O'Brien and the Dalcassians maintained their ancient rights at once attracted his attention. He marched an army against them in 1555, but was promptly met in his way through the Queen's County, and was compelled to enter into a treaty, the terms of which were, that the Irish and the English of Munster should live in peace with each other, neither encroaching on the actual possessions of the other. Here we find the renewal once more of the claim of the Dalcassian prince to rule over Munster.

Sussex, however, was but borrowing time. The right of Conor O'Brien, under the patent of Henry VIII., was not to be abandoned if English force and fraud could—as well it could—maintain it. He gave himself full time to strike with effect. Leading a powerful force, A.D. 1558, into Thomond, he seized the castles of Bunratty Clare[1] and

---

[1] The Four Masters give its proper Irish name, "Clare-mor," signifying the great or chief timber-ford or bridge. This was on the narrowest part

Clonroad. Donal made no resistance. He fled with his family for protection to Maguire of Fermanagh. Sussex then publicly proclaimed Conor Earl, with full feudal rights over all Thomond, in return for which Conor renounced the Dalcassian title; and others of the leading men of the O'Brien clan with him solemnly vowed fealty on the relics, and with bell, book, and candlelight, as the heralds' certificate declares,[1] to the English Queen, in the cathedral of Limerick after High Mass on the 10th of July, A.D. 1558. Thus the cathedral built by one of his ancestors, a King of Munster, was witness of the voluntary surrender of all Irish rights to a foreign potentate. Now for the first time did the reality of the great change in their condition break in on the minds of the people, not only of Thomond, but of all Ireland. They were, in the graphic words of the Four Masters, "seized with horror, dread, fear, and apprehension of danger; and the descendants of Con and of Cathoir, the descendants of Heremon and Heber, of Ir and Ith, were alarmed at this change."

As might well be expected, this surrender on the part of Conor met with violent opposition. The first to resist were the sons of that same Morogh who was himself the first to yield obedience to the English. Of these, Donogh held possession of the castle of Inchiquin, while the other, Teigue, went to seek assistance from his cousin, the Earl of Desmond. Conor besieged the castle, but the approach of the Earl of Desmond's forces compelled him to raise the siege, and he withdrew to Galway to claim the aid of his kinsman and co-earl, Clanrickard. Their united forces returned to the fray. Desmond, after advancing as far as Inchiquin, and finding that castle relieved, turned back and rested for the night at Ballyalla, where the two earls came up with him. In the early morning both armies began skirmishing,

---

of the Fergus, which in those days, not being hemmed in by dams, frequently overflowed its banks, turning the flat stretch of country towards and above Ennis into a lake. It was from its position, a place of such importance, that after the English occupation it gave its name to the whole country.—O'Donovan's *Four Masters*.

[1] Lenehan's *Hist. of Lim.*

keeping up a running fire—the first that is mentioned in the *Annals*—on each other, with a view to secure the advantage of position. At the place now incorrectly called Spancil Hill,[1] Desmond and Teigue O'Brien gave battle. The latter gained a very decided victory. The numbers slain are not given, but the Four Masters say that very many of note fell on the side of the two earls, among them not only O'Briens and MacNamaras, but also MacSwineys, who are called constables of Clanrickard and Thomond. Probably that clan, like the Swiss,[2] lent their swords in those days for pay. It is hard otherwise to account for their presence. This was the first time, too, as the Four Masters remark, that the Dalcassians yielded in the fight to the Geraldines; but with the latter there was a strong contingent of his own race under Teigue O'Brien. Desmond returned in triumph; and Donogh and Teigue remained unmolested in Inchiquin. This battle of Spancil Hill was fought in the month of June 1559, during the reign of Elizabeth, who had ascended the throne the previous 17th of November.

[1] It should be "hill of the cold wood."—O'Donovan's Four Masters.

[2] This appears almost certain from the fact that, in the following year, in a battle between the O'Briens of Arra in the county of Tipperary, and the O'Carrolls of Ely, there fell "O'Brien's constable, Heremon MacSwiney."—Four Masters.

CHAPTER XVI.

FROM 1559 TO 1576.

Internal Conflicts — The Castles of Ballyalla and Ballycar captured by the Earl of Thomond and the English — Introduction of Clan Sheehy and Clan Sweeney — Subdivision of Clare between the Contending Parties — Execution at Tuaclea, near Lisdoonvarna — Morogh of Ara, the stripling, first Protestant Bishop of Killaloe — Malachy O'Molony, Cornelius O'Mulryan (Maol-Ryan), Catholic Bishops — First Assize at Ennis Monastery, A.D. 1570.

THE opening of 1560 found the fortunes of those who strove for the old order of things on the wane. Teigue the son of Donal, who fled to the Maguire country, died there, and the other Teigue, who had, with Desmond, defeated the Earl of Thomond at Spancil Hill, was captured at Limerick, as was believed, through the treachery of the earl, and carried prisoner to Dublin. The latter, following in so far the bad Irish custom, made raids on the O'Flaherties of Connemara, who were the enemies of his ally Clanrickard, and on the O'Connors Kerry and FitzGeralds along the Shannon from below Limerick to Glin, but with very little success. Soon other work was cut out for him. Donal, who had fled to Fermanagh, re-entered Clare with Teigue, who managed to escape from Dublin, and both took up arms against the earl. Then again Clare became the theatre of a furious and destructive civil war, while the English looked on with, doubtless, no little satisfaction.

The fighting commenced with a nocturnal attack on the earl's forces at Ballymacregan, in the parish of Dysert. Many of them were slain, and some spoils captured. The O'Deas came to the aid of the earl, and, pursuing the victors, came up with them at MacGorman's Fort close by, where the conflict was renewed. A running fight was kept up from thence over Scoolhill to Rath-Blathmac.[1] Here a fierce engagement took place, in which the earl's force was defeated with great loss. Many prisoners were taken; among them Brian Duv, grandson of Conor-na-Srona, for whose ransom[2] the castle of Shallee, where his grandfather held his court as prince of the Dal-Cas, was delivered over to Teigue O'Brien. This occurred A.D. 1563. In the year following, the Earl of Thomond renewed the conflict. The English came to his aid with some cannon from Limerick, with which he battered and demolished the castle of Ballyalla, which remained in the possession of Teigue and Morogh O'Brien since their victory at Spancil Hill. Ballycar also fell into his hands. The county was now rather evenly divided,—the eastern portion, from Ennis on, mostly supporting the earl, while the western and north-western supported the claims of his rivals.

In the midst of all this clamour, MacBrody, Ollav of Ibricken and Inchiquin, who lived undisturbed in the midst of the contending parties at Ballybrody, near Dysert, went to his account, and was succeeded in his office by his brother.

Donal, the returned prince, and Teigue his brother, who had been chosen Tanist of Thomond, united their forces with those of Morogh and Teigue of Inchiquin, and assumed once more the offensive. It appears that the Earl of Thomond was then residing at Rosroe in Clancuilean,[3] relying a good deal on the support of the MacNamaras. A swoop was made in that direction, with the hope of capturing him as well as plundering Clancuilean. About one hundred of his troops were slain, but he escaped. The whole country, as the Four Masters put it, from Cratloe[4] to Kilkeady, and from Rinanna to Scariff, flew to arms. The invaders, however, made good their retreat without loss, carrying with them great booty.

[1] So called from the old church of Rath, near Corofin, dedicated to St. Blathmac, whose feast used to be celebrated on the 9th of July. --Calendar of the O'Clerys. *Feeluire Aenguis.*

[2] Four Masters.

[3] A place still well known, lying between Quin and Six-Mile-Bridge.

[4] The old Irish name—Sliebh Oidheadha-an-Righ—is given by the Four Masters. It was so called because of the death there of Crimhthan, monarch of Erinn, by poison, in the latter part of the fourth century.

It is apparent that the English-made earl was not warmly supported even by those over whom he held nominal sway. No attempt was made to pursue the victors. These did not return to the attack, but they procured, probably through the intervention of their ally, the Earl of Desmond, the services of the Clan Sheehy and Clan Sweeny from beyond the Shannon; who, as mercenaries, raided over East Clare, and succeeded in taking with them more of the cattle of the country than they left behind them. It was a sore humiliation to the clans of East Clare. To put an end to this state of things, the earl had to enter into terms of peace with his opponents, leaving Morogh and Teigue in quiet possession of what they held, and giving to Donal full sway over Corcomroe, some plundered Church livings, among them the rich Abbey of Corcomroe, and other lands in various parts of Thomond. Neither the O'Connors of Corcomroe nor the O'Loughlins of Burren were of the Dalcassian race. They were of the Ulster Rudricean race, a colony of whom had settled down in that district about the time that Luighaidh Meann had driven out the Firbolgs. It may be inferred that they welcomed among them Donal, on the ground that he was the elect of the Dal-Cas, to whom they were subordinate for so many centuries. He resided in, and probably built, the castle of Ennistymon.

A branch of the O'Briens of Tromora had settled down in Aran since the period of the treaty, already referred to, between them and the merchants of Galway,[1] for the protection of that port. Mahon, their chief, had in 1560 made a raid into Desmond, but, on returning, his vessel was wrecked on the Galway shore, over a hundred men being lost; only Mahon, with three others, escaping.[2] In 1565 he was treacherously slain by some of his own people. The merchants of Galway sought to avenge the murder of their protector. The guilty parties fled before them in their ship from Aran, and took refuge in Corcovaskin, landing in the Bay of Ross, near Loop Head. Donal, hearing this, determined to assert his sovereign authority. Hastening southwards, he captured the greater number of the murderers, probably with the aid of the MacMahons, and brought them back prisoners

---

[1] Hardiman, *Hist. of Galway*, p. 52, note *d*.   [2] Four Masters.

to Magh-Glae, now Tooclea, within view of the scene of their crime; and there hanged some of them, and burned others, according to the measure of their guilt.[1] When such summary justice could be executed by an Irish chief so late as 1565, it cannot be said that even Elizabeth's strong hand had yet fastened its grasp on Clare.

During all those years of conflict, the inhabitants of West Clare—the MacMahons, the O'Gormans, the O'Connors, and the O'Loughlins—had observed a strict neutrality. If the saying be true that "happy is the country which has no history," then these clans were to be envied. This Arcadian bliss was not, however, to last any longer. In 1568, Teigue MacMahon, called Caoch, or "blind," from some defect, or perhaps, as some think, because he was over-shrewd, succeeded Brian in the chieftaincy. He was the first of that clan in a very long period to attract any attention. The slow but sure advance of the English brought him, as we shall see later on, into some prominence.

In 1569 the first formal attempt to introduce Protestantism into Clare was made. The Lord Deputy, Sir Henry Sydney, entered it with a formidable force, and marched through it on his way to Galway, meeting with no opposition, except at two castles, Cloonoan, near Kilkeady, and Ballyvaughan.[2] These he reduced with little difficulty, and an order was made that henceforth Clare should be governed as part of the province of Connaught. This order was afterwards, as we shall see, withdrawn. The death of Turlogh, or Terence, O'Brien, Bishop of Killaloe, in this year, gave the coveted opportunity for the appointment of a queen's bishop. He had led, at least in early life, a very disedifying career. The shame of it fell upon him in his old age. The Deputy, Sir Henry Sydney, wrote to the Privy Council, stating the complaint of the merchants of Galway, that "on the borders of Thomond, certain outlaws, being bastards of the Bishop of Killaloe, robbed all travellers, and had put a ward in a castle, which they meant to defend. I marched thither, and, after it was attempted, the ward in the night came away and left the place, which was committed to the custody of Sir Roger

---

[1] Four Masters. [2] Ibid.

O'Shafnis (O'Shaughnessy), Lord of that country—an obedient and dutiful servant of the Queen's Highness—one of the best to be liked in all Connaught."[1] On the death of the bishop in 1569, MacO'Brien of Ara, on the east side of the Shannon, having made submission to the English, now asked for his son, though under age, the appointment to the bishopric. The queen was only too glad to have her headship of the Church thus recognised by an Irish chieftain, and at once not only granted the request, but also issued letters patent constituting himself owner in English feudal fashion of the clan property.[2] An order was made to apply the revenues of the diocese for the education at Oxford of his stripling son Morogh, or Maurice, O'Brien. His qualification for the office was thus described by the Lord Deputy in his letter dated August 1574: "The said Maurice his father and himself (besides his sufficiency and zealous disposition to the true religion) have and do at this time of stir show themselves as well by good advertisement as otherwise very well and dutifully affected to Her Majesty's service." Again: "Upon the said Maurice's return, well commended from my Lord of Canterbury, Her Majesty has appointed him Bishop of Killalowe now void, and wills and commands . . . letters patent and writs to be issued under the Great Seal for his consecration and admission to the said bishoprick, with all rights, duties," etc.[3] In such orthodox fashion did the Virgin Queen provide for the apostolic succession in the diocese of Killaloe!

In the meantime Rome was not silent. Malachy O'Molony was "appointed by Papal provision, 10th January 1571, and held the see till he was translated to Kilmacduagh on the 22nd August 1576, when Cornelius O'Mulrian was appointed to Killaloe."[4] This bishop, O'Molony, had been tracked and arrested in London on his way home to his diocese. He was confined in the Marshalsea, and a spy named Herle, pretending to be a fellow-prisoner, tried all he could to convert him to Protestantism. For a year and a half he was kept in this dungeon, during which time he contrived to "give Papish counsel[5] to some of the Archbishop of Canterbury's servants."

[1] State Papers.
[2] *Rot. Pat. de anno* xii. *Eliz. d.*
[3] State Papers.
[4] Brady's *Bishops*.
[5] State Papers.

He is accused of making recantation in order to secure his release; but this is scarcely consistent with the acknowledged fact that after his release, or, more probably, escape [1] with the aid of those to whom he gave "Papish counsel," he went directly to his diocese and administered it as a Catholic bishop till his translation in 1576 to Kilmacduagh. From the very important part played by his successor, Cornelius O'Mulrian (properly Maol-Ryan), it may be inferred that room was made for the latter, as one of far more vigorous character, to stimulate opposition to the aggressive policy of Elizabeth.

In 1570, the notorious Miler MacGrath, a member of the Fermanagh family, appeared in Thomond as Elizabeth's Archbishop of Cashel. More about him will appear later on. It is curious that, like Luther, his descendants became Catholics. Some of them were transplanted by Cromwell into Clare. His wife, an O'Meara of Lisbonny, near Nenagh, was all along Catholic, and, it is said, had him reconciled to the Church before his death.

From an entry in the Four Masters, under the year 1570, it appears that Brehon law still prevailed in Clare. MacNamara, Lord of Clan Cuilean, "a noble and majestic man," died, and was succeeded, not by his own son, but by "Donal Reagh, son of Cumeadha."

The first attempt to hold a court of English law in Clare was made this year, and it was anything but a success. It was arranged between Sir Edward Fitton, President of Connaught, and Teigue O'Brien, son of Morogh of Inchiquin, who had accepted the office of Sheriff of Clare (he was the first called to it), that the court should be held in the Franciscan monastery at Ennis. Conor O'Brien, Earl of Thomond, being in his castle of Clare only two miles away, looked on with a jealous eye. As he did not attend, a force,

---

[1] In a letter dated August 30, 1590, from Sir D. Rougham to Burghley, treating of a charge made against Sir John Perrot of over-leniency to this bishop, the writer says: "All the world that would scan, see, or hear this, would not believe that Sir John Perrott, Her Majesty's Deputy, would pardon a Roman bishop, and one that confesseth to have a Bull from the Pope."

consisting of English cavalry [1] and members of his own family with their retainers, was sent on the third day to summon him. He allowed some of the party within the gate; then, closing it quickly, he made prisoners of them, and attacked those outside, killing such of them as were unable to escape by rapid flight into Ennis. The president broke up the court, and fled precipitately towards Connaught, being guided by Teigue and Morogh O'Brien through the difficult passes of that rocky region. The earl pursued them hotly, and only desisted when they had reached the shelter of the castle of Gort.

When Lord Justice Sir Henry Sydney heard of this outrage against the queen's representative, he despatched at once a large force, under the command of the Earl of Ormond, into Clare, to reduce the stubborn Dalcassians once more to submission. Being a first cousin of the earl, Ormond entered into a parley with him, and induced him to yield up without a blow the castles of Bunratty, Clare, and Clonroad, reserving to himself but one of his strongholds — that of Moy, in Kilfarboy. No sooner had he done this than he repented of such a tame surrender; but, not being able to keep the field against the English, or recover his castles, he fled first into Kerry, then into France; but finally, going into England, he humbled himself to Elizabeth, and was restored to favour. On his return to Ireland the following year, 1571, he put himself into communication with Sir Edward Fitton, yielding up the castle and town of Moy, which he had, on the former occasion, reserved to himself. The latter, having now the co-operation of the earl and his followers, opened a court at Ennis on St. Patrick's day, and for eighteen days presided over it. The jurisdiction of the court extended over the Clanrickard as well as the Dalcassian territory. This was the first formal recognition by the Dalcassian chiefs of English, as opposed to Brehon, law in Clare. The people generally had no part in it, and subsequent events proved that they were opposed to the surrender of this, as well as other rights, made in their name.

In the following year a similar court was held under the

[1] Four Masters.

same president, at Galway, where such causes as were presented from Clare were heard. He turned these occasions to good account in his own interest. His cruelty was so dreaded that bribes poured in upon him. "It would not be easy," say the Four Masters, "to enumerate all the hundreds of kine that was given to the president during the two years he remained in Thomond." When this became known at the English court, his recall was determined on.

No sooner were these assizes at an end, and Sir John Perrot with his strong escort out of the country, than evidence was afforded of the very slight impression made by these events on the minds of the Dalcassians. The right of making war at their own will was resumed by them, and the wretched spectacle was once more displayed of O'Briens plundering and slaying O'Briens. A petty quarrel between two of their chiefs set them at each other's throats. Calling to their aid with the promise of plunder the disbanded gallowglasses[1] of the Geraldines, with some of the Butlers and MacSwineys, who were mere soldiers of fortune fighting for pay, the O'Briens of South Clare made an incursion on those of the north of the county. They swept through the whole northwest, and, taking the inhabitants by surprise, seized and carried away without opposition all they could lay hands on, even plundering the church of Kilnaboy.[2] Nor did they stop till they reached, late at night, the hill of Knocachip, at Moy, near Lahinch. In the meantime a rapid muster of the people was made by Teigue, son of Morogh of Inchiquin, and Donal of Ennistymon, of whose vigour mention has been already made. They had with them some of the Burkes, the MacSheehys, and even of the MacSwineys. While gathering their strength, they kept their opponents in view, and encamped for the night about three miles east of them at Carn-Mic-Tail, now called

---

[1] The gallowglasses were heavy-armed infantry, wearing iron helmets and coats of mail for defence, and carrying a long sword and a broad axe with keen edges.—Ware's *Antiquities*, by Harris, p. 161.

[2] This is the modern form of "Cill-inghin-Baoith," its ancient name, signifying the "Church of the daughter of Boeth"—a Saint formerly much revered in Clare and Limerick, her father being of the royal line of Cormac Cas, ancestor of the Dalcassians.—O'Donovan's Four Masters.

Carn Connachtagh.[1] A close watch was kept on their assailants, and at early morning they rushed on them with fierce determination. A sudden panic seized on the latter. They fled precipitately along by Lahinch to Inagh, abandoning all they had, and falling, the Four Masters say, " by twenties and thirties, by twos and threes." A small party under Turlogh O'Brien, brother of the Earl of Thomond, took refuge in the castle of Caherush beyond Milltown-Malbay, while a good number, including some of the chiefs, were wounded or taken prisoners. Two years later on, A.D. 1575, the earl and his brother Turlogh took revenge for this defeat by a savage raid on the country towards Kildysart, then under the jurisdiction of Teigue of Inchiquin, seizing or destroying both lay and Church property. With the enemy at their gates, such was the suicidal policy of the degenerate O'Briens of that day.

---

[1] This is a conical heap of stones near Kilshanny, about three hundred feet in diameter at the base and twenty-five feet high; and is believed to have been the place where O'Connor, Prince of Corcomroe, was inaugurated.

CHAPTER XVII.

FROM 1576 TO 1590.

Clare, annexed to Connaught in 1569, is reannexed to Munster in 1576—The Dalcassians for the first time consent to pay Tribute—How Clare and Tipperary became at last an English Possession—The last Tanist of Thomond — The Protestant Earl of Thomond cuts asunder the Allied Northern and Southern Catholics—Donogh of Ennistymon, ancestor of the Dromoland O'Briens, hanged at Limerick, A.D. 1582 —Fate of Donogh Beg O'Brien—Tripartite Deed—MacNamara and other Chiefs refuse to sign—Stout Resistance of Mahon O'Brien of Cluanoon (ancestor of the Clare Mahons)—Owners of Castles in Clare at this period—Suppressed Abbeys.

IN this year Clare was reannexed to Munster under the presidency of Sir William Drury, by order of the Lord Deputy, Sir Henry Sydney. The latter, with a considerable force, proceeded from Cork towards Limerick, where he was met by some of the Dalcassian chiefs.[1] They went with him voluntarily through Clare on to Galway. He broke faith with them, bringing some of them, as well as the sons of the Earl of Clanrickard, to Dublin as hostages. Donal O'Brien must have been party to this treachery to his kinsmen, as Sydney appointed him governor of Clare. He ruled with great firmness, repressing disorder with much severity; so that, "while he continued in office," say the Four Masters, "it was not found necessary to place watchmen over cattle, or even to close doors." Sir William Drury gave him effective co-operation. Coming to Limerick, he then held an assize, at which "several of the gentlemen and common people of the O'Briens, and many others besides, were hanged."[2]

In the following year, 1577, some notable events occurred in Clare. Teigue of Inchiquin, after his stormy career, and

[1] Four Masters.   [2] *Ibid.*

MacGorman, chief of his clan, died. Sir William Drury, bringing with him a large force of the English and Irish of Munster, held an assize for eight days in the monastery of Ennis. He endeavoured to secure the payment by the Dalcassians of a regular tribute, and, on their refusal, let loose on them the large body of troops who were with him in Ennis. It needs no great effort of fancy to realise what that meant. Under such pressure they had to succumb, and for the first time [1] in their long history they agreed to pay tribute. Not much was demanded,—only ten pounds from each barony,— but the thin end of the wedge was in at last.

The work of submission now proceeded apace. As on two former occasions, so too at this crisis, the head of the O'Briens was the first of the Dal-Cas to strike his colours. On no one of these occasions did he look for, nor could he count on, the consent of his clan. Their sense of loyalty to their chief was trafficked on at their cost for his aggrandisement under the English connection. As we have already seen, the Earl of Thomond, after a fitful opposition to the English invaders, made a complete surrender of his strong places. He sent his son Donogh to the English court as a hostage for his future good behaviour, and to receive an English and Protestant education. Now he went over himself to render his submission complete. Elizabeth gladly received him, recognising at once how useful a tool he could be in her hands. We have her own account, in a letter to Sir Henry Sydney, dated October 7, 1577, of "the humble suit made unto us by our right trusty and right well-beloved cousin, Conoher Earl of Thomond." Such a flattering reception boded no good for the people at home. It appears from this letter that he bargained for "freedom from cesse on all his own lands within the said county of Thomond, which, he says, are comprised in eight baronies, besides the barony of Ibreckan." He then sought the "wardship of heires after the decease of the chiefs of every name." This Elizabeth, as might well be expected from her character, wisely refused; preferring to reserve to herself the plucking and bringing up of such youths. He secured "the customs of Clare (Clarecastle) and

[1] Four Masters.

Clanrode;" and also that "so much of the bonnagth for the wages of the gallowglasses, as hath been leviable upon the earl's particular and proper lands, shall be remitted to him as in suspense, while the service of that gallowglass shall cease, if you, our deputy, shall know no cause to the contrary." Nor was he yet satisfied. He had already part of the Church land belonging to Clare Abbey, granted "by the king, our father, of noble memory, King Henry VIII." Now he looks for the rest of it, and with it "the territories of Ince (Ennis) and Coheny (Quin), the chantries of Termon-Shenin (Killone), Termon-Tolloughe (Tulla), Termon-Moynoudh (Moynoe), and Termon-Skenoway."[1] The complacent Elizabeth sees no difficulty about sweeping all the Church property—" abbey lands, frieries, and chantries,"—gifts bestowed by the pious donors for the use of the poor more even than for the service of religion—into his net, seeing that there is reserved to herself " such a rent as by the survey shall be allotted." The people of the Clare of to-day must not complain, since they have workhouses under a Poor Law Board as substitutes for those relics of the benighted Middle Ages! He furthermore sought a grant of the island of Iniscatha,[2] but this was refused, on the ground that it commanded the approach to the city of Limerick. All these grants made to him, "in consideration of the dutiful mind the said erle pretends to bear to us and to our service," were only conditional. To fetter him the more, and bind him neck and heels to the English interest, it was left to the discretion of Sir Henry Sydney to confirm them or limit them as he thought fit.[3] Here are the queen's words: " Yet we refer to your consideration the manner of our grants, to pass under our seal, and to be limited as you shall think convenient for our service, and his reasonable relief." He could now feel reasonably secure, though at the cost of conscience and honour. His title and

---

[1] Or Iniscronan.

[2] This island was granted, six years later on, A.D. 1583, by Elizabeth to the Mayor and Corporation of the city of Limerick.

[3] This discretion was, to some extent at least, exercised; as a grant in fee of the Abbey of Quin and its possessions was made by letters patent, dated December 14, 1583, to Sir Turlogh O'Brien, son of Donal of Ennistymon.

ill-gotten possessions, as far at least as Church lands were included, were recognised by the English queen; and no one, from the Irish point of view, challenged his claim to the headship of his clan, since Donal of Ennistymon—the last who laid claim by the law of Tanistry to the principality of Thomond—had surrendered it. The English policy had now gained considerable ground in Clare. The Earl of Thomond was no longer The O'Brien—only an English-made noble. His son and heir received his training and his religion from Elizabeth; and another O'Brien, son of O'Brien of Ara, had just been appointed, after an English education, Protestant Bishop of Killaloe. All political resistance had ceased, and for the first time Clare might be said to be an integral part of the British Empire.

It has been already stated that the Bishop of Killaloe, Malachy O'Molony, was translated to the see of Kilmacduagh, to make room for Cornelius O'Mulryan, a Franciscan friar. The latter was the brother of the chief of that name. His great abilities were availed of by Pope Gregory XIII. in support of the Catholic cause, championed chiefly by the Earl Desmond in the South, and later on by O'Donnell and O'Neill in the North. Since his appointment to the see of Killaloe in 1577,[1] he employed all his energy in organising, with the aid of the Pope and the King of Spain, an expedition in support of Desmond. He set out for Ireland from Rochelle, to prepare the way, with Desmond, for the landing of the expedition, but his vessel fell into the hands of pirates, and he was glad to be allowed to escape, with his life only, back to France. Thereupon Desmond [2] wrote to the Pope, still pressing for aid. It was strongly recommended that the Bishop of Killaloe should accompany the troops, to direct them where to land and to guide them through the country. His arrival in Ireland was at once notified to the queen by Sir William

[1] Seven years later on, in 1584, his metropolitan, Dermot O'Hurley, Archbishop of Cashel, fell into the hands of the English, and suffered a glorious martyrdom in Stephen's Green in Dublin.

[2] The Pope issued a Bull, as did others of his successors, calling on all Irish Catholics to take up arms for the faith, and granting them the same indulgences that were offered of old to those who fought for the Holy Land.

St. Leger, then President of Munster, in a letter from Cork, dated 1582, describing him as "a traitor called O'Mulrian—a lewd prelate," etc. It is easy to infer from this that the English regarded him as a formidable opponent, and spared no pains to get him into their power. For years he shared in all the rigours and perils of the Desmond insurrection, and, not being able to enter into his own diocese, had to administer it as best he could from a distance. For the purpose of this history, it will be enough to state here the well-known fact, that this insurrection, having for its object the protection of the Catholic Church and people against the violent efforts made by Elizabeth to introduce Protestantism, ended in disaster. After its final collapse with the tragic death of Desmond, the bishop succeeded in escaping to Lisbon, and from thence wrote to Cardinal de Como in 1584, describing the calamities that had befallen them. An extract from this letter may be given here, as it affords a picture, from the Catholic point of view, of the condition to which the country had been reduced :—

"The creation of bishops just at present is quite useless unless a fleet be sent. Indeed, it is injurious, because bishops cannot be easily consecrated or sent forth on the mission in Ireland or in England, except in some parts of Ulster; because, in either case, they have only to hide themselves or appear disguised in secular dress, or must adopt the soldier's, carry a sword or halbert, without being either shaven or shorn, without any clerical habit, without revenue or obedience [1] rendered by their subject faithful. And then, if they are convicted of being bishops, they suffer capital punishment—nay, even their own parents and blood relations who give them shelter lose all their chattels and estates, which go to the royal treasury." [2]

As might well be expected, this bishop died in exile, without being once able to enter his diocese. Not only were the English eager to get hold of him as, in their view, a traitor,

---

[1] That is, of course, in public; as it is well known that never was such obedience rendered to priest or prelate, as by the faithful Irish flocks to their clergy during all the years of bitter and untiring persecution.

[2] *Spicilegium Ossoriense.*

but he had for mortal enemies the Irish who wielded power in Clare. The Elizabethan Bishops of Killaloe and Kilfenora[1] were both of the O'Brien blood. Though they certainly did not touch the hearts or consciences of the people, they could, with the forces at the command of their relations and the English, collect the revenues of the dioceses, and make either side of the Shannon too hot for the Catholic Bishop of Killaloe. He died A.D. 1617.

From the scanty records supplied by the Four Masters,— all or nearly all others having disappeared, — we can get only glimpses, during some of those years, at the principal personages in Clare. At the year 1578 the death is given, in honoured old age, of Scaive, great-great-grand-daughter of Brian Catha an Aenagh, and wife of Brian MacMahon of Corcovaskin; as also of Sioda MacNamara of Clancuilean East, who was slain near Mountshannon while in pursuit of a marauding party from the Clanrickard country. Another remarkable entry appears under the same year: "John, son of Donal, son of Thomas, son of Teigue MacClanchy, chief Brehon to the Earl of Thomond, died. There was no son of a lay Brehon in Ireland, in his time, who had better tillage, or a better house, than he." This is proof of the respect paid in such troubled times to the office of Brehon, or judge, which had not as yet been entirely replaced by English law. In the following year, 1579, Donal of Ennistymon died. He was the last Tanist of Thomond. The system of selecting their prince according to Brehon law, practised by the Dalcassians for two thousand years, was brought to an end. Primogeniture got the better, for better for worse, of Tanistry. The change told unquestionably in favour of stability, though not unfrequently at the cost of firmness of rule. Conor, Earl of Thomond, did not long survive him. He died at the comparatively early age of forty-five, A.D. 1580, and was laid with his fathers, notwithstanding his apostasy and plunder of Church property, in the monastery of Ennis.

The career of this earl was one of which no Irishman,

[1] Murtogh, son of Donal of Ennistymon, recommended, A.D. 1573, by the Lord Deputy to the queen.
[2] State Papers.

above all, no descendant of the Dalcassians, can be proud. Falling upon a critical period of Irish history where men's souls were tried, his whole policy seemed centred in himself and his immediate family. No man in Ireland better served the English and Protestant interests. Except for one brief outburst, at the opening of the first assizes in Ennis, his place all along was at the feet of Elizabeth and her deputies, suing for everything, sacred or profane, that he could lay hands on. Had he thrown in his lot with the brave and spirited Earl of Desmond, another story might have to be told.

The evil he did grew into greater magnitude after his death. His English-reared son Donogh cut across the vigorous opposition offered to Elizabeth's aggression through the West and North of Ireland. O'Neill and O'Donnell, combining with the Geraldines of the South and a considerable force of the Dalcassians of Thomond, reduced her to such straits that she was compelled twice to sue for peace, offering the most honourable terms. True, they did not trust her, and kept on the struggle for faith and fatherland. Donogh, the young Earl of Thomond, faithful to his training, took the English side all along, and helped in a very great degree to upset and defeat the Irish confederacy. The wrong he did his country lies, however, mostly at the door of the father who had him educated to play such an un-Irish *rôle* in the national struggle.

Sir Nicholas Malley, President of Connaught, was directed by the queen to take Clare into his jurisdiction, to divide it into baronies, and to fix upon either Killaloe, Quin, or Ennis as the capital of the county. Clarecastle would have been selected, as being on the navigable part of the Fergus, but that the Earl of Thomond reserved it for himself. The fact that assizes had been held in the monastery of Ennis brought it into such prominence that it was fixed on as the capital, and henceforward it became a town of some importance. The county, which before was divided into five great districts, Corcovaskin, Corcomroe, Hy-Cormaic, Hy-Fearmic, and Hy-Caisin, was now split up, A.D. 1579, into the baronies we have at present.

In the following year the sons of the Earl of Clanrickard

took up arms against Elizabeth, and were supported by the greater part of the Dalcassians. The Earl of Thomond and Turlogh of Ennistymon, Sheriff of the county, took no part in the struggle. Whatever was considered English property in the northern and eastern parts of the county, from Burren to Limerick, was seized; but the insurrection soon collapsed. Turlogh O'Brien, uncle to the earl, and one of the sons of Clanrickard, fell into the hands of the English,—the latter, as the Four Masters relate, by treachery,—and both were hanged in Galway, A.D. 1580. Donogh of Inchiquin, from whom the Dromoland family trace their descent, surrendered under promise of a free pardon; but, finding some flaw in the wording of the promise, they broke faith with him. He was hanged at the gate of Limerick on the 29th of September 1582, by the Sheriff, Sir George Cusack, and Captain Mortaunt or Mordaunt, who was marshal of the county.

Up to this time the MacMahons of Corcovaskin, owing to their remote and secluded position, took little part in the affairs of the county. One of them, the son of MacMahon of East Corcovaskin, now Clonderalaw, signalised himself two years before this by a deed of great treachery and cruelty in favour of the English.

The Earl of Desmond was still holding out against the English south and east of the Shannon. One of his bravest captains, David Purcell, with sixteen more, rowed across for some reason not specified, perhaps being hard pressed, and rested for the night in Iniscatha. MacMahon, hearing this, surrounded the house in which they were, set fire to it, and as they came out, unarmed, asking for mercy, they were all captured. Bringing them with him to his castle of Colmanstown, in the present parish of Kilofin, he hanged the soldiers on the following day, and handed over Purcell to the garrison of Limerick, by whom he was soon put to death.[1] It would appear from this that he too, like the Earl of Thomond, had thrown his lot in with the English.

Very little of note occurred during the following four years in Clare. We find mention made, but only bare mention, of a Dean O'Grady as a man of great power in Church

[1] Four Masters.

and State; and of Maolin MacBrody, "Ollav to O'Brien in history."

It will be borne in mind that MacNamara, Prince of Clan Cuilean, had accepted a knighthood on the same occasion on which Conor O'Brien renounced his Irish title for an English earldom. Nothing more was heard of it. It seems probable that on his return home he repented, and resumed, in Irish fashion, the headship of his clan. Certain it is that no MacNamara afterwards assumed the English title, while we find them maintaining their old one. The Four Masters note at the year 1584 the death of "the son of MacNamara of the western part of Clancuilean—a man of all the Clan Cuilean the most dreaded by his enemies in the field of battle;" and we will find his father stoutly refusing, with some other Clare chieftains, to sign the agreement entered into with Sir John Perrot in the following year. The knighthood thus relinquished was conferred on Turlogh, son of Donal O'Brien of Ennistymon, by Elizabeth, in 1583, as a reward for his services, and was long after retained in the family. This naturally stimulated his zeal in the English interest. He turned his attention, soon after arriving home from London, on his neighbour, Turlogh O'Loughlin of Burren, who had taken part in the Clanrickard uprising, and, seizing him, carried him off to Ennis, where, after a mock trial by martial law, he was put to death by Captain Brabazon in 1584. Another of those who had taken a leading part in the insurrection, Donogh Beg O'Brien, met with a far more terrible fate. He fell into the hands of Cruise, then Sheriff of Clare. The new Lord Deputy was at this time on a tour from Dublin round by Athlone to Galway, and back through Clare towards Limerick, to receive the formal submission of the insurgent chiefs. He rested for a night in Quin, and there committed an act of barbarous cruelty. The unfortunate Donogh O'Brien was delivered up to him by Cruise. He had him first half-hanged from the shafts of a car. Then his bones were broken by strokes of a heavy axe, and his mangled body, while he was still alive, was fastened on with ropes to the top of the tower of Quin Abbey, as a feast for the birds of the air.[1]

[1] Four Masters.

The King of Dahomey could hardly venture into the lists for refined and inhuman cruelty with Sir John Perrot,[1] the illegitimate son of Henry VIII., Queen Elizabeth's Lord Deputy for Ireland. With such tools in her hands, commanding superior force, it is no wonder that she awed into submission the broken and betrayed clans of Clare, Tipperary, and Galway.

Sir John Perrot, having now disposed of all the enemies to the queen's policy west of the Shannon, summoned a Parliament to sit in Dublin on the 26th April 1585. The Four Masters give the names of all who attended this Parliament from all parts of Ireland. There attended from Clare, among the peers, Donogh O'Brien, Earl of Thomond, Morogh O'Brien of Inchiquin, and the queen's Bishop of Killaloe, Morogh, son of O'Brien of Ara; among the commons, Sir Turlogh O'Brien and Boetius Clancy. There came also, not as members, but to watch their own interests, John MacNamara, Lord of West Clancuilean, Rossa O'Loughlin, son of the O'Loughlin of Burren, and Turlogh O'Brien of Ballycorick. With the acts of this Parliament we have no concern in this history; but following it soon after, and very probably arising out of its deliberations, a meeting was held at Ennis, which claims from Clare people more than ordinary attention, as its avowed purpose was to effect a complete change in the land tenure all through the county — to substitute, in the most formal way, English for Brehon law.

The statement of the alleged agreement entered into at this meeting between the Queen of England and the people of Clare, is given in full in the Appendix, as it appears in what is called Sir John Perrot's Tripartite Deed, for the reason that it gives a kind of photographic view of the Clare of that day.[2]

It is a significant fact that little more than half of those named in it signed this truly revolutionary document. The

---

[1] He afterwards planned and executed the ignoble scheme by which the sons of O'Neill and O'Donnell were lured into a ship in Lough Swilly, and carried off to the dungeon of Dublin Castle.

[2] I take the liberty of quoting it from Canon Dwyer's valuable *Diocese of Killaloe*.

clansmen who were most concerned in it, inasmuch as it filched away their ancestral rights, had, it need hardly be said, no hand whatsoever in it. In their regard it was an act of spoliation pure and simple. The Four Masters, at the year A.D. 1585, note specially that MacNamara of West Clancuilean refused on the spot to affix his signature. Their own words are worth giving here:—

"They deprived of title and tribute every head or chief of a sept, and every other lord of a triocha-ched throughout the whole country (with the exception of John MacNamara, Lord of the western part of the district of Clann-Coilein), who did not subscribe his signature to this ordinance of theirs. They acted a like ordinance in the counties of Galway, Roscommon, Mayo, and Sligo."

The following were those who actually signed. For clearness' sake the names are here given as they are now spelled.

Donogh Thomond.	Owen O'Loughlin.
Mauritius Laonensis.	Rossa O'Loughlin.
Marie for her son, the young Baron of Inchiquin.	Edward White.
	George Cusack.
Turlogh O'Brien.	James Neylan.
Murtogh O'Brien.	Boetius Clancy.
MacNamara Rua.	Conor MacGilreagh (Gallery).
Teigue MacMahon.	Donogh Clancy.
Turlogh MacMahon.	Conor O'Brien.
Mahon O'Dea.	George Feminge.
Mahon O'Brien.	

Another, Donald Syne, appears third on the list, next after the Protestant Bishop of Killaloe, and probably is intended for Donal, Protestant Bishop elect of Kilfenora, a son of Donal O'Brien of Ennistymon.

From this document it appears that Sir John Perrot had the county, consisting of nine baronies, divided into "one thousand two hundred and fifty-nine quarters and a half, and one third part of land, estimating every quarter with his pasture, meaddow, woode, and bogge, of a hundred and twenty acres." The amount made payable out of each quarter of one hundred and twenty acres, as given accurately by the Four Masters, was ten shillings to the crown as public revenue, and five shillings to the Earl of Thomond, or such others of the chiefs temporal or spiritual as were in favour at the time. This was the origin of what is now known as crown-rent and head-rent. In addition to this crown-rent, they had also to bind themselves, their heirs, successors, etc., to provide for the service of the crown "forty good able horsemen and two hundred footmen well-armed upon their own proper costs and charges," together with fifteen horse and fifty foot for general hostings. The Earl of Thomond, the Baron of Inchiquin, and the Bishops of Killaloe and Kilfenora, however, were not included in this provision. In return for this, it was stipulated that, with some exceptions, all the "charges, taxes, exactions, boarding of soldiers," etc., that had grown up from custom or the Brehon law should altogether cease. But it must be borne in mind that for these "exactions" was substituted that claim for rent, on the part of those who received the English title to the land, which grew and grew until it has made the occupier's and tiller's life more intolerable than ever. In return for this claim, which will be just now more fully specified, "the names, stiles, and titles of captaines ship, Tanist ship, and all other Irish authorities and jurisdictions heretofore used by the said chieftaines and gentlemen, together with all election and customary divisions of lands, occasioning great strife and contention among them, shall from henceforth be utterly abolished, extinct, renounced, put back within the said county of Thomond for ever." A clean sweep, in fact, of all that was distinctively Irish in favour of the English system!* Have the people profited by the change?

And now for the bribes offered to these chieftains and gentlemen to secure their assent to the new condition of things, as shown in this Indenture. To begin with, the queen seized upon all the property belonging to the suppressed abbeys, and distributed it in a great measure among them. The "Abbey of Tulloe," only a few stones of which can now be traced, owned, as Sir John Perrot testifies, twelve quarters of land, Tomgraney eighteen, Moynoe four, Killone three, Clare fifteen, Corcomroe twelve and the two-thirds, and Kilshanny one; in all sixty-five and the two-thirds quarters, of one hundred and twenty acres of land each. All this was diverted from the service of religion and the poor to the use of the queen and her "chieftains and gentlemen." The bishopric of Killaloe had been largely endowed in the days of the generous past. It owned five quarters of land at Truagh, nine at Tradaree, seven at Dromlyne, twelve at Clonderalaw, thirty-seven at Moyarta, nineteen at Tullaghodea, and two and the one-third at Burren; in all ninety-one and the one-third, when Sir John Perrot wrote out his Indenture. The Bishop of Kilfenora had sixteen and a half quarters in Corcomroe, with one for the Dean, and fifteen and the one-third in Burren. How much of this went to provide the revenues of the Protestant bishops of those sees, cannot be easily ascertained or identified; but it is safe to say that, though the chieftains and gentlemen got their share, the people were the sufferers. They had, and have still, to provide for their own bishops.

The Earl of Thomond, as might be expected, came in for the greatest share of the spoil. He got large slices of the baronies of Islands and Bunratty, and the whole of the barony of Ibricken, "and all the goods and chattels of persons attainted of felony within those lands, and all other casualties and amerciaments that shall grow from time to time within the same;" together with a head-rent of five shillings per quarter over nearly all the rest of the county. The Baron of Inchiquin was well provided for in the baronies of Inchiquin and Tulla. The Bishop of Killaloe got five quarters as a domain to his house or manor of Killaloe; and the Bishop of Kilfenora, four quarters as a domain adjoining his houses of Kilfenora and Kilaspuglinane, as well as the goods and chattels of felons within the same.

Sir Turlogh O'Brien was made owner of fourteen quarters attaching to his castles of Ennistymon, Ballynalacken, and Liscannor, and five shillings a quarter over the rest of the barony of Corcomroe, with all the goods, chattels, etc., of felons convicted from the barony. MacNamara of East

Clancuilean and MacNamara of West[1] Clancuilean had similar grants in the baronies of Upper and Lower Tulla, but with the express condition "that the rents, duties, and customs challenged to be belonging to the name MacNamara, shall, at his decease, be utterly determined and extinct for ever." This shows that they had not at that time, like the O'Briens, formally surrendered those claims, and we learn from the Four Masters that John MacNamara of West Clancuilean refused later on to sign this agreement.

It will be enough to add, for brevity's sake, that the two MacMahons, the two O'Loughlins,[2] Mahon O'Brien of Clonduain, Sir Edward Waterhouse of Doonas, Dr. James Neylan of Ennis, Boetius Clancy of Knockfynne,—both of whom were evidently in high favour, doubtless for special services in the English interest,—Edward White of Cratloe, and George Cusack of Dromlyne, were all recognised as owners of castles and considerable domains in their several localities, on the same or nearly the same conditions. And though Mahon O'Dea of Dysert, Conor MacGilreagh of Cragbrien, Donogh Clancy, Conor O'Brien, and George Feming, are not specially mentioned, it is quite probable, as we find their names appended to the Indenture, that they too were well provided for. Much more remained still to be disposed of, and applications came pouring in, especially from various branches of the O'Brien family residing in Ballycorick,

---

[1] It appears from the wording of this Indenture that in those days Dangan, in the MacNamara country, was, like Clarecastle, a town of some importance. It gave name to the barony now called Bunratty, but, like Bunratty, not a trace of it now remains.

[2] Canon Dwyer gives in the appendix to his work two curious deeds copied from the MacCurtin MSS., both bearing evidence of being the handiwork of that Boetius Clancy, who, being the Brehon of the chief families of the O'Briens, had made himself useful in the scheme for despoiling the Clare clans. One purports to be an abject surrender, on the part of the O'Loughlins of Ballyvaughan, of all they had, to the Earl of Thomond. The other, in barbarous Latin, records an equally abject surrender of all their rights, titles, and claims, alleged to be made by ten gentlemen of the O'Connors of Corcomroe, to Turlogh O'Brien of Ennistymon. They could not have signed such documents voluntarily if they knew their contents. It is not unlikely that they were forged as a pretext for the clean sweep made of the properties of those families.

Cahermonane, Drumlyun, Ballycar, etc. The occupiers and tillers of the soil were left to settle as best they could with those who received the English titles to the land. Their title, coming down to them from time immemorial under the operation of the Brehon law, began from the date of this Indenture to be utterly ignored. Here we find the origin of that war between landlords and tenants which has continued, with results highly injurious to both classes and to the whole country, down to our own time.

Besides MacNamara of Clancuilean West, there was one other of note who would have no part in this surrender. Mahon O'Brien alone among the O'Briens, from whom the Mahons of Clare are called,[1] held out stoutly from first to last against Sir John Perrot. It was a bold and manly stand, but devoid of the smallest hope of final success. Sir George Bingham, Governor of Connaught, was ordered to besiege him in his castle of Cluanoon, the remains of which may still be traced in the parish of Kilkeady, about six miles north-east of Corofin. It was then a place of considerable strength, as the resistance to the large force provided with artillery brought against it clearly proved. For three months the small garrison kept them at bay. If desperate and rash, it was certainly a glorious defence. Finding that the cannons took little effect on the strong walls of the castle, and that all his assaults on the fortress were so vigorously repulsed, Sir George Bingham endeavoured to undermine it. Sharpshooters were so placed as to command every point where the besieged might expose themselves, while engaged in flinging down stones and other missiles on their enemies underneath. By one of these Mahon was shot dead on the battlement of the castle. The garrison then surrendered quickly, in the hope of receiving quarter. A really brave man readily recognises bravery in an enemy. They were all, however, put to death, and great part of the castle was razed to the ground. This was not Bingham's only act of cruelty. He spared no one.[2] Not only did he hang all of the fighting men who at any

---

[1] Four Masters.

[2] He first signalised himself in Ireland at the treacherous and bloody massacre of Dun-an-oir, near Smerwick, in Kerry, in 1580. Yet this is

time fell into his hands,[1] but the Four Masters assert that even "women, boys, peasants, and decrepit persons" were killed by the soldiers under his command. He was not alone in the work of butchery. Rivals worthy of him in this respect crop up in almost every chapter of the English progress in Ireland.

Towards the close of this century, in Clare, the death of another son of John MacNamara of West Clancuilean is recorded,[2] and the slaying, at the doorway of the monastery of Ennis, by the O'Griffys of Ballygriffy Castle, of a son of that Doctor Neillan who had all along actively supported the English interest.

We have been following, in the preceding pages, the steps taken by the agents of Elizabeth to Anglicise Clare. It will be interesting to consider the state of Clare just before the process began. We have a description of it from the pen of Sir T. Cusack, written in 1574, and preserved in the library of Trinity College.[3]

The following summary conveys as clear an idea of it as can well be gathered from the English spelling of the Irish names :—

"The Barony of Tullaghanaspul conteyneth MacNamara's country by east, the Baron of Inshyquyn, and Donal Reogh MacNamara, chief in the same; the castles are thirty-eight in number." Of these, three, Tomgraney, Moynoe, and Truagh, belonged to the O'Gradys; one, Castlelogh, to the Baron of Inchiquin; one, Castle Callogh, to the Earl of Thomond; three, Glanoradone, Fomeara, and Tyredagh, to Turlogh O'Brien; one, Dunass, to John the Dane (Waterhouse); all the others, twenty-nine in all, beginning with Tulla, where the chief lived, to the various branches of the MacNamara family in the east.

the man the inscription on whose monument in Westminster Abbey begins with, "To the glory of the Lord of Hosts."

[1] About seventy were hanged in Galway alone, among whom were Teigue, the son of Donal MacNamara of East Clancuilean, and the son of O'Connor Roe.—Four Masters.

[2] In Sydney's *Letters*, fol., vol. i. p. 102, we read : 'The two MacNamaras, if the countrie were quiet, might live like principal knights in England.'

[3] MS. marked E 2. 14, and the Carew MSS. vol. 611.

"The Barony of Dangen conteyninge West MacNamara's country. Shane MacNamara, chief in the same. Castles forty-three." Of these, the Earl of Thomond owned three, Bunratty, Clounmoney, and Rossmanaher; other O'Briens, five; the MacClancys, six; the Neylons, three, Ballyshannon, Ballycastlea, and Ballyalla; Shane O'Mulconry, one, Ballynagun; Donogh O'Grady, one, Cluanagh; MacInerny, one, Ballynacraggy; Shane MacMahon, one, Corbally; twenty-two in all; the rest belonged to the MacNamaras.

"The Baronie of Cloyntherala conteyninge East Corkewasten. Tege MacMahon, chief in the same. Castles seven." Of these, five, Clonderalaw, Dangen y Burke (Ballynacally), Cahircon, Ballymacolman, and Derracrossan, belonged to the MacMahons; and two, Dunagrogue and Coruberigane, to the O'Briens.

"The Baronie of Moyartha which conteyneth West Corke-Waskin. Terlogh MacMahon, chief in ye same. Castles eight." Of these, four, Carrigaholt, Moyarta, Dunlicky, and Dunsumayn, belonged to the MacMahons; two, Dunbeg and Dunmore, to Sir Donal O'Brien; one, Ballyket, to James Cahane; and one, Iniscatha, to Charles Cahane.

"This man by inheritance is called a Courboc," *i.e.* steward to the monastery—literally, cowherd.

"The Baronie of Tuogh Morey Conor conteyninge Corcomroe. Sir Donal O'Brien, knight, chief in ye same. Castles twenty-three." Of these, one, Tuomolyn, belonged to MacClancy; one, Ennistymon, to O'Connor; the rest, twenty-one in all, to the O'Briens. They wrested these from the original owners, who were mostly O'Connors.

"The Baronie of Gregans conteyninge the country of Burren. O'Loghlin, chief in the same. Castles twenty." All of these belonged to the O'Loughlins.

"The Baronie of Tullagh Idea. Sir Donal O'Brien, knight, chiefe. Castles twenty-four." Of these, three, Ballynalicky, Magowna, and Dysert, belonged to the O'Deas; one, Ballygriffy, to O'Griffy; three, Dunmulvihil, Carigathoher, and Ballynafircruane, to the MacSwineys, who answered to the modern militia; the rest, seventeen in all, to the O'Briens.

"The Baronie of Cloyneraude conteyninge ye troghkied of

Cloynerade and ye Ilands. Therle of Thomonde, chiefe in the same. Castles nineteen." Of these, one, Enenshy (Inch), belonged to MacClancy ; one, Island Magrath, to MacGrath ; two, Cragbrien and Tirmaclane, to MacGillaroe (Gallery) ; the rest, fifteen in all, to the O'Briens. "There are eight Baronies, seventy-nine parish churches, and one hundred and seventy-two castles, and eight Abbeyes.

"The Abbeyes and Religious Houses are :—

"The Abbey of Clare, possessed by Sir Donal and Teige MacConor (O'Brien), his brother. Inish by James Nillan. St. John's, a nunrye, by ye Baron of Inshiquyn. Corcomroe Iland Chanens (Canon Island), by Therle of Thomond. Kiltsna (Kilshanny), Quynhye (Quin), occupied by ffriers. The Abbey of Inis Cronan."

Who can say that the people who built all these castles, churches, and abbeys were the semi-barbarians English writers represent them?

CHAPTER XVIII.

FROM 1590 TO 1602.

The Earl of Thomond joins the English in an Attack on the Northern Princes—Driven back—Besieged in Armagh and Newry—O'Brien of Ballycorick hanged—Defeat at Ballyshannon—Uprising in Clare—O'Donnell's Raid in Clare—Sieges of Carrigaholt, Dunbeg, and Dunmore—Second Raid of O'Donnell, A.D. 1600—The Earl of Thomond reduces Clare to submission.

THE English sway was now unchallenged in Clare. The queen's writ began to run there. Two of the vessels of the ill-fated Armada having been wrecked, A.D. 1588, on the coast, with six hundred men on board, local tradition has it that Boetius MacClancy, acting as sheriff, seized and executed the few Spaniards who succeeded in reaching the shore at Spanish Point—so named from this event. To this day the people point to mounds close to the sea, called by them the "Spaniards' Graves."

Sir Turlogh O'Brien of Ennistymon was commissioned, with the sheriff, by the Lord Deputy, to hunt up the Spaniards, with power "to use torture in process of this inquiry." So terrified were the people, that water was refused at Kilrush and Liscannor to a vessel which weathered the gale, though an equal quantity of wine was offered for it.

An epidemic of some kind must have raged through Clare in 1591 and the following years, as we find recorded in the Four Masters the death of considerable numbers of the principal persons among the O'Briens, MacNamaras, and MacMahons.

The base plot by which Sir John Perrot succeeded in seizing and carrying off to Dublin Castle the young princes, O'Donnell and O'Neill, led to the next commotion in Clare. After their romantic escape, the whole North combined against the treacherous English. The Lord Justice, Sir William Russell, summoned to his aid the Earl of Thomond, and both proceeded at the head of their combined forces into Tyrone. Here they found the Northern army so strongly posted, that, not daring to attack, they withdrew hastily to Armagh. The Irish went in pursuit, and for fifteen days watched without being able to assault the town, which was well fortified. Leaving a garrison within the fortress, the English, with their Clare contingent, contrived to elude the vigilance of their foes, and retreated to Newry. Here again the pursuing Irish found them within strong entrenchments, but, after a week's delay, finding that the Lord Justice could not be induced to risk a battle, they returned to their own country.

Soon after this, Sir John Norris, who was left in command, and his brother, Sir Thomas Norris, the President of Munster, determined to recover the lost English prestige. They strove to take the Northern princes by surprise, but were promptly met in their rush through Monaghan, and were forced to retreat after severe loss. Both were wounded; and here occurred the personal encounter, described so graphically by O'Sullivan Beare,[1] between Hugh O'Neill and a huge cavalry officer named Segrave, in which the latter was slain.

Another great mishap befell the English this year. While a large consignment—one hundred and twenty-four barrels —of powder from England was being conveyed through Dublin, it blew up accidentally, and caused great havoc and loss of life and property in the city.

Fighting in the Northern army were two of the O'Briens, Teigue and Conor of Ballycorick, who were dissatisfied with the Clare settlement. In the hope that the Irish successes under O'Neill and O'Donnell would inspirit the people of Clare, they returned there, but failed in the attempt, and were captured and hanged.

In the year 1597, Lord Borough was sent to replace the incompetent Russell as Lord Justice. His first act was to deprive Sir John Norris of the command of the army, and

[1] *Hist. Cath. Iber.* tom. iii. lib. 3, c. 11.

assume it to himself. He then marched northwards, and, guided by a traitor, Turlogh O'Neill, he succeeded in passing the Blackwater into O'Neill's country. Here, however, he was attacked with such vigour and skill in a series of skirmishes night and day, that he was unable to penetrate farther, and, suffering considerable loss,—the Earl of Kildare being of the number,—he was compelled to retreat to Dublin.

In order to divide the Northern forces, he had issued instructions to Sir Conyers Clifford, the Governor of Connaught, to attack, with all the forces he could muster from that province and Clare, O'Donnell at Ballyshannon. The Earl of Thomond, the Baron of Inchiquin, the Earl of Clanrickard, the Baron of Dunkellin, and a large following of the Irish and English, met him by appointment at the monastery of Boyle on the 24th of July. A proud sight for the English invader! Irishmen against Irishmen once more. Trusting in their numbers, their discipline, and their superior equipment, they hastened to the attack. O'Donnell stoutly resisted their crossing the river Erne, but had to fall back upon his fortress of Ballyshannon. In the passage, the Baron of Inchiquin fell while leading on his troops. Now began the real struggle. A ship sent round from Galway landed some heavy ordnance for the assault on the castle. For three days it played on the stout walls without effect, and then the scene changed. The besieged became the besiegers. Hemmed in between the fortress and the river, the principal ford of which was covered by the castle, and in want of the supplies which O'Donnell took good care to cut off, the Governor found himself and his army in a most critical position. After long deliberation, retreat was decided on. In the early morning they began the recrossing of the river. As soon as their design was perceived, the exulting Northerns fell upon their rear, and turned their flight into a rout. They had to abandon their cannon and whatever else would impede their retreat. O'Donnell pursued them across the river, and had the proud satisfaction of seeing the enemy, after suffering great loss, scattered before him. It was some consolation for the treachery of his captain, and the indignities of his long imprisonment. We may be sure there was little welcome at their return home to Clare for the leaders who brought the proud Dalcassians into such ignoble plight.

A curious bye-battle took place on the banks of the Shannon in consequence of this Dalcassian defeat. The Burkes, who had seized on O'Conaing territory, now known as Castleconnell, encouraged by the death of the young Baron of Inchiquin, determined to add on to it, if they could, the adjoining district of Portcroissi, which had always belonged to his family. This design of theirs becoming known, a considerable force crossed the Shannon, at the bringing in of the harvest, to defend the rights of the widowed baroness and her children. A fierce conflict took place, many falling on both sides, among whom is specially noted from Clare—the first time the name figured on that side of the Shannon—" Hugh O'Hogan, son of a chieftain distinguished for goodness and wealth."[1]

Meanwhile the Lord Justice, driven to desperation by the repulses he suffered at the hands of O'Neill and O'Donnell, resolved on one more trial of strength before the winter would set in. O'Neill had been harassing the garrison left in the stronghold built by Borough on the Blackwater. He went with all his available force to their support, but was once more hurled back, this time dying, by the vigorous Northern prince. So complete was the success of O'Neill and O'Donnell, that Elizabeth sued for peace. The Earls of Thomond and Ormond were deputed by her to proceed to the North and offer them the most favourable terms, including a recognition of their independence. They did not believe, and with good reason, in her sincerity; but, after a three days' conference, a truce, till the following May, was agreed on. The Earl of Thomond went to the queen to receive further instructions; and the respect in which the brave Northern princes were held by the Leinster Irish, who were up in arms against the English, is shown in their laying down their arms at their request during the term of the truce.

May 1598 came, and with it, the truce being now at an

[1] Four Masters.

end, the renewal of hostilities. Hugh O'Neill laid siege to the fort built by Lord Borough on the Blackwater. An army of four thousand foot and six hundred horse, under the command of Marshal Bagenal, was sent against him. It is not necessary here to give details of the celebrated battle of Bealanaithebuidhe, in which more than half of this army, with its leader, was left dead on the field. When the news reached Clare, those there who were discontented with the settlement of 1585 flew to arms. Among these were Teigue O'Brien, brother to the earl, who took from Margaret Cusack, Baroness of Inchiquin, the bridge and adjoining lands of Portcroissi, as well as the castles of Scariff and Cluain, near Tulla; Turlogh O'Brien, son of Mahon, killed at the defence of Cluanoon, who slew George Cusack, to whose father, Sir Thomas Cusack, Mahon's confiscated property was made over; Teigue Caoch MacMahon, of Carrigaholt; and many other men of note in the county. The Earl of Thomond could count upon the active assistance in the English interest of the Inchiquin and Ennistymon families, who, like himself, had been enriched at the expense of so many others. His youngest brother, Donal, held for him the castle of Kilmurry Ibrickane. One of the first incidents of this civil turmoil was a nocturnal attack upon this castle by Teigue Caoch, who seized it, and, slaying many of the defenders, carried off Donal a wounded prisoner to his castle of Dunbeg, which he had a short time before wrested back from a Limerick merchant to whom it had been mortgaged. He kept him only for a week, and then set him at liberty without ransom. This same Donal it was who afterwards became his son-in-law and successor at Carrigaholt. Possibly the lady had procured his liberation. Here would be the origin of the romantic story still told in West Clare of their stolen interviews, and his escape from the enraged father, by swimming his horse across the bay of Carrigaholt.

About this time Teigue seized an English vessel, with its crew and cargo, which had drifted in on his coast. It played a strange part in his after history, which will be narrated in its proper place.

The county was once more the theatre of civil war from the

sea to the upper Shannon. O'Neill sent his son Con southwards to organise a combined resistance against the English. He entered into a correspondence with Teigue O'Brien among others, and prepared him and his party in Clare for the advance to be made . soon after by O'Donnell against Elizabeth's adherents in the county.

A very interesting description of this raid is given by the Four Masters, annotated by Dr. O'Donovan, so as to identify all the places named. Marching southwards with great rapidity, O'Donnell encamped, on St. Bridget's night, A.D. 1599, in the heart of the Clanrickard country, near Athenry. Before dawn he pushed on to a wood called Ui Flaney, in the parish of Kilkeady. Here he divided his forces, sending one division under O'Rourke and MacSweeney into Burren, another under Maguire straight towards Inchiquin, a third sweeping the country southwards by the great wood of Ballyhogan, in the parish of Dysert, on to Tully O'Dea; while O'Donnell himself, with the main body, pushed through to Kilnaboy, "in the upper part of Dal-Cas." Towards night, those who went southwards rejoined him. Here he remained for the night, laden with spoil; and on the next day, wheeling round by Inagh and through what was called Breutir, or the Fetid District of the Fearmacigh and the Cormacigh, up to the base of Mount Callan, he swept the whole country by Ennistymon as far as Kilaspuglinane (Bishop Flannan's Church), and met, at Kilfenora, Maguire and O'Rourke returning from Inchiquin and Burren. Another halt was made here for the night. "When O'Donnell saw the surrounding hills covered and darkened with the herds and numerous cattle of the numerous territories through which his troops had passed, he proceeded, the next morning, on his way homewards over the chain of rugged-topped mountains of Burren, and, passing by Nuaghaval Turlach, the monastery of Corcomroe, and Carcair-na-g-Cleireuch ('Narrow Pass of the Priests'), arrived at Corranrua,[1] in the west of Hy Feachrach-Aidne (near Kinvarra), where he stopped for the night."

[1] This castle, belonging to O'Heyne, fell to the ground, A.D. 1755, at the very moment that the earthquake happened at Lisbon.—O'Donovan.

It is not to be supposed that all this was done without bloodshed on both sides; but, as the surprise was so complete, no organised opposition could be offered in that rugged district. One incident relieves somewhat the uncivilised character of their inroad. MacBrody, the hereditary historian and poet of the Dal-Cas, by a little judicious flattery, secured the restoration of his cattle. He declared to O'Donnell that this devastation of the O'Brien territory was in consequence of the curse of St. Columb-cille, for the ruin wrought by the great-grandson of Brian Boroimhe on the Hy Niall fortress of Grianan-Oiligh. This allusion to the Saint of his race softened O'Donnell's heart.

When Sir Conyers Clifford, Governor of Connaught, heard of this success of O'Donnell, he determined to counteract it. He sent next month seven or eight companies of soldiers from Galway, under the command of Theobald Dillon, Captain Lester, and Richard Sherlock, Sheriff of Clare, with instructions to put themselves at the disposal of Sir Turlogh O'Brien of Ennistymon. For the sake of effect, they wisely followed the same route that O'Donnell took, and not without success. Some of Teigue O'Brien's troops lay in ambush for them on the road between Kilkeady and Kilnaboy. A sharp encounter took place; but though the English suffered more than the Irish, they forced their way through and joined hands with Sir Turlogh at Ennistymon.

Teigue O'Brien saw that it was now time to submit. O'Donnell was far away in the north with his rich booty, and the English were at Ennistymon. He sued for peace, and, being the brother of the Protestant earl, his terms were accepted, and he sank henceforth into obscurity.

The united English and Irish first turned their attention to the castle of Caherminane, a few miles from Ennistymon, and a troublesome neighbour to Sir Turlogh, and soon reduced it. They then marched southwards through Kilfarboy, keeping a safe distance—as far as the bog of Monemore would permit—from Dunbeg and Dunmore, with a view to win over to their side Teigue Caoch MacMahon, who was a nephew of Sir Turlogh. He was too much attached to the Irish and Catholic cause to yield; so they had to content themselves with what plunder they could seize on, and, proceeding on to Ennis, held an assizes, at which rough-and-ready justice was dealt out to the queen's enemies. This was some short time before Easter, in the month of April.

The Earl of Thomond now appeared on the scene, and resolved to make himself felt. He had a special grudge against MacMahon, because of his seizure of his own castle of Kilmurry and the wounding and imprisonment of his brother. With all the force he could collect, he marched to Carrigaholt, besieged it, and, at the end of four days, captured it, with the town surrounding it. Having procured ordnance from Limerick, he next sat down before Dunbeg, which the garrison surrendered without a blow, having, in fact, no cannon to defend it. He showed his magnanimity, as might be expected from his bringing up, by hanging them up face to face. Dunmore next fell to him. His vengeance on MacMahon, who, taking to his ship during the siege of Carrigaholt, had crossed the Shannon to his ally Desmond, was now complete. Sending back the cannon to Limerick, he went eastwards to take formal possession of the castle of Derryowen, in Kilkeady, and Cluain and Lisofin, near Tulla, which his brother Teigue dared no longer to hold; and so Clare once again was in every part under the English yoke.

His next movements were not so successful. At the head of his troops, he joined the Earl of Essex, and shared in the ignominy of his defeat at the hands of the brave Desmond. When Essex was recalled and replaced by Blount, Lord Mountjoy, an effort was made to detach O'Moore of Leix from the Irish and Catholic cause. An interview was arranged between him and the Earl of Ormond. The latter invited Thomond, who was one "of the counsellors to be assistant to the Lord President of Mountster, Sir George[1] Carew," to the conference. A long time was spent in a vain attempt to come to terms. Ormond, who had with him a bodyguard of three hundred men, but at some distance, as were O'Moore's gallowglasses of an equal number by preconcert at the other side, very rashly insisted on seeing "that infamous Jesuite Archer." As soon as he came, the earl and he

[1] *Pac. Hib.* chap. i. p. 34.

fell into an argument whereon he called Archer "traytour."[1] Some of the Irish, suspecting evil intent against Father Archer, had crept up after him, and, hearing those hot words, rushed to his rescue. A scuffle ensued, in which the Earl of Thomond received a pike-thrust in the back; but he and Sir George Carew and the others on Ormond's side made their escape, owing to the strength and fleetness of their horses, leaving Ormond a prisoner in the hands of his exasperated enemies. Some time after, he was liberated for a ransom of three thousand pounds. This wears all the appearance of treachery, though O'Sullivan Beare insists that both parties met at their own peril, "no pledge of security having been given on either side;" but such breaches of faith were not all, or nearly all, either then or any other time, on the Irish side. The castle of Glin was soon after attacked by the English, under the command of Sir George Carew and the Earl of Thomond. The Constable, who, with a small garrison, was charged with its defence, held out with as much fortitude and bravery as was afterwards displayed by MacGeoghogan in the much better known siege of Dunboy. His name does not appear, but it is certain he was a Clareman,[2] as he sought and obtained an interview, as such, with the earl. His object was to induce him to raise the siege, assuring him, as one naturally anxious for his safety, that a large force was at hand ready to fall upon the English. This artifice, if artifice it was, did not succeed. Fire was opened upon the castle, which was briskly returned, even though the besiegers, with refined cruelty, held up before them a child of the Knight of Glin, six years old, which had fallen into their hands. The fate of the poor child is not stated. When a breach was effected, the small garrison, rather than surrender, fought from storey to storey up to the battlements, and flung themselves at last into the water underneath. Some who surrendered were soon despatched. As usual, no mercy was shown; all who were captured were slaughtered. This first Protestant Earl of Thomond did credit to his training. No English commander butchered prisoners with greater alacrity. He was a worthy precursor of his kinsman Inchiquin, and the godly Cromwell.

[1] *Pac. Hib.* chap. iii. p. 44.   [2] *Ibid.* vol. i. chap. vii. p. 115.

To return to Clare. There was apparent quiet there, but it was only on the surface. How could there be real rest where force was so recently used to uproot all the old and revered institutions, including religion itself? The condition of the people was more unsettled than ever; and, to add to their misery, they had to pay dearly, without their sharing in it, for the Protestant and pro-English policy of their chiefs. The splendid victory of O'Donnell at the Curlieu Pass—where, on the 15th of August, A.D. 1600, with only four hundred men, he fell upon the advancing English force of more than two thousand trained soldiers, slaying, with the help of O'Rourke, who came up while the battle was proceeding, over one thousand eight hundred of them, including the Governor of Connaught, Sir Conyers Clifford himself—left the north of Clare entirely unprotected and open to attack. The Earl of Thomond, true to his English training, was all this time, and long afterwards, away from Clare on the queen's business through South Munster. O'Donnell determined to strike at him in his own country. His last attack was confined to his subordinates of Inchiquin and Ennistymon. Leaving his eastern and southern frontier in charge of O'Doherty and O'Neill, he crossed the Erne, and, gathering to his aid the clans of Connaught, English as well as Irish, he proceeded rapidly towards Clare—keeping this time more towards the Shannon. Entering it through Moynoe, Scariff, Tomgraney, and Tulla on a Sunday morning, when because of his well-known religious disposition his onslaught was totally unexpected, he halted not bringing with him all he could seize till he pitched his camp on the banks of the Fergus, west of Clonroad [1]—probably on the site of the present Diocesan College. He left nothing in Ennis untouched except the monastery. He did not, however, come so far unscathed. Though taken so completely by surprise, the Dalcassians knew how to hit hard back. "Among those of their chiefs," the Four Masters are careful to say, "who were mortally wounded at this time were O'Boyle and O'Clery, both accidentally, by another party of O'Donnell's people, as they were attacking Clarmor (Clare Castle). From

[1] Four Masters.

this Clar (meaning a timber bridge) the county of Clare is named."

Starting early the following morning, they swept the rich plains down to Clondegad, then struck across to Cahermurphy, near Kilmihil, and, taking in the whole range of country to the sea, along by Kilmurry, Caherush, Kilfarboy, and Moy, spread ruin and devastation everywhere on their route. They rested for the night at Ballygowan Castle, now called Smithstown, in the parish of Kilshanny. The next day they came upon the ground they had traversed on the previous occasion, along towards Inagh, and back by Corofin, Inchiquin, Leimaneigh, and Kilfenora, till they reached the calm retreat of Corcomroe. What revelling there was that night within those rock terraces on that green sward round the deserted cloisters, built up by one O'Brien for Catholic purposes, and now ruthlessly and sacrilegiously confiscated by another! The following morning O'Donnell crossed "the white hills of Burren," by the Priest's Pass, at his leisure, with the plunder of the greater part of Clare; while the Earl of Thomond, who had shattered its power of resistance to external attack, was away in the distance, doing the queen's work zealously in Leinster and South Munster.[1]

Nor was O'Donnell yet satisfied with the punishment and humiliation he had inflicted on the queen's O'Briens and their followers. In October of the same year he set out once more for Clare, and had reached as far as Ballymote before he learned that his kinsman and brother-in-law, Niall Garv ("the Stubborn") O'Donnell, with his three brothers whom he had left in charge of his territory, had gone over to the English. Sir Henry Dowcra, who was cooped up in Derry and Lifford, had been for some time tempting Niall, and at last succeeded. The promise of being recognised as The O'Donnell was the price of his treachery. His defection was the occasion of freeing Clare from another incursion. O'Donnell speedily returned.

---

[1] In *Pac. Hib.* vol. i. chap. vii. p. 101, it is stated that with eight hundred foot and sixty horse he issued from Limerick, fell upon the O'Donnell's rear, slaying many, and recovered great part of the cattle. The line of retreat, given so circumstantially by the Four Masters, at such a distance from Limerick, renders their account far more probable.

The disorganised condition of the county during the transition from the Irish to the English system of government invited attack. Some of the disappointed Burkes and O'Briens conspired together to carry off as much as they could of what was left after O'Donnell. They swept through Feacle and Tulla, and along the course of the Fergus by Ballyalla, and rested for the night with their plunder at Kilrachtis. The following day they were pursued by the MacNamaras and some troops in the pay of the Earl of Thomond; but, with the loss of some men, and the wounding of two of the leaders, one of whom, Teigue O'Brien, a near relative of the earl, died soon after, they escaped into Galway.

The earl, after all this loss to the county, which may be fairly ascribed to his policy, appeared on the scene for a short period in the beginning of 1601, and signalised his presence by holding an assize at the monastery of Clonroad, and hanging sixteen persons for various offences.[1] He then went to England, from which he returned towards the end of the year with reinforcements for Lord Mountjoy, who was then besieging Kinsale.

The disastrous defeat of O'Neill and O'Donnell, who marched south to relieve the Spaniards besieged in Kinsale, does not properly find a place in this history. The only one of note from Clare who took part in it on the Irish side was Teigue Caoch MacMahon, who, after his flight from Carrigaholt, took refuge with O'Donnell, and fought under his banner. At the door of another MacMahon,[2] Brian of Monaghan, lies the shame of the betrayal of the Irish. He should not have been trusted, for he was one of those who sent sons to be brought up at the feet of Elizabeth. The request, secretly conveyed, for a bottle of whisky, was apparently the signal, prearranged between him and Sir George Carew, that important information was about to be conveyed. His position as one of the council of war in the Irish army enabled him to give Carew some hours' warning of the contemplated night attack. That betrayal, as well as the confusion the army were thrown into by going astray in the darkness, gave the Irish

---

[1] Four Masters.
[2] *Pac. Hib.* vol. ii. chap. xxi. Moryson, vol. ii. chap. ii.

and Catholic cause a blow from which it never fully recovered. It will suffice to quote the Four Masters as showing how it told on the Irish mind.

"Manifest was the displeasure of God and misfortune to the Irish of fine Fodhla on this occasion; for previous to this day a small number of them had more frequently routed many hundreds of the English, than they had fled from them in the field of battle, in the gap of danger, in every place they had encountered, up to this day; immense and countless was the loss in that place, although the number slain was trifling; for the prowess and valour, prosperity and affluence, nobleness and chivalry, dignity and renown, hospitality and generosity, bravery and protection, devotion and pure religion of the island, were lost in this engagement."

After the surrender of Kinsale, and the retreat homewards of the Northern Irish, a vain but gallant attempt was made by O'Sullivan Beare to hold his own castle of Dunboy. Teigue Caoch MacMahon, faithful to the end, and brave to a fault, threw in his fortunes with O'Sullivan; and here he found himself once more besieged by his old enemy, the Earl of Thomond. An act of insubordination brought his stormy life to an end [1] in a most tragic way by the hand of his own son. O'Sullivan wanted the vessel of which we have heard before to sail for supplies to Spain. MacMahon, whose son was in charge of her in the harbour, refused to let her out of his own reach. O'Sullivan took a boat with some men to board her himself, into which MacMahon also leaped. When close to the vessel, he called out to his son to fire. It was his own death-summons. He received a bullet, from which he died soon after. The son, overwhelmed by such a misfortune, sailed away to Spain, from whence he never was again heard of. With him disappeared the family that ruled for more than a thousand years in West Corcovaskin.

The glorious though unsuccessful defence of Dunboy needs no recounting here. It stands out in history as one of the most heroic and the most brilliant on record.

---

[1] "There was no barony in Ireland of which this Teigue was not worthy to be lord for bounteousness, for purchase of wine, horses, and literary works."—Four Masters.

O'Sullivan Beare, seeing all was now lost, determined, however, not to sue for terms or surrender. At the head of about one thousand followers, he set out for the North. He had to fight his way literally inch by inch. The retreat celebrated by Xenophon was not so full of adventure. When they came upon the Shannon at Coill-fhire, a wood near Portland, in the parish of Lorha, not finding boats to ferry them over, they killed all their horses, made corachs of their skins, and succeeded, strangely enough, in crossing on such frail boats, carrying with them as much as they could of the flesh to serve as food in their great extremity. Being now in the Clanrickard country, they were hemmed in on all sides by the English and their allies, the Burkes. Fighting against great odds, but with the courage of despair, they cut their way through, and finally reached the friendly shelter of O'Ruarck's territory—thirty-five in all out of the thousand who started with their chief from Glengariff.[1]

The defeat of the Catholic Irish was now complete for the present at least; but it was resolved to renew the struggle if only reinforcements could be procured from Spain. O'Donnell proceeded there for this purpose; and, notwithstanding the total failure of the attempt to relieve the Spanish garrison of Kinsale, he was received at court with the highest marks of distinction. The hope was held out to him of yet one more attempt to rescue the Catholic Irish from the grip of the Protestant English queen. The Irish army under O'Neill was still to be counted on. They had made their way back to the North, little knowing that they had in their company a traitor—MacMahon, to whom their defeat was largely due.

While these events were occurring in the South, a considerable number of the discontented in Clare took arms once more. Among these were some near relatives of the Earl of Thomond, who seized on the castles of Derryowen, in Kilkeady, and Castletown, in the parish of Doura. When, however, he returned with considerable force to Clare, they did not attempt to hold out against him, especially as he gave them promise of safety for a fortnight, within which to

[1] Four Masters.

put together and carry away what they could of their property. No sooner had they crossed the Shannon into Duharrow, than O'Brien of Ara—that pliant tool of the English policy—set upon them, captured most of them, and put them back into the hands of the earl at Killaloe. Here, on the pretext that their fortnight had expired, he hanged them face to face [1] on the nearest trees—a favourite method of his, as was shown before at Dunbeg and Dunmore. He could now write to his mistress Elizabeth, who was then on her dying bed in that awful agony of conscience of which English history tells us, that the Catholic Dalcassian race of Clare, Limerick, and Tipperary was, mainly through his effort, at the feet of a foreign Protestant potentate. Truly a noble boast for the head of that valiant, proud, and, for twenty centuries, free and freedom-loving people.

In the year A.D. 1602 died that John MacNamara, Lord of West Clancuilean, who had refused to sign the formal surrender of their lands and their rights proposed to the Clare chiefs by Sir John Perrot. MacBrody also died, than whom, say the Four Masters, "there was not in Ireland a better historian, poet, or rhymer.'

On the 24th of March 1603, Queen Elizabeth ended her stormy and, from a worldly point of view, most successful career. She was succeeded on the throne by James VI. of Scotland and I. of England—the son of her cousin, Mary Queen of Scots, whom, in her jealous hate, she had so foully and so unnaturally brought to the scaffold.

[1] Four Masters.

CHAPTER XIX.

FROM 1602 TO 1641.

Recusants—Priests flung overboard at sea after leaving Scattery (Iniscatha) Island—Parliament in Dublin A.D. 1613—Interesting State of Protestantism in Thomond, as described by Protestant Bishops—First Great Confiscation.

WHEN James ascended the throne, he found all Ireland reduced to at least outward submission. His accession was a cause of almost as much joy to the Catholic Irish as was the death of Elizabeth. They hoped great things from the son of a mother who suffered death for their faith, and a prince who had Irish blood in his veins. Never were a people so cruelly disappointed. At the outset the gage was thrown down to them. Their leading men were called upon to take the oath of loyalty to the king, including an acknowledgment of his supremacy as head of the Church. Those who refused were called *recusants;* and measures were soon taken to deprive them of their lands and such offices of emolument or honour as they held. The king gave himself up blindly to the avarice and cupidity of his counsellors. The rage for dispossessing the Irish and transplanting English into their places took full possession of him. To crown all, the "Act of Uniformity" of Elizabeth, prohibiting attendance at Roman Catholic worship, was again solemnly promulgated; and on the 4th of July 1605, a further proclamation was issued by His Majesty, declaring to his beloved subjects of Ireland "that the freedom of worship they were led to expect was not to be given them, and ordering all Catholic bishops and priests out of the kingdom."

The first to suffer from these tyrannical measures were the Earls of Tyrone and Tyrconnell, the latter the brother of the brave Hugh O'Donnell, who died soon after landing in Spain. These, having been presented to the king by Lord Mountjoy and created earls, had begun to be reconciled to their dependence on the English throne, when suddenly, both on the score of religion and as having only their old Irish titles to their broad lands, they found themselves marked out for spoliation and ruin. That most interesting book, *The Flight of the Earls*, by the Rev. C. P. Meehan, gives a graphic picture of the fall of those descendants of a hundred kings.

Like the rest of Ireland, Clare too, though in a certain sense under the protection of that Earl of Thomond, who may be said to be more English than the English themselves, was plunged in all the miseries of a protracted period of political and religious transition. The old landmarks had been by foreign law swept away; and a new system of land tenure and of religion was being forcibly thrust upon an unwilling people. The Protestant Bishop O'Brien might, with the aid of his own family on one side of the Shannon, and of the dutiful Earl of Thomond on the other, collect the revenues of the diocese of Killaloe, but he could not reach the hearts of his supposed ecclesiastical subjects; while the Catholic Bishop O'Mulryan dared not set foot within the realm. He, as the active supporter of the Earl of Desmond, was a special object of aversion to the English and Protestant interest. He might well expect the fate of Redmond Galcory, Bishop of Derry, who was seized by English soldiers and killed without any form of trial; or of Conor Devany, Bishop of Down and Connor, who, though about eighty years old, after a mock trial,[1] was hanged, beheaded, and quartered in Dublin; or, coming nearer home, of O'Hurley, Archbishop of Cashel, who was brutally burned at the stake in Stephen's Green, A.D. 1582. Priests and religious were so persecuted in those years in Clare, that some of them, losing courage, petitioned for a vessel to take them to some other country. Their request was granted. A vessel called at Scattery to

---

[1] Four Masters. O'Sullivan Beare. No Irishman could be induced to do the horrid deed. An Englishman, sentenced to death, saved his own life by becoming his executioner.

take them on board, but when well out at sea, all of them, numbering forty-six, were flung overboard. The perpetrators of this treacherous deed sought and received Church property as a reward for such a meritorious act.[1]

We have from the pen of Sir John Davies, after his circuit through the South *distributing justice*, a description of the methods by which English rule was upheld and the Protestant faith preached in Clare. It was not considered enough to exact the oath of supremacy. Those who betrayed their conscience so far, as well as the far greater number who refused to do so, were subjected to fines for non-attendance at the Protestant religious service. Writing of some who had been indicted upon the statute for not coming to church, he says, " We required them to pay the penalty of the laws, viz. twelve pence for each Sunday and holiday."[2] It appears from this that holidays were still kept, perhaps to add to the number of fines. By this ingenious contrivance, which was worked through this and the succeeding reigns, far the greater part of the people were made liable to constant and harassing exactions.

The same report gives us a glimpse into the inner life of the Clare of that day. Though from an unfriendly pen, it is well worth quoting. " In the county of Clare, which contains all Thomond, where I beheld the appearance and fashion of the people, I would," he writes, "I had been in Ulster again; for these are as mere Irish as they, and in their outward form not unlike them; but when we came to despatch the business, we found that many of them spake good English and understood the course of our proceedings well. For the justices of Munster were wont ever to visit this country, both before my Lord of Thomond had the particular government thereof and sithence. After the despatch of the gaol, which contained no extraordinary malefactors, our principal labours did consist in establishing sundry possessions of freeholders in that county, which had been disturbed in the time of the rebellion, and had not been settled sithence. The best freeholders, next to the O'Briens, are the MacNamaras and the O'Lancey, (O'Clancys), the chief of which families appeared in a civil

---

[1] *Hibernia Dominicana*.   [2] C. S. P. Ireland, p. 467, 1603-9.

habit and fashion, the rest are not so reformed as the people of Munster.[1] But it is to be hoped that the example of the earl, whose education and carriage your lordship knows, and who indeed is served and waited on very civilly and honourably, will within a few years alter the manners of this people, and draw them to civility and religion both."[2] The writer then proceeds to describe with great zest the hunt after the "notorious thief or rebel, Redmond Purcell," who had held high command under the Earl of Desmond; the imprisonment of Sir Turlogh O'Brien, brother of the Bishop O'Brien, whom the latter accused of harbouring this rebel; and, finally, his betrayal by one MacHurley, "so that now we hear he is executed by martial law."

In the same report complaint is made of the inefficient manner in which Protestant teaching is conveyed. "If our bishop and others were but half as diligent in their sacred charges as these men (the priests) are in the places where they haunt, the people would not receive and nourish them as now they do.[3] That unconscious touch, "the places where they haunt," reveals the bitter spirit of persecution which marked the attempt to propagate the Reformed religion, and which was persevered in for more than two centuries, with what result the Catholic Clare of to-day testifies. The Earl of Thomond did all he could, by a rigid enforcement of the laws against the Catholics, and by encouraging[4] Protestants to settle in Clare, to plant the new faith there. Very little advance, however, was made. The people would still gather to the hunted priests, though they had at the same time to pay tithes to the Protestant teachers, no small part of which found its way into the pockets of lay patrons. The bishop who succeeded O'Brien, John Rider, had to repair to the English court, to complain of "the great decaies, and unconscionable concealmte and usurpacons of the tem-

---

[1] Clare had been, for some years previous, reunited to the government of Connaught, but when the Earl of Thomond was made President of Munster, A.D. 1617, it was again made, and continued ever since, part of that province.

[2] Sir J. Davies, *Car. Cal.*, May 1606.   [3] C. S. P., 1603, p. 8.

[4] Sir A. Chichester in C. S. P., 1606, p. 34.

poralities, tythes, advowsons, and other spiritualities of that Bishopricke, to the utter overthrow of the state thereof."

To make matters worse, all the old enactments against the Irish dress, language, and names were now, for the first time, put in force in Clare. Fines, ranging from £6, 13s. 4d. (a large sum in those days) downwards, were imposed on "such as shall be shorn or shayen about the ears, or use the wearing of hair upon their heads like unto long locks called glibbes,[1] or have or use any hair growing upon their upper lips, or have or use any shirt, mocke, kercher, bendel, or linen cap, coloured or dyed with saffron—ne yet in any of their shirts or smocks above seven yards of cloth, to be measured according to the king's standard. Or that no woman wear kyrtle or coat tucked up; or embroidered or garnished with silk, or couched ne laid with usher, after the Irish fashion."[2] This, and such like, were the enlightened laws which the Earl of Thomond, as Governor of Clare, was bound to enforce, to the best of his power, among the Dalcassian clans.

During the early years of the reign of James, the Catholic Irish abandoned all idea of a resort to arms as hopeless. However, they maintained all along an attitude of sullen, passive resistance to his repressive measures. With wonderful courage and constancy, they risked all the grave penalties attaching to the refusal of the oath of supremacy, and non-attendance at Protestant places of worship. With a view to overawe them and impress them with the fulness of his authority and power, James resolved on convoking a Parliament in Dublin. To make sure of a majority in this assembly, he created not less than forty boroughs,[3] most of them small towns where English and Protestant voters predominated. In the teeth of all this, a large body of recusants, not less than one hundred and one out of a total of two hundred and twenty-six, were returned to the House of Commons. This Parliament met on the 18th of May 1613. Its first proceeding—the election of a Speaker—was the

[1] Hence Carolan's beautiful air, "The Coulin."
[2] *The Statutes of Ireland.* Newly Perused and Printed by the Society of Stationers.
[3] O'Donohue's *Memoirs*, chap. xviii. p. 252.

signal for a fierce contest. Sir John Davies, Attorney-General, was the candidate of the king and his party. The Catholics supported the claims of Sir John Everard, who resigned his office of Justiceship of the King's Bench rather than take the oath of supremacy. Objection was made at once to the right of sitting for the newly-created boroughs. While the dispute was proceeding, the Catholics placed Sir John Everard in the chair. The Protestants, failing to force him from it, actually placed Sir John Davies in his lap. Amid such disorder nothing could be done. The Catholics, after this protest, retreated in a body, and sent a deputation, foolishly enough, to state their case to the king; while Sir A. Chichester sent a counter-deputation, among whom was the Earl of Thomond, on the part of the Protestants. The result was just what might be expected. The king's party were all right; the other all wrong. Some of the latter were sent to the Tower, and others summoned over to answer for their behaviour. Among these were the brother of the earl, Sir Donal O'Brien, who had received his title, with the forfeited MacMahon estates, from Queen Elizabeth, and Boetius Clancy, the two members sent from Clare. Though both of these had taken with the earl the English side in the late struggles, they yet held to the Catholic faith, to which fact they probably owed their election for Clare. Sir Donal proved his zeal in the cause by helping Sir William Burke to hold Sir John Everard in the chair. James contented himself with administering a sharp reprimand, and sent them back with a warning to resume the work of Parliament in a more obedient spirit. This had the desired effect; but, after the voting of supplies, the Parliament was dissolved, probably to prevent another outbreak.

The Earl of Thomond, as the reward for his many services to the English and Protestant cause, was made President of Munster, A.D. 1617, and had Clare reunited once more, and finally, to the Southern province.

Three documents, which have been rescued from obscurity by the patient industry of Canon Dwyer, and given by him, in their original form, in his work on the *Diocese of Killaloe*, throw much light incidentally on the internal condition of

Clare at this critical period. One of these was a return of the state of the diocese of Kilfenora, made by Adams, Bishop of Limerick and Kilfenora, for the royal visitors, A.D. 1615; another, a similar return made by Rider, Bishop of Killaloe, on the same occasion; and the third, a much more detailed and minute and exceedingly methodical return of the state of the diocese of Killaloe, "presented to His Majesty's Commissioners at Dublin, July 1st, 1622, per Johannum Laonensem Episcopum."

We find in these documents very interesting lists of the names of decanates, parishes, incumbents, vicars, churches, and of the sums payable from all the parishes, but very little, except by inference, as to the numbers of professing Protestants. The decanates still followed the lines, and kept up the names, of the old great clans. For instance, Omullod and Ogaskin were but corruptions for Uim-Bloid and Ui Caisin, the tribe names of the O'Briens and the MacNamaras; but the names of the parishes and their boundaries are still substantially the same. The churches were already suffering in the conflict between the old and the new religion. It is sad to come upon such notes, monotonously repeated, as "church and chancel down," "church down, chancel ruinous," "walls up, uncovered," "church and chancel uncovered," "all these churches ruined" (Kilfenora), etc. Nearly all the fine old structures were in ruins; and if we find any attempt to repair or rebuild recorded, and that only in a very few instances, we will be told "my Lord of Thomond hath undertaken it," or it was done "by ye help of ye fines of ye Recusants." It will be easy to gather from this alone that the Reformation did not present itself in a very Christian form to the people of Clare. It was the "dog in the manger" for them. It did nothing for the preservation of the churches, and took them out of the hands of those who would do it.

Looking over the names of the incumbents and vicars, we find, as might well be expected, that the English largely predominate. Out of a total of forty-nine, including the two bishops, only eleven bear Irish names. Of these, Hugh O'Hogan was Dean of Killaloe in 1622, Patrick O'Hogan

Archdeacon, and Daniel Kennedy Precentor and Prebendary of Tulla. Another was Dean Donnellon of Kilfenora, but, it is noted, " he is revolted back to Popery."

The influence of the Earl of Thomond may be traced in the appointment to those dignities, or may they have been rewards wisely meted out to encourage converts? They are certainly out of all proportion to the relative numbers of the two nations.

It is not easy to discover what service the Protestant clergy rendered for the incomes they received. Very few of them knew Irish, and very few of the Irish knew English; and nearly all the churches had been allowed to fall to ruin since the priests were compelled to abandon them. It must be inferred that most of the benefices were practically sinecures. This appears, too, from the manner in which they were multiplied in the hands of individuals. For instance, Bartholomew White, who is described as " a minister, a native, a man of good life,"—probably a member of the Cratloe family, of whom we have heard before,—was at the same time " Rector and Vicar of Kilnaboy, Parson and Vicar of Killonanogham, in the diocese of Kilfenoragh, and Vicar of Rath, of Dysert, and of Kilfarboy." But this plurality pales into insignificance before the fact recorded in this return, that Adams, Bishop of Limerick, was also "Incumbent of Tomgraney, of Kilraghtis, of Kiltulla, of Templemaley, of Kilmormogal (Kilmore ?), of Inniscronan, of Cluana, of Tulla, and of Doora"! The Protestants, if there were any in those parishes, must have consoled themselves for the absence of their rector in the knowledge that he was no less than a live bishop. One is inclined to ask whether the kindness was reciprocated. Did John Rider, Bishop of Killaloe, get so many fat incumbencies in the diocese of Limerick?

In reply to the question, " What livinge and means ye incumbents and curates have ? " the Bishop says :—

" First, for ye incumbents, theyre means are set downne in ye several value of every man's livinge in ye answer to ye third article above throughout ye whole."

" Secondly, for ye curats of ye Benefices, Presentative,

Collative, and Appropriate, they have sufficient allowance to theyr content." That speaks well for the allowance.

"But for ye impropriators" (laymen holding the fruits of benefices), "eyther they have no curats at all, or els they allow them nothing but what they get burying, marrying, and christening, and scarce that same either."

The Bishop has a word to say of his predecessor, Mauritius O'Brien.

He accuses him of having "fraudulently surrendered into ye hands of ye Kings Matie that now is, about ye yeare of Or L God, 1610," the patronage to certain benefices, and of making leases "by consent of ye then incumbents of divers Parsonages, Vicarages, and Prebends wthin ye diocese, whereby ye service of God and good of ye people is much hindered"—a poor compliment to his ultra-Protestant Majesty.

Special complaint is made of "certaine Rectories appropriat ad mensam Episcop" (mensal parishes) "leased away by ye last Bishop, or withheld by others, viz.:—

"Rectory of Dola,[1] leased to Daniell O'Brien gent. for twenty-one years in Ano 1611 (Feb. 12) for fifteen shillings p. annum; and it is worth yearly 20 markes st.

"Rectory of Shainborloe, in ye parish of Quin, leased in Ano 1587 for three score and one years to Daniel Mac-na-mara of Dingane-Wiggen (Dangan) in ye county of Clare gent. for eighteenpence p. annum; it is worth yearely ten pounds Sterl.

"Rectory of Dromleen, in ye county of Clare, ditained from me by ye Earle of Thomond, L^d. President of Munster; it is worth p. annum twenty pounds sterl."

Considering the great value of money in those times as compared with the present, that was no small fish which the earl, good Protestant as he was, kept in his own net.

He next complains of "ye temporall lands anciently belonging to ye Bishopricke now made away in lease or fee farme by ye former Bishops, or at least withheld from

[1] It cannot be Tulla, as it already belonged to the Bishop of Limerick. I cannot identify it with any rectory now known in Clare. The name is still found near Nenagh.

me by others." Then follow the names of the Church lands and the persons holding them—a goodly long list indeed.

The Earl of Thomond and Sir Donal O'Brien secured for themselves far the greater portion of the booty. A large number of townlands, easily recognisable now, even in the uncouth spelling, lying in Moyarta and Clonderalaw, were leased to them at nominal rents by the generous Protestant bishops and rectors, probably for fines paid down. We find, too, that some others, Donogh Clansha, Dermot and Owen Cahan, Owny and Edmund Swiny, Donal and Dermot O'Gorman, Donal and Turlogh Roe Mahoone, Teigue and Turlogh Donel (the Mac and O dropped), etc., came in for a share, but only in a comparatively small way. Farther east, the earl gets a lease of twenty-one townlands in Dromcliff, Rath, and Kilnamona, all Church property, worth in those days £230, "at 9d. per an. for 100 yeares," and of four townlands in Kilfarboy and Kilmurry, worth £40 a year. Nicholas Darcy takes Kilkeady; and the heirs or executors of Bp. Neiland, Bp. of Kildare,[1] are pretty well provided for in Kilnaboy and Aughanish, five ploughlands, with the town, worth £60 a year, falling to their share. Sir John[2] and Daniel MacNamara also had four and a half townlands in Killuran, Kiltulla, Tuaimfinloe, and Ballinacleiry; and John Loghlen, who must have been either an O'Brien or, more probably, a MacNamara, leased no less than twenty-two townlands at Garranboy, and on round the Bay of Scariff, up to Clonesker. Besides those already named, various other townlands were set to the Earl of Thomond in different parts of the county; and some few to the Earl of Clanrickard, Richard Burke, Conor O'Flannery, and three Hogans, Patrick, Daniel, and Thomas, near relatives very likely of the Dean. That Earl of Thomond who shared so largely in Church plunder, in this as in other ways, has now no direct descendant. His house has been blotted out; so too has it been with nearly all, if not all, the others;

---

[1] Probably son or grandson of the Dr. Neilan who got a grant of the Abbey of Ennis.

[2] This is the first mention made of this title in the family since the dropping of it on his return by the MacNamara who received it in London from the hands of Henry VIII.

while the patrimony of the Church, intended in a large degree for, and loyally given to, the poor, has passed into families inheriting neither the blood of those who seized it nor the faith of those who originally granted it. This was the first fruits of the Reformation in Clare.

Bishop Rider, to the inquiry, What has His Majesty or any of his predecessors done for education, or charity, or religion in Clare? answers laconically, Nothing; but saves himself by saying that "no doubt His M$^{tie's}$ noble progenitours and predecessors" gave all that had been actually given by O'Briens, MacNamaras, MacMahons, etc. Truly a diplomatic lie!

The rest of this valuable return is made up chiefly of several special complaints.

Naturally the first is, that so much of the former revenue of the Bishop of Killaloe, consisting of "lands, many castles, halls, stone houses, other tenements, services, fishings, refections, and other profits thereto belonging, are all deteined" from him in the manner already described. He cannot recover by process of law, because "when any Church business comes to triall, ye jurors (who are for the most part recusants) are very scrupulous in giving any verdict for ye Church." As a remedy, he proposes that, in order to be left to his studies and his episcopal duties, the king should take all these, which he computes as worth £2000 a year at least (in reality nearly £4000), and to cause "foure hundred pounds sterl. to be paid yearely, by four equall portions, out of His Highness' Exchequer, unto me, ye now Bishop of Killaloe, and my successors, yt we might ye more freely spend ourselves and our times in ye immediate service of God." A modest proposal certainly; very advantageous, on the face of it, to the crown; but it does not appear that the king took a mean advantage of it!

The bishop next lays stress on the fees due from the dissolved abbeys and monasteries, but withheld from him, and on the great number of rectories and vicarages "impropriat." He holds that, with some diligence, flaws might be found in the titles of the "impropriators." He instances one case, that of Oliver Grace ("who is ye greatest Impropriator for number of benefices in my Dioces "), and points out how his title could be broken. The king did not take the bait.

The next complaint is best given in full: "Seventhly, I complain that there are divers *Abbies or Monasteries* dissolved in my Dioces, wherein yet ye people do bury theyr dead out of ye ordinary place of Christian buriall, to ye contempt of religion and maintenance of theyr superstition. And besides that, to these places many ffriars and Priests doe ordinarily resort, and sometimes in ye yeare great concourse of people publickly, as in the abbey of Quin in ye county of Clare; and abbey of Inshenamcoh in ye county of Tiperary; and in Inishgealtragh or ye Island of Seven Altars standing in ye midst of ye river of Shanan, bordering ye county of Galway."

The good bishop is indignant that most of the officers under the sheriffs—nay, that the sheriffs themselves—are sometimes recusants, and hence it follows:

"ffirst, they execute not truly ye Capias against Recusants indicted according to ye Statute of 20 Elizab. in this kingdom of Ireland, whereby God is dishonoured, religion made a scorne, and ye pious intendements of His Majesties lawes are frustrated"!

"secondly, they doe not truly execute ye writ de excommunicate capiendo wch sometimes I get forth against Recusants, with whom I have preceded, and other notorious offenders; but by theyr putting off ye said writ into ye hands of theyr Popish officers, ye parties offending p'santly have notice of it, and they doe shun that sheriff during his time: and at ye end of his yeare ye writ is not delivered over to ye next sheriffe; and so ye writ is lost, or concealed among them, to the contempt of religion." Those passages cannot be beaten by anything in Bret Harte or Mark Twain.

"The multitude of Popish priests," too, were giving him trouble—"hindering ye minister in ye worke of his calling, and drawing back those whom ye minister had formerly gained."

He finds out their names, and parishes, and places of residence, and "interteiners," and duly supplies them to His Majesty. Among them we find names familiar to us. John O'Halloran looked after Quin and Cluana; Hugh Hogan, a full namesake of the Protestant Dean, had charge of Kilmore. Thomas Oge Gorman wickedly entertained Teig O'Rowhan in Kilmurry Clonderila, as did Murtagh O'Meahan his own son Loghlin in Kilmaley; and Donogh MacGilpatricke (Fitzpatrick now), Conor O'Daoine in Kilfarboy. Donnell MacBroodan gave up his writing history to risk his liberty and his life as parish priest of Kilnaboy and Kilkeady. Teigue Mac-Gilpatrick ran like risks for the people of Dromcliffe and Clarecastle, as did Donogh O'Malone in Kilmihil, Donogh O'Connor in Doura, and Donogh O'Loghlen in Killaloe. Father MacKennedy was sheltered by his own father in Kilmacduagh, and Teigue MacOwen by Henry Blackwell in Moyarta. William O'Clery was known to be in charge of Killurin and Clonilea, and Morgan O'Coman, of Kilfinaghta (Six Mile Bridge). These, with four or five others, whose names (excepting O'Haighshy of Quin Abbey, *Anglicè* Haugh) are not now recognisable, were all, out of the "multitude," the bishop could get tidings of in Clare; a fact which speaks well for the care with which the others were concealed. "One Nethemias Nestor, who tookt upon him to be ye Pope's Nuntio," cannot be more definitely located than "in ye baronies of Insiquin Burren and Corcomroe;" but Sir John MacNamara, Kt., is denounced for frequently harbouring an Irishman, "Mahoon MacGrath, Vicar-General from the Pope over ye whole diocese, who takes upon him to order priests and to dispense in cases of matrimony and other cases, as is to be shewne and proved." The zealous bishop was not to be blamed if, after such precise information, these Popish priests were allowed much longer "to goe on unbridled and unlimited in theyr wicked and superstitious courses." He is naturally very wroth at "ye despising of my jurisdiction to wch very few are obedient at this day. Priests and Popish lawyers who hold ye people in hand yt there shall be liberty of conscience;" and blames the recalling of certain warrants for the fact that "ye natives that came to church in severall parishes are all gone backe again." The coercion of that day in matters religious had the same effect that coercion in politics has in our own time. It ends in failure.

It is not easy to discover how far the bishop's requests were complied with. We have, however, on record that the king, in June 1620, granted him and his successors " the territory called Termon-i-grady als Tomgrany, containing twenty-one qrs. of ploughlands."

This document throws a flood of light on the face of Clare at the beginning of the transition period. It reveals the heartless system of plunder which was sprung upon the people in the sacred name of religion. They not only saw their churches in ruins, their clergy proscribed, their faith mocked as a superstition, but they found themselves also subjected to a constant drain in the shape of fines, as long as they refused to play the part of hypocrites. It may be questioned whether even Mahomet's methods were not preferable. He did not adopt any disguise. With sword in hand, he thrust the Koran down the throats of the vanquished. Here, however, there was the pretence of a process by law. The mere Irish had no good cause of complaint, whereas their consciences were duly regulated for them by statutes of Henry VIII., Queen Elizabeth, and their anointed successors.

King James was not satisfied with the plantation of Ulster. The flight of the earls gave him and his ravenous courtiers an excuse for the forfeiture of the counties over which they and their ancestors for twenty centuries had ruled. The English and Scotch cities and towns were scoured of their most worthless inhabitants, in order to provide sound Protestants as "undertakers" for the 385,000 acres out of which the "mere Irish," now that their natural leaders had left them, were ruthlessly driven. This was not enough. The defeat of the Earl of Desmond had left most of South Munster in the hands of the English, and it only remained to take over Clare and Connaught. It was found that the English titles to the clan lands, accepted by the Clare chiefs in 1585, were not duly registered. Here, then, was the opportunity at hand. An attempt to rectify the mistake, backed up by a sum of three thousand pounds, did not succeed; and so, when Charles came to the throne at the death of James in 1625, he found the whole county in as unsettled a condition, from the legal point of view, as a rapacious king and court could desire. The Earl of Thomond, whose whole history is a blot upon the national character, had also passed away; and it is a significant fact that, notwithstanding his lifelong service to the English and Protestant cause, even his family claims were not considered secure. This may be inferred from the fact that his younger son, Sir Barnabas,—a new name, given plainly in compliment to the new religion,—was prominent among the discontented. Sir Thomas Wentworth, Lord Deputy, allowed the growing feeling of uncertainty to seethe on, with ulterior objects in view.

The conspiracy against the rights of the Clare Catholics came to a head in the year 1637. Secretary Coke writes to the Lord Deputy from Whitehall[1] on the 3rd of May: "You may take the opportunity the time offers to you to go on with the plantation in the county of Clare, and from His Majesty you may expect encouragement and support." Lest he should cool down, he is spurred on, a few weeks later, on the 17th of June: "If you clear anything in the county of Clare, the study is well employed, and you may believe His Majesty doth not think you to be asleep, when he heareth you have watched almost your eyes out of your head." It is no matter for regret that the eyes of both plotters, and the heads with them, went out on the block some time afterwards. He did not sleep in the project, as is proved by a letter dated 15th August 1537, in which he writes: "His Majesty's title to the two Ormonds is found. I am most confident we shall have like success for Clare, where we are able to make a clear and undoubted title of ourselves." In this plot to rob all round, the Earl of Thomond, a true son of his father, was busily engaged. "My Lord of Thomond," writes Strafford on the 23rd of August, "Lieutenant-Governor of that county, hath been exceeding diligent and forward in this service; not only leading himself, but persuading others into this good conformity." "Good conformity," writes the layman— "God's honour and obedience to His Majesty," wrote the cleric Rider a short time before—and both to cover as unscrupulous and unjust plunder as the history of any country records.

[1] *Strafford Letters*, vol. ii. p. 76.

The events of the next four years in Clare were so unimportant as to call for little if any notice. The people were crushed. The renegade Earls of Thomond made combination among the clans for the purpose of defence impossible. Religious and political persecution had full swing, and dull despair took the place of the old Dalcassian activity. An English ecclesiastic named Bramhall, who became afterwards Bishop of Derry, accompanied Wentworth, now Earl of Strafford, into Clare, to spy out defects in title.

Meanwhile Charles was getting into trouble with his Scotch and English subjects. A Parliament was convoked in Dublin, with the view of strengthening the king's hands. While willing enough to vote supplies which taxed the people, the members of this Parliament wrangled mostly about their own personal titles and privileges. They could not properly be called representatives, so limited was the franchise. Many of them, among others two O'Briens, scrambled in more for the purpose of defeating the designs of Strafford and Bramhall upon the claims they had set up on their own part so unjustly against their clansmen, under the arrangement with Sir John Perrot, than to secure the public good. Strafford was called back to counsel the king, whose despotic rule had driven first the Scotch, afterwards the English, into open rebellion. In his absence the members for Clare in Parliament had little difficulty in counteracting the plantation policy, but the march of events was now so rapid, that its sittings were brought abruptly to an end. Before, however, dissolving, this Parliament of 1640 presented to the Lord Deputy a complaint of "the many grievous exactions, pressures, and vexatious proceedings of some of the clergy of this kingdom, and their officers and ministers, against the laity, especially the poorer sort, to the great impoverishment and general detriment of the whole kingdom." Then follow the specific complaints. The nineteenth runs as follows, and will give a fair idea of the rest, as well as of the spirit in which the preachers of the new religion approached the down-trodden people:—

"19. From a poor man that hath but one cow they take that for a mortuary. From one that is better off, his best garment for a mortuary, if a woman her best garment. And a gallon of drink for every brewing by name of Mary gallons. Then come hide and tallow and lamb-muttoe, soul-money, portion-canons, Patrick's-ridges, rood sheaves, book-money, beggars' mortuaries, and parish-boundary dues."[1] This was but a part of what the English invasion of Clare brought upon its inhabitants. Can any one wonder, after perusing this parliamentary document alone, at the uprising of 1641? In other parts of the kingdom the provocation was still greater. This is how the king's archbishop, Adam Loftus, writes on the 16th of February 1641: "We have indited of treason all the noblemen, gentlemen, and freeholders in the counties of Dublin, Meath, Kildare, and Wicklow, which I hope will be a great advantage to the crown, and good to this poor kingdom, when those rascals shall be confounded, and honest Protestants planted in their places."[2] I do but touch upon a few of these State Paper revelations. Few as they are, they are quite sufficient as an explanation of the fierce religious and race animosity which has ever since subsisted between the English intruders and the native Irish.

[1] *Journal of the House of Commons*, A.D. 1640, p. 248, second edition.
[2] State Papers. Letter to Sir R. King.

CHAPTER XX.

FROM 1641 TO 1646.

The Rising—Sieges of Ballyalla, Inchicronan, and Tromoroe—Swearing of Affidavits—Curious Incidents—Proposed Extermination of Catholics—John O'Malony of Killaloe surprised near Quin—Siege of Bunratty—Cardinal Rinuncini—His Description of Bunratty—Thomond freed once more of the Foreigners.

IF ever a revolt was justifiable in any country, it was that of 1641 in Ireland. The grievances of the English and Scotch against Charles I. were but sentimental when compared with those of the native Irish and Catholic Anglo-Irish against the English Government of that day. The revolt began in Ulster, which had just been partitioned out among adventurers, most of them taken from the lowest class in English and Scotch towns and cities. Though not to the same extent, the same policy of plunder and Protestant plantation had been carried out over a great part of South Munster. We have seen how Adam Loftus had been plotting with the English court, in the beginning of that year, for the indictment, on a charge of treason, " of all the noblemen, gentlemen, and freeholders of Dublin, Meath, Kildare, and Wicklow," in order to " confound these rascals, and plant honest Protestants in their places." Only Clare and Connaught remained. The plan adopted for these was to bribe into submission the most powerful, as they were the most subservient, of the native proprietors, and, having thus warded off organised opposition, to take one-fourth of their lands from all the rest. We have this under the king's own hand to Strafford, from "Westminster, 2nd March, in the 15th year of our reign."[1] The latter had reported " the readiness shown by Morrogh, Baron of Inchiquin, to advance and further the plantation in the

---
[1] State Papers.

county of Clare," wherefore "we are pleased to extend our grace to him, that he may not, in course of plantation, have the fourth part of his lands in that county taken from him as from the others, the natives there." The same favour was extended to the Earl of Thomond.

No sooner did he succeed to the title, than he began to follow in the footsteps of his brother and father. His efforts to plant English and Protestant settlers in Clare were not, however, very successful. Lord Clanrickard writes of him to the king in January 1641: "My Lord President of Connaught is forced to retire to the castle of Athlone. . . . My Lord of Thomond is in little better condition, as I am informed, and all his English and Dutch plantations forsaken." The revolt did indeed interfere with and retard for a time their pretty scheme of wholesale plunder, but only to render it, later on, more general and more effective.

The mine thus laid in all parts of Ireland, north, south, east, and west, by the English, sprang upon themselves towards the end of this fateful year. Before describing its effects in Clare, it may not be amiss to quote what the best living authority, fresh from a long and exhaustive study of the State Papers of the period, himself a Protestant, J. P. Prendergast, B.L., says of this struggle. It had been the fashion with English writers, as indeed it still is with the majority of them, to speak of it quite confidently as "the Irish Massacre." This he calls "an historical falsehood."[1] And when taken to task for this by a writer of such mark as W. Goldwin Smith, he replies: "But even supposing his (Smith's) conclusion to be right, he still commits a great injustice by using such terms as that 'the Catholics had begun the war by a great massacre of Protestants,' for he then includes in the charge three-fourths of the inhabitants of Ireland of that religion, who were entirely free from it, even by the admission of their enemies, as the scene was confined to Ulster. And if the Irish of Ulster, being Catholics, and, by his own statement, 'deeply wronged and oppressed' by the English, being Protestants, were thus forced into resistance and rebellion, it is surely misleading to

[1] *Cromwellian Settlement*, second edition, Preface.

speak of a massacre of Protestants by Catholics, instead of English by Irish. They were attacked, not as heretics, but as oppressors — not as Protestants, but as plunderers."[1] What a loss to Ireland — yes, and to England too — that there are not more Prendergasts and fewer Goldwin Smiths!

As far as can be ascertained, there is no proof whatever forthcoming that this general uprising was preconcerted. The fuel for it was there, and it but needed the touch of the match to cause the conflagration. When the news was spread of the success of the Northerns, the Catholics, whether of Irish or English blood, took heart, and determined to make one bold effort to recover the property of which they had been plundered. There is no reason to doubt that they drove out, wherever they could, the Protestants who had so lately forcibly intruded themselves on their lands. These, flying in terror, circulated absurd stories of a general massacre, accompanied by the most disgusting cruelties, including even cannibalism. The cold light of impartial history has stripped the rising of all these ghastly details; laying bare, however, as might well be expected, a sufficiently exciting picture of widespread violence; attended in only too many instances, where force met force, with bloodshed. Terrible as it certainly was, how far it fell short of the well-authenticated, cold, measured cruelty of the Cromwellian suppression a few years after!

It is not easy to come at the facts of this struggle, as the Protestants, when victorious, found it their interest to magnify their losses. It was the surest way to secure a share of the spoil. The wildest and most absurd stories of pillage and murder were set afloat, and were sworn to. We will examine into some of these as we proceed.

The first contest in Clare took place at the castle of Ballyalla, near Ennis. An Ennis merchant named Cuffe, ancestor of the present Earl of Desart, had a lease of this castle from Sir Valentine Blake, probably as payment for goods. How Blake himself came to own it is not specified. The few Protestants who were in Ennis and around fled there for safety. One of the MacNamaras proceeded to the North,

[1] *Cromwellian Settlement,* second edition, Preface, viii.

in the hope of being supplied with cannon to assault this and any other castles that might be held for the English. At this time, so well had the work of plundering the native Irish been carried on, that no less than thirty-one of the castles of Clare were, nominally at least, owned by Englishmen; among whom, not without reason, were reckoned the Earl of Thomond and Donogh O'Brien of Newtown.[1] The only other names appearing in this list, that would be now recognised in Clare, are those of "Luke Brady, Esq., Toumgraney; Richard Keaton, Balenacragen; William Costolow, Lisofin; James Marten, Castell Keale; and George Colpis, Balycare." We find mention, however, in the narrative of William and John Bridgman, the sons-in-law of Parson Twimbrock (whose deposition is worth notice, and will be given later on), and Mr. Hickman and Mr. Burton, as being deprived of their cattle and goods by Colonel Connor O'Brien of Lemaneigh and Teigue O'Brien of Dromore Castle.

MacNamara failed to secure the cannon, so the siege of Ballyalla had to be carried on in a very primitive manner indeed. We have a description of it from Cuffe's own pen. The castle "had a reasonable strong wall, and well provided notwithstanding the country's malles (? misfortunes probably), as the poorer sort of people, specially some of Mrs. Cuffe's and her son's tenants, would furnish privately with some fresh provision for money, as hennes egges, geese, lambs, and the like. This, however, is put a stop to."

On the 21st of February, Captain H. O'Grady summoned the castle in the name of the king to surrender, but was fired on and wounded by "Andrew Chaplin, minister." This was a declaration of war to the knife. Having no ordnance, the besiegers put together a large wooden structure on wheels, thirty-five feet long and nine feet broad. This was euphoniously termed "a great sowe," under shelter of which to approach and endeavour to undermine the castle. It had a highly pitched roof, "covered over with two rows of hides and two rows of sheepskins, so that no musket bullet or steel arrow could pearse it, of which trial often was made."

---

[1] *Narratives of the Contests in Ireland in* 1641 *and* 1691. Printed in London for the Camden Society.

They made also a " leathern piece of ordenance about five feet in length, which, being loaded with 13 lbs. of powdhar," it is needless to say, burst at the first discharge. With such appliances no progress could be made, and so the siege had to be raised.

Towards the end of the same year, another attempt was made, and this time a successful one, by Donal O'Brien of Leimaneigh, and Teigue Roe O'Brien, brother to Lord Inchiquin, to capture the castle. It was again defended with great spirit; but, provisions failing, and one of the Cuffes having been captured, and a gallows erected before the castle, upon which to hang him and other prisoners, it was at last surrendered on the 26th of September 1642.

It speaks well for the humanity of the Irish that no revenge was taken upon the prisoners who fell into their hands. There is not so much as a hint of cruelty to the prisoners, much less of a butchery like that which took place after the capture of the castles of Dunboy and Glin. Even the parson Chaplin, who shot O'Grady at the first parley, was allowed to escape. He made a deposition afterwards, in which he accuses the Earl of Thomond of aiding the insurgents; but it is easy to infer, from the terms in which the charge is made, that he only interfered to protect the people of the county from the violence of the well-armed and organised English. In another deposition, made by Edward Mainwairing, the same charge is repeated. It is not at all unlikely that the design was to have his huge property also confiscated. It was well known that, before the title fell to him at the death of his brother, his leanings were with the Irish and Catholic cause.

The castle of Inchicronan was taken by a joint force of the O'Gradys and the O'Shaughnessys. A sortie made by the besieged was repulsed with loss, upon which the place was surrendered.

Colonel Ed. O'Flaherty came across from the Arran islands and laid siege to the castle of Tromoroe, which was then held by Peter Ward. They stormed it from Sunday night to Wednesday morning. Ward's wife was killed by a chance shot through the window. His son held a parley

with O'Flaherty. The latter offered them (the parish priest
—the Unionist of that day—being, curiously enough, of the
number) their lives, but Ward obstinately refused to surrender.
He was soon overpowered and slain, and the castle taken and
plundered. Some of those captured asked to be allowed
to go in safety to the house of Richard White, of Kilmurry,
where they found shelter.[1] This does not look like the
savage warfare described in the depositions.

A little careful inquiry into those depositions will disclose
the fact that they were, for the most part, bold efforts of the
imagination. When it is borne in mind that money in those
days was at least five times its present value, the losses sworn
to must have been very great indeed. They exceed, in fact,
all belief. For instance, William Chambers, of Kilrush,
British Protestant, swears he was robbed of his goods and
chattels, worth £1519, also his cattle; and Max Graneer,
Dutch settler, declares his loss at £2389! while bitterly
complaining of the violence of Charles and Owen O'Cahane.
Ann Usher, of Killimer, swears she was robbed of goods to
the value of £994. "And after many raids upon her cattle
and garrons, her house was rifled and pillaged by Charles
O'Cahane of Termon. *Jurat*." George Waters, British Protestant (a strong claim that), had taken from him £2047,
and John Pring, of Latoon, £1354, etc. Multiplying these
figures by ten, or, even at the lowest computation, by five,
one would not find in the Clare of to-day many of its
inhabitants so blessed with the world's goods as were, at
their own showing, those Protestant settlers of 1641.

Here is another specimen too good to be passed over. The
Reverend John Twembrooke, of Dysert, swears "he was, last
Christmas, robbed and despoiled of goods and chattels to his
loss and damage in £348, besides his church living, worth
£200 per annum, cows, horses, mares, heifers, turf, books,
linens, woollens, hay, corn, leases, debts, by T. O'Brien of
Tullamore." In the return of Bishop Rider, already referred
to at some length, this parson's living is put down as £20 per
annum. Which of the two statements is the correct one?
Nor is he entirely absorbed in his monetary losses. His

[1] O'Flaherty's *West Connaught*. Edited by Mr. Hardiman.

religious instincts are alive. He denounces, on oath, the following: "John Love, Thesaurus of Kilfenora; Patrick Lysaght of Ballywire, Chancellor of same; Owen Nellane of Killaspuglinane, clerk; O'Hirley, Vicar of Glanina, and divers others; Robert Cox, clerk, and Pierce Butler near Cashel, clerk—all of them, since the rebellion, turned Papist as this deponent is credibly informed. *Jurat,* 24th June 1642." (Dep. 472.)

The swearing goes on in all parts of Clare. James Vandeleur swears (792) to a loss of £1836, and names O'Brien of Dromore, MacNamara of Rossroe, MacNamara of Cratloe, and MacNamara, Ralahine, as the delinquents. It is significant that Vandeleurs are owners of Ralahine at the present; but where is that branch of the MacNamara clan?

Again, we find a good strong oath recorded (788) of William Culliner, Barony of Bunratty, shoemaker and British Protestant—none of your mere Irish. He is robbed and despoiled to the value of £132, 8s. Shoemaking must have been a profitable business in the Clare of that day. I fear no one with such a hoard could be found in Bunratty now. He carefully adds on the 8s., to save his conscience of course, and then "further saith"— But this must be passed over; it is too hotly spiced for present consumption. He comes down, too, on some who relapsed back into Papistry, and sets the Puritan zealots on their track.

Anthony Heathcote was a sorely-tried man. If his story, on oath, can be credited, he had amassed among the wild savages of Clare property to the value of £3278, or say from £15,000 to £30,000 of our money, and all this was swept away from him. But the worst treated man of the whole lot was Gregory Hickman of Barntick, in the parish of Clare, a British Protestant. He enters into a long description of his woes, all on oath. The wife of O'Hehir of Cahir came with her servants and took away his poultry, household stuff, furniture, worth at least £10, not even leaving him his own brass kettles. O'Brien of Ballymacooda threshed his corn under his nose. O'Grady Rhua drove away his cattle. His wool was plundered from him. His servants were either murdered, or else stripped naked and couverted into rebels! Boetius Clancy, the model English-Irishman, seized upon his cows, his bull, and his gelding. And what all these left after them, Conor O'Brien, gentleman, of Leimaneigh, " in a most rebellious manner " laid hands on. He took deponent's corn, and wickedly turned the same to his own use. He seized on four hundred of his sheep; and, to crown all, his wife, the famous Mauria Rhua, came with MacLaughlin Oge and one MacCasey, yeoman, and marched off at the tails of his fourteen English pigs (" British Protestant " had to be dropped in this connection), together with his household stuff. He estimates the loss of all these goods and chattels at the modest figure of £3672, 7s. 8d. to the penny! With *jurat* at the end, the seal of accuracy, which it would be rank heresy to call into question, is fixed to the doleful tale. If W. Gregory Hickman did not fall in for a good share of the confiscated lands of Clare, it was not for want of making a good case. He took some satisfaction, however; in denouncing divers relapsed Papists, especially the aforesaid Rev. Patrick Lysaght; and in deposing to the hanging of four men by John O'Griffen, while O'Hehir, whose wife took away his household goods, looked on from horseback.

Many more such "depositions," made in all parts of Clare, could be quoted, but those few will suffice to give a fair idea of the commotion in the county resulting from the 1641 rising. If all that was told of it be true, one asks how so many who were at the mercy of the Irish, lived to tell their tales. Mr. Prendergast, admittedly the most accurately informed and best living authority on the subject, in his invaluable work, *The Cromwellian Settlement*, quotes the report of the Commission, dated 23rd December 1641, and argues from it in the following unanswerable manner against the long-prevailing legend of a general barbarous massacre:[1] " It was, in its original form, to take an account of the losses. It was amended on the 18th January 1642 to include murders, so that was an afterthought, a thing scarcely possible

[1] *Crom. Set.* p. 60, quoting from the originals in the "Remonstrance" by Doctor Henry Jones, Agent for the Protestant Clergy of Ireland. London, 1642.

if there had been a general massacre. The first Commission recites 'that many British and Protestants have been separated from their habitations, and others deprived of their goods;' the Commissioners are accordingly to examine upon oath concerning the amount of loss, the names of the robbers, and what traitorous speeches were uttered by the robbers or others. The second adds, 'and what violence was done by the robbers, and how, and what numbers have been murthered, or have perished afterwards, on the way to Dublin or elsewhere.' And the Remonstrance shows that the outrages, in spite of the Commissioners' attempt to present the most terrible pictures, were for the most part only such as necessarily followed the stripping of the property of the English, and driving them from their possessions, as those planters had driven the Irish from theirs thirty years before; and that the murders were fewer than have occurred in similar insurrections, where, of course, some would be slain resisting the pillagers of their homesteads. The Commissioners seem unconscious of any general massacre." Any impartial reader can draw from the report of those Commissioners no other conclusion than that no reliance is to be placed on the raw-head and bloody-bones stories told in those depositions, of which only mild specimens are given above.

Most of the Anglo-Irish Catholics, finding that a design was on foot, as already related, to strip them of their lands and properties, threw in their fortunes with the insurgent Irish. Out of this union for their common interests sprung the celebrated Confederation of Kilkenny. Lord Mountgarret was chosen president. Owen O'Neill got command of the Northern forces, General Preston of those of Leinster, Colonel Burke of those of Connaught; while General Barry was in supreme command in Munster, with Sir Daniel O'Brien, uncle of the Earl of Thomond, in charge of Clare. The confederates professed loyalty to the king, but demanded the restoration of their plundered properties and freedom of Catholic worship, as they proclaimed similar freedom for Protestant worship. The Earl of Ormond was at this time General of the King's Forces in Ireland. The spirit in which their demands were met may be inferred from the following direction sent to the earl :[1]—

"It is resolved, That it is fit that his lordship do endeavour with His Majesty's forces, to wound, kill, slay, and destroy by all ways and means he may, all the said rebels, their adherents, and relievers; and burn, spoil, waste, consume, destroy, and demolish all the places, towns, and houses where the rebels are, or have been relieved and harboured; and all the hay and corn there; and kill and destroy all the men there inhabiting, capable to bear arms. Given at His Majesty's Castle of Dublin, 23rd February 1642.

" R. Dillon		Tho. Rotheram	Ad. Loftus
  F. Willoughby	J. Temple		Robert Meredith."

In reference to the above, Leland, a Protestant clergyman, says :[2] "In the execution of these orders the justices declare that the soldiers slew all persons promiscuously, not sparing the women, and sometimes not the children." Nothing of the kind is alleged against the Irish of Clare, as we have seen, when in fair open war Protestants fell into their hands. Some private acts of vengeance are spoken to, but no massacre or slaying of captives by the organised Irish force.

The Earl of Thomond took no part in the struggle. He retired into England, leaving his castles of Bunratty and Clare in the hands of the king's forces; in the former of which a sum of not less than £2000 was discovered, and, needless to add, turned to their own account. He afterwards tried, but failed, to have this regarded as a debt. He observed throughout a prudent caution, not making himself very obnoxious to the Irish, while appearing always on the side of the English.

The occupation of Limerick by the Confederate army under General Barry and Lord Muskerry, and the surrender of the castle when undermined some weeks after, left Clare as well as Limerick practically in the hands of the Irish. One check, however, they sustained in Clare. John O'Molony, Bishop of

[1] Carte's *Ormond*, vol. iii. p. 61.   [2] Leland's *Hist.* Book v.

Killaloe, while organising the Catholics near Quin, was surprised by the English from Bunratty, defeated with some loss, and very nearly captured.[1] The success of the Irish at and around Limerick could not therefore be regarded as assured while Bunratty remained in the hands of the English; so, though they were provided with but little ordnance for the assault on so strong a castle, it was determined at all hazards to capture it.

Meanwhile the struggle between the king and the Parliament was progressing in England. Ormond was directed to negotiate a peace with the army of the Confederation, so as to secure its services for the king. One of the conditions demanded by the Irish, and conceded by Ormond, was embodied in the Sixth Article of the peace in the following words: "That the plantation of Connaught, Kilkenny, Clare, Thomond, Tipperary, Limerick, and Wicklow, may be revoked by Act of Parliament, and their estates secured in the next sessions." This was but an act of justice. Had it been carried into effect by either the king or the parliamentarians, attended by freedom of worship, how much of the subsequent misery, and race-hatred, and bloodshed, would have been avoided! The two nations might have been linked in the bonds of peace, and would assuredly have grown happier and stronger side by side.

The conclusion of this peace changed the whole aspect of the war in Ireland. The Irish were henceforth fighting for the king, as well as for their own rights. As the garrison of Bunratty, consisting of 800 foot and 60 horse, under the command of Colonel M'Adam, and well supplied with provisions in view of the inevitable coming conflict, was on the side of the Parliament, it was necessary to besiege the place. A force of 3000 foot and 300 horse, under the command of Lord Muskerry, was sent into Clare for that purpose; and so important was the reduction of this fortress considered, that Cardinal Rinuncini himself, who had some time before been despatched from Rome with considerable supplies both in arms and money (2000 swords, 500 petronels, 20,000 lbs. of powder, and five or six small trunks of Spanish gold, all

---

[1] Carte's *Ormond*.

landed at Kenmare, after a narrow escape from an English ship of war), took his place among the troops. Not only have we a good idea of the size of this fortress and its outworks, from the fact that 800 foot and 60 horse, with the usual followers of such a force, were accommodated within it; but we have a picture of its internal appearance and surroundings from the pen of the Cardinal, showing how an Irish chieftain beyond the Shannon could support his style and dignity in those days.

"I have no hesitation in asserting," he writes, "that it is the most beautiful spot I have ever seen. In Italy there is nothing like the palace and grounds of the Lord of Thomond. Nothing like its ponds and park, with its 3000 head of deer."

And yet all in those parts were "wild Irish." The massive castle, still imposing even in ruin, standing on the Shannon, seven miles below Limerick, on the Clare side, tells its own tale.

The siege was protracted, owing as well to the naturally strong position of the castle as to the stubborn resistance offered by the garrison. It was open to the Shannon, from which supplies were poured in.

The river Raite, from which it takes its name, spreading out into marshes, encircled it on the south and east. The only assailable point was on the north-west, where a high spur of land overlooked the castle; and here a strong earthen mound was erected, upon which were placed four cannons. Muskerry had with him three officers of great ability, who had served for many years in the German wars—Major-General Stephenson, Lieutenant-General Purcell, and Colonel Purcell. The attack was maintained with great vigour, especially after the arrival of two pieces of heavy ordnance from Limerick. The besieged, on the other hand, did not confine themselves to a mere defence. They sallied out from time to time; and on one of these occasions had very nearly thrown the whole attacking force into confusion—the Irish outposts flying before them in a panic, for which Lord Muskerry court-marshalled and executed some of the leaders. The arrival of Cardinal Rinuncini in the camp threw great spirit into the troops. He went into the trenches, keeping up the courage of the men by sharing their danger. A constant fire was kept up day and night on the castle without making much impression. It so wearied, however, the defenders, that when their commander, Colonel MacAdam, was mortally wounded by a stray shot, they lost heart, and offered to surrender. On the twelfth day after his arival in the camp, the Cardinal had the satisfaction to receive the keys of the fortress, allowing the garrison to depart in their ships for Cork. Though no special mention is made of it, the castle of Clare also must have been included in the surrender. Leaving a sufficient force in the castles, he returned in triumph to Limerick, where the victory was celebrated by a solemn Mass and *Te Deum* in the cathedral. To add to their joy, news soon arrived of the capture of the castle of Roscommon by General Preston, and the great victory of Owen Roe O'Neill over Monroe, at Benburb, where no less than three thousand of the enemy were slain, with a loss on the Irish side of only seventy killed and two hundred wounded.[1] These rapid successes raised the hopes of the Confederate Catholics to the highest pitch. In the summer of 1646, Clare had not so much as an openly hostile foot on her soil.

[1] Haverty. To inflame the English mind, it was described in print on the walls of London as "the bloody fight at Blackwater on the 5th of June, by the Irish rebels against Major-General Monroe, when five thousand Protestants were put to the sword."

CHAPTER XXI.

FROM 1646 TO 1651.

Morogh na Thothaine—Cromwell—Ormond in Clare—Council of the Confederation takes refuge in Ennis—Ireton—Betrayal of the Irish Cause—Ludlow at Inchicronan—Surrender of Limerick—Mauria Rhua.

THERE looms up now, in the history of this protracted struggle, on the English side, a Clare man whose exploits have secured him the unenviable title of Morogh na Thothaine—"Morogh of the burnings." He was grandson of that Lord Inchiquin who lost his life, as already related, at the Erne, in the expedition against O'Donnell. Succeeding to the title while yet a minor, he was brought up, as a ward of the English crown, in the Protestant faith, and married, when he came of age, the daughter of Sir Anthony St. Leger, President of Munster. He was true to his training during the early period of his life, for never was there a more savage or bitter anti-Irishman. Having served for awhile on the Continent, he was appointed to a command under his father-in-law, and, having displayed great vigour and ability in repulsing an attack of the Irish on Cork in the April of 1642, he was entrusted by the Lords Justices, Sir John Borlase and Sir William Parsons, with the command of the army of Munster, vacant by the death of St. Leger, in the July of the same year. He was then but twenty-four years of age. He went to the king to solicit a formal appointment to the presidency of Munster, the duties of which he had been discharging since the death of his father-in-law; but, finding the Earl of Portland already named to it, he so resented the slight as to turn upon the king and take service under the Parliament. He addressed a Remonstrance to the Parliament against the truce for a year agreed upon in 1644 by Ormond on behalf of the king, and Muskerry for the Confederation; and received as his reward from the Parliament the prize he so coveted, being appointed President of Munster. As we shall see later on, the king's was not the only cause he betrayed. It was to him that his cousin, the Earl of Thomond, after refusing the terms offered him by Sir Daniel O'Brien of Carrigaholt, his uncle, and Daniel O'Brien of Duagh, on the part of the Confederation, had surrendered Bunratty before his departure for England, and with it a much-needed supply of good horses for cavalry. These he brought with him to his headquarters at Cork, leaving Colonel MacAdam, as already related, in command of a strong garrison. In the year following, 1647, he issued from Cork at the head of a well-appointed army, consisting of five thousand foot and fifteen hundred horse. With this force he had little difficulty in capturing the weakly-supplied fortresses of Dungarvan and Cappoquin. Receiving a large reinforcement of men and material from England, he next invested the strong fortress of Cahir.[1] A base stratagem enabled him to seize it with little loss. The commander of the garrison, yielding humanely to the entreaty of a wounded prisoner, allowed an English surgeon to be sent for. Inchiquin sent in disguise one of his officers, Colonel Hippsley, who had some surgical skill. He noted carefully the weakest point upon which an assault could be made, and, finding the garrison over-confident, he urged Inchiquin to surprise them by scaling the walls on the side which he found vulnerable. The assault succeeded beyond his most sanguine expectations. Flushed with these successes, he rushed upon Cashel. The inhabitants fled in terror to the cathedral on the Rock. Cooped up here, they were able to offer but a weak, disorganised resistance. They were literally butchered without mercy by fire and sword in the sacred sanctuary itself. History has no more bloody or infamous tale to tell than the slaughter by Inchiquin of about three thousand men, women, and children, in and around the cathedral of Cashel. Twenty priests were

---

[1] It was considered the strongest castle in Munster, and had held out for two months in Elizabeth's reign against Essex, with an army of twenty thousand men.

included in the massacre. Their blood bespattered the altars upon which they had often offered the Holy Sacrifice.

The news of this disaster filled the Confederates with fierce indignation. The Commander-in-Chief, Lord Taafe, was sent with a force of seven thousand foot and one thousand horse to intercept Inchiquin on the way to Cork. They met at Knocknoness, near Mallow, and here Inchiquin's superior skill and energy inflicted, with inferior numbers, enormous loss on his opponent. Nearly half the Confederate army was destroyed, and all, or nearly all, their war material fell into his hands. The Parliament, elated at this victory, voted £10,000 to carry on the war, and £1000 to Inchiquin himself.

It was his last victory in the cause of the Parliament. Once more, for reasons which it is not necessary to probe, he changed front. Negotiations were set on foot with the Marquis of Ormond on behalf of the king; and when that nobleman landed in Cork, on the 29th of September 1648, Inchiquin brought over his force with him to the side of the king, but only to learn soon after that the king was beheaded. The step taken was, however, irrevocable, and he soon gave proof of zeal in the Royalist cause. He is next heard of surprising and cutting to pieces with his cavalry a strong detachment sent by the Parliamentary General Jones from Dublin to reinforce Drogheda. That fortress, after a short siege, fell into his hands. He next rushed upon Dundalk, compelling Monk, the future restorer of the English monarch, to surrender it to him. It was his last notable success. The king's cause being completely lost in England, Cromwell was sent over to take supreme command in Ireland of the Parliamentary forces. Inchiquin, leaving garrisons in those towns, returned southwards to confer with Ormond, and the notable events following quickly after the arrival of Cromwell pushed him out of public life in Ireland.

Inchiquin died a Catholic in 1674, at the, for so varied a career, early age of fifty-six. He was, by his own request, buried in St. Mary's Cathedral in Limerick.[1]

[1] While repairs were being effected some years ago in the cathedral, a coffin covered with frieze was dug up. On opening, no remains were

The new title of Earl of Inchiquin was continued in his descendants. In 1800, Morogh, the fifth earl, was created Marquis of Thomond, the elder branch of the O'Briens having been extinct since 1741.[1] The title did not last long. By the death without issue, in 1846, of William, Marquis of Thomond, the house of Morogh the Burner was wiped off the face of the earth.

We have now to return to the regular sequence of events in the county itself. The comparative calm which followed upon the capture of Bunratty and the occupation by Irish troops of the castle of Clare, continued for about two years. It was only the lull before the storm. The coming of Cromwell was an end of it. Cruel and savage and sanguinary as Inchiquin was, his exploits paled before the ruthless deeds of this psalm-singing apostle of the Reformation.

" I believe we put the whole number of the defendants to the sword. I do not think thirty of the whole number escaped with their lives. Those that did are in safe custody for Barbadoes. . . . And now give me leave to say how it comes to pass that this work is wrought. It was set upon our hearts that a great thing should be done, not by power or might, but by the Spirit of God. And is it not so already? Thereupon is it good that God alone should have all the glory." This is his own description of the massacre of Drogheda, in which not only the armed defendants, about three thousand of the flower of the Irish army, but women and children,[2] young and old, were for five days and nights butchered without mercy. Hence onward during his stay in

---

found within. It is believed to have been Morogh O'Brien's, and that his body was taken from it by night and flung into the river by some of the citizens, who regarded it as desecrating the holy place.

[1] "It—the earldom of Thomond—was revived A.D. 1756 in the person of Percy Windham, the nephew-in-law of the last lineal marquis, to whom it was made to appear, by a forged will, that he left the reversion of his estates. But the title became extinct with him in 1774 (as Brian Boru was glad to see)."—O'Donovan's *Letters, R. I. A. Ord. Sur.* p. 104.

[2] This was but carrying out the enactment of the English Parliament quoted in Borlase's *Rebellion,* p. 139, and Hughes' *Abridgment of Acts,* p. 165. Borlase significantly adds, p. 214, "The order of the Parliament was exceeding well executed."—*Vid.* Fr. Murphy's *Cromwell in Ireland,* p. 184.

Ireland his cry was, No quarter, wherever the slightest resistance was offered. Wexford next fell into his hands, affording him another opportunity to emphasise his policy of indiscriminate slaughter. These evidences of inhuman barbarity produced a widespread terror. With the exception of Waterford, the siege of which he was obliged to raise, nearly all the Southern strongholds surrendered. Even Kilkenny, so long the centre of the Confederation, made little better than a show of resistance, owing in no small degree to the ravages of a pestilence within its walls. He next turned his attention to Clonmel, where he for the first time met with a serious repulse. The brave commander of the garrison, Hugh O'Neill, nephew of Owen Roe, hurled back his troops again and again from the walls. So impressed was he with the bravery and stubbornness of the defenders, having lost nearly three thousand of his soldiers, that he gladly offered favourable terms to the mayor for the surrender of the town. His chagrin may be imagined, when, on entering the town, he discovered that the garrison, under Hugh O'Neill, having, in common with the townspeople, concluded that the fortress could not hold out any longer,[1] had slipped away under cover of night to Waterford. The way to Limerick and Clare was now made clear; but just then despatches reached him, urging his immediate return to England, where a storm from the North was threatening. He sailed from Youghal at the end of May 1650, leaving the completion of his work in the hands of one as fanatic and ruthless as himself, his son-in-law Ireton. Before leaving, however, he tried to secure the neutrality of Limerick, offering the citizens freedom of religion and the secure possession of their property, on condition of their allowing his troops to pass into Clare,[2] where Ormond's army was located. These terms having been rejected, Ireton had only to fight his way into the doomed county.

The first practical intimation the people of Clare got of the turning of the tide of war towards them, was the flight into

[1] "After a siege of nearly two months, both ammunition and provisions had run out."—Father Murphy's *Cromwell*, p. 337.

[2] Carte's *Ormond*.

Ennis of the Parliament of Kilkenny,[1] followed soon after by Ormond's forces. So much was he distrusted, though fighting on the same side, that he would not be allowed within the walls of Limerick, and on Clare was thrown the burden of supplying this, almost the last, remnant of the Royalist army. The Irish bishops, among them John O'Molony, gave voice to the general mistrust by calling on Ormond to resign, and as he refused, sentence of excommunication was pronounced against all who would recognise his authority. The Bishop of Killaloe summoned to his aid his Clare kinsmen. They were directed to meet near Quin; but Ormond promptly despatched Colonel Wogan with sufficient force to mar this movement.

Before the Claremen could organise, they were set upon and dispersed—the bishop himself being taken prisoner. Not less than fourteen hundred pounds, a considerable sum in those days, probably committed to him for war purposes, fell into Ormond's hands. Content with his success, and too politic to excite further odium, he released[2] the bishop.

Meanwhile Ireton was preparing for the siege of Limerick, where the brave Hugh O'Neill held command. Desiring to invest it on all sides, he detached a strong force to seize the pass at Killaloe. Ormond had given Lord Castlehaven two thousand men to watch and defend the Shannon from Killaloe to Doonas. The ease with which the Cromwellians crossed the river in the face of so many well-disciplined troops, gives colour to the charge of treachery brought against the Royalist officers, Captain Kelly and Colonel Fennell, who were in immediate command at O'Brien's Bridge and Killaloe. The earthworks thrown up for the defence of those passes were abandoned almost without a blow. The disheartened Royalists retreated into the county of Galway, without apparently being aware of the fact that Ludlow was at the same time investing the castle of Gurteensheguara, near Gort, and almost in their line of march towards the city of Galway. Had they been able to intercept and dispose of Ludlow, the siege of Limerick

---

[1] Two of the MacNamaras, Daniel of Doon and John of Moyriesk, had represented Clare in the Supreme Council of the Confederation.

[2] Carte's *Ormond*.

might have ended differently. He, however, succeeded in an assault on the castle, after a brave defence, and, sweeping Burren and North Clare of cattle and provisions, brought timely aid to Ireton's army. Colonel David Roche had crossed into Clare with a view to collect, if possible, a force sufficient to fall on Ireton's flank. He secured the hearty co-operation of Conor O'Brien of Leimaneigh, who had been appointed Commander-in-Chief of Clare by Lord Inchiquin. Before the hastily summoned Claremen could be fully organised, Ludlow was despatched to attack them. An encounter took place at the pass of Inchicronan, which was vigorously defended [1] by O'Brien. His men, seeing him fall early in the fight mortally wounded, retreated precipitately, bringing with them the body of their chief. Ludlow, satisfied with this success, which he rightly judged would hinder any further interference with the operations on the Clare side of Limerick, returned to Ireton's aid. The city was now invested on all sides—the troops under Lord Muskerry sent to raise the siege on the Limerick side having been defeated by Lord Broghill.

It is no part of the purpose of this history to enter into the details of the siege. Suffice it to say that, after a gallant defence, made doubly difficult by the ravages of a frightful plague in the city, and the treachery of Fennell, who contrived in some unaccountable way to get command of John's Gate, looking towards Clare, and threatened to open it to the enemy, a parley was sounded. O'Brien, Bishop of Emly, who was the soul of the defence, offered to give himself up, if the lives of others less obnoxious to Ireton were spared. The latter, knowing well to what an extremity the city was reduced, insisted on excluding from pardon all who would be proved to have been prominently opposed to capitulation; and these hard terms had to be accepted. The troops under arms were allowed to march out; those willing to reside in the city were promised protection of life and property; but twenty-two, including Bishops O'Brien and O'Dwyer, and Generals Hugh O'Neill and Purcell, were condemned to death. Hugh O'Neill's life was spared, not by Ireton, but by the council of officers. Bishop O'Dwyer escaped. He was suspected of having made

[1] Ludlow's *Memoirs*, vol. i. p. 360.

private terms with the English for his own safety. Bishop O'Brien and all the others were executed—the bishop publicly reproaching Ireton for his cruelty and bloodthirsty bigotry, and summoning him in the most solemn manner to final judgment for his crimes. Within a month[1] this fanatic died miserably of the plague, raving of the murdered bishop.

With the fall of Limerick on the 27th of October 1651, the resistance to the Cromwellian invasion of Clare and Connaught practically collapsed. Ludlow turned his attention to the only two strongholds in Clare still garrisoned for the Irish and Catholic cause—Clarecastle and Carrigaholt. So disheartened were their defenders, that, when summoned by him, they made scarcely any show of resistance. Both surrendered, and then Clare lay at the feet of the invader. As evidence of the terror generally felt, it may be mentioned that the notorious Mauria Rhua, daughter of MacMahon of Clonderalaw and wife of Conor O'Brien of Leimaneigh, who fell at Inchicronan, when her castle was seized on and garrisoned by Ludlow,[2] rode down to Limerick after him, and offered herself, as token of complete submission, in marriage to any officer selected by him. The curious offer was accepted, and in this way a Colonel Cooper came to be installed at Leimaneigh, as the successor of the unfortunate Conor O'Brien. There are those who think, judging from what is traditionally told of Mauria Rhua's character, that the property was dearly purchased.

[1] On the 26th of November 1651, just four weeks to a day.
[2] Having raided Burren for the second time on this occasion, Ludlow wrote of it : "It was a country in which there was not water enough to drown a man, wood enough to hang him, nor earth enough to bury him, which last is so scarce that the inhabitants steal it from one another."

CHAPTER XXII.

FROM 1651 TO 1690.

Formation of the Irish Brigade—Second Great Confiscation—Expulsion of Priests—Destruction of Clare Castles—Families transported to Clare—Partial Recovery of Properties at the Restoration of the Monarchy—Bishops of Killaloe—Curious Lettings—Clare Representatives in King James' First Parliament—Burgesses of Ennis—Officers of King James—Battle of the Boyne—Athlone—Limerick—Sarsfield—Clare's Share in the Defence.

VÆ VICTIS.[1] The country was now entirely subjugated. With the surrender of Limerick and Galway the ten years' war was at an end. Over thirty thousand Irish soldiers accepted the terms offered them, and, laying down their arms in Ireland, were carried over the sea to serve in the armies of the Continent. The terms of surrender of the Brigade of Thomond were made by Major-General Sir Hardress Waller, Colonel Peter Stubbs, commanding the Royalist English forces in Clare, Colonel Thomas Sadler, Lieutenant-Colonel John Nelson, Governor of Killaloe, and the rest of the council of war, on the English side; and Colonel Mortogh O'Brien, Colonel Daniel MacNamara, and Lieutenant-Colonel James FitzGerald, on the part of the Irish, now being formed into the well-known Brigade. The substance of these conditions was that acts of war, as distinct from murder, were not to be indictable, and that the "Romanist clergy in orders," having *no other crime* laid to their charge than officiating as priests,

---

[1] At Nenagh, in 1651, there were executed four O'Briens of the old ruling stock, Donogh, James, Bernard, and Daniel, as well as two O'Kennedys, James and John, both of noble birth. In Limerick, Major-General Purcell; Fanning and Stritch, mayors; Barron and Galway, knights, with others, shared the same fate. In Galway, Tralee, and all the chief towns, men of most note were done to death. The crime of having fought well was all-sufficient.—*Morrisonii Threnodia.*

shall have liberty and passes to go beyond the sea. Thus was the first flight of the Wild Geese from Clare settled upon. Then came the rush for plunder. Two sets of claimants made their appearance—the adventurers who had given money to carry on the war, and the officers and soldiers who had engaged in it. The former had been promised one thousand acres of good land in Ulster for every £200, in Munster for every £450, and in Leinster for every £600. To meet these claims, as well as those of the men who engaged in the war, all the lands of the defeated Irish Catholics were seized. Those of the latter who escaped death or banishment to the Barbadoes were ordered to remove with such property as was left them into Clare and Connaught, where portions of the confiscated deserted lands were allotted to them. All priests and bishops were ordered out of the country, under pain of death at sight, and any Catholic found outside the Shannon line of boundary after the term allowed for transplantation, May 1654, had elapsed, was also declared liable to death by an Act of Parliament passed on the 26th of September 1653. The design plainly was to make Ulster, Leinster, and Munster entirely Protestant, and to starve out Catholicity for want of pastors in Clare and Connaught. The Cromwellian policy towards Catholics found apt expression in the well-known phrase, "To hell or to Connaught."

Clare was reduced almost to a wilderness. Famine followed on the footsteps of war to the degree that, if a contemporary writer [1] is to be believed, not only did the unfortunate people resort to horse-flesh for food, but in their extremity, in some cases, used even human flesh. Only about forty townlands out of thirteen hundred, and these mostly in the barony of Bunratty,[2] could be said to be inhabited in the June of 1653. To make the desolation more complete, an order was issued to destroy nearly all the castles. Commissioners sat at Loughrea to superintend these operations,[3] as well as to parcel out the confiscated lands to

[1] "Mercur Politicus," June 8, 1653, p. 2516.

[2] S. P. $\frac{A}{1}$, p. 205.

[3] A man named Edmund Doherty had his bill for £82, 10s., vouched

the English claimants and the Irish who were driven out of the other provinces. For the soldiers among the former was reserved a belt of land four miles wide all along the sea and Shannon, with the manifest intention of isolating the latter and cutting them off from all outer communication. The foregoing is but a bare outline of the drastic measures adopted to smother the national and Catholic spirit of the people; yet that spirit not only survived, but became intensified. It grew with the wonderful growth of the despised and down-trodden race; and it is not too much to say that Clare has emerged from the Cromwellian desolation and subsequent persecution more wedded than ever to the national traditions, and as sincerely Catholic as any part of the Christian world.

Instructions[1] were given to the Loughrea Commissioners to send those transplanted as far as possible from their old homes, and to scatter to different places the members of the same clans. This was with a view to render return difficult, and to prevent combination. Hence it was not allowed to the inhabitants of Kerry, Cork, or Limerick, to settle in Clare, nor to those of Donegal, Cavan, Fermanagh, or the other northern or north-eastern counties, to seek new homes in North Connaught. This accounts for the considerable numbers of families bearing Ulster names, such as O'Donnell, MacDonnell, O'Neill, MacGuire, etc., now living in Clare. The old clans, however, O'Briens, MacNamaras, MacMahons, O'Deas, MacInernys, etc., have held their ground, in spite of all efforts to exterminate them. They still form a large majority of the population.

The worst was not yet over. A war tax, in the shape of a monthly contribution of £510, was levied on the depopulated and impoverished county. Troops were despatched regularly from Limerick and the garrisoned towns of Clare to enforce the payment of this, for the time and circumstances, enormous impost. It is easy to imagine the scenes of plunder and rapine which must have followed in all parts by them as correct, for "demolishing thirteene castles in ye county of Clare, at £2, 10s. each castle."—S. P. vol. x. p. 158.

[1] S. P. $\frac{A}{64}$, p. 364.

of the county. Clare was being remorselessly bled to death. An entry in "The Order Book of the Commissioners of Lymerick, Joshua Bennett, Thomas Carpenter, Thomas Harden," who had charge of the taxation, is eloquent on the subject. It runs thus: "May 12th, 1653—Upon serious consideration had of the present poverty and disability of the whole County Clare, and the starving condition which the few poor remaining inhabitants are in, and the impossibility there is of getting in the monthly contribution, their whole substance being engaged for their arrears hitherto," etc. A reduction not specified was ordered, "until the further pleasure of the Commissioners," signed by H. Ingoldsby, W. Skinner (not inappropriate), and S. Clarke.

Here is another significant entry: "May 31st—Gyles Vandeleur is authorised from time to time to join with the other applotters of the Barony of Bunratty for the public business."

The exhausted condition of the county did not save it from further "applotting," as the following entry in the same disastrous year testifies:—

"22nd July—The Commissioners are satisfied that Clare is so destitute, and the substance so slender, that the contribution is reduced as before."

The transplanting into the county made up, however, to some extent for the drain in the population. The return ordered in 1659 gives—Families: English, 440; Irish, 16,474. In this "Book of Survey and Distribution," from which the numbers are taken, the names of the families are also given.[1] The presence of such names as O'Callaghan, Callinan, O'Hea, Cullinan, Hennessy, Hogan, Hurley, O'Dwyer, Glissane (Gleeson), Hickey, Ryan, Keogh, Kennedy, FitzGerald, etc., in considerable numbers, shows that Cork, Limerick, and Tipperary contributed their quota of hunted Catholics; while names such as MacTeigue, MacLoughlin, MacShane, Sweeney, and MacSweeney, as well as those already noted, O'Donnell, O'Neill, MacGuire, etc., point unmistakably to a Northern

---

[1] The full list, comprising the whole population of Clare in that year, will be found in the Appendix. It cannot but be of deep interest to all their descendants.

origin. The Burkes and O'Kellys from Galway had, by intermarriages, settled down, long before, in all parts of Clare. The first intention was, as already noted, to reserve Clare for those most remote from it. At a later period, 1656, this order was in some degree modified. It ran thus: "The inhabitants of the counties of Kilkenny, Westmeath, Longford, King's County, and Tipperary, to be transplanted into the baronies of Tullagh, Bunratty, Islands, Corcomroe, Clonderlaw, Moyfartagh, and Ibrickan, in the county of Clare." It was specially ordered that "Irish widows of English extraction" should be sent to the baronies of Tulla and Bunratty.[1] Owing to the ever-increasing difficulties of the transplanting, the repeopling of Clare was effected from the adjoining counties and Cork, as the names given above sufficiently testify.

Some of those were specially favoured. Pierce Creagh, of Limerick, being hated by his countrymen "for his former known inclination to the English Government," was allowed a "secure place in Clare neare the English quarters," in the forfeited MacNamara territory; and Edmund Magrath, of Tipperary, who had acted as a spy, had conveyed to him, with special protection, property in Clare, at Tyredagh, near Tulla, where the people, through dislike of him, began at once cutting down the woods. He also got back his original property of eight hundred acres of Ballymore in the barony of Kilnamanagh. It was probably part of Miler Magrath's ill-gotten goods.[2]

The death of Cromwell in 1657, followed by the weak rule of his son Richard, prepared the way for the restoration of the monarchy. On the accession of Charles II. to the throne, the hopes of the Catholics ran high, but were soon dashed to the ground. Those, however, who had followed the fortunes of the exiled Stuarts to the Continent were at once taken into the royal favour, and restored to their estates. Among them, the most prominent in Clare were the Earl of Inchiquin,[3] Sir Daniel O'Brien of Carrigaholt, who, though over

---

[1] *Cromwellian Settlement*, pp. 162, 163.   [2] *Ibid.* pp. 378-382.

[3] Inchiquin recovered 39,961 statute acres; Lord Clare, 87,113; the Ingoldsbys, 1349 in Bunratty; and Pierce Creagh was allowed to retain 1718 at Dangan and Lisdoonvarna.

eighty years of age, was created Viscount Clare, with remainder to his grandson, Daniel; John MacNamara of Creevagh; Daniel O'Brien of Dough; John MacNamara of Cratloe, who became Sheriff in 1686; Sir Henry and Sir Richard Ingoldsby; Pierce Creagh; Daniel MacNamara of Doon; John MacNamara of Moyriesk; Captain Michael Morrissy; Captain Murtagh Clancy; Ensign Turlogh O'Hehir, and others.

They were put at once, by the Act of Settlement, into possession of the estates they had forfeited. Those, whether English adventurers[1] and soldiers, or Irish transplanted Catholics, who had acquired portions of their properties, were removed to other parts of the county. To make room for these, all who had acquired rights during the war, or by transplantation, were bound, by the Act of Explanation, to surrender one-third of their landed possessions. It is easy to imagine the confusion that this redistribution caused from end to end of Clare. The Earl of Orrery, better known as Lord Broghill, who had been made President of Munster, tells how one MacMahon boxed the ear of the High Sheriff while in discharge of duty; and a MacNamara ran his sword through a justice of the peace.

There was hope that, with the return of Catholic noblemen and gentlemen to their estates in Clare, the Catholic religion would be at least connived at. Priests began to appear in the open. The Abbey of Clonroad was reoccupied, and probably with it their religious houses through the county. So much can be inferred from the severe measures adopted later on by the Earl of Orrery. He ordered the Sheriff to seize on four friars who had branched off from the parent house at Ennis to a place called "Rooscagh, in the district of Brentree," and in the parish of Dysert. They were subjected to the Star Chamber process by John Gore, Esq.,[2] one of His

---

[1] In the *Cromwellian Settlement*, p. 403, etc., a list of these, copied from the original roll, is given, numbering 1360, with the sums contributed by each, varying in amount from the modest £10 of "James Bricdell, of London,"—a name still surviving in Clare,—to the £6100 of the ambitious "Richard Wade, of London, Carpenter."

[2] Cromwellian, but wisely royal when the turn came.

Majesty's justices of the peace for the county. "In their sworn affidavits, Murtogh O'Gripha and Teigue O'Hehir are made to admit that they are priests ordained by Maelaghlin Kelly,[1] Archbishop of Tuam—being a bishop of the Roman See; that Flan Broody is guardian and head of their convent" (he appears to have escaped); "and that the place where they keep their convent was given to them by one Morrice O'Connell, gent.; and that they are of the convent of Inish Clondrode." William Browne and Richard Lysaght, lay brothers, give similar testimony;[2] and all four were cast into Ennis jail, but liberated on giving bail for future good behaviour. The real cause of the lenity shown them was the unsafe condition of the jail. They were probably glad to get off with their lives out of the country, as we hear nothing more about them. The lesson taught was intended for all the "insolent Papists" of Clare.

During the remaining years of the reign of "the Merrie Monarch," no Papist dared to officiate publicly in any part of Clare. The tithes and Church property were made over, by a clause in the Act of Explanation, on the Protestant bishop and clergy, "having actual care of souls" — which care must have been of a very light kind. The Catholic bishop, John O'Molony, who was one of only nine bishops residing in their sees in all Ireland in 1649,[3] died in 1655. Two Vicars Apostolic, Dionysius Harty and John De Burgho, administered as best they could, at the risk of their lives, to the spiritual wants of the Catholics of the diocese, till, in 1671, another, John O'Molony, and of the same family, was consecrated bishop at the urgent request of the people. His fame as a doctor in the University of Paris had reached the county from which he had been an exile almost since his infancy. His appointment was strongly recommended by the doctors of the university, as well as by French and Irish

---

[1] It should be Quealy, a Clareman, who was highly recommended for the bishopric of Killaloe, when it was conferred on John O'Molony. Later on, he reached the dignity of Archbishop of Tuam. He took the field with the Catholic army, and met a soldier's death in Sligo.

[2] Orrery's *Memoirs*, vol. ii. p. 109.

[3] Brady's *Episcopal Succession*, vol. ii. p. 120.

bishops and archbishops. He had to run all the risks of residence in his diocese, for "on the 30th of July 1675," the Propaganda granted the Bishop of Killaloe " six months' leave of absence from his diocese, to enable him to go to France on urgent private affairs."[1] Probably the private affairs were the steps necessary to establish, at his own expense, those burses in the Irish College for students of Killaloe, for which he is still gratefully remembered—a marble monument there recording his munificence, as well as his escape from the plots of his pursuers. He received charge also of the diocese of Limerick, and lived through all the troubles to a good old age, dying in 1702.

Some light is thrown on this transition period of Clare history by another Protestant bishop — Worth — in the description given by him of his management of the Church property which fell into his hands. We have again to thank Canon Dwyer for bringing it to light in his *Diocese of Killaloe*. A perusal of the whole document, and others of a similar kind following, will well repay Clare and Tipperary readers. I can but give a few selections from it here.

The good bishop, after some wrangling on the subject, gives over the ferry-boat at Killaloe to "Mahon O'Nihill and his partners, to whom I have set the same for this year at the rent of £16 sterling, with other additions."

He sets "fishing weares," too, to the same industrious "Mahon O'Nihill and Co." for £28 sterling, but requiring him to bring down his timber wood (from Craghill[2] probably), and also to furnish his house with fish every Wednesday, Friday, and Saturday. Here we have a relic of the Papist times.

He also sets the royalties of the barony of Tulla, "right of his sea-heriots, weaves and strayes, felons' goods, fines for battery and bloodshed, customs and tolls," etc.

He finds that his predecessor, the Elizabethan Mauritius O'Brien, began a nice job, by leasing for 101 years to another

---

[1] Brady's *Episcopal Succession*, vol. ii. p. 121.

[2] If credit be given to local tradition, many ships of the British Navy, to which mainly England owes her supremacy, were built of the splendid oak trees that grew on this hill.

Reformation bishop, Daniel Neylan of Kildare, probably one of the family which plundered the Ennis Franciscan Abbey, "the isles of Aghnis, and five quarters of the land of Killinaboy, with the town of Killinaboy, for 12d. yearly;" that these fell into the hands of his son William, and Sir Roger O'Shaghness, who married the former bishop's widow; that "when I came to the Bishoprick these lands were in the possession of one Patrick Allen of Dublin, merchant, who, pretending an old lease by Bishop Jones to Robert Casey, whose relict he married, obtained a decree in the Court of Claims. . . . as I saw no ground to confirm his new lease . . . as soon as I was consecrated I entered on the lands of Killinaboy, and distrained for the rent due 24th March 1660, most part whereof W. Blood received for me; but rent due 29th September was received by Allen."

He finds two leases for the mensal lands at Dromlyne, in Bunratty—one to John MacNamara, made in 1587, for sixty-one years, at 2s.—a good bargain, but now expired; and another to D. MacNamara, given in 1633, for twenty-one years, at £10 a year.

In Moyarta, among other lettings for small sums, there is one to Sir D. O'Brien, of lands at Ballyket, with "a good castle and good storehouse." There is scarcely a trace of either now. Another at Dunaha was let to the same Sir D. O'Brien at £2 per annum; also the town, hamlet, village, and fields of "Carrigahoulie, *alias* Rinaneaderrick." The latter name is still preserved among Irish speakers.

Other lettings, and for mere trifles, are noted at Kilkee to MacSweeney, "whereon stood a castle;" and at Moyarta, Kilfeera, Killenagallagh, Kilcashel, and Lisdeen, all to Sir D. O'Brien. The same practice in regard to Church property prevailed all over the country, so that the bequests of Catholics in past times for religious and charitable purposes, fell, under English rule, like the clan lands, into the hands of the chiefs who made submission and forwarded English interests.

Nor did the good bishop forget himself. Thirteen hundred acres were set for £55 per annum to members of his own family for long periods.

"The Primary Visitation of Thomas (Price), Archbishop

of Cashel, held at St. Flannan's Cathedral, 29th September 1667," to be seen in the Record Office, shows, if correct, but a small number of Protestant clergy in Clare at that date—only seventeen in all; and all these, save D. Driscoll, bearing English names. Four of them—Blood, Cox, Whitston, and Bayllie—are still represented in the county. The others have disappeared. The trifling sums set opposite their names, under the heading of "Scedula procurationum," being supposed value of glebe lands only, and varying from Dean Jasper Pheasant's £2, 10s. 10d. to Cornl. Sherin's £10, 3s. 4d., do not, of course, represent their whole incomes. These were made up from various sources, but mostly from tithes wrung from unwilling Catholics. Fines, too, were exacted for non-attendance at Protestant worship and other misdemeanours, one of which at least is of too curious a nature to be described here. Suffice it to say that a certain sin gave occasion for it.

All the elements for strife were abundantly present in Clare during the whole reign of Charles II. It might with truth be said that almost every man's hand was against his neighbour in the distracted county. Protestant was against Catholic, Englishman against Irishman, adventurer against transplanter, and nearly all against the restored exiles—such were amongst the consequences of English invasion. Nor did the accession of James II., on the death of Charles in February 1685, mend matters. It only made them much worse, as the sequel will show.

James II. was a devoted Catholic, and soon made his determination to act justly by Catholics known. Their hopes ran high, when, in 1687, Talbot, Earl and afterwards Duke of Tyrconnell, was sworn in Lord-Lieutenant of Ireland. He at once opened up all the offices of State to Catholics. They were no longer excluded, as in previous reigns, from the army, the bar, the bench, or the other learned professions, but the appointments made were not in excess of what their numerical superiority and public services might fairly lay claim to. This even-handed justice excited the hatred of the Protestants, and contributed much to the unpopularity of the king in England.

To understand the sequence of events, it must be borne in mind that James's two daughters by his first wife—the daughter of Lord Chancellor Hyde, whose wife had been in her youth a servant in London—were brought up Protestants, and given in marriage by Charles II. to Protestant husbands. Mary was the wife of the Prince of Orange, her own first cousin, and Anne had for husband George, Prince of Denmark. The Princess of Orange would then have succeeded to the throne after the death of James if he had no male issue. He had, however, married secondly the daughter of the Duke of Modena, and the birth of a son dashed the hopes of the Protestants. An intrigue was set on foot, with the result that his nephew, William of Orange,—the husband of his daughter Mary,—landed in England, at Torbay, Devonshire, on the 5th November 1688, with a large force, on the pretence of protecting Protestant interests, but in reality to seize the throne. James, being abandoned by his army, fled to France, claiming and receiving the protection and support of Louis XIV. Tyrconnell, having heard early of the arrival of William, put Catholics in command of the principal places in Ireland, and called upon the Catholic lords and gentry to arm their retainers and prepare to defend their king and their own newly-recognised rights. He communicated with James, and the latter, collecting as many of his supporters as he could, including a French contingent, set sail from Brest, and landed at Kinsale on the 12th March 1689. A short time before, on the 20th of February, the Prince of Orange was proclaimed king within the walls of Derry. James hastened to invest the city. Every one knows how gallantly the defenders foiled every effort made to capture it, till at last the siege was abandoned and James retired discomfited and discredited to Dublin. Here he assembled a Parliament on the 7th of May following, which sat in the King's Inns, and consisted of forty-six peers, including six Protestant bishops, and two hundred and twenty-eight commoners. Lord Clare, who had been made with Boileau, a trusted French officer, a joint-governor of Cork, attended amongst the peers; while the county of Clare was represented by Daniel O'Brien and John MacNamara of Cratloe; and the borough of Ennis by Theobald Butler and Florence MacCarthy.[1] After some opposition, an Act of a far-reaching character was passed. It was a repeal of the Acts of Settlement and Explanation. It enabled those who were in possession of property before 1641 to prosecute their claims to it. Another Act declared all those who had fled the kingdom, and would not return before the 1st of November following, liable to the charge of high treason and the forfeiture of their lands. To define still further the position, freedom of worship was solemnly proclaimed. This largely-Catholic Parliament, while vindicating the Catholic claim to religious liberty, imposed no religious disability whatsoever on any section of their fellow-countrymen.

It would be out of place here to enter much into details of the struggle that ensued. No period of our history is better or more widely known. The contest was one not merely between James and his son-in-law and nephew for the possession of the crown: it was still more a desperate effort of the Catholics of Ireland to recover possession of their lands, and to secure freedom of worship. The justice of their cause cannot be called into question, whatever may be said of their prudence or political wisdom.

William determined to try out the issue with James on Irish ground as soon as possible. The first contingent of his army, under General Duke Schomberg, arrived at Bangor, in Co. Down, on the 13th of August 1689. The followers of William in the North rallied to his standard, and an army of about 30,000 men, composed of well-trained Dutch, Danes, French Huguenots, and English, was ready to take the field. After some not very important successes, they were sent into winter quarters, where almost one-third, some say, succumbed to sickness arising from insufficient supplies and the inclemency of the weather. James's army, numbering about 20,000 Irish and French, being better supplied, was in far better fighting condition. He in vain offered battle to Schomberg, and is blamed for not forcing it at all costs; but the courage

---

[1] This is, I think, a misprint for Florence MacNamara, who was certainly one of King James's burgesses for the borough of Ennis.

[2] D'Alton, p. 34.

for which he was noted in his early career as Admiral during his brother's reign, neither then nor afterwards displayed itself.

As the winter advanced, the state of affairs in both armies was reversed. The Duke of Schomberg received abundant supplies from England; while the Irish began to run short, especially of provender for their cavalry. The arrival of William himself at Carrickfergus, on the 14th of June, with a large reinforcement of men, money, and war material, was the signal for a final and decisive struggle.

The story of the battle of the Boyne has been often told, and by writers of every shade of political opinion. It is generally admitted that William's army, as well in number as in war material and discipline, was far superior to James's. The latter had levied a tax of £20,000 for war purposes, per month, over all Ireland. The sum fixed on Clare, being £1798, 5s. 6d., covered the three months following the 10th of April 1690. The assessors named for the collection of the tax were the High Sheriff, Sir Donogh O'Brien, John MacNamara of Cratloe, Donogh O'Brien of Dough, Daniel MacNamara, John MacNamara of Moyriesk, James Aylmer, Florence MacNamara, Samuel Boyton, John MacNamara, and the Provost of Ennis, David White. In a letter, dated April 20, 1690, written by Donogh O'Brien, High Sheriff of Clare, and addressed "To the Right Honble. the Earl of Lymerick," he explains the course adopted by him, in conjunction with Lieut.-Col. MacNamara, to secure a supply of good horses for the service of the king. He issued warrants to the barony constables for the seizure of such horses as might be found with the persons whose names were attached. It will be of interest to those now living, two hundred years later on, to give the names in this list of "the chief gentlemen and ablest persons in the Coy.," before the third wave of confiscation swept over unhappy Clare.

Barony of Tulla.

Thomas Spaight, Teigue MacNamara of Legort; Simon Purdon, Esq., John Grady, James Grady, Florence MacNamara, Esq., Henry Thornton, Danl. MacNamara, Esq., Donogh MacNamara, and Capt. Teigue MacNamara of Ranna ; Nicholas Magrath, Henry Tuey, Henry Bridgeman, John Cusack, James Stacpole, John Magrath, Ambrose Pery, Edward Nayle, Patrick Arthur, Teigue Malony, Donogh MacNamara of Derryada.

BARONY OF BUNRATTY.

John MacNamara, Esq., Sir D. O'Brien, Bart., Thos. MacNamara, D. MacNamara of Gra; T. MacNamara, John MacNamara of Moyriesk, Esq. ; Roger MacNamara, Edward Uniacke, Managh Grady, Andrew Creagh, John Mayer, David Bindon, Capt. Ed. Fitzgerald, Capt. John Fitzgerald, Ed. Pympton, Ignatius and Patrick Connell, Ed. Delahoyde, D. MacNamara, Francis O'Brien, John Clanchy, D. MacNamara, Giles Vandeclure, Wm. Reyall, T. Dillon, Wm. Butler, Henry Coopp, Ml. Comyn, H. Destare, Rich. Gline, John Resine, Peter Warge, John Colpoyse, Sir Oliver Burke, Mau. Grady, L. Grady.

INSEQUIN BARONY.

Thos. Blood, Ed. Hogan, M. Dea, D. Grady, Pierce Butler, D. O'Kearyn, H. Hehir, Ed. Hehir, M. Griffa, Lt.-Col. Donogh O'Brien, Capt. D. Neylan, L. Hehir, Ri. Connell.

CORCOMROE BARONY.

Donogh O'Brien, Esq., Ennistymon, John Hurley, Bryan Hanrahan, Thos. O'Connor, James Coffer, Wm. MacDonogh and his two sons, Durmod O'Teigue, James Fitzgerald, Murtogh O'Bryan, Dl. Clancy, Thos. Clancy, And. Hehir, Ml. MacDonogh, Boetius Clancy, Capt. Ml. Lynch.

BURREN BARONY.

Col. Terlogh O'Loghlen, his son Dan. O'Loghlen, Murtogh O'Brien, Constance and Hugh M. Davoren of Ballyvowhugh, James Davoren, George Martyn, William Davoren, Wm. Lamer, Ed. Breen, John MacDonogh, D. Roe O'Loghlen, J. O'Daly, John Mariaghaun, M. Davoren of Nuohaval, J. MacDonogh.

Ibricken Barony,

Augustine Fitzgerald, And. White, Ed. Dwyer, Patrick Comyn, P. Quillinan, The Lady Dowager of Clare, MacNihill.

Moyfarta Barony.

J. MacDonnell of Kilquee, Henry Hickman, Ed. Mulrooney, C. Considyn, Bryan Cahan, John Vanhugard, Ri. Creaghe, the Town of Kilrush, Murtogh MacMahon, Dermot Considyn, Ri. Scott, Pa. Wolfe, J. MacNamara.

Clonderalaw Barony.

Montiford Westropp, Thos. Crofton, J. Linchey, T. Considyn, P. White, Conor MacMahon, Rob. Peacock, Henry Lee, Dan. Fynucan, T. MacMahon, Theo. White, Geo. Mellon, Geo. Rosse, Ri. Henn.

Island Barony.

The Provost and Borough of Ennis, Wm. Herrott, Mich. Wolfe, Sam. Burke, James Creagh, Owen Considyn, L. Curry, T. O'Brien, James Aylemer, James Bedowel, J. Hickman, Geo. Stamer, S. Hehir.

Most of the families above mentioned are still represented in the county.

It is not a matter for wonder that such raw levies, thus hurriedly put into the field, were far from being efficient at the Boyne. It is stated that Lord Clare's Yellow Dragoons behaved badly there. The original regiment which was raised at Carrigaholt, was considered, from its thorough discipline, the flower of King James's army. It was sent north, the year before, to share in the operations which culminated in the collapse at Derry, but, having been drawn into an ambush at Lisnakea, on the 26th of July 1689, was literally cut to pieces. Those, then, of the same name who fought at the Boyne were for the most part a raw levy, from whom much could not be expected. We know how badly the Americans of both armies fought at Bull's Run; but, like those Clare dragoons, as every one knows, they gave abundant proof of conspicuous valour throughout their after career.

The following is part of a letter, written at Cork, August 10, 1689, by Lord Clare to Donal O'Brien of Ennistymon. It shows the distrust with which Protestants, as such, were regarded; and the hardships to which, in consequence, they were subjected.

LETTER from DANIEL, VISCOUNT CLARE, to DONAL O'BRIEN, Esq. of Ennistymon, D.L.

"CORK, *Aug.* 10, 1689.

"DEAR COUSIN,—For your comfort I have only to tell you that yesterday came to me here a gentleman who belongs to the King (James II.), and comes with letters from the King of France. He left Brest on Monday last, where he saw a hundred capital ships and fire-ships under sail, going towards Plymouth, to seek the English and Dutch fleet, and from thence to come to us. He says we shall have in Kinsale this night or to-morrow three frigates laden with arms and ammunition; and our men which were in the Isle of Wight and a great many French officers are coming. . . . Speak to Father Teigue, and send to all the clergy in the county, to pray for their good success. You are to remove all the Protestants from Clare Castle, and to keep them confined at Pierse Creaghe's house, with a guard of your militia and townsmen, except G. Stamer . . . and Thos. Hickman, who are both to remain at Clare Castle, as well as W. Purdon, under the charge of Hugh Sweeney. And herein fail not to confine without delay Bindon, Hewitt, and such other townsmen as are in the county, though you have them not in the list returned from Dublin, as Colpoys, young Lee, young Vandaleur, Smith, and all such, especially when you hear of an invader. . . . Ye ould folks may not be so strictly used. But leave not a young Protestant in the county without streight imprisonment, for which this shall be your warrant." (Signed) "CLARE." [1]

[1] Canon Dwyer, pp. 386–389.

Clare evidently wanted thoroughness. The English method of dealing with such as these would be to string them up, or shoot them at sight.

At this period, the following were among those who had fled the county, and whose properties had been declared forfeited by the Act of Parliament mentioned above, unless they returned to their allegiance before the 1st of October 1689. They had not returned:—The Earl of Inchiquin and his two sons, Lord Ibricken and William O'Brien, Conor O'Brien, Hy. Hickman, Js. Hamilton, Thos. Hawkins, Hugh Brady, Samuel Lucas, F. Gore, John Drew, John Bayley, G. R. Barrett, Wm. Babbington, Geo. Barnett, Thos. Birchos, Hy. Brady, Ml. Busteed, Ro. Cox, Stephen Colbourne, Ml. Lysaght, A. Purdon, Geo. Syng, Tho. Smyth, S. Walton, John White, John Walkens, and Sir J. Ingoldsby.

These, as will be seen, were all restored; and most of them, if not all, received large slices of the confiscated properties of the defeated Catholics.

During the short reign of James in Ireland, the following constituted the corporation of the town of Ennis:[1]—

David White, merchant, *Portreve.*

Burgesses 12.

Daniel, Viscount Clare.
Dennis O'Brien of Dough, Esqr.
Florence MacNamara, Esqr.
John MacNamara.
Pierce Creagh, merchant.
James Casey, do.
Peter Rice, do.
And. White, do.
And. Woulfe, do.
Obadiah Dawson, apothecary.
James White, merchant.
John Lentall, vintner.

Denis Casey, *Town-clerk.*

As a matter of much deeper interest, especially to those

[1] Patent Rolls of the Court of Chancery. Harris. Dwyer.

bearing the same names, I give here, quoting from D'Alton, the list of officers, A.D. '1689, in Clare's famous regiment of dragoons. Many of them perished in the fatal fight of Lisnakea, but their cause and spirit were well maintained by those of their blood and religion who filled up their places in the battlefields of Ireland and the Continent.

Colonel Daniel O'Brien, Lord Clare.

Captains.	*Lieutenants.*
The Colonel.	Turlough O'Bryen.
James Philips, Lieut.-Colonel.	David Barry.
	John Hurley.
Francis Browne, Major.	John Ryan.
Florence MacNamara.	Murrogh O'Bryan.
Redmond MacGrath.	Owen Cahane.
Morris FitzGerald.	Silvester Purdon.
James MacDonnell.	William Lysaght.
Nicholas Burke.	Joseph Furlong.
Roger Shaughnessy.	Patrick Hehir.
Teigue O'Brian.	Richard Bedford.
Thady Quin.	

Cornets.	*Quartermasters.*
Daniel O'Bryan.	James Neylan.
Thos. FitzGerald.	William Hawford.
Murtogh Hogan.	James White.
Hugh Perry.	James Ryan.
Thos. Donnell.	Chris. O'Bryan.
Nicholas Archdeken.	Ed. Bohilly.
John Burke.	Gerald FitzGerald.
William Neylan.	Dan. MacNamara.
Laurence Dean.	Dermot Sullivan.
Hugh Hogan.	James O'Dea.
Thos. Clancy.	Thomas Lee.

Nearly all these names are to be found also in the lists of other regiments. They figured, of course, much more numerously among the rank and file, which was composed of the Clare clans, amalgamated with the Catholics who had been driven into the county by Cromwell.

The battle of the Boyne was the turning-point in the war. The Irish army, though defeated, retreated to Dublin in good order, after inflicting, according to the most reliable accounts,[1] on the superior forces of William a loss in killed and wounded fully equal to its own. James fled ignominiously. This was not a war for the dynasty alone, so the flight of James did not put an end to it. The plan agreed on by the Irish generals was to concentrate all their forces on the line of the Shannon, from Athlone to Limerick, and there wait William's attack, in the hope of being meanwhile reinforced from France. Lauzun, however, who had command of the French, who were the allies not of the Irish but of James, believing or affecting to believe "that Limerick could be battered down by roasted apples," withdrew to Galway, leaving all the glory of the subsequent defence to the Irish. The first attack made was upon Athlone by Lieut.-Gen. Douglas with twelve thousand men and fourteen pieces of artillery. It was gallantly foiled by the garrison under Colonel Richard Grace. The English, hearing of the approach of Sarsfield, and fearing to be cut off from their main body, retired upon Limerick, and here the final struggle of this year's campaign was entered on.

The English forces mustered, according to their own historian's account,[2] 38,000 fully equipped men; while the Irish had about 20,000 infantry, half of whom only were well armed, and 3500 cavalry, who were posted a few miles from the city, towards Six-Mile-Bridge, in the county of Clare.

The first exploit in the conflict was the one which probably decided its fortunes. With this gallant exploit, and the brilliant defence which followed it, the name of Patrick Sarsfield is imperishably wedded in history. Having learned that William's battering train, consisting of six twenty-four-pounders, two eighteen-pounders, and a large supply of

---

[1] Story and Berwick, who were both present, one in each army. Story gives four hundred of the English killed, which, with the wounded, would fully amount to the thousand stated by Berwick in his memoirs as the total loss of the Irish.

[2] Griffith's *Villare Hibernicum*.

ammunition and provisions, with ten boats and other necessaries for investing the city on all sides, was being conveyed under escort from Waterford, he determined at once to try and destroy it. Leaving Limerick with five hundred picked horsemen on the night of the 10th of August, he crossed the Shannon at Killaloe, and, under the guidance of O'Hogan, a Rapparee leader, who knew the country well, reached the northern slope of Keeper Hill before daylight, and halted at Silvermines. Here he lay concealed for the day. A traitor named Manus O'Brien, called by Story "a substantial country gentleman," brought word next day to the English camp of Sarsfield's movement across the river, but could not further describe its object or direction. William suspecting it sent out a detachment under Sir John Lanier to meet the convoy, but as he did not leave the camp till two o'clock the following morning, he was forestalled. Sarsfield, resuming his march late in the evening, found his quarry reposing in fancied security only eight or nine miles away from William's army at Ballyneety,[1] near Pallas, now a station on the Waterford and Limerick line of railway, and, falling on them early in the morning of the 12th August, cut down all who attempted resistance. Filling the heavy guns with powder, then fixing their mouths into the ground, and heaping round them all the ammunition and other materials for the siege, he laid a train of powder on to a safe distance. Then, setting fire to it, he and his brave followers had the satisfaction to see the war-supplies[2] upon which William counted so securely for the destruction of the walls of Limerick, blown to atoms. The terrific explosion shook the earth around, and was heard not only by the advancing English escort, but in the camp and through the city, bringing dismay to the army of William, and raising high the hopes of the Irish. Sarsfield retraced his steps as speedily as possible, and was received by his fellow-countrymen with acclamations that must have been

[1] Ballyneety is Irish for White's Town.
[2] Consisting of 8 pieces of heavy cannon, 5 mortars, 155 waggons of ammunition, 12 carts of biscuit, 18 tin pontoons, 400 draught horses, and 100 fully accoutred. The Irish probably carried off as many as they could of the horses.

heard in William's camp. The garrison and citizens were still further encouraged by the arrival of Baldearg O'Donnell, whose appearance seemed to verify the prophecy that "a red-handed O'Donnell would free Ireland by winning a great battle at Limerick."

It is not within the scope of the present work to dwell at any length on this, or the following, siege of Limerick. Those who desire detailed accounts will find them in Lenihan's painstaking and sympathetic *History of Limerick*. William's army lay entrenched at Singland, around the slope of land a little north of the city, and not far from that interesting relic, the portion of the Black Battery now standing near St. John's Cathedral. From here he advanced closer and closer, by throwing up earthworks almost to the very walls, and keeping up a continuous cannonade from his field-pieces. Here, again, as at the Boyne, according to Dean Story, who vouches for it as having on both occasions occurred under his own eyes, a well-directed cannon-ball grazed William, who was himself fearlessly directing the operations. Had he been killed on either occasion, there was an end to the war, for some time at least; and English as well as Irish history should have taken a very different turn. The good Dean believed that his hero, the pious William, was under the special protection of Divine Providence. It is no easy matter now to reconcile this with the fact of his relations with Barbara Villiers, and their illegitimate son, raised by him to a foremost place among the English nobility.

The guns did their work well, in spite of the constant and well-directed fire from the walls. A breach was effected near the Black Battery, and through this breach, on the morning of the 27th of August, the picked men of William's army stormed the city. Large bodies succeeded in forcing their way through the breach, and then took place the hand-to-hand fight inside the walls, which has been, and will be to all time, the pride and the glory of the citizens of Limerick. It is beyond question that not only the men, but the women also of the old city by the Shannon, threw themselves, along with the garrison, on the invaders. Every kind of weapon was grasped. Even stones did their work, for Dean Davies, who was an eye-witness, writes that Lord Charlemont and the Earl of Meath came back "bruised with stones." No nation in the world has a nobler record than that furious onslaught by unarmed men and women on the best disciplined forces then in Europe. The lanes and streets poured out their frantic defenders, while the Irish soldiers met the enemy foot to foot and eye to eye. Small arms played on them from the walls, the roofs of the houses, and every point of vantage. Fierce and fanatic and brave, undoubtedly, as these Dutch and Danes, and Brandenburghers and English were, they had to give way before the furious Irish; and, while retreating in confusion through the breach, the havoc made of them was completed by the blowing up of a mine, which Sarsfield had with great foresight prepared for such an event. Those who escaped took refuge in their trenches, and William met and saw with his own eyes such a discomfiture under Limerick's walls as he never experienced elsewhere in his whole warlike and stormy career. With the loss of prestige, as well as of nearly two thousand of his choicest troops,[1] in this one engagement alone, he felt that the hope of capturing Limerick was vain. Calling a council of war, and throwing the blame on the bad weather, it was resolved to abandon the siege. Clare had her share in the glory of this successful defence. From every part of the county supplies poured into the city. The cavalry posted on the Clare side took care that any attempt to cross the river and fully invest the city should be resolutely resisted. The blood of Claremen flowed freely in the defence, and once more, as in 1646, the foreign foe was shaken off. Her hills were ablaze with light, when it was seen that the army of the invader of Irish and Catholic rights was in full retreat from the walls of the gallant city, part of which stood on her soil.

[1] Harris. Story.

CHAPTER XXIII.

FROM 1690 TO 1703.

Second Siege of Limerick—Butchery on Thomond Bridge—Treaty of Limerick—Flight of the Wild Geese—Clare reduced to a Desert—The Third Great Confiscation — Plans for Plunder—Those who secured it—Sums paid for it—Origin of Titles of most of the Present Owners.

THE last chapter opened with the tale of the surrender of Limerick to Ireton, and its dire consequences to the people of Clare. This one has for its starting-point the flight from the walls of the rescued city, of a general far abler than Ireton, and a king among the most powerful then in Europe. The position in Clare was once more reversed. The old inhabitants—the descendants of a hundred generations of Clare freemen — had fought for and won their national birthrights. The English intruders and despoilers lay at their mercy. There is no evidence that they resorted to reprisals in the interval between the two sieges of Limerick.

The struggle was by no means at an end. It was continued through the rest of Ireland, and it was well known that it would be resumed in Clare at the first opportunity. William, baffled for the time, despatched fresh troops with munitions of war into the country. The garrisons of Cork, Kinsale, and other towns still in the hands of the Irish, surrendered on honourable terms to the overwhelming English forces, and surely and steadily the tide of war during the winter and spring of '90 and '91 turned towards the Irish stronghold—the line of the Shannon. Sarsfield remained in Limerick repairing the fortifications. Tyrconnell, who had gone to France, returned in January with provisions and ammunition, and was followed by St. Ruth, a French general of great ability, who took over supreme command by orders of King James. He also brought with him supplies sufficient to equip an army of 25,000 men, and was accompanied by other French officers of note. It is not necessary here to enter into the details of the siege of Athlone, or the battle of Aughrim. It will be enough to say that, owing in no small degree to the supercilious treatment of Sarsfield and, the other Irish commanders by the proud and too-confident St. Ruth, with the fall of the latter, the Irish army was left without any one in supreme command; and at the very moment when victory at Aughrim seemed assured, it was thrown into disorder for want of generalship, and suffered a severe defeat. The way was now open into Clare, and it was determined by the victorious English to invest on all sides the lion-hearted city of Limerick, from whose walls they had been flung back only a few months before. A march, however, on the western side of the Shannon would have been both difficult and dangerous, owing to the hilly and barren character of the country, as well as to the certainty of being harassed by the Irish, who had retreated, with better knowledge of the route, in that direction. The approach, then, was made along the eastern side. Ginckle had taken the precaution of bringing with his army a supply of tin boats, with which he hoped to construct a pontoon bridge somewhere near the city. The little island above Athlunkard Bridge facilitated this design. Local tradition has it that a fisherman named MacAdam pointed out a rock on the Clare side upon which the chains necessary to complete and secure the bridge could be fixed. The rock is since called Carrig-a-Clouragh, or "Chain Rock." He received, after the surrender of Limerick, to which he so materially contributed, a grant of land along the river side.

Sarsfield had posted some troops, under Brigadier Clifford, to watch this point. It is stated, and proofs are offered, that he and Colonel Henry Luttrell had determined to betray the cause. The latter was well rewarded by William, but met a traitor's doom, being killed years afterwards at his own door. Certain it is that the passage across was effected on the night of the 15th September, little or no resistance being offered, though a large force of Irish cavalry, who were in camp at Cratloe, only a few miles off, could easily have been summoned to the support of the defenders. It is not easy to understand why the lodgment made and maintained on the Clare side was not attacked with more vigour by the Irish, as it was so plain that it would be availed of to cut off from the city communication with the rest of Clare, which was the main source of supplies. In a week after, on the 22nd of September, Ginckle, having made all his preparations, forced a passage across, in the face of the Irish fire, at the head of ten regiments of foot and all his cavalry, with fourteen guns, and bringing provisions, which he well knew the Clare people would keep out of his reach. He ordered an attack upon Thomond Gate. The defenders, to the number of 850, were obliged to retreat. While they were crossing the bridge, the French officer in command of the fort on the city side, fearing that the English, who pressed hotly on their rear, would enter with them, gave orders to raise the drawbridge, leaving the brave fellows to their fate. At the hands of a foe that never knew pity, this meant butchery. Story, their own historian, who was all along an eye-witness, writes that "before killing was over" (in spite no doubt of cries for quarter), "they were laid in heaps upon the bridge, higher than the ledges of it, so that they were all either killed or taken, except about a hundred and twenty that got into the town before the bridge was drawn up, and many of these"—the good Dean notes, with evident satisfaction—"cut and slashed to the purpose." This was a crushing blow to the hopes of the defenders. Now, after six weeks of a death-struggle, gallant and determined on both sides, the Irish found themselves completely hemmed in. With their base of supply completely cut off, and after looking in vain for the promised support from France by the river, which showed them only the English flag flying,— distrusting, too, the French in the city, since the massacre on Thomond Bridge,—it became clear that any further defence would be fruitless, and only a useless waste of human life. A parley was sounded. Negotiations were entered into, and with no little difficulty were concluded on the 3rd of October.

Late in the evening of that eventful day, the celebrated Treaty of Limerick was signed. The terms granted to the Irish, being all that they could in reason expect,[1] show how anxious Ginckle and his council were for the surrender of the city. It is only necessary to read through the treaty—a copy of which is given at full length in Lenihan's *History of Limerick* —to see in the light of the events which followed how basely that treaty was violated. The repudiation of this solemn compact, "before the ink wherewith 'twas writ was dry," was shamelessly persevered in, till the Claremen of 1828—one hundred and thirty-seven years afterwards— forced the English Government to reconsider their policy towards the Catholics of these kingdoms, and to grant them part, at least, of their natural rights.

According to the terms of the treaty, the Irish soldiers were at liberty either to return to their homes or to take service on the Continent. They were drawn up, the 5th of October, on the King's Island, and there they were asked to declare their choice. Ginckle gazed on these splendid troops with a hungry eye, and through his agents offered them the most tempting terms if they would join his army. About one thousand, mostly from the North, under that Baldearg O'Donnell about whom such hopes were entertained, and who proved such a fraud, accepted his offer, and were sent into England. About two thousand took passes, and returned to their homes. The great bulk, however, of the army, including the whole Clare contingent, had made up their minds to take service in France, with the hope deep in their hearts that all was not yet lost, and that an opportunity would be given them to renew some day, on Irish soil, the fight for faith and fatherland. They little knew of the heartlessness of kings and the callousness of diplomacy. Their bravery was their ruin. The French king, once he got hold of them, took good care to keep them in his own service. He thought no more of Ireland, steeped as it was in misery; and so those gallant

---

[1] For instance, the 25th Article provided that the garrison should march out "all at once, or at different times, as they could be embarked, with arms, baggage, drums beating, match lighted," etc.,—in a word, with all the honours of war.

men shed their blood or fretted out their lives far away from the dear old land, giving to it nothing ever more but the lustre and the glory of their brave deeds in the European wars.

Nearly twenty thousand men voluntarily expatriated themselves. The greater number sailed in French and English ships lent for the purpose, in accordance with the terms of the treaty.

There is hardly in history anything more touching than the parting of these brave men with their wives, their children, their families, and last, not least, the land of their love, for which they had so often risked their lives. Wives and sisters and daughters clung to them, tried to force their way into the boats that conveyed them to the ships, and yielded only when they were forcibly driven back. It is to be hoped that the story told of their hands having been slashed with swords to make them loose hold of the boats is not true. What a sad sail that 16th of October down the Shannon! Many were looking with fond gaze on the hills and valleys of Clare, in which they had spent the merry days of youth. One of the ships foundered near Kilrush, with the loss of about one hundred men. All the others weathered the gale, and, passing under the frowning cliffs of Clare, turned their prows southward round the majestic Brandon mountains, and joined the fleet that had sailed from Cork, all laden with a living cargo of stout though sorrowing hearts for the battle-fields of Europe. The spirit in which they went is well described in an Irish song, written soon afterwards, the first verse of which is thus rendered into English by Mangan:—

> "Farewell, O Patrick Sarsfield! may luck be on your path;
> Your camp is broken up, your work is marred for years;
> But you go to kindle into flames the King of France's wrath,
> Though you leave sick Eire in tears."

The fortunes of the Thomond contingent of that gallant army of exiles, Clare's famous dragoons, under Lord Clare as colonel, and John MacNamara and James Philips as lieutenant-colonels, must not be lost sight of; but the fate of Clare itself, now finally at the mercy of the conquerors.

claims first attention. The castle of Clare, which was garrisoned by a troop raised at the expense of Teigue MacNamara of Ayle, near Tulla, was surrendered, as stipulated for in the treaty, MacNamara being allowed to return to his estate. Lord Clare chose to abandon Carrigaholt Castle and all his vast possessions rather than submit and swear allegiance to William and Mary. Such of the people as still remained had now but to wait the will of their victorious enemies. The county was practically a desert. Taking the population of all Ireland in 1641 given by Sir William Petty in his *Political Anatomy of Ireland*, as 1,466,000, and reduced by war to 850,000 in 1652, we can infer that half a million would be as much as could have survived all the disasters of the succeeding years, culminating in the surrender of Limerick. That would leave in all Clare probably not more than about fifteen thousand of both sexes reduced to utter subjection and despair. In a return sent by Ryder, Protestant Bishop of Killaloe, to Dublin Castle in 1693, for the publication of which we have again to thank Canon Dwyer, the following significant entry appears: "John Lawson, Englishman," being appointed to the "Rectory and vicaridge of Quin, Rectory and vicaridge of Tulloe, Rectory and vicaridge of Cluony, Rectory and vicaridge of Dowry, Rectory of Templemaley, Rectory of Kilraghtis, Rectory of Kilmurry-negaul,"—in a word, to seven of the finest parishes in the heart of fertile Clare,—has placed opposite to his name, "No cure served at present; noe church in repaire; the county all wast." This was mostly MacNamara territory. The principal families of this once powerful sept, refusing to abandon their faith, or swear allegiance to William, have altogether disappeared, some during the progress of the wars on the Continent, others reduced to penury and obscurity for safety's sake among the peasants in Clare.[1] A few of the minor branches, having

---

[1] The present writer heard from many sources in his youth the tradition relating to the disappearance of the Rafoland or West Clancuilean family, the lineal descendants of the founder of Quin Abbey. Having made vain resistance, and killed some English troopers who were out on a foraging expedition, they had to fly precipitately, and conceal themselves from the coming vengeance. Their descendants are still traced among families in

conformed to the Protestant faith, contrived to cling on to what was but small remnants of the once wide MacNamara domains. Not one of their descendants in the direct line holds now a single acre in fee of the old Clan Cuilean principality. The best blood of the race runs in the veins of the farming class in Clare.

Another wave of confiscation and plunder now swept unopposed over the face of the impoverished and thinly populated county. Not only those who fought and lost, and would not swear allegiance to one whom they regarded as an usurper, forfeited their estates, but Catholics, *as such*, in spite of the solemn compact at Limerick, were soon after deprived of all rights of property and citizenship. It is not within the scope of this history to reproduce all the well-known diabolical enactments of the Penal Laws. The loathing and indignation aroused by the reading of them in honest-minded Protestants must be more acute even than the sense of their injustice felt by Catholics. It will suffice to trace their working out in the social and political life of the county during the coming years.

The representatives of the adventurers and Cromwellian soldiers, whose hold of the confiscated lands had been disturbed by the Acts of Settlement and Explanation, as well as those who received grants for their services in the late war, could now step in and secure their claims. There was no one to gainsay them. The four-mile-wide line along the sea and Shannon, reserved for Protestants only, had been increased on the Shannon side to ten miles, by a Proclamation of the Lords Justices of Ireland, dated September 26, 1790. Before entering into further particulars of the Williamite Confiscation, it will be interesting to take a bird's-eye view of the titles to Clare properties, established by the Acts of Settlement and Explanation in the reign of

the parishes of Tulla and Feacle. I found a curious corroboration of the story, in discovering among the Royal Irish Academy records a name familiar to my memory, Harrison, as one of those who shared the spoils of the fugitive MacNamaras. The Earl of Thomond must have seized on the abandoned property, for he leased the rich corcass lands down to the river to this Harrison for a fine of £10 at only £30 a year, showing clearly a defective title. It was secured by being enrolled, October 26, 1703.

Charles II., as found in the records of the Royal Irish Academy, marked $\frac{14}{B\ 19}$. Only the principal ones can be given here.

Daniel O'Brien, afterwards Lord Viscount Clare, had confirmed to him in Clare, 84,339 statute acres, at a rent to the crown of £790; and in Limerick, 2774, rent £26. Most of this had been MacMahon property, lying in the baronies of Moyarta and Corcovaskin, but some of it lay in East Clare, notably about Newmarket, including Carrigoran and Urlan, now owned by the FitzGeralds. He got also a grant of the castle, manors, fairs, and markets of Ballyket, near Kilrush, as well as the castle and manor of Carrigaholt, and a lease from the Protestant Bishop of Killaloe of Killimer and Burrane. Enrolled June 16, 1667.

Murrogh, Earl of Inchiquin, was secured a little earlier, March 22, 1666, in 39,961 acres, at a rent of £374. In this grant were included the castle, manor, town, and lands of Inchiquin and Corcomroe; the "courts leet and baron seneschalship, fishing weares, ferry," and other privileges held in the "manor of Bryansbridge;" the parsonage and vicarage of Clondegad, and half tithes in other parishes, twenty-two ploughlands in the parish of Killone, and seventeen in the parish of Dromcliffe.

Ed. Worthe, Protestant Bishop of Killaloe, got 955 acres, rent £9, on February 14, 1667. Edmund MacGrath, 5799 acres, north and east of Tulla, rent £54, enrolled June 29, 1667. Bartholomew Stackpoole, 3041, rent £28, with power to hold two fairs at Stackpoole's Court of Enagh yearly for ever on the 20th of July and 6th of December, "and ye eve of each day with a Court of Pye Powder and the tolls, 5s." John MacNamara of Creevagh got 2370, rent £22, at Moyriesk and Ballyhickey, in addition to considerable portions of other townlands. Donogh O'Brien of Dough got 4340, rent £41, together with the castle, manor, town, and lands of Dough O'Connor (now Liscannor). Henry Ivers got 2133, rent £19, with the castle and town of Kilkishen, with power to hold fairs and markets at Mount Ivers and Knocklough, rent for each fair and market, 5s. Donogh O'Brien of Leimaneigh, 3750, rent £38, but of these, two ploughlands were to be for the use of Samuel Burton, probably only a life title. William Lysaght got 1239, rent £11, October 4, 1678. John Cusack got 967, rent £9, February 28, 1679. John Blake and Marcus French got 1778, rent £16, together with the manor, town, and lands of Ballyalla. Theobald Butler got 236, rent £2, 16s., and 649, rent £6. Cornet John Gore got 401, with the MacClancy's castle of Knocfin, rent £3, 15s. Cornelius Clanchy got 1000, rent £9, with the curious proviso that the Irish names should be changed to Castle Bridgeman, Bridgeman's Town, Bridgeman's Grove, and Mount Ambrose. These names have disappeared with that branch of the family. Various members of the White family are down for grants in Bunratty and Clonderalaw—Stephen White for 486, rent £4, 11s.; Jenette White for 549, rent £5; Henry White for 420, rent £3, 18s., and 359, rent £3, 2s.; and David White, 162, rent £1, 10s. Nicholas Burke got 4512, rent £43, 11s.; John Sarsfield got 1438, rent £13, 9s.; Donogh MacNamara, 319, rent £3; Daniel MacNamara, 234, rent £2, 4s.; Matthew MacMahon, 713, rent £6, 13s.; James Butler, 718, rent £6, 12s.; Sir Richard Ingoldsby, 1349, rent £122, 6s.; Captain William Hamilton, 5290, rent £49, 11s.; Colonel Willoughby, 1399, rent £13; Colonel Cary Dillon, 2117, rent £19, 16s.; John Eyre, 2221, rent £15; James Nixon, 1037, rent £9, 14s.; Mortogh MacMahon, 270, rent £2, 10s.; Conor O'Brien, FitzDonogh, 1674, rent £15; William Ryan, 706, rent £6; Pierce Creagh, 1718, etc. etc.

These are but specimens of a list too long to be inserted here. It will be seen at a glance that many of these were natives of the county, while others were outsiders rewarded for their services to the Stuarts. A considerable number of both classes of owners had, in the meantime, thrown in their lot with William, and so not only saved their properties, but were able, for small sums, to purchase portions of the confiscated lands of their unfortunate neighbours. It will cause no surprise to find, after their past well-known temporising policy, that the chief families of the O'Briens—notably the Earl of Thomond, the Earl of Inchiquin, and the Dromoland O'Briens—were of this number. Of Lord Clare alone, or almost alone, among them can it be said that he could taste—

> "The fierce joy that warriors feel
> When all but life and honour's lost."

We have now to consider and take note of the third confiscation of Clare property within a period of less than sixty years. History, except in Ireland, affords no parallel to it. The second—that under Charles II. and James II.—was but, on the whole, a recovery of their old possessions by the native Irish and Anglo-Irish. The third, under William, was, in the main, a confirmation of the first under Cromwell, in favour of the English and Protestant interest. William made liberal grants of the confiscated and deserted lands to his own followers; but, falling somewhat into disfavour with the English people, on account of his partiality to the Dutch, the Parliament appointed Commissioners to investigate and modify or annul some of these grants. Among those so favoured was Joost Van Keppel, whom he had created Earl of Albemarle, and to whom he granted the greater part of the vast property of the Lord Clare. He, anticipating the change coming over William's English subjects, disposed of such title as he had to three purchasers, Nicholas Westby, Francis Burton, and James MacDonnell, for the nominal sum, for such a property, of a little over two thousand pounds. His letters-patent were issued in February 1698, and the sale was effected within a fortnight after. The Commissioners took note of this, and ordered a re-sale. The same parties having, it is to be presumed, some right of pre-emption, again purchased for the sum of £10,161, thus securing the Parliamentary title in March 1702, under which they were enabled to enter upon, and transmit to their descendants to the present day, the valuable estates forfeited by the chivalrous Lord Clare. It must be said that there are more questionable titles than this in the county. The one already alluded to in a footnote above, under which the Earl of Thomond leased over the lands of Donogh MacNamara of Rafoland and Mouhane to Harrison, was surely one of these.

The foregoing affords an example of the way in which very

many of the owners of property in Clare acquired their titles. There was practically no public competition at these sales. It is not too much to believe that, between the Commissioners who had charge of the sale of the forfeited lands, and the buyers, who were for the most part Williamites, like the Earl of Thomond and Sir Donal O'Brien of Dromoland, or followers of the Stuarts who had conveniently changed their politics or their religion, all alike feathered their nests well. If the reader cares to look over the list of names already given as having secured properties under the Stuarts, he will, if a native of Clare, recognise easily some present owners whose ancestors belonged to the latter class. Of the former, next to the O'Briens, the Vandeleurs fared best. Their ancestor, John Vandeleur, a younger son of the Ralahine family, having been appointed to the vicarages of Kilrush, Kilfeeragh, and Killballyowen, where there were hardly any Protestants, had time to devote himself to martial pursuits. He acquired distinction at the battle of Aughrim, and, with such a reputation, found it easy, on his return to West Clare, to negotiate for a large slice of the broad domains there which had fallen into the hands of the victors. Another purchaser to whom, unlike Vandeleur, an evil fame popularly attaches, was John Cusack of Kilkishen. It is traditionally believed of him that he set himself to "discover" and betray those who, having property, still strove in private to cling to the old faith,[1] using for this purpose disguises, so as to worm his way into the houses where Mass was secretly offered.

Among purchasers at this period was Nathaniel Lucas of

---

[1] His remains lie in the graveyard of Clonloum, near Kilkishen. The popular belief is that a tombstone without any inscription having been placed over his grave, some rural poet cut on it, in Irish, the lines thus translated—

> "God is pleased when a sinner ceases to sin;
> The Devil is pleased when he a soul doth win;
> The world is pleased whene'er a bad man dies:
> Now all are pleased, for here John Cusack lies."

His family removed the tombstone, so that no trace of his grave remains. He had no son, but it is commonly believed that through his daughters some of the Gore and Studdert families inherit his property.

Clonmel, who for the small sum of ten pounds secured 220 acres of the prime land of Glanquin and Tullacommon, in the barony of Inchiquin, and who probably was the father of the celebrated Dr. Lucas. The Westropp and Ivers families, who are still represented in the county, purchased largely; but it is fair to add that they did not deal harshly with those who had to accept tenancies under them. Similar purchases were made in every barony of the county. Not less than 72,426 acres of what was then regarded [1] as profitable land, together with the far greater portion set down as unprofitable, but rendered profitable since in no small degree by the unaided industry of the tenants, passed over for insignificant sums to the predecessors of the present owners. Nearly all of the best-known families of the old septs were swept out, or settled down in obscurity to till, under the new comers, the lands owned by their ancestors for over two thousand years.

. The ownership of Clare lands became still further changed, by the sale in 1712 of great portion of the Thomond property. The earl, having no direct issue, and being probably in monetary difficulties, sold on fee-farm titles, under a Special Act of Parliament, considerable portions of O'Brien territory, of which English feudal laws made him sole owner, at the cost of the clan. Protestants only could purchase, and thus these lands also fell into the hands of the families already named, the Burtons, Gores, Westbys, MacDonnells, Westropps, Stackpooles, Henns, Scots, Gabbetts, etc. The titles acquired, as related above, are those under which, *as their origin*, most of the Clare properties are held at the present day.

[1] Report of the Commissioners of Public Records.

CHAPTER XXIV.

FROM 1703 TO 1770.

Working of the Penal Laws in Clare—Government Tools—Bishops in the Penal Times—Curious Elections—Cutting of Woods—Irish Brigade—Letter of Lord Clare—Thomond Marshal of France—Flag presented by Louis XVI.—Charles Lucas.

THIS chapter must cover a much longer period of time than any preceding one in the Christian period, for the reason that, for more than a century following, Clare can hardly be said to have a history. Its people, beaten to the ground, trampled on, and stripped of all proprietorial and civic rights, sought safety in obscurity. The policy of William, who died from a fall off his horse in 1702, or rather of the party who made William king for their own purposes, was continued during the whole reign of Queen Anne and her successors. It may be summed up in the short sentence—ferocious, savage religious and civil persecution of the defeated Irish Catholics. No other country claiming to be regarded as civilised—Russia alone hardly excepted—has such a black record on the face of its history as England has in the working of the Penal Laws of the eighteenth century. I can find no better way of describing the condition of Clare during all this time than by a recital of the conditions—they cannot be called laws—under which the people were compelled to live. As already stated, the whole population of Clare at this period must, in all probability, have been under thirty thousand. Sir Richard Cox, the bigoted author of *Hibernia Anglicana*, writes exultingly in a letter,[1] dated October 25th, 1705, that "the youth and gentry of the Irish were destroyed in the rebellion, or gone to France; those who are left, destitute of horses,

---
[1] Southwell Papers.

arms, money, capacity, and courage. Five out of six of the Irish are poor, insignificant slaves, fit for nothing but to hew wood and draw water."

Before going into the particulars of the iniquitous code of laws which reduced the people of Clare and of all Ireland to the condition described above, it will interest the reader to have before his eyes the very words of the Treaty of Limerick, solemnly made with those same "Irish" on the 3rd of October 1691, only fifteen years before, while they had still arms in their hands, and Patrick Sarsfield to lead them.

1st. "That the Roman Catholics of this kingdom shall enjoy such privileges in the exercise of their religion as are consistent with the laws of Ireland; or as they did enjoy in the reign of King Charles the Second; and their Majesties [as soon as their affairs will permit them to summon a Parliament in this kingdom] will endeavour to secure them such further security in that particular as may preserve them from *any disturbance* upon the account of their said religion."

2nd. "All the inhabitants or residents of Lymerick, or any other garrison now in possession of the Irish, and all officers and soulders now in arms under any commission of K. James, or those authorised by him to grant the same, in the several counties of Lymerick, Clare, Kerry, Cork, Mayo, or any of them [and all such as are under their protection in the said counties [1]]; and all the commissioned officers in their Majesties' quarters that belong to the Irish regiments now in being, that are treated with, and who are prisoners of war or have taken protection, who shall return and submit to their Majesties' obedience, they and every of their heirs shall hold, possess, and enjoy all and every their estates of freehold and inheritance, and all the right, title, and inheritance, privileges and immunities which they, and every or any of them held, enjoyed, or were rightfully entitled to in the reign of King Charles the Second, or at any time since by the laws and statutes that were in force in the said reign of King

---

[1] The words within brackets were omitted either by mistake or design from the first draft of the Treaty prepared for signature, but had to be added at the remonstrance of Sarsfield while the French fleet was believed to be sailing up the river.

Charles the Second. . . . And all and every the said persons, of what trade, profession, or calling soever they be, shall and may use, exercise, and practise their several and respective professions, trades, and callings as freely as they did use, exercise, and enjoy the same in the reign of K. James the Second, . . . provided that no person whatsoever shall have or enjoy the benefit of this article, that shall neglect or refuse to take the Oath of Allegiance made by Act of Parliament in the first year of the reign of their present Majesties, when thereunto required." This Oath of Allegiance imposed no religious restriction whatsoever — simply allegiance to the sovereigns ruling in England.

There was, it must be admitted, a certain vagueness in the wording of the first of these articles; yet it bears on its face the promise of liberty of worship so long as the just laws of the kingdom were not violated. It cannot possibly be distorted into the meaning that Roman Catholics were to be freemen in Ireland only when they became Protestant. That this was the policy adopted towards them in the years following is so well known that it requires no proof. However, a few specimens of the Draconian code enacted against them, originating in the very next Parliaments after the Treaty, will find a fitting place here, if only to contrast them with the words of the Articles given above.

In 1693, Lord Capel came to Ireland, two years only after the Treaty, and, being made soon after Lord Deputy, began to curtail in every way the rights secured by it to the Catholics. To enable him the better to carry out the fell purpose for which he was appointed, he called a Parliament in Dublin in 1695. Among the Acts of this Parliament, passed unanimously, so well had he packed it with the most bitter enemies of the people, were one for "banishing all Papists exercising any ecclesiastical jurisdiction, and all regulars of the Popish clergy, out of the kingdom before the 1st of May 1698;" another "to prevent Papists being solicitors;" another for "restraining foreign education;" another "to prevent Protestants intermarrying with Papists," etc. etc. The penalty upon clerics remaining in the kingdom was imprisonment until they could be transported beyond the seas; and execution for high treason if they dared to return. If any person concealed or entertained a cleric after the 1st of May 1698, he was to be fined £20 for the first offence, £40 for the second, and for the third he should suffer the loss of all real and personal property, half of which, if it did not exceed £100, was to go to the informer, the rest to the king. The penalty for sending children out of the kingdom for education, or for instructing children at home or abroad in the Romish religion, was "forfeiture of all legal rights, as well as of all real and personal property." Out of the lands thus seized, William made grants to his mistress, Elizabeth Villiers, worth in all about £25,000 per annum.

The members for Clare in this Parliament were—for the county, Sir Donogh O'Brien and Sir Henry Ingoldsby; for Ennis, Francis Gore and Francis Burton. With these were associated for the purpose of collecting the poll-tax struck in this Parliament, the Hon. John O'Brien, Simon Purdon, Augustine Fitzgerald, James MacDonnell, Edmund Perry, Henry Lee, Thomas Hickman; Neptune Blood, Dean of Kilfenora; John Hawkins, Clerk; James Hamilton, Walter Hickman, and William Smith, Provost of Ennis.

Again, in 1703,—the Duke of Ormonde being Lord-Lieutenant,—a Bill "for preventing the further growth of Popery" passed through the English and Irish Houses of Parliament. It would appear from this Bill, that, in spite of the exodus of the Irish army and the numerous recruits following it from the land, the Catholics were still increasing in number. It was not deemed sufficient to have pains and penalties of the worst possible kind imposed on those who practised Catholicity. The open acceptance of Protestantism was made obligatory by the famous "Sacramental Test" included in this nefarious Act of Parliament. This clause excluded from all civil rights—in fact, made outlaws in their country—those who did not receive the Sacrament according to the rite of the Church of England, thus renewing the Act of Elizabeth. The Catholics claimed to be heard by counsel at the bar of the House. A Clareman, Sir Theobald Butler, together with Sir Stephen Rice and Counsellor Malone, were, as if in mockery, accorded this barren privilege. Their arguments, grounded on the sacredness of treaties and the rights of conscience, fell on deaf ears. Not a single member of the Irish Parliament uttered a word of protest against this sweeping measure, and so it became what was called law. Other Acts of a similar tendency followed in quick succession. The Catholic child was tempted to rob his father, the Catholic wife to despoil her husband. Either had only to pretend to become a Protestant, and immediately became the owner in law of the property. If a Protestant became a Catholic, the property passed to the next Protestant relation. Popish secular clergy were obliged to register themselves — the regulars having been all banished—for particular parishes, but dared not say mass openly. This registration could have no other object than to enable official attention to be turned upon them, and to have their movements well and carefully watched. A reward of £50 was offered to the priest-hunter who discovered any person exercising ecclesiastical jurisdiction, such as a bishop or vicar-general; £20 for a priest not registered; and £10 for any Popish schoolmaster. These rewards were levied in fines on Papists alone. A penalty of £20 could be recovered from any one who refused to disclose the names of priests who said mass or persons assisting at it. The learned professions were rigidly closed against Catholics. They could not purchase lands or take leases for more than thirty-one years. If the profits of any farm worked by a Papist exceeded the rent by one-third, he could be deprived of the surplus in favour of the Protestant discoverer. Catholics were not allowed to settle on the forfeited estates except as labourers or cottiers, with holdings worth less than thirty shillings a year. From time to time orders were issued to have these barbarous enactments, and many others of a similar kind, rigidly enforced. This would point to a generous unwillingness on the part of some local Protestants to use against their down-trodden Catholic neighbours the horrible engine for practising cruelty towards them placed by statute in their hands.

Such measures, and others, all of the most elaborate kind, for oppressing Catholics, were passed from time to time in the Irish Parliament during the whole reign of Anne. She died in 1714. In the reign of her successor, George I., a struggle of a constitutional character arose between the Irish and English Houses of Peers. It originated in a law-case — Sherlock *v.* Annesley — upon which appeal was made to the English Parliament, and ended in the famous declaration of that House, in A.D. 1719, "that the Irish Parliament was not possessed of independent authority even in matters relating to Ireland, but was subject to the English Parliament." I give here for brevity's sake the substance, not the exact words. This encroachment on the ancient rights of Irish Parliaments was tamely acquiesced in, and remained in force till Grattan and the volunteers tore it to shreds in A.D. 1782. It did not lessen the appetite for persecution. A new measure for still more effectively "preventing the growth of Popery" passed readily through Parliament, 1723; but, having to be submitted to the Parliament of England, it was found to contain a clause of such an inhuman and brutal character against the Irish clergy, that, though hating them intensely, those English gentlemen felt constrained, for decency's sake, to reject it.

What is given above does not nearly exhaust the black list of oppressive enactments against the disarmed Irish Catholics placed on the Irish and English Statute Books during the reigns of William and Anne, and the Georges. No others need be quoted. They speak for the rest; or, if their common character be looked for, it is best summed up in the well-known words of Edmund Burke, The Penal Laws, he wrote,[1] were "a machine of nice and elaborate contrivance, and as well fitted for the oppression, impoverishment, and degradation of a people, and the debasement in them of human nature itself, as ever proceeded from the perverted ingenuity of man."

Under such conditions the people of Clare had to drag on existence as best they could, for the greater part of the eighteenth century. They had no voice in the selection of members for Parliament. The honour—such as it was—of representing the county and borough was enjoyed by only about half a dozen families. The franchise was limited to

[1] Letter to Sir Hercules Langrishe.

staunch Williamite Protestants. These alone, and they were but a few, were represented in those treaty-breaking Parliaments. It must be said of them that they knew their men; for not one of the members for Clare or Ennis showed the slightest disinclination to rivet the chains on the necks of their Catholic fellow-citizens. Not a word of manly protest was raised even against the brutal punishment proposed for priests already referred to, and which the English conscience, intensely Protestant as it was, could not stomach. From a speech delivered far on in the century, A.D. 1764, by one of those so-called representatives, Sir Lucius O'Brien, member for Ennis, glimpses may be had both of the spirit animating them, and of the condition of the people of Clare. After stating that then Clare was "extremely well peopled," he says farther on:[1]—

"I need not show the political disadvantages that arise in this country from the number of Papists among us. It is necessary to lay the Papists under some restraints from which the Protestant is free." The vivid picture given by Edmund Burke of the working of the Penal Laws against Irish Catholics is neatly toned down by this degenerate Clare O'Brien to "some restraints on the Papists from which the Protestant is free"!

We gather from this speech that in spite of all the "Acts to prevent the growth of Popery," Popery was still growing in Clare. The occasion of the speech was a motion made by Sir William Osborne in the House of Commons for a return of the names of non-resident incumbents. Sir Lucius O'Brien, supporting the motion, states that "there are in Clare no less than seventy-six parishes, and no more than fourteen churches; so that sixty-two parishes of the seventy-six are sinecures;" and that, "when the number of the churches is so small, the rectors of most of them are non-resident. Yet such is the fact, and so much greater regard have the clergy to the tithes than to the souls of their parish." He laments that owing to this "they must have recourse to Popish priests. The priest, sir, must marry those who would enter into the nuptial contract; the priest must baptize the children;

[1] *Memoirs of the O'Briens*, by O'Donohue, p. 539.

and the priest must bury their dead; or they must cohabit like savages in the recesses of Africa, the child must be considered a mere denizen of nature, under no covenant with God, and the dead must be deposited in the earth without any memorial of a resurrection." A pretty picture this of Clare after seventy years of enforced Protestantism and of violent and unceasing efforts to root out Catholicity!

The names of those who were necessarily most prominent in sustaining the old cause on the soil of Clare through those evil days find a fitting place here.

From 1702, when John O'Molony died, to 1713, the diocese of Killaloe was ruled by vicars. In that year Eustace Browne was elevated to the dangerous dignity of bishop, and was succeeded in 1728 by Sylvester Lewis Lloyd.[1] He was succeeded in 1739 by Patrick MacDonogh, who ruled the diocese for only four years, and had for successor in 1743 William O'Meara. Patrick O'Naghten was appointed in 1752. He had been for sixteen years President of Douay College, which owed to him much of its celebrity. He died the same year, and was succeeded by Nicholas Madgett, President of the College of St. Bàrbara at Paris. An exchange of dioceses took place between him and another William O'Meara, who had been Bishop of Ardfert, each one probably preferring the diocese of his nativity. This bishop lived till 1765, when he was succeeded by Michael Peter MacMahon, who lived till 1804. It is believed that he was one of the family from which Marshal MacMahon sprang, and used to receive from his French relatives a gift of wine every year. How these bishops and the priests who worked under them contrived to discharge their functions in spite of the Penal Laws, no one can tell. They had to live in concealment, and so left no record. But all the same they did their work well, as the Clare of 1828 abundantly proved.

It has been already stated that the Parliamentary constituency of Clare was very limited during the eighteenth century. We have evidence of this in a petition presented to Parliament by Henry O'Brien and Nicholas Westby in 1715, against the return of Francis Gore and John Ivers,

---

[1] Brady's *Episcopal Succession*, p. 128.

who had been declared members for the county. The objections lodged were [1] that Arthur Gore, son of Francis Gore, being High Sheriff, gave only six days' notice, at a court held at Ardsollus, of the time and place of the election—that one hour before the time fixed he called for a poll, not at Ardsollus, but at Mount Ivers, near the house of one of the candidates, where only about twelve voters were present, and then declared his father and John Ivers duly elected—that before the hour named about one hundred and fifty Protestant freeholders arrived on the scene and demanded a poll on behalf of the petitioners, and were not only refused, but fired on by the Sheriff's men; and that afterwards the Sheriff went to the house of one Stephen Bagwell, and did there take the votes of some other supporters of his father and John Ivers. In support of these charges, a similar petition was presented to the committee appointed to investigate the matter, by George Colpoys, Robert Harrison, and Neptune Blood, Dean of Kilfenora. It is a curious commentary on the methods of the time, that in the face of such apparently circumstantial evidence the sitting members held their seats, and so about a dozen voters gave to Clare its parliamentary representatives.

Another noteworthy incident occurred in connection with the next election, which took place on the accession of George I. in 1727. Another petition was presented against the members returned, Francis Burton and George Purdon. The Sheriff now was Thomas Stothard—the first of the name now so widespead in Clare as Studdart I could find any trace of. This time nearly two hundred votes were cast, and, after a searching inquiry, Sir Edward O'Brien was declared elected in room of George Purdon, on the grounds that some of the latter's voters had married Popish wives *who had not become Protestants within one year after marriage.*

Keeping the foregoing facts, coupled with the pressure of the Penal Laws, before our eyes, it is easy enough to draw a picture of the abject condition of the Catholics of Clare during the eighteenth century. For them it was one long night of a worse than Egyptian bondage. Round them everywhere

---

[1] *Memoirs of the O'Briens,* p. 381.

were the ruins of the churches built and endowed by their forefathers; or if some still stood,—the most notable of which were St. Flannan's Cathedral and the more ancient shrine of St. Molua at Killaloe,—they had the mortification to see them converted to Protestant uses. A Catholic could hardly call what he had his own. If real property, he held it absolutely at the will of his Protestant landlord; and if personal, he knew not the moment when the "discoverer," or the "priest-hunter," would pounce on him for Popish practices. He dared not have a horse worth more than five pounds, nor give his children any Catholic education, except such as could be snatched from hunted priests and teachers in lonely, out-of-the-way places. The hedge-schoolmaster became an institution in those dark days, and left a name that should be a name of honour in all succeeding generations. Some families deserve special notice in this connection—the Curtins or MacCurtins, the MacBrodys, the MacClancys, and the MacGraths. They carried on, in the face of persecution, the honourable traditional calling of their clans. One of these, And. MacCurtin, who lived at Moyglass, in the parish of Kilmurray, in 1730, wrote an Irish dictionary; a quaint Irish poem, calling on Don, the fairy king, to make him his gilly or horse-boy, as the poetical profession *had gone out of fashion*; an exquisitely-written copy of the *Cathreim Turlogha*,[1] now in the library of Trinity College, and other works. Another MacCurtin, Hugh, published in Louvain, A.D. 1728, *The Elements of the Irish Language Grammatically Explained in English.* Members of this family were all along, down to our own time, remarkable both as priests and teachers.

The county at the beginning of this century, in spite of all the political changes, was still beautifully wooded, even

---

[1] Extracts from this work, written by Magrath in or about 1459, have already been given. Though in a very turgid style, it gives internal evidence of fidelity to truth and facts, and dealing as it does with Clare history for a period of nearly two hundred years, from the reign of Donogh Cairbreac O'Brien down to nearly the writer's own time, it throws light and life on various places in the county, the names of which, as found in this book, are still retained in the language of the people. It exhibits the MacNamaras specially as hardly second in power and influence at that period to the O'Briens.

along the sea-board. I have found in all parts of it rooted stumps of trees standing still where they had been growing in the not very distant past. In Shaw Mason's *Statistical Survey of Ireland*, he writes that "almost the entire county about Ennistymon was, within the recollection of an old man, aged one hundred, who died about thirty or forty years ago (1810), covered with woods, mostly oak and ash full grown, and that he frequently shot wild pheasants in those woods." All that country, and indeed nearly all West Clare, is now bare and naked. The writer heard from his father that his grandfather used to tell how, when cattle strayed away in his youth, so covered with trees was the whole country between Tulla Quin and Kilkishen, that search had to be made for them through the glades of the woods. It is nearly all bare now. He heard himself, from old people near Bodyke, that the old people of their young days told of the slopes of the hills, all the way from Tomgraney to Broadford, being so thickly wooded that "a man might go from one place to the other along the branches of the trees almost without coming to the ground." There is not a tree there now. The new owners easily found markets for such valuable timber. It is traditionally stated that some old owners too, notably the absentee English O'Briens, stripped the hills round and above Killaloe of the noble oaks which adorned them, and of which were built some of the finest ships in the English navy.

The gloomy condition of plundered and downtrodden Claremen at home during all those years is relieved by the lustre which the exiles from the county shed on the name of Clare in the battlefields of Europe.

Lord Clare's regiment, forming part, and no inconsiderable part, of the famous "Old Brigade," numbered, on their arrival in France in 1691, sixteen hundred men, and was recruited from home, according as gaps were made, and not infrequently made, in its ranks. A letter from Lord Clare to one of the recruiting officers is well worth a place in any history of the county:—

"Paris, *Oct.* 1746.

"Dear MacDonogh,[1]—I congratulate you on your marriage, but trust it will not induce you to retire from the Irish Brigade. I hope you do not forget the memorable day they had at Fontenoy, and the other glorious days in which they had a share. Your promotion goes on, and all are wishing for your return. With your assistance and O'Brien's, the ranks are near filled up. I hope to see you soon. How does my old friend and relation, Cap. Dermot O'Brien, get on ? Is he in good health, and permitted to live and pray in peace ?
—Yours, Clare.

"To Mons. A. MacDonogh,
  Co. Clare, Ireland."

Notwithstanding their chivalrous devotion to the fallen fortunes of France's ally, the exiled Stuart, the Irish officers had to submit to a reduction of rank in the French service. All the same, they fought nobly. Far from home, but with hearts and eyes longingly and lovingly turned towards the old hills of Clare, their colours floated over most of the battlefields of the Continent during that stormy period. Many a brave fellow, dying on foreign soil and in an alien cause, must have felt as Sarsfield did when he uttered the pathetic exclamation, "Would that this blood were shed for Ireland !" To follow their fortunes through all their wanderings would be out of place here. Whoever desires full information will find it in detail in O'Callaghan's *Irish Brigades in the Service of France*. It may be enough to note here that every man of Clare blood should carry engraved in his memory the names of Embrun, and Marsaglia, and Valençay, and Blenheim, and Ramillies, and Dettingen, and Fontenoy; in every one of which, and in other fields of less note, the valour of Claremen was conspicuous. It must be added that they were at times wild and unruly. This gave occasion for a complaint

---

[1] This was, I think, the MacDonogh who established a thriving smuggling trade in West Clare, and upon which in no small degree, as I have been told, the MacNamara property in Doolin and Ennistymon was built up. Wines and silks were received in exchange for wool, hides, and tallow.

of them and reply to it which should not be, and will not be, easily forgotten. The French king, being in conversation with Lord Clare, who, on the death without issue of the Earl of Thomond, had assumed that title, and was known by it on the Continent, and had also risen to the rank of marshal, said to him,—

"Marshal, your countrymen give me great trouble."

"Sire," replied he, "your enemies make the same complaint of them everywhere."

It is nothing short of a national loss that this brave soldier's line also became extinct. The clash of incessant war left him no thought of marriage till late in life. He married into a noble French family, but the children born to him did not long survive him, and thus dropped out of Clare history the one family—the solitary conspicuous family of a noble stock—which had proved true in trying times, and at enormous sacrifice, to principle and to patriotism. Other O'Briens there were, indeed, and not a few, but not so prominent, who during all this century proved themselves worthy of the better traditions of their race.

This brief outline of Claremen, exiled because of their devotion to faith and country, may be brought to a close with the testimony given to them by the unhappy Louis XVI. Having to disembody the Irish Brigade in his fallen fortunes, he presented to them a banner with the proud motto—

"1692—1792."
"*Semper et Ubique Fideles.*"

At home, the only or almost the only bright spot on the page of Clare history was the lustre shed on it by the career of Charles Lucas. He was born at or near Corofin in 1713, and was probably a son of the Nathaniel Lucas who acquired property in that locality, as already narrated in the last chapter. An apothecary by profession, he settled down in Dublin, and, becoming successful there, found it easy to obtain admission to the Corporation. Here he soon made his influence felt while exposing and denouncing the jobbery of that venal body. Fortunately he did not limit his inquiries to the misdeeds of the Corporation of Dublin. He soared higher, and, with eloquent voice and able pen, turned the fierce light of public opinion on the malpractices of Dublin Castle and Parliament itself. Though the Catholics had neither vote nor voice in the affairs of the nation, and were outside his range of vision, yet they viewed with delight his vigorous attacks on their tyrants. He stirred up a spirit of patriotism in the breasts of even the narrow-minded, bigoted ascendancy party. Songs and ballads were written and sung in his honour through the length and breadth of the land. The humble Clare apothecary became the idol of the people as the champion of nationality against foreign dominion.

The Government and Parliament naturally feared and hated this bold intruder on their preserves. When an effort was about being made to elect him to fill a seat for Dublin, that became vacant in 1749, it was determined not only to oppose him but to crush him. That weapon always at hand for Government lawyers—a prosecution for libellous and disloyal publications—was directed against him. He evaded it by crossing over into England. They, glad to get rid of and silence him, allowed it to drop, but the slavish House of Commons was got to pass a resolution declaring him "an enemy of his country."

At the death of George II. in 1760, a new Parliament was called. Lucas took advantage of the change to return to Dublin, where he was received with popular rejoicings, and at once elected member for the city. In this capacity he worked energetically for the redress of grievances in the House, and the creation of a purely Irish spirit in the country. He may be truly said to have paved the way, with Molyneux and Swift, for the Declaration of Independence, which, alas! he did not live to share in. He died in 1771. The following epitaph is on his tomb in St. Michael's Cemetery, Dublin :—

"Lucas, Hibernia's friend, her joy and pride,
Her powerful bulwark, and her faithful guide,
Firm in the Senate, steady to his trust;
Unmoved by fear, and obstinately just.

Born 26th Sept. 1713.
Died 4th Nov. 1771."

This new spirit of Irish nationality infused into the people compelled the House of Commons to commit a kind of suicide. Hitherto, Parliaments were unlimited as to time, and consequently practically irresponsible to the people. The last one had sat for thirty years. Pressure was so brought to bear on that which met on the accession of George III., that it was compelled to petition the king for a seven years' limit as in England. It was too much to expect that what even loyal Irish asked for should be granted, but the case made was so strong, that eight years was fixed as the life of future Irish Parliaments. This change necessitated a new election, at which Sir Edward O'Brien and Francis Burton were returned for the county of Clare, and Lucius O'Brien—a son of Sir Edward—and Thomas Burton for the borough of Ennis. This Lucius O'Brien being a man of considerable ability, employed it largely in promoting Irish interests, which meant of course Protestant interests only, in Parliament. Of his views regarding Catholics we have already a specimen given above. He succeeded to the baronetcy on the death of his father in 1765.

The other most important measures with which his name as member for Clare was associated were the independence of the judiciary, and some salutary checks put upon the wasteful and dishonest expenditure of public moneys. Before this chapter, which covers the worst period of the Penal Laws, closes, it is but common justice to record the constancy with which the great bulk of the people of Clare clung to the old faith. Some, indeed, bent before the storm. Their names, with the dates of their submission, appear on lists still preserved in the British Museum, called the "Egerton MSS. 77," and from which they have been published in Lenihan's carefully compiled *History of Limerick*. I do not care to reproduce them here, because I find on examination that most of those families have either disappeared entirely, or are now represented by Catholics. At the present time there are not three per cent. of the whole population non-Catholic. This fact speaks for itself. It bears silent but eloquent testimony to the utter failure and collapse of the Penal Laws in Clare.

CHAPTER XXV.

FROM 1770 TO 1801.

Condition of Clare — Dilapidation—Commerce impeded — Population increasing — Families from Neighbouring Counties—Public Spirit reviving—First Signs of Toleration—Building of Catholic Chapels—Clare Members of Parliament on the side of Liberty—Relief Acts—Nationalist Meeting at Ennis—Spanish Admiral O'Kuoney—Donogh Rua MacNamara—And. Magrath—Thomas Dermody—Other Clare Celebrities of the last century.

EVEN at this period, A.D. 1771, so long after the Williamite subjugation, the county had scarcely yet begun to recover from the prostrate condition into which it had been flung. The means of communication between the people were of the worst kind. Roads were few and bad, and badly kept. They were run invariably against the hill-tops for the purpose of securing at little cost a solid foundation. Produce was carried to fairs and markets on the backs of horses, or dragged on rude sleighs over the ill-constructed, narrow roads. Eugene O'Curry mentions, at p. 369, *Ordnance Survey*, that his grandfather, Melaghlan O'Curry, a large farmer, employed his men, horses, and *sledges* in burying the victims of the famine of 1741. Dean Kenny of Ennis, with whom the writer lived for some time, told him that even at the beginning of the present century these primitive modes of conveyance were still in use. The almost equally rude and inconvenient block-wheeled carts began to be used first about this time. Some of them are yet preserved as relics of this transition period. The wealthiest of the gentry owned heavy four-wheeled carriages, but seldom used them, because of the difficulty of drawing them up and down the steep and dangerous roads. Spring cars were totally unknown. Pillions, upon which the gentleman's or farmer's wife sat behind her husband on horseback, took their place, and were much used far on into the present century. The need for strong and sure-footed horses for saddle-work in such circumstances stimulated the breeding of high-class animals, and thus Spancil Hill Fair acquired celebrity all over Ireland.

The general state of the county was still in a very sorry condition. The traces of the long and disastrous conflict were abundant on every side. The ruins of churches, monasteries, and forsaken homes, covered the land, while very little was done in the way of reconstruction. The towns and villages were mere rows of thatched huts, and without buildings of any architectural character to relieve their dreariness. It is related that when Paul Liddy, the Feacle freebooter, who, like another Clareman, MacNamara of Cong, levied blackmail on the English intruders, and was generous with it to the dispossessed, was arrested and lodged in Ennis jail, his gang found it easy to set a great part of the town on fire, and while all available hands—those in charge of the jail included—were busily engaged in quenching the flames, they actually broke through the jail walls and liberated him.

The poorer people, entirely cowed and at the mercy of the new-comers, burrowed in unsightly cabins in out-of-the-way places, and lived on the potato almost exclusively. The good things of the land went in the shape of rent to supply delicacies to the tables of its new owners. They knew practically nothing of the outside world. Education was at the lowest ebb. Their whole intellectual training was confined to what they snatched at intervals from the hedge-schoolmaster, or heard at Mass-time from the carefully-concealed priest. How it was that in such depressing conditions the love of learning, as well as of country, was transmitted so vigorously, can only be explained by the admittedly strong elastic tone of the Celtic mind.

As the century waxed on, some little religious toleration began to be displayed. In this respect Clare was much better off than the sister-county Tipperary, more especially the northern—the Dalcassian—half, with which this history is so much concerned. There the Cromwellian conquest had been complete, and a Puritanical element of the most overbearing and insolent type had been largely implanted. It was not so in Clare. A considerable number of the gentry were of the old stock. They had indeed abandoned the old faith, but with them in some degree "blood told." For instance, Sir Donogh O'Brien became legal owner of the Clenagh and Ballylean property, only to protect it and restore it honourably to the MacMahons. A large number, too, of the new proprietors, though of English blood and faith, were only purchasers, and had not come into direct collision with the despoiled. For these reasons a better feeling began to grow up, and though the repressive enactments were still there, and hung like a millstone round the necks of the peasantry, inasmuch as they could be at any time appealed to, they were not rigidly enforced. The Catholic religion began to be practised a little more openly. Priests felt more secure; and though they dared not put themselves much in evidence by building stately churches, or turning to account any of those that had been seized and unroofed, they commenced putting up those little thatched chapels all over the county, mostly in remote spots, the last of which—those of Kilclaran in Feacle, and Toovara near Lisdoonvarna—have only lately given place to edifices more worthy of the purpose to which they are dedicated.

No suitable provision was yet made for the education in Ireland of the Catholic clergy. The sons of the Catholic gentry, as well as professional and mercantile aspirants, had still to go abroad, or else receive their education in an atmosphere so saturated with aggressive Protestantism as that of Trinity College and kindred institutions. Not a few of these succumbed to the temptation of falling in with the wealthy and favoured professors of the new faith; and their descendants are still easily recognisable in Clare. Of those who went abroad some fell under the influence of French infidel teaching. They found no difficulty in dropping the Catholic religion, and with it the brand of inferiority which had been fixed on it in these countries.

Meanwhile the population was again rapidly increasing. It received numerous accessions in Cromwell's time and since from the neighbouring counties. There were always close relations, friendly or unfriendly, between the people of South Galway—the O'Kellys, O'Shaughnessys, O'Donnellans, and Burkes—and those of Clare; and so those names are found scattered all over the county. O'Connells, O'Sullivans, and O'Scanlans came in from Kerry, and O'Donovans, O'Sheas, Conways, and O'Callaghans from Limerick and Cork. From Tipperary, many families of Hogans, Slatterys, Corbetts, Ryans, Keatings, Gleesons, settled down in Clare. All the foregoing, and others who had assumed English surnames after the last siege of Limerick, intermarrying largely with the old Clare stock, contributed to the pronounced Celtic character of the vast bulk of its population. Another name that should find a place in this enumeration is that of Murphy. Families of the name in every class of society are widely scattered not alone over Clare, but over all the counties of Ireland. This is due to the fact that it has its origin in the Christian patronymic Morogh, used very generally in the families of Irish princes and chieftains. In the parish of Kilmihil, about eight miles from Kilrush, a stone-fort of unusually large dimensions occupies a commanding position on the top of a hill. It is now called Cahermurphy, and gives its name to the townland, but in the language of the Irish-speaking people it is still "Cahir-Morogha."

At the time of which we are now writing, George III. had been for some years on the throne. As has been already stated, one of the first Acts forced on the Irish Parliament by the strong feeling through the country after his accession, was to limit the duration of Parliaments to eight years. Under this new system the first members sent by the very restricted constituency of Clare were—for the county, Sir Edward O'Brien and Francis P. Burton; for the borough of Ennis, Lucius O'Brien, son of the former, and Mr. Thos. Burton. Sir Edward, dying in 1765, was succeeded by his son in the baronetcy, and by Mr. Charles MacDonnell as M.P. for the county. The limiting of the duration of Parliaments brought them into more frequent touch with the constituencies, and so created more popular interest in their working. Other elements were not long wanting to add intensity to this interest. We are now entering on the initial stages of the agitation among the despised Catholic Irish for the restoration of religious freedom with which the name of Clare is indelibly associated.

Frederick Lucas, following boldly on the lines of Swift and Molyneux, had stirred up the national sentiment, directly in the breasts of the Protestants of his native Clare, and indirectly in the hearts of their much more numerous Catholic neighbours. Now came the news of the American War of Independence to inspire still more [1] both alike. The Irish Parliament was after all but the shadow of a Parliament. Poynings' Law had it still in its iron grip; until that grip, so forcibly insisted on as we have seen earlier in the century by the English Parliament, was relaxed, there could be no true liberty in Ireland. The effort to relax it under the banner of the Volunteers met with such support from Clare as will be now once more recorded.

It is satisfactory to know that the voice of Clare, both at home and through some of her representatives in Parliament, was for the cause of freedom. Sir Lucius O'Brien had become, with Mr. Burton, M.P. for the county, and Mr. Crofton Vandaleur, with Mr. Charles MacDonnell, was returned for the borough of Ennis. Sir Lucius must have been a man of great ability. He took a very leading part in the resurrection of the Irish Parliament. The Clare members were all of what was called the "country," or patriotic, as against the "Court," or English party. They could be counted on in every advance made, slowly at first, but afterwards with great vigour, towards the Declaration of Independence. Sir Lucius O'Brien was particularly useful in matters relating to finance, and the curtailment of wasteful or corrupt expenditure. To him, too, was committed the honourable task of proposing the Bill to render judges independent of the Crown, which he carried successfully through.

Some halting measures of Catholic relief began to be introduced. The first was one enabling them to take an oath

---

[1] "A voice from America shouted 'Liberty!' and every hill and valley of this rejoicing Ireland answered 'Liberty!'"—Flood.

of allegiance without renouncing the spiritual jurisdiction of the Pope, but it was hampered by insulting insinuations attributing to Catholics the holding of doctrines which they need not and did not hold. It opened the way in some measure to the securing of positions of emolument which required the taking of an oath, and later on to the exercise of the franchise. Arising out of it, too, came another Act, with which Sir Lucius O'Brien's name is honourably connected, enabling those who had taken the oath of allegiance to contract for leases of land for 999 years, transmissible of course to their posterity. This was a relief, as well to the landlords as to the tenants, inasmuch as they could now get substantial tenants willing to pay large fines and heavy rents for the privilege of working farms with security. Some of the restrictions on trade with England and the colonies were also removed again, through the energy and practical work of Sir Lucius O'Brien in Parliament; but it was reserved for the Volunteers, a few years later on, to hang round their cannons' mouths the famous threat—" Free Trade or else—"

Among the first to take the oath of allegiance so altered [1] were Dr. Michael Peter MacMahon, Bishop of Killaloe, and the priests of the diocese. I fancy some of them, if not all, must have made wry faces while going through the process; but we must not weigh in the same balance as our own, men who were only just escaping from under the iron heel of oppression. The attitude they assumed could hardly bring them any personal advantages. Its effect was to create a better feeling between their flocks and the governing authorities.

Meanwhile, an incident had occurred in the House of Commons which threw all Ireland at a bound into what may well be called a revolution. Though in the agony of her struggle with the gallant Americans, England made a feeble effort to extract money from the Irish Parliament, while withdrawing the last remnant of the defensive force of the country. One of the members for Wexford, a man of impetuous character, springing to his feet, moved that the Bill should not only be

[1] Letters of Sir Lucius O'Brien in O'Donohue's *Memoirs*, p. 411.

rejected, but burned by the hands of the common hangman at the doors of the Parliament Houses. This extreme measure was not resorted to; but the feeling spread that the country should arm in its own defence. Ogle began with his own tenants and neighbours. Others rapidly followed his example; and thus sprung out of the earth armed men, calling themselves proudly Volunteers, banded together not only to defend Ireland in case of foreign attack, but to protect and forward her internal interests. England looked on the movement with ill-concealed jealousy and fear, but was powerless to interfere. Before long an army of sixty thousand Volunteers, largely added to afterwards, entirely independent of English influence, stood sentinel over the country; and with such a force at its command, the Irish party brought steadily forward and carried measure after measure for the freeing of the limbs of Ireland from the shackles imposed on her, not only by English, but by previous Irish Parliaments.

The first great measure was the one already referred to, Free Trade, not only with England, but with all countries not at war with England. There had been for some time a special dispute with Portugal on this head. Clare spoke its mind through its representative, Sir Lucius O'Brien, who had the manliness to propose that the King of England, as King of Ireland, should wage war with Portugal, relying on an army and navy to be provided by Ireland itself. The effect produced by the proposal on the House and on the country was electrical,[1] though it was not further pressed. There was no need of it when the restrictions upon the trade of the kingdom were, as soon after they were, to the intense joy and relief of people of all classes, removed.

Passing over measures of lesser importance, we come now to the crowning one of all—that for the legislative independence of Ireland. It does not properly come within the sphere of a county history to enter into the particulars of or to detail the personal efforts made during the struggle. The names of the prominent actors are engraven in indelible letters in the history of Ireland. The 15th of February found the delegates

[1] Sir Jonah Barrington.

of the Volunteer corps of Ulster deliberating at Dungannon, and proclaiming with one voice that it was not competent for any body of men other than the King, Lords, and Commons of Ireland to make laws for the people of Ireland. They also declared, with only two dissenting voices, that the hour had come to relax the Penal Laws in force against their fellow Roman Catholic subjects. They were bound in honour to make this declaration in return for the active support given by the Catholics in every county of Ireland to the Volunteer movement. It was of importance that these resolutions should be adopted by the other provinces. In the county of Clare a general meeting of the gentry, clergy, and freeholders, at the suggestion of Sir Lucius O'Brien and Ed. Fitzgerald, Esq., M.P.s for the county, was held at Ennis on the 6th of April 1782. The High Sheriff, Poole Hickman, who convened the meeting, was moved to the chair, and the following, among other resolutions, were unanimously passed :—

"1. That it appears to us to be absolutely necessary to declare that no power on earth has any right to make laws to bind this kingdom, save the King, Lords, and Commons of Ireland.

"2. That a claim of any body of men other than the King, Lords, and Commons of Ireland to make laws to bind this kingdom is unconstitutional, illegal, and a grievance. . . .

"9. That the thanks of this meeting are due to those wise and virtuous men who so firmly demanded and so strenuously contended for the declaration of our rights and redress of our grievances. . . .

"11. That it is our unalterable determination to seek a redress of these grievances; and we pledge ourselves to each other and to our country, as men of honour, that we will at every ensuing election for our county support those only who will support us therein; and that we will use all constitutional means to make such, our pursuit of redress, speedy and effectual."

The meeting concluded with a vote of confidence in their representatives, noting pointedly their fidelity "at a time when venality and corruption influence so many members of Parliament," and another of thanks to their chairman.

The above resolutions ought to be interesting and instructive and inspiring to all generations of Claremen. The descendants of those who figured most prominently and so honourably at that meeting are for the present, but it is to be hoped not permanently, estranged from the national principles to which their forefathers gave such manly and unequivocal expression.

Not further back than 1770, when war was imminent between France and England, Lord Clare's regiment was sent out to the French possessions in India. It was the privilege of that regiment, so largely recruited from Clare, to be allowed to take the front wherever and whenever English soldiers were to be encountered. Such was the feeling abroad. At home, since the partial relaxation of the Penal Laws, Catholics began to enter not only the ranks of the Volunteers, but to take service in the English army. Major Sir Boyle Roche beat up for recruits at Limerick in 1775, when about five hundred men, many of them doubtless from Clare, joined the ranks.[1] Lord Kenmare, a Catholic, as a proof of his loyalty to England, and to encourage this movement, gave each of the recruits half a guinea additional bounty. The French Government regarded these first approaches to reconciliation with a jealous eye. It was clearly seen that those Irish regiments which had done such splendid service could not be much longer kept up. The decline of stupid Protestant bigotry in the hour of England's dire necessity was the cause, by a strange fatality, of the decline of the Irish Brigades in the service of France.

France was not the only country that profited by the ability and bravery of Clare exiles. There is in use at present in the parish of Liscannor a silver chalice, which has on it the following inscription in Latin :—

"The most illustrious Lord Daniel O'Kuoney, now Governor of Ferrola under the Catholic King, and who had command of his navy elsewhere on many occasions, bestowed this chalice on his native parish of Killanaspuglenane in the year 1756."

The church and parish, though in the diocese of Kilfenora, were dedicated to the patron saint of Killaloe—the name

[1] O'Callaghan's *Irish Brigade*, p. 613.

signifying "Church of Bishop Flannan." The Admiral's name, O'Kuoney, is found yet as Cooney in many parts of Clare. Had he remained supinely at home under the beneficent sway of England, he would have lived and died in the obscurity of peasant life. The Spanish service opened up to him a field for his ability and talents denied to him in his native country.

It is not necessary to enter here into the details of the remarkable events that crowded round the epochs, so fraught with good and evil to Ireland, of 1782, 1798, and 1800, and the intervening intervals. The white light of criticism has already beaten on them from every point of view. Sir Jonah Barrington, in his *Rise and Fall of the Irish Nation,*—and no phrase could more fitly describe the whole series of events,—provides food for thought to men of Irish blood in all generations. We have seen above that Clare, through its parliamentary representatives, its gentry, clergy, and freeholders, did contribute in an outspoken way to the "Rise" of the Irish nation. Francis MacNamara did disgracefully, in his own person, contribute to the "Fall" of Ireland for "cash, and a private pension paid by Lord Castlereagh."[1] Outside of him, no other man of Clare blood figured in the shameful traffic of our country's liberties. The Colonel Burton, Colonel M'Donnell, and J. O. Vandeleur in the "Black List" were not, the writer believes, members of the Clare families of those names. On the other side, in the list of honour representing the true sentiment of the county, are found Sir Edward O'Brien, son of Sir Lucius, who died 1785, Nicholas Westby, and the Prime Sergeant, the Right Hon. James Fitzgerald, who sacrificed his high and lucrative position, and of whom Barrington records that "he could *not* be bought."

Beyond what has been just described, the writer cannot find that Clare made any appreciable mark on that stormy period. During the terrible struggle of 1798 she was quiet. Clare was the last county in Ireland subdued by the Williamite arms. The traces of that calamitous overthrow had not yet disappeared. The grandfathers of young men living in 1798 could tell them, and assuredly did tell them, of the dreadful

[1] *Rise and Fall*, p. 492. First Edition.

experiences of their own early youth. This knowledge, coupled with the remoteness of the county from the scene of conflict in those days of difficult travelling, contributed much to the peaceful attitude of its people. The yeomanry too—that name of sinister import—had something to say to it. Armed by the Government, and fired with the zeal born of anti-Irish and anti-Catholic prejudice, they tramped about the county, creating terror among the unarmed peasantry. Woe to the man upon whom the suspicion even of sympathy with the United Irishmen could be fixed. Outrages upon these were committed, but they stopped short, except in one instance, as the writer has been told, of taking life.

Drum-head court-marshals were held at Limerick, before which the accused from the surrounding counties were brought for trial. Some of these were hanged on the new bridge; but most of them got off with transportation or whippings. Among the latter were about a score brought in from Killaloe by Major Purdon's corps of yeomanry, and a few captured by Captain Studdert's near Kilkishen. One of the Lysaghts of Kilfenora and Thomas Frost of Rossmanaher, with others, were transported for life.

The infamous Judkin Fitzgerald was busy with the lash and the pitch-cap and the rope through Tipperary. It is a singular fact that the last of his descendants in the male line—a boy of nine or ten years of age—hanged himself accidentally some years ago, while showing his young companions how his grandfather hanged the Croppies in 1798. The poor lad paid dearly for the teaching he evidently received at the hearthstone.

To the yeomanry of that period is attributed the wanton disfigurement of what had been, according to Wakeman,—no mean authority,—judging from the small part that escaped, a work of real art over the high altar in Quin Abbey. There it stood, exposed to and braving the elements for a century since the church was unroofed, so well and perfectly was the fresco executed, till the bullets of those Vandal fanatics were poured on it, not sparing even the figure of the Saviour on the crucifixion. The marks of the bullets remain there to the present day. It is matter for congratulation to Claremen at home and abroad, that the whole beautiful structure, as well as the Abbey of Corcomroe, has been placed as a national monument under the care of the Board of Works. In all probability no Vandalism will ever again desecrate one or the other. Why the more ancient and still more interesting ruins on Iniscatha (Scattery) and Iniscaltra (Holy) islands have not a like privilege is beyond comprehension. It is to be hoped that Ireland, under the Home Rule now impending, will stretch her protecting arms around these and other such relics, everywhere through the land, of a glorious past.

To turn now to subjects of a different character, some Claremen of note who figured—I might perhaps say flourished—during, or immediately after, this period, claim attention at our hands in a history of the county. Donogh Rua MacNamara was born at Cratloe early in the century. He was sent to France, like so many others, to study for the priesthood. It became abundantly evident, during his collegiate course, that his tastes did not lie in that direction, so he was sent home still a layman. Being fairly educated, and not having a patrimony to fall back on, he joined the ranks, pretty numerous during the whole century, of rambling and rhyming[1] schoolmasters. Some of his effusions are given in the *Poets and Poetry of Munster*, translated by unhappy Clarence Mangan, and edited by the late Rev. C. P. Mechan. One of them at least is of a humorous kind. He wielded the ferula for a while in foggy Newfoundland, and falling in on an occasion with a jovial company of English soldiers and Irish emigrants, he was asked for a song. It was produced extempore, but must have been polished somewhat afterwards. The lines in the verses are alternate English and Irish. In the English, he is civil enough to the soldiers and their king, but he greatly amused his bi-lingual Irish companions by scathing denunciation in the Irish lines of King George and every one and everything English.

In the same very interesting collection, another of his songs, having the true ring of poetry about it, is given in full. Its title, "The Fair Hills of Eire, O," declares its purpose; and the longing of the exile's heart for the land of his

[1] "The jealous, waspish, wrong-head, rhyming race."—POPE.

birth and his love finds in every verse eloquent expression. He preserved a vigorous intellect into extreme old age. In his ninetieth year, he wrote a Latin eulogy on the death of another remarkable Irish teacher and poet, Teigue Gaelach O'Sullivan, the first lines of which may be given here in proof of his scholarly ability.

> "*Thaddeus hic situs est; oculos huc flecte, viator
> Illustrem vatam parvula terra tegit.*"

He spent most of his life in the counties of Cork and Waterford, and died, A.D. 1814, at Kilmacthomas. It is certain that he lived into his hundred and fourth year.

Another of the same class, and still more noted for his poetic vein, was Andrew Magrath, who, though born in the county of Limerick, near the Maigue,—the southern boundary of the Dalcassian principality,—was of the Clare family of that name. He was popularly known as the "Mangaire Sugach," "Jolly Pedlar," and justified the appellation by his roving disposition and the licentiousness of his life and his songs. Some of these—notably the "Shanduine," or "Old Husband"—are still only too well known. He was regarded as the truest Irish poet of the century. The Press was not a power in his day, as it is in ours. For those writing in Irish it was non-existent. They wrote under conditions the most unfavourable, and yet their songs and poems are still popular—no small testimony to their merit. Magrath, like MacNamara, died in extreme old age. Unlike so many others, the "Uisce Beatha"—"Water of Life"—was for them no misnomer.

The two MacCurtins, Hugh and Andrew, had made their mark in a more legitimate manner earlier in the century. These were followed by James Considine, born near Mullagh, and Bryan Merriman, a native of Kilmihil, who, while teaching a school in Feacle, wrote a piece called "Courth-Ban-Oithe," which possesses considerable literary merit, and, though not in print, lives in the memory of the Irish-speaking people of the county.

One other Clare poet, but in the English tongue, Thomas Dermody, born at Ennis in 1775, far outshone the others in the brilliancy of his genius and the wondrous character of his acquirements. His father, a native of Clonmel, had settled down in Ennis, and there taught a classical school. From his fourth year upwards, young Dermody was literally "crammed" with Greek and Latin, and yet, strange to say, he grew to love passionately those learned languages. Before his eighth year, he was able to assist his father as usher in the school. His poetic talent soon developed. This Ennis lad wrote true poems in his tenth year— earlier in life than either Moore or Chatterton. He ran away from home, and, though penniless, made his way to Dublin. Here a gentleman passing one of the bookstalls noticed the child of eleven years, in rags, poring over one of the classical authors, and, questioning him, learned with amazement that he was quite familiar with them. He was placed in an academy, kept by a Mr. Austin, who undertook to edit a volume of his poems. The fame of this almost infant prodigy soon spread. A sum of £150 was subscribed, and confided to his patron for his support. Being tempted in an unlucky hour to write a few satiric lines on Mr. Austin, in revenge for punishment inflicted on him, he was expelled from the academy, and the money given for his maintenance was, in a cruelly vindictive spirit, sent back to the subscribers. His poems remained for a time unpublished. His wonderful talents, however, attracted the attention of lovers of learning, while his wretched and forlorn condition touched their hearts. In spite of all that was done for him, the demon of drink, even so early in life, began to bring about his ruin. He had imbibed the love of it in childhood from the bad example set him by his intemperate father. It grew upon him to that degree, that time after time he fled from the shelter provided for him by his generous admirers to the lowest haunts of vice. He entered the army, and, getting wounded in Flanders, he was retired on a small pension. He now sought a field for his literary labours in London, and there, as in Dublin, soon sprang into fame. His evil habits, however, pursued him, and brought him to an early grave. He died in extreme poverty and want at London, in his twenty-seventh year, A.D. 1802.

It is true to say of this son of Clare that he was one of nature's prodigies. Had he controlled his passion for drink, he would probably have taken a foremost place in the world of letters. In the wide range of his acquirements from infancy upwards, as well as in the variety and charm of his writings, there was the true stamp of genius. A passage from a short poem written by him when he was *only ten years of age*, and occasioned by the death of a brother, will not be out of place here as a specimen of what he could do even so early in life, and of what might reasonably be expected from him in his maturity, if his natural powers were carefully developed and cultivated:—

> "CORYDON—A MONODY.
>
> "Oh, Shannon,[1] thy embroidered banks can tell
> How oft we strayed beside thy amber wave,
> With osier rods arching thy wizard stream,
> Or weaving garlands for thy liquid brow.
> Ah me! my dearest partner seeks the grave;
> The ruthless grave, extinguisher of joy.
> Fond Corydon, scarce ripened into boy,
> Where shall I ever find thy pleasing peer?
> My task is now (ungrateful task, I ween)
> To cull the choicest offspring of the year,
> With myrtles mixed, and laurels varnished bright;
> And scattering o'er thy hillock green
> The poor meed, greet the gloom of night."

Another and a much better known Clare poet of the last century was jovial Ned Lysaght. He was a barrister of eminence, and was regarded as one of the leading wits of a witty period. He wrote many capital songs, some of them of a patriotic character, the best known of which is "Our own little Island"—a great favourite with the Volunteers, and still widely sung.

A very remarkable individual in his day was MacNamara of Moyriesk, who bore the significant appellation of "Fireball." He was a notorious duellist, and so dexterous with the sword, as well as sure with the pistol, that no opponent could escape him. He gave the name of Fireball to his family, not one of whom now lives to carry it on. The last of them was a John

---

[1] Poetic for Fergus.

MacNamara, an attorney of so easy-going a disposition that he was called "John the Soft." He was stung into a duel with a Mr. O'Callaghan[1] by his pointedly offensive remarks while professionally engaged against him. The duel was fought at Spancil Hill. It is related that on his way to the trysting ground O'Callaghan invited those whom he met to come and see him shooting the "beggarly attorney," and that he was warned in reply to take care of the "Fireball" blood. He received a fatal wound, of which he died within a few days. The then parish priest of Quin, Father MacMahon, who became afterwards Bishop of Killaloe,—uncle of the present parish priest of Quin, Father Daniel Corbett,—was hurriedly called, and administered to him the last consolations of the Catholic Church.

Two others of the same name were very prominent in London life at the end of the last century. They acted as agents in both a legal and political capacity for men of the highest position in both countries; and of one of them Lord Cloncurry states in his Memoirs, that though an Irishman and a Catholic, his house near London was the rendezvous for the *élite* of the metropolis—the heir to the throne being a frequent guest there.

Among Clare celebrities on the border-land between the last and present centuries Macready stands in the first rank. He was born in Ennis towards the end of the last century. He is justly recognised as one of the first painters of the age. There also Power (Dion Boucicault) first saw the light, but many years after. His sphere was on the stage, where, whether as actor or composer, few equalled him, fewer still surpassed him.

The county which gave those men birth in troubled times should not wish to let their names lie in oblivion.

[1] Called the Great O'Callaghan, grandfather of the celebrated Jesuit, Dr. O'Reilly.

CHAPTER XXVI.

FROM 1801 TO 1828.

The false Lord Clare—The Forty-Shilling Freeholders—Influence of Napoleonic Wars on Clare—O'Connell—Clare Protestants in favour of Catholic Relief—O'Connell's Duel with D'Esterre—Major Mac-Namara—Famine of 1822—Tom Steele—"Head Pacificator of Ireland"—The O'Gorman Mahon—Amusing Incidents—Vesey Fitzgerald—Father Murphy of Corofin—Ennis besieged—Nomination Speeches—Droll Story against O'Connell—Obstruction Tactics of the Protestant Party—Declaration of the Poll—Clare killed with one blow Protestant Ascendancy and the Catholic Association.

ON the 1st of January 1801 the Irish Parliament ceased to exist. Corruption of the most shameless character began the work of its destruction, and a despairing civil war, fomented for the purpose by English craft and cruelty, completed it. The two prominent pliant tools in the hands of the English Prime Minister, Pitt, were Lords Clare and Castlereagh, and all three will go down in history to the latest times as among the most unscrupulous conspirators the world has ever produced. Of the three, Clare was the worst. It is something to have to record, that though he usurped the name of the county, he had no other connection whatsoever, either by blood or property, with it. The last who had a legitimate claim to the title, the son of the celebrated Comte de Thomond, Marshal of France, had, as already stated, died under age in 1774. John Fitzgibbon, made Earl of Clare for his treachery to his country, was of an obscure family. His father had been partly educated for the Catholic priesthood in France, but, finding little scope for his ambition in that dangerous calling, he became Protestant, studied for the bar, became a success there, and gave to Ireland in his son one of her worst, if not her very worst, enemies. No more appropriate specimen of the raven in the eagle's nest can be found in all history, than in the assumption by this man of the title of Earl of Clare.

His treason to his country brought with it its own punishment. Pitt and Castlereagh had the decency to resign, as the promises of measures of relief, in the United Parliament they held out to the Catholics to wean them from active opposition to the Union, were utterly ignored by the King and his other advisers. The new Ministry cared little for Clare now that his base work was accomplished, and he had the mortification to find himself neglected, and perhaps despised. He was bitter to the last. The Castlereagh correspondence described him as a strong advocate for the continuance of martial law in Ireland. Broken down in spirit, he died two years after the fulfilment of his treachery. In revenge for his alleged boast that "he would whip Ireland into a tame cat," the populace of Dublin flung dead cats on his coffin and into his grave. He has now no male representative. The title which he was given as a reward for the betrayal of his country did not long survive him. It is now and for many years extinct.

Arising out of the dalliance with the Catholic body, the Bishops of Ireland were invited in 1801 to send to the Government statements of the condition of their several dioceses. This was the first notable move in the direction of the insidious attempt to secure the "Veto" in the selection to bishoprics in return for liberal annuities to the episcopate and Catholic clergy. Every one knows how ignominiously it failed. It is not unlikely—it is in fact certain—that some of them understood its drift, but most of them did not fully realise it.

Some of the bishops gave rather elaborate descriptions.[1] The Bishop of Killaloe, Dr. Michael Peter MacMahon, then in extreme old age, and having for a coadjutor Dr. O'Shaughnessy, answered curtly enough a series of questions put to him. They had reference chiefly to the discipline of the Catholic Church and the incomes of the clergy. The replies disclose nothing that is not now thoroughly well known. At that time, along with the seculars there were nine regulars in the diocese, six Franciscans and three Dominicans.

[1] *Memoirs of Viscount Castlereagh*, vol. iv., beginning at p. 97.

During the early years of the present century nothing of historic interest occurred within the borders of the county. The Napoleonic wars had a double-edged effect. They vastly improved the condition of the food-producing classes, while they bore hard on all others. Provisions ran high in what was to some extent a state of siege. Though England was supreme on the high seas, France was still able to check, and did check, the operation of commerce. There grew up under these conditions, strange to say, silently and unobserved, unfelt even by those possessed of it, a power in the county which was destined to come into conflict with the King, Lords, and Commons of Great Britain, generalled by the conqueror of Napoleon, and to come victorious out of the conflict. It had on its side, it should in fairness be added, the public opinion of the vast bulk of the people of Ireland, marshalled by another conqueror—a conqueror not on the field of battle, but in the higher field of the mind, Daniel O'Connell.

In 1793 the Irish Parliament passed into law what was called a "Relief Bill." It widely enlarged the franchise, giving to every one having a freehold of the value of forty shillings, irrespective of religion, the right to vote for members of Parliament. No Catholic, however, could pass the threshold of either House of the Legislature without abjuring his Catholicity, so the Catholic voter had to choose between Protestant candidates solely. His crushed condition at that period, both before and after the Union, and his ignorance in nearly every case of the real issues involved, left him at the mercy of his landlord. He would be for or against the Union or any other measure just as his landlord dictated. He could not have a choice of his own, so he allowed the one to whom he had to look up to make the choice for him. It clearly became the policy of landlords in such a condition of things, to secure on their estates as many obedient subservient freeholders as possible. The increased value of land, owing to the exigencies of war, contributed to the development of this policy. Thus the despised Catholics gradually acquired political power, which proved when the time came for it a mine under the feet of their oppressors—dug and charged by their own hands.

The career of Napoleon in those years captured the Irish Catholic imagination. It was watched with eager curiosity. Little as he deserved it, he was regarded by the Irish people as their hero, and possibly their future deliverer. In their songs and ballads he began to take the place of the exiled Stuarts—the last of whom, the Cardinal of York, had actually become a pensioner on the bounty of the English King. Every victory of his was hailed with almost as much joy amid the hills of Clare as on the plains of France. His success meant loss and injury to the English; and though Irishmen filled the ranks of the English army, and fought bravely, as Wellington himself afterwards testified, yet strangely enough all this was forgotten, and the Irish sentiment went heartily with the French legions. Since '91 the Irish Brigades had been incorporated in French regiments, and lost their exclusively Irish character, but they were not forgotten at home. When at last Napoleon fell, the hopes of the Irish Catholics fell with him. In another and more practical way his ruin brought ruin on a large class in Ireland. The rents had gone up with the prices. The father of the present writer, who remembers well the events consequent on the defeat of the French at Waterloo, told him that the farmers of Clare in many instances hastily secured what they could of their crops and cattle to avoid distraints for rents they could no longer pay, and left their farms derelict.

There was growing up, too, in those same years, another who would take the place of Napoleon, and become much more their idol. The Catholic Committee, formed under the leadership of Lord Fingal, Arthur O'Connor, Dr. MacNevin, and John Keogh, which had done good and bold work in trying times, was becoming somewhat timid. Nor was this to be wondered at. Every prominent man on the Irish side, even though undoubtedly free from participation in the United Irish and Robert Emmett movements, became at once an object of suspicion in Dublin Castle. Just then there stepped to the front the young Kerry barrister. His wonderful abilities gave him early in life the lead at the bar. His monetary success, unequalled before his time, did not induce him to look coldly on the wrongs and sufferings of his fellow-countrymen. Like another Moses, he boldly took his stand with his own people. With the full and accurate knowledge of the law he was possessed of, he contrived to keep clear of the many pitfalls provided for those who would dare to interfere with the privileged classes. He lost no opportunity that presented itself of waking up his fellow-Catholics to a sense of the wrongs and injustice to which they were subjected, and inspiring in them the hope that by peaceful combination within the law, stringent as it was, the redress of their grievances could be secured. Slowly but steadily he welded all classes of Catholics together, and brought all the popular forces of the country under his own potent, inspiriting influence. The titled and proprietorial Catholics—always timid and hesitating—were a drag-chain upon the movement, but the enthusiasm of the populace more than counterbalanced their weakness. He so riveted attention on the Catholic claims, that Whigs and Liberals began to make half-hearted efforts in Parliament to consider them. Measures of relief, but only of an insignificant character, were from time to time proposed, but little or no advance was made in the first twenty years of the century towards the full restoration of civil rights to the Catholic body.

The activity thus aroused by the unceasing efforts of O'Connell on the Catholic side provoked a counter-movement on the part of especially the Orange element on the other side. False stories were circulated of a Bull alleged to have been addressed by the Pope to the Irish Bishops, exhorting them to excite in their flocks a hope of freedom at the hands of Napoleon; and of a solemn promise said to have been made by him to establish Catholic ascendancy in Ireland. The spreading of such absurd rumours was but a ruse to cover their real design, which was to create alarm, and so prevent any extension of freedom to their Catholic fellow-countrymen. The Orange party were elated at having a brother of the King —the Duke of Cumberland—for one of their shining lights. It is matter of history that they even intrigued later on to disturb the succession to the throne by placing him there instead of the rightful successor, the daughter of his elder brother.

This spirit did not, however, animate all the Protestants. Many, if not most of them, desired justice to be done to Catholics, and it is to the credit of the Protestants of Clare, that as early as 1807, so soon after the 1798 and 1803 convulsions, they held a meeting in Ennis to demand the liberation of the Catholics from the penalties imposed on them by law.

Meanwhile O'Connell was forging on. No opportunity was missed by him of forcing public attention on the grievances of the Catholics. Nor did he lose sight of the evils inflicted by the Union on the industrial interests of the country as well as its national character. Repeal of the Union and Catholic Emancipation were themes exalted and grand enough for his master mind. "Keep pegging away at the Union" was the motto of Grattan, and while Grattan and Curran lived it was never lost sight of. Their matchless eloquence, more polished but not more powerful than O'Connell's, was employed in supporting against all odds the Catholic claims, as well as the restoration of the Irish Parliament; but when both died,— Curran in 1817 and Grattan in 1820,—all the energies of the nation were directed by O'Connell to the securing in the first place of Catholic Emancipation. He regarded this as the great indispensable step towards a Repeal of the Union.

Every one has heard of his duel with D'Esterre in 1815. That barbarous practice was still in full swing: It enabled his political enemies to lay an insidious plot against his life. The officer trained to arms was believed to be more than a match for the untrained barrister, and was incited, as was generally believed, to provoke the contest. O'Connell was weak enough, in obedience to the false sentiment of the day, to pit his valuable life against his worthless opponent's. He chose for his second Major MacNamara, a Clare officer deeply in sympathy with the popular movement, and it was believed that O'Connell owed his life largely to the skill with which he managed the duel. D'Esterre fell. O'Connell, filled with compunction at having taken the unhappy man's life, was said to have placed an annuity of £300 a year at the disposal of his widow and children. The news of the affair spread like wildfire, and made the people wild with joy. He was now a hero in their own sense of the word. His success over his opponent was regarded as an augury of victory over the party whom he represented. In Clare especially it was hailed with acclamation, as a Clareman figured in it so creditably in the popular view of it. Major MacNamara was held high in the esteem of the people for his share in it, and is still remembered with a feeling of pride.

In the year 1822, one of those periodical evidences of English rule in Ireland, a famine, decimated the country. It must have been for the time it lasted nearly as disastrous as that of '47 and '48. Its march was not so well observed as in the latter instance, but we can imagine what dreadful suffering there must have been in Clare, whereas nearly 100,000 [1] of its people were dependent on charity for their daily bread. This unhappy record affords evidence also of the enormous increase of the population since the termination of the wars.

O'Connell had been thwarted time after time in his efforts to solidify the whole people, by what was called the Convention Act. This penal statute forbade any meetings of delegates or persons holding a representative character. To steer clear of this Act, O'Connell founded in 1823 the Catholic Association. Though purely voluntary and unrepresentative, the Government, alarmed at the vast proportions it at once assumed, found some excuse for suppressing it in 1825; but O'Connell, who knew well, as he himself expressed it, how "to run a coach and six through any Act of Parliament," soon revived it, under the name of the "New Catholic Association." The members paid a penny a month, which was called the "Catholic Rent," and the numbers enrolled may be estimated from the fact that for a long time as much as £500 a week was paid in. This Association lived on, and gave blood and life to the popular uprising at the famous Clare election of 1828.

The two men who next to O'Connell figured most prominently at this election, O'Gorman Mahon and "honest Tom Steele," both Claremen, deserve some notice here. The latter, though a Protestant, was, like William Smith O'Brien, then

[1] Alison's *History of Europe.*

representing Ennis in Parliament, a member of the Catholic Association, and personal friend and enthusiastic admirer of O'Connell. He held property between Tulla and Kilkishen, on which was the family residence, picturesquely situated over Cullane Lake. He practised also as an engineer, but threw profession and property almost to the winds in his ardour for the national cause. Being a man of fine physique, though always ready to fight himself, he undertook the task of quelling that spirit in others for the sake of union in their own ranks. O'Connell gave him the title of which he was very proud—" Head Pacificator of Ireland." His being a Protestant, a man of good family, and holding property in the county, apart even from his energy of character, gave him great weight in the struggle. He will be found as we go along working most disinterestedly, seeking no emolument nor parliamentary honours in the long struggle for Repeal of the Union.

The O'Gorman Mahon was a much more remarkable figure in political life during the greater part of the present century. Born at its opening in Mill Street, Ennis, he came early in life into the possession of considerable landed property bought by his father, a prosperous merchant in that town. His real name was James Patrick Mahon, which he had to don always when seeking parliamentary honours, but he started in public life with the title of The O'Gorman Mahon, assumed from his mother's family, and woe betide the man who called his right to it in question. A dozen paces before the mouth of his pistol or a sound thrashing was the alternative. From his personal appearance in extreme old age, when the writer came to know him first, it was easy to infer that in his youth and manhood's prime he must have been a splendid specimen of humanity.

He was one of the first few Catholics appointed to the commission of the peace, and an incident that occurred in connection with it, told the writer by one who was present,[1] illustrates at once the character of the man, and a custom up to that time prevailing, but long since gone out of use. Some of the Protestant gentry had a monopoly of presenting for the

[1] Rev. D. Corbett, P.P., Quin.

making and keeping in repair the roads. They made a nice thing out of it, until William O'Connell of Toureen, near Ennis, a relative of his great namesake, one of the largest and most successful farmers in Ireland, and grandfather of the present Daniel O'Connell, J.P., of Kilgorey, near Tulla, took heart to interfere with the blackmailing practice. He put in a presentment at the Road Sessions for so much a lower figure than the others, that it could not in common decency be thrown out. They determined to die hard. They set their men to obstruct O'Connell's men, and of course a free fight ensued. Summonses were issued. The case came on at Petit Sessions in Quin about 1824, and O'Gorman Mahon was asked to come there and see justice done to O'Connell's men. He stalked in with dogs and gun, having walked across shooting from Newpark, near Ennis, where he then lived. The case had been for some time at hearing, and one of Mr. O'Connell's men was giving evidence.

"You say you struck the man?" interposed O'Gorman Mahon fiercely.

"Begor I did, your honour, but he struck me first."

"Then what the d—— else would you do, man?" shouted the lately appointed justice of the peace.

Result: applause in Court, consternation on the Bench, and much subsequent civility on the part of the other magistrates.

To the last day of his long life he maintained a fighting attitude, making no secret of his readiness to take up the pistol at a moment's notice, though usually courteous and polished. It was said that a visit in that spirit to Dromoland procured him the deputy-lieutenancy of the county.[1] Thackeray caricatured him unmercifully in his picture of The O'Mulligan, for the which the wonder is that he was not promptly called out.

Such were the men who proved themselves the left and right hands of O'Connell in the Clare election.

The Catholic Association had adopted a resolution pledging itself to oppose, when occasion offered, every member of the

[1] Shiel's description of the court-house scene with High Sheriff Molony is too well known to need reproduction here.

bitterly anti-Catholic and anti-Irish Wellington Administration. The first opportunity given was on the appointment of Mr. Vesey Fitzgerald to the Board of Trade. This necessitated his re-election for the county of Clare. No one imagined that any serious opposition would be given to a gentleman who was himself deservedly popular, a member of a popular family, the son of the Prime Sergeant who lost his highly-paid office because of his opposition to the Union, and an excellent landlord. In fact, O'Connell proposed that in this one case no action should be taken, but, fortunately for the cause, he was overruled. Major MacNamara, O'Connell's second in the duel with D'Esterre, was fixed on as a Protestant member of the Association, who would, as such, and from his position in the county, be likely to prove a strong candidate. After some delay, he declined, on the grounds of his friendship for the Fitzgerald family. Then, not knowing where else to turn, O'Connell, by a happy inspiration, resolved to offer himself to the constituency, and if returned, to go over to London and literally "beard the lion in his den." The idea was caught up with enthusiasm. The gage of battle was flung in the face of Protestant Ascendancy, and then there was precipitated amid the hills and valleys of Clare a fierce struggle, constitutional in its character, but as momentous and as far-reaching in its issues as if the red hand of war were engaged in it.

Not a moment was lost. The forty-shilling freeholders formed the great bulk of the constituency, and to move them to action and to encourage them to strike out against their landlords was the work of the hour. Hitherto landlords regarded the votes of their tenants as much their own as their rents. Interference with them was considered a personal affront. Steele and O'Gorman Mahon hastened to the county for the express purpose of canvassing those tenants, but began by declaring their readiness to give any gentleman who chose to feel aggrieved satisfaction in the usual way at the pistol's mouth. They were not troubled. We cannot measure in our prosaic day the full value to the cause of their pluck and daring. It infused life and courage into the hearts of the down-trodden tenantry.

Other zealous workers in the people's cause followed quickly, either as volunteers or sent down by the Catholic Association. Among the former, the most celebrated and best known were "Honest Jack Lawless," editor of the *Irishman* of Belfast, and Father Tom Maguire, the recognised and revered champion of Catholicity. They found before them, ready to hand, in the persons of the priests of the county, with one solitary and, as the future showed, sad exception, as earnest and influential a body of canvassers as any cause could supply. Sheil's well-known description of Father Murphy of Corofin may be taken as applying to every one of them; for whatever of passionate feeling or eloquence in word or act was in them was stirred to its utmost depths. From every altar went forth appeals, mostly in the soul-stirring Irish tongue, to strike one good blow for God and Ireland, and the appeals were not made in vain.

The days before and during the election were days of intense excitement. As the polling for the whole county should take place in Ennis, that little town teemed literally day and night with a surging population; and the old courthouse, which stood on the site where stands now the O'Connell monument, had riveted on it the minds of the millions in the United Kingdoms. A large body of police and soldiers were ready for any emergency, but their services were not called for. Perfect peace prevailed. The Catholic Association had voted a considerable sum out of the "Catholic Rent" to provide entertainment for all who required it, but strong drink was strictly forbidden, and the warning went forth to the people not to allow themselves to be provoked into a quarrel. An amusing instance of what came of the warning will illustrate the prevailing feeling.

A friend of Mr. Fitzgerald had said or done something which one of the brawny MacNamaras from the neighbourhood of Tulla considered an affront. "Look here, sir," said he, "do the same to me *after the election*, and I'll give you the best pig I have at home to pay the rent."

The spirit of mutual forgiveness and brotherhood among the people evoked by this contest was well described in Banim's beautiful poem. Two men are represented standing before the altar in a Clare country chapel—one, an old man whose only son was killed by the other in a faction fight.

The last verse may be given here:—

> "But the old man he looked around him,
> And thought of the place he was in,
> And thought of the vow that bound him,
> And thought that revenge is sin.
> And then, crying tears like a woman,
> 'Your hand!' he cried—'ay, *that* hand;
> And I do forgive you, foeman,
> For the sake of our bleeding land.'"

The nomination gave an occasion of a display of strength and eloquence on both sides. Mr. Fitzgerald was surrounded by the massed gentry of the county, hardly one of whom was not under personal obligations to him for place or office bestowed on some member of the family. O'Connell had the priests and the people. Sir Edward O'Brien and Sir Augustine Fitzgerald proposed the Cabinet Minister. O'Gorman Mahon and Tom Steele proposed the Demagogue. Mr. Fitzgerald, a polished and eloquent speaker, delivered a most effective speech, recalling all he and his father had done in the cause of the people, and bringing tears into the eyes of many of his opponents while describing in faltering accents his father, who had lost so much for Ireland, now on his dying bed, waiting for a verdict at their hands. Never before had O'Connell such a difficult task as to undo the impression made by this speech, and he did undo it in a way all his own. Seeing that he could not contradict the statements made so skilfully by his opponent, nor make any charge against him individually, he turned upon some of his supporters a whole torrent of sarcasm, till in the shouts of laughter he provoked the previous speech was almost forgotten. Then, pouring out all the vials of his wrath on Peel and Wellington, and painting in glowing terms all the wrongs and insults inflicted on them as Irishmen and Catholics by this Ministry of which Mr. Fitzgerald was a member, he asked them in tones of thunder, were they going to rivet with their own hands the chains on the necks of seven millions of Catholics by returning the man who posed as their friend at home, but was the paid official of

Ireland's enemies in Parliament. There could be but one answer to such an appeal. In the unanimous "Never! never!" the Protestant Ascendancy party began to read the "writing on the wall."

When the booths were opened, a bit of sharp practice was put in play which helped to exasperate the popular party. Before a Catholic could vote, he might be asked, and was asked in every instance on this occasion for the first time, to produce a certificate signed by a magistrate that he had taken an oath of loyalty to the House of Hanover. Neither the forms for the purpose nor the magistrates were forthcoming the first day of the polling; but on the second day the men were ranged in long lines, they responded to the words of the oath read out for them, and neither Steele nor O'Gorman Mahon had much scruple in certifying that the oath was duly taken. They were then sent in batches to swell the rather thin roll of voters on the popular side recorded the day before.

A good thing occurred in connection with this voting by batches which is worth setting down here. It must be premised that the "ne'er-do-weels" on both sides of the broad western Shannon cross over occasionally to let matters cool, and are not welcome in their new quarters. While O'Connell, Father Kenny, parish priest of Kilrush, and some others were standing chatting on the square before the court-house, one of Father Kenny's organisers rushed up in a state of excitement, and, having eyes for no one but the parish priest who gave him charge, cried out, "I have all my men, Father John, but one — that Connell; and I never knew a good man of the name! 'Tis that Connell from Kerry, too, where no honest man ever came from." All present roared with laughter, no one so boisterously as O'Connell himself.

The cause of obstruction being disposed of, the polling went on apace. The result was at last declared:—

O'Connell,	2057
Fitzgerald,	1075
Majority,	982

The county went wild with joy. The whole country followed. For a long time afterwards the fact of being a Clareman made one popular at a bound in any part of Ireland. The county had made a great breach in the hitherto unassailable battlements of Protestant Ascendancy. O'Connell's return to Dublin was one long triumphal procession. Seven millions of people regarded his victory as their own, and began at last to see the dawn of freedom after a long and weary night of bondage.

The Catholic Association was dissolved. It had, as a first wise move, some years before, sent a petition with 800,000 signatures to Parliament, asking and securing the removal of certain disabilities under which the Dissenters laboured. Now, in a sense, it had set its own house in order by the Clare victory, and the special work for which it was called into existence being accomplished not fully but to some extent, it voluntarily fell out of sight.

CHAPTER XXVII.

FROM 1828 TO 1851.

Bill of 1829 for Catholic Emancipation—Petty Restrictions—O'Connell at the Bar of the House claiming to sit as M.P. for Clare—O'Gorman Mahon succeeds him in '30—Unseated on Petition for Bribery—Quarrel with O'Connell—"Terry Alts"—Classical Schools—National System—Workhouses—Monster Meeting at Ballycoree—From Life to Death—The Famine—Drowning at Poulnasherry—The *Times* becomes a Balaam—Statistics of Evictions and Deaths—Letter of Very Rev. Dr. Kelly, P.P., V.G., Kilrush—Father Malachy Duggan.

THE Clare election, combined with the determined spirit it had evoked from end to end of Ireland, brought home to the minds of Wellington and his Administration the conviction that there should be either a large measure of Catholic Emancipation or civil war. For the latter they were not prepared, so they felt themselves compelled to eat all their previous declarations against granting civil rights to Catholics. The King, too, who had publicly sworn, "so help me God," never to yield on this point, had to give way; and when Parliament met next, in February 1829, a measure, inadequate indeed, but for the time startling enough in character, for the emancipation of Roman Catholics in Great Britain and Ireland, was introduced in both Houses. To gild the pill for Protestant bigotry and intolerance, certain restrictions were still to be maintained. No Catholic should be Lord-Lieutenant of Ireland, nor—more important still, for the appointment to the magistracy was vested in the office—Lord Chancellor. The Catholic Association, which had already dissolved, was to be declared illegal; and, worse than all these put together, the brave forty-shilling freeholders were to be disfranchised. The men who had by their votes in Clare compelled a radical change in the British Constitution, were stripped of the weapons with which they had won their famous victory. Why O'Connell seemed to acquiesce—for he remained silent—in the reduction of the Catholic electorate to about one-tenth of what it had been, is almost incomprehensible. By a cunning and shabby device, too, he was compelled to seek re-election. The Act was not made retrospective, so that, when he advanced to the table of the House of Commons, he was confronted with the old intolerable oath, declaring the King of England the Head of the Church, the sacrifice of the Mass impious and idolatrous. He refused, of course, and demanded, what could not be denied him, the right to be heard at the Bar of the House in defence of his claim to sit after a duly-declared election. This gave him the opportunity of delivering, on the 15th of May, before the closely-packed curious senate, a splendid harangue, the pith of which was contained in his impressive and eloquent declaration—"Part of this oath I know to be false; the rest I do not believe to be true." All his reasoning and eloquence fell on ears that would not hear. He had to come back to Clare to qualify for taking the amended but still offensive oath approved of in the Act of Emancipation.

This time, though his former friends the forty-shilling freeholders—fully nine-tenths of the Clare voters—had been made incapable of giving him support, his return was unopposed. This was probably advised by the Government as a tribute to the strong public opinion aroused by the crisis in the three kingdoms. Daniel O'Connell then took his seat as member for Clare, the first Catholic in either the Irish or English Parliament since the reign of James II.

After a storm a calm. Comparative quiet reigned in the county for some subsequent years. Owing to the death of George IV. in 1830, and other causes, election followed upon election within short intervals, but of a tame kind compared with that of '28. In the election of 1830, O'Connell felt called on to resign the safe seat of Clare, in order to give a final blow to the Beresford influence in Waterford. O'Gorman Mahon succeeded him. Having married a very wealthy lady, Miss O'Brien of Dublin, and not being a lover of money, he spent money, or it was spent for him, so freely that he was unseated on petition. The voters under the new ten-pound franchise had not, as a rule, the splendid spirit of their poorer brethren, and, being much less numerous, the doubtful among them were unfortunately secured by bribes. Maurice O'Connell, the son of the Liberator, as O'Connell was after the victory of '28 universally called, was sent down. The magic of the name secured his return; but at the next election a split occurred. O'Gorman Mahon asserted his right to stand for the county, and, having money still to dispose of, he was able to bring a mob with him from Ennis in opposition to the Liberator himself when approaching the town. · A scuffle ensued, which so incensed O'Connell, that, declaring himself no longer safe there, he passed through to Galway. These occurrences threw O'Gorman Mahon out of public life for some years.

The "Terry Alt" system—one of those calamitous secret societies which have brought from time to time so much ruin and misery on the country, and on the dupes who are entrapped into them—spread rapidly in Clare. It took its name, as was said, from a shoemaker living in Corofin, and perhaps for the fantastic reason that he had nothing to say to it. The rumour was industriously, and of course untruthfully, spread that O'Gorman Mahon was at the head of it, and this contributed largely to increase its numbers. It had its origin in disputes about land. Since the '28 election, the landlords in most instances were at open war with their tenants. Increased rents were demanded and exacted from tenants at will. Then in the natural course evictions followed, and then murders, and then hanging. A typical instance of what was taking place through the county was the atrocious murder of Neptune Blood—descendant of the parson who had secured, as already related, confiscated property—outside his own door, avenged by the erection of a gallows on the same spot, to hang three men convicted of the murder.

A state of alarm and terrorism prevailed for some years. It gradually died out towards the end of the decade, owing partly to the more prudent, as well as more just, relations of the landlords with their tenants, and still more to the great and beneficent change brought about among the people by the Father Mathew and Repeal movements.

The educational condition of the county was still deplorable in the extreme. The love of learning was there, but very little to satisfy it. Elementary education was given in what was little better than the hedge schools of the preceding century. Those who aspired to higher branches had to depend entirely either on the Erasmus Smith school, established in Ennis, or on classical schools maintained entirely by the fees of the pupils. Of the Erasmus Smith College all that need be said is, that some few privileged Catholics were taught there gratis, but with great danger to their faith. It was a decided advantage to Protestant aspirants to the various learned professions. It is no longer in existence; but before it was merged in the more liberal educational programme lately adopted under an Act of Parliament, it could boast of having given to the wide world of letters of this generation one of its most popular writers, Richard Ashe King, son of its late Principal, the Rev. Dr. King. It is only fair to say here that, though being brought up in such an exclusive school, and writing mostly for an English public, his tone displays nothing of the bigot or the anti-Irishman. On the contrary, it is in a very marked and, it may be added, courageous way sympathetic whenever he touches on Irish topics.

A very successful classical school was kept about this time in Ennis by Mr. O'Halloran. Mr. Magrath taught later on with great advantage to youths whose parents could not afford to send them to boarding-schools outside the county. How this want of suitably equipped schools was supplied within the county will appear in its proper place.

Among the best known and most sought after of the classical teachers of this transition period were Mr. Curry and Mr. Tuohy. On these, and such as these, Catholic parents who desired to educate their sons for the various professions, had largely to depend; and well, all things considered, they did their work. They moved about from place to place, according as the need for their services grew more pressing in different localities. Mr. Tuohy's two sons still keep up the good old tradition in their well-taught school at Killaloe.

The first move made by the State towards educating the descendants of those whom it robbed of lands and learning alike, was in 1831. Lord Stanley introduced his Bill to establish what was, euphoniously but not truthfully, called National Education. The world knows now, since the publication of Archbishop Whately's Life by his daughter, as indeed had been surmised before, that it was the insidious aim of that eminent ecclesiastic, and his brother Commissioners of National Education, by means of school-books suitable for the purpose, to de-Catholicise and de-Nationalise the youth of Ireland. How they signally failed, mainly through the watchfulness of the episcopacy and priesthood of Ireland, is now matter of well-known history. With hardly an exception, the National teachers of both sexes worked hand in hand with their managers, and, by their intelligent and hearty co-operation, helped largely to turn to good account the system adroitly planned for sinister purposes.

Following closely upon the building of the new National Schools in Clare came the erection of workhouses. The Poor Law provisions had about them an air of philanthropy. In neither system were the feelings of the people for whom it was introduced taken into account. With very few exceptions, an Englishman legislating for Ireland scorned to consult the wishes of its people. In this case, O'Connell and his party strongly opposed the proposed method of relieving want, but it was forced on, and became law. Thus this soulless, callous, unsympathetic, and grudging system began its evil course. Whatever may have been the aim of its promoters, it was so worked as to merely keep soul and body together, with very little comfort, at the least possible cost; and, worse still, to degrade the poor in their own eyes. They were compelled to wear the uniform of pauperism, and carry its brand on their persons like criminals in jails. This was the substitute for the broad spirit of Christian charity which had worked so well in the past. The convents and monasteries endowed by voluntary generosity for the relief of the poor, as well as for religious purposes, which had covered the land, were robbed and ruined, and we have got instead of them those glaring and unsightly bastiles ironically called workhouses.

While these changes were being wrought in their midst, the people of the county were not politically idle. They did not rest on their '28 laurels. The Anti-Tithe Movement met with their active support, till that unjust and hateful impost was removed indeed from sight by the Tithe Act of 1838, but left still on the shoulders of the tenants in the shape of increased rents.

But the topic that, like Aaron's rod, swallowed all others, was the movement for the Repeal of the Union. Year after year it grew in volume and intensity of purpose, till it fairly eclipsed that for Catholic Emancipation. One of the members for the county—the landlord member, Sir Lucius O'Brien—was opposed to it. The other, Cornelius O'Brien of Birchfield, was returned in support of it. The then close borough of Ennis was represented by William Smith O'Brien, who, though with strong popular sympathies, looked shyly at it for awhile. During this period of suspense he came into collision with Tom Steele. A duel was fought. Fortunately no blood was spilled, and honour was satisfied. In time he was converted. Being a man of well-known strength and purity of character, and a member of one of the oldest houses in Europe, his adoption—his energetic and enthusiastic adoption—of the demand for the Repeal of the Union gave it a new impetus in the country, but above all in his native county.

The Catholic Association was now transformed into the Repeal Association, and on its headquarters, Conciliation Hall, in Dublin, the whole mind of Ireland was focussed. The priests of Clare stepped once more to the front, and, by encouraging Repeal literature, kept themselves and the people in touch with the central organisation. They were active in collecting the Repeal Rent. Repeal buttons and Repeal hatbands and badges were to be seen everywhere. The rapid spread of the Temperance movement under the guidance of Father Mathew, who seemed Heaven-sent at such a crisis, cleared the people's brains for the work that O'Connell with ever-increasing energy set before them. In Clare the climax was reached, when it was announced that O'Connell himself would address a Repeal meeting in Ennis of the people whom he led to victory in the cause of Catholic Emancipation.

The whole county was astir from end to end. This truly "monster" meeting was held in 1843. It was plain that no town nor city could afford adequate space for the multitudes sure to attend, so the hill of Ballycoree, about a mile to the north of Ennis, was chosen as a centre for the immense assembly. Newspaper reports of the day gave about seven hundred thousand as the probable number present, but this was certainly an exaggeration. The whole population of the county was only about half that, even in that year of its highest land-mark. But it must have been, notwithstanding, a huge gathering, for all accounts agree in stating that the great bulk of the people of the county, backed up by large and numerous contingents from Kerry, Limerick, Tipperary, and Galway, were present. All the roads leading to Ennis were black that whole summer morning with people, some of whom, to make sure of being in time, had been travelling through the night. "Clare was the rallying point of Ireland," wrote an eye-witness, "the focus of Irish patriotism, the centre of Irish feeling."[1] It is well that no one can forecast the future. What dismay would have seized on that vast multitude, if some one in whom they believed could tell them that within four or five years many thousands present there in the prime of life, and with high hopes of the future, would be struck down to the earth, not before the cannon's mouth, with pike or gun in hand, fighting as many were fully prepared to fight for Irish liberty, but helplessly, despairingly, gasping out their lives in the jaws of famine and pestilence! The terrible impending calamity was mercifully hidden from their view.

O'Connell, with some friends, including three French gentlemen, had been entertained and slept the night before the meeting at Deerpark, near Six-Mile-Bridge, the residence of Dr. Kennedy, Bishop of Killaloe. On their way next day to Ballycoree, they were met at Newmarket by an immense but well-organised procession, brilliant with Repeal and Tem-

[1] *Limerick Reporter.*

perance banners. Over a hundred bands enlivened the proceedings throughout. The day being very fine, gave full effect to the vast and varied concourse. When at last the platform was reached, the chair was taken, on the motion of Hewitt Bridgeman, M.P. for Ennis, by Cornelius O'Brien, M.P. for Clare. Animated and eloquent speeches were delivered by the Bishop, Fathers Sheehan, Comyn, MacMahon, and Quaid, Caleb Powell, M.P. for Limerick, Tom Steele, D. O'Connell of Kilgorry, and others; but the great event of the day was O'Connell's own splendid speech, delivered in his happiest mood. No accident marred the proceedings, which wound up with a banquet given in the Old Chapel of Ennis, one feature of which was the presence of some magistrates who had been deprived of the Commission of the Peace for their action in connection with the Repeal movement. Caleb Powell, M.P., Dillon Browne, M.P., for Mayo, and John MacNamara of Moher, represented those who had received from the Government[1] this mark of distinction. Among those present were, beside those already named as at the meeting, Hugh O'Loughlin, J.P., Fort; John MacMahon, J.P., Firgrove; Maurice O'Connell, J.P., Kilgory; J. P. Molony, J.P., Tulla; M. Canny, J.P., Clonmony; Ed. M'Grath, Kilbarron; Dr. Foley, Kilrush; M. Canny, C. O'Connell, etc. etc. Father Sheehy of Tulla delivered a most eloquent speech, in the course of which he announced that £1200 would be handed the following morning to the Liberator, as the Clare contribution to the Repeal Rent, and was complimented highly by him for his talented and spirited address. One sentence only of O'Connell's speech may be given here as indicating the tone of the whole: "I am proud of Clare—ever-glorious Clare. I am proud of the conduct of the people everywhere, and particularly so at the feeling of scornful indignation with which they reject every thought that would make this a party or sectarian question."

Dr. Kennedy's splendid speech on this occasion was chiefly

---

[1] Wm. Smith O'Brien, to mark his contempt for the petty spite of the Government, had written the Lord Chancellor a manly letter resigning the Commission of the Peace. He had not yet formally joined the Repeal movement.

remarkable for the vehemence with which he denounced the evil spirit of landlordism, which was already pauperising the whole county by the exaction of excessive rents, and the heartless eviction of those who could not pay them. Here was the shadow of the coming trouble.

Other and even greater meetings followed quickly. O'Connell confidently declared that this should be the Repeal Year. He and most of his followers in Parliament had resolved to stay at home and organise the country. The Government grew alarmed, and introduced an Arms Bill to *disarm* the people. Smith O'Brien moved and ably spoke to an amendment asking for an inquiry into the cause of discontent. He was voted down. Every one knows what followed. The last of the meetings—that of Clontarf, announced for Sunday the 8th of October—was proclaimed late on the preceding evening. With great difficulty the deeply-laid plot for a carnage of the unarmed people was thwarted. Then came the prosecution of O'Connell and others, among whom was his ever-faithful "Head Pacificator—honest Tom Steele." Another Clareman destined to take a prominent part to the end of his life in public affairs, Sir Coleman O'Loughlin, was among the junior counsel for the defence. His father, Sir Michael O'Loughlin, a scion of the old princely Burren clan, was the first Catholic raised to the judicial bench, notwithstanding his having given evidence before the House of Lords of the shameful practice, known to himself as a lawyer, of packing juries in Irish political trials. He became Master of the Rolls, and died[1] all too soon, a few years before. His son had now a similar experience, for not only every Catholic, but every known liberally-minded Protestant juror, was challenged by the Crown. The result was a foregone conclusion. O'Connell and his associates were sent to Kilmainham prison. On appeal to the House of Lords, the judgment was reversed in the well-known words of Lord Denman, that such a packing of a jury as in this case was "a mockery, a delusion, and a snare." The liberation of the prisoners sent a thrill of joy through the country towards the close of 1844,

[1] His statue adorns the entrance hall of the new Court-house in Ennis.

but the Repeal Year was past, and Repeal had only received a blow from which it never recovered.

With the turning over of what is but a page in history—the events of two or three unimportant years—what a contrast presents itself! The high and bounding hopes of '43 and '44 yield place to the blank dismay and despair of '46 and '47. No free country ever rushed, or could ever so rush, from one extreme to the other, except perhaps in the case of disastrous war. But then Ireland was not a free country. Our way here lies only through Clare, and it is a sufficiently sad and weary one. When it became known that the potato —the sole food of millions of the Irish poor—had rotted in the pits at the end of '45, a cry of terror rose from the land. True, the workhouses were there,—one in Ennis, another in Scariff, another in Ennistymon, and yet one more in Kilrush, —and the whole county was found mapped out in electoral divisions for the relief of distress. For the first year or two of the famine this system was of some advantage, but as want deepened year after year, it completely broke down. England, which had forcibly introduced the uncertain land tenure which rendered such a calamity natural, stood aloof, folded in the mantle of political economy. With the exception of some very inadequate grants for relief works, managed mostly, or rather mismanaged, by English officials, the terrible strain fell on the local rates. The poor were condemned to eat the poor. Charitable contributions indeed began to pour in from America and England, but failed to stem the torrent of ever-increasing want. Deaths from famine or famine fever grew so frequent over the whole county, that they created neither comment nor surprise.

Since the disfranchisement of the forty-shilling freeholders, the policy of giving leases was reversed, and those who cultivated the soil were made tenants at will. The law afforded every facility for eviction, and evictions became the order of the day. Whole villages in some instances were unroofed. The half-starved occupants had to find refuge in *scalps*—huts erected in dykes out of the debris of the broken-down houses. Needless to say, the workhouses in Clare were soon crammed. A new one was erected in Tulla, and auxiliaries added on to the others. These all were filled as fast as they could be built, and from overcrowding and insufficient food became traps for fever and pestilence. To add to the horrors of the situation, cholera broke out and swept away its own victims. The world outside of Ireland could afford no parallel to the misery that reigned in Clare during that awful period.

The condition of the Union of Kilrush specially attracted attention. A benevolent Protestant clergyman, S. Godolphin Osborne, aided by Captain Kennedy, the most humane Poor Law official in Ireland, brought out in bold relief, in the pages of the *Times*, the depth of misery prevailing there, and the supineness of the Guardians in dealing with it. He was writing so late as 1850, when the worst was past. Here are some of his published statistics :—

"Pauper accommodation in the workhouse for 4654. Actual number in it in the month of March 1850, 5005. Deaths in three weeks of that month, 203. The published statement of deaths in the half-year ending September 29, signed ' C. M. Vandeleur, Chairman,' gives a total of 1014. Average weekly cost per head—food, $11\frac{1}{4}$d.; clothing, 2d." No wonder the paupers died—and not from overfeeding.

The writer severely blames the Board of Guardians for the "improper diet of the indoor paupers, and the insufficiency of outdoor relief given to the destitute." He concludes his letter with the following words :—" When, the other day, I looked on the Crystal Palace, and thought of Kilrush workhouse as I have seen it and now know it to be, I confess I felt, as a Christian and the subject of a Christian Government, utter disgust."

It was about this period that as many as forty poor creatures, returning from the Kilrush Board of Guardians to Moyarta, without having been able to procure entrance to the workhouse or outdoor relief, were nearly all drowned while attempting to cross the Shannon inlet in the overcrowded ferry-boat.

The Society of Friends were busy in those evil days. For their humane exertions on this and similar occasions they deserve the everlasting gratitude of the Irish race. They did not, like another body whose deeds must soon be chronicled, take advantage of the dire distress for proselytising purposes. They sent two of their number in January '47 to see with their own eyes the condition of West Clare. Though the population there was somewhat more numerous than in the other parts of the county, there was no difference in the depth of poverty. A few sentences from their published report [1] will give an idea of the prevailing misery:—

"The scenes which we witnessed and the stories which we heard in these abodes of human misery will not be easily effaced from our memory. All were poor in the extreme— some deplorably so; but it was the same sad tale we heard from all: their potatoes had failed, and, their scanty stock of oats being all consumed, they are now solely dependent on the wages received from the road works. The applicants for employment are so numerous that in most instances only one man in a family, and in some cases one, a *boy, woman,* or *girl*, can obtain it. All work alike on the roads!" (The making of, in very many instances, useless roads, was the clever device of the English officials to stay the progress of the famine!) "The pay of a man is tenpence, a woman eight-pence, and a boy sixpence per day; and when you consider that there may be broken days from sickness or severe weather, and that families here average about seven individuals, you will not be surprised when we state that they can scarcely support life under their many privations. Indeed, their week's wage, when exchanged for food, is not more than sufficient for three or four days' consumption. They endeavour, however, to stretch it over the week; but it is no uncommon thing with many families to be without food for twenty-four or thirty-six hours before the succeeding pay-day comes round, with the exception of the man or boy who is at work. And to prevent his strength (upon which all their living depends) from failing, the scanty subsistence of the others is still further reduced, to provide him with sufficient to sustain him."

That was a true picture of all Clare in that year, when the worst had not been yet reached. And yet Ireland was forced into a union with Great Britain, the richest country on the

[1] *Transactions during the Famine in Ireland,* '46–'47, pp. 179, 180.

globe, on the distinct assurance of British statesmen that a career of prosperity should henceforward open out before her!

To the flippant and heartless statement that the misery of Ireland was due to the facility of subsistence on the potato, the Society of Friends gave the following unbiassed, unprejudiced reply [1] in 1852:—

"Such does not appear to us to be the case. The people lived on the potato because they were poor; and they were poor because they could not get regular employment. This want of employment seems in great measure to have arisen from the state of the law and the practice respecting the occupation and ownership of land."

The "law" and the "occupation and ownership of land" was England's gift thrust on an unwilling Ireland.

O'Connell, William Smith O'Brien, and the other leaders of the people, had been proclaiming aloud that a self-governed Ireland would need no external help even in such an awful extremity—that her own resources were more than sufficient to meet it. Strangely enough, the *Times*, of all papers, which had published a letter from its own commissioner, dated at Ennis, August 1846, finding little to complain of but "gombeen men," in its issue of February 25, 1847, corroborates their declarations in the following vigorous terms:—

"Property ruled with savage and tyrannical sway. It exercised its rights with a hand of iron, and renounced its duties with a front of brass. 'The fat of the land, the flower of its wheat,' its 'milk and honey,' flowed from its shores, in tribute to the ruthless absentee, or his less guilty cousin, the usurious lender. It was all drain and no return. . . . England stupidly winked at this tyranny. Ready enough to vindicate political rights, it did not avenge the poor. It is now paying for that connivance."

The Corn Law Act of 1845 contributed to the impoverishment of Ireland. The cultivators of small farms found their profits from the growth of corn greatly diminished, and thus the rich English consumers benefited at the expense of the Irish starving poor. A desperate effort was made, when the

[1] *Transactions*, p. 9.

famine deepened, to keep what was still grown of it in the country. In the county of Clare some horses were shot while conveying it to market. Police in civilian dress were then sent to escort it, and found it easy to arrest the half-famished creatures engaged in this outrage against the law. They were then duly transported for trying to realise Dean Swift's idea of building a "wall of brass round Ireland," for the protection of the starving poor of the country.

This dismal subject may be dismissed with a couple of extracts. One shall be from the evidence before a Parliamentary[1] Committee of the Captain Kennedy already mentioned. He, as well as the Rev. S. G. Osborne, had severely censured the Kilrush Board of Guardians, one of the consequences of which was a challenge sent by Captain Kennedy to Colonel Vandeleur, chairman of the Board. Instead of a duel, the colonel sensibly and prudently tried out their differences in an action for libel at the Cork Assizes, but failed to secure a verdict. Here is part of his sworn evidence :—

"The state of some districts of the Union baffles description. . . . Sixteen houses, containing twenty-one families, have been levelled in one small village in Killard division. . . . As soon as one horde of houseless and all but naked paupers are dead, or provided for in the workhouse, another wholesale eviction doubles the number. . . . As cabins become fewer, lodgings become more difficult to obtain; and the helpless and houseless creatures . . . betake themselves to the nearest bog or ditch with their little all, and, thus huddled together, disease soon decimates them.

"Notwithstanding that fearful, and I believe unparalleled, numbers have been unhoused in this Union (Kilrush) within the year (probably 15,000), it seems hardly credible that 1200 more have had their dwellings levelled within a fortnight."

To facilitate the work of eviction, grappling-irons were flung over the roofs and hauled away, dragging them down with one sweep. It was alleged that in one of these humane proceedings, a child, having been forgotten in the hurry of

[1] *Blue Book*, No. 1089. May 7, 1849.

removal, was suffocated. Much was not made of this, as a life in those days was hardly of any consequence.

The *Limerick Reporter* had a leading article on the subject in the same year, from which the following may be quoted:—

"The landlords of the Union (Kilrush), to whom high rents were paid, pounced, tiger-like, on the people after the potato crop failed, and put out nearly TWENTY-FOUR THOUSAND of the working farmers, out of a total of 82,000, to perish in the *scalps.*"

Without any desire to exaggerate the horror of the situation, it may be fairly assumed that, in proportion to population, very little if anything short of similar devastation was made over the whole face of the county. Can it be a matter for wonder that there are burning memories among those still living at home and abroad, of the awful privations endured and the wrongs inflicted on them and theirs during that disastrous period? Many of them have oftentimes bitterly regretted that the people did not adopt the despairing course urged on them by William Smith O'Brien and the Young Ireland party. It would have been more manly, it could hardly have cost more loss of life, if they had flung themselves, all unarmed as they were, on the bayonets of the British soldiery.

The following correspondence may well be allowed to conclude this dark chapter in the history of Clare:—

"KILRUSH UNION.

"LETTER from the Very Rev. Mr. KELLY, P.P., Kilrush, to His Excellency the EARL OF CLARENDON, Lord-Lieutenant General, and General Governor of Ireland.

"KILRUSH, *Dec.* 13, 1849.

"MY LORD,—Fully sensible of your pressing engagements, I am unwilling to trespass on your Excellency; yet, from the heartrending scenes which have occurred in this district within the last few days, I feel it a duty briefly to offer our distressed situation to your Excellency's consideration.

"In this Union (Kilrush), the poorest in Ireland, during the summer months *thirty thousand persons, half the present population*, received out-door relief. Of these nearly *twenty thousand* have been, within the last year, thrown houseless and homeless on the world. I shall not harrow your Excellency's tender feelings by a description of their miserable state; whole families being huddled together in miserable huts, in appearance more like corpses from the sepulchre than animated beings. Several philanthropic Englishmen who have visited the district, and seen with their own eyes our condition, have, I presume, already given your Excellency a faint idea of our state. Yet the cup of our misery has only within the last fortnight been filled up. Not a single ounce of meal or any out-door relief has been administered for the last ten days. Our poorhouse contains over two thousand inmates; of these, nine hundred are children of a delicate frame and constitution; yet the young as well as the old are fed on *turnips* for the last week. Thousands from the neighbouring parishes, deprived of out-door relief, crowd about the Union workhouses; there disappointed, they surround the houses of the shopkeeper and struggling farmer; and their lamentations —their hunger shrieks—are truly heartrending. But, my Lord, I am gratified to say that no property is touched—no threat held forth. I know whole families in this town to lie down on their beds of straw, determined rather to *starve* than to *steal*. It is true that no means are left untried to alleviate their miseries by many, very many, charitable persons, of whom it may be said that, if they could coin their hearts into gold, they would give it to the poor in their present extreme necessity. Yet what avail their efforts to meet the present awful destitution!

"It was determined that a public meeting would be held to address your Excellency; but when a report—alas! a true report—reached us, that thirty-five paupers from Moyarta parish, a distance of fifteen miles, in the hope to be relieved at the workhouse, were all—all drowned whilst crossing a narrow ferry, I considered it my duty not to lose a moment in communicating to your Excellency our awful situation, which may be imagined, but cannot be described. *One week more*, and *no food!* The honest, peaceable poor of this district fall like leaves in autumn.

"I feel, in thus addressing your Excellency, I take a bold step; but your sympathy for the poor has encouraged me. Never, never be it said, that during your Excellency's Administration half the population in a remote and wretched district were suffered to starve. I write in a hurry—I write in confusion. My house at this moment is surrounded by a crowd of poor persons, whose blood has become water, seeking relief, which, alas! I cannot bestow.

"Anxiously and confidently expecting at your Excellency's hands a remedy, I have the honour to be your Excellency's obedient and humble servant,

"TIMOTHY KELLY, P.P., Kilrush."

HIS EXCELLENCY'S REPLY.

"DUBLIN CASTLE, *Dec.* 18, 1849.

"SIR,—In acknowledging the receipt of your memorial, the Lord-Lieutenant has directed me to state that his Excellency has received, with deep regret, the intelligence of the melancholy loss of life which has occurred at the ferry of Kilrush, and of the destitution stated to prevail in that Union. He regrets that the Guardians have not put rates in course of collection, from which funds could be afforded for the relief of the poor, the responsibility of providing which rests with that body.

"Your communication has been referred to the Poor Law Commissioners.

"I am, sir, your most obedient humble servant,

"T. N. REDINGTON."

Nothing more came of it!! The people still died of hunger under the paternal sway of the United Kingdoms of Great Britain and Ireland.

This amiable and high-souled priest, of whom there is a lifelike statue in the Kilrush church, told the writer that while the cholera raged in that "black '49," he and one of his curates, Father Mechan, afterwards the well-known parish priest of Carrigaholt, had to leave Kilrush and go through the parish of Carrigaholt administering the last sacraments, when word was brought them that the parish clergy were all down in the epidemic. In that one day they attended not less than about forty cases of cholera and famine fever. The parish priest, Father Malachy Duggan,[1] who had himself attended eighteen cases only two days before, died of cholera within a few days.

[1] Lever, who was then a medical officer in Kilrush, afterwards vilely caricatured those priests in one of his novels. Death in the discharge of duty did not avail to save Father Duggan from his anti-Catholic pen.

CHAPTER XXVIII.

FROM 1851 TO 1893.

Effects of the Famine—William Smith O'Brien's Career — O'Gorman, O'Donnell, and Doyle—Proselytism in Clare—Springfield College leading on to Diocesan College—Contests on Independent Opposition Principles—Six-Mile Bridge Massacre—Narrow Escape at Tulla—Uncertain Tenure and Unrest—Distress in '63 and '64—Fenianism—Its Consequences—Amnesty—Home Rule—Farmers' Club and Land League in Clare—Parnell—Meetings at Ennis and Milltown-Malbay—Phases of the Land Struggle—An Irish Parliament at last within reach.

THE events to be recorded in this concluding chapter belong for the most part to the history of our own times, and are too well known to require more than brief notice. The prosecution of O'Connell gave a death-blow to the Repeal movement. He tried bravely to carry it on, but, though he had succeeded in reversing the conviction, two facts had been plainly placed before the country: England would not yield Repeal without a fight, and O'Connell would not fight. The movement had been carried too far, and was too widespread, and had stirred up the hopes of the people too much, to admit of a craven surrender. The more ardent spirits among the Repealers came now to the front. Clare and Tipperary gave to this whole-souled band of earnest patriots, William Smith O'Brien, M.P., Richard O'Gorman, Richard Dalton Williams, O'Donohue, and Father Kenyon, a priest of the Diocese of Killaloe. The *Nation* sprang into being to give voice to the new advanced policy. No man was more fit to throw life into the pages of a journal than its first editor, Charles Gavan Duffy. He had on his staff a brilliant band of enthusiasts; Davis, Kenyon, Mitchell, Dillon, and others such like, writing not for pay, but to infuse their own national inspirations into the minds of the young men of Ireland. In their hands it became probably the best-written and the most attractive journal in the British Empire. The advanced policy, so ably advocated, gave birth to what was soon known as the Young Ireland Party. From the start they scarcely concealed their design of a resort to arms if driven to it by a final refusal of Irish autonomy. Williams, while yet a student in the College of Carlow, wrote that splendid ballad, "The Munster War Song," which, though affecting to treat of a past period, was well understood to apply to the living present. Lyrics of a similar character quickly followed, from the pens of Davis, Duffy, M'Carthy, O'Hagan, Doheny, and others, till in the *Songs of the Nation* not only did the youth of Ireland find thoughts to set their souls on fire, but the Irish race became possessed in a few years of an enduring literature of which any nation might be proud.

O'Connell and the "Old Irelanders," as they came to be called, looked askance at this dangerous development. Almost insensibly at first, but steadily the cleaving asunder began to be made manifest in Conciliation Hall itself. Thomas Francis Meagher's famous "Sword Speech" was the eloquent impromptu reply to the "not one drop of blood" policy. William Smith O'Brien came into almost open collision with O'Connell. He had refused to obey a summons to attend to his parliamentary duties which O'Connell submitted to, both having declared their preference for work in Ireland among the starving people. O'Brien was imprisoned in the cellar of the House of Commons for contempt. When released, he was feted at Kilrush and Limerick. The open approval of his action was regarded by O'Connell as a slur upon himself. Then followed a debate in Conciliation Hall towards the end of 1846, on the question of censuring the advanced policy advocated in the *Nation*, which ended in an open rupture— O'Brien, Meagher, O'Gorman, Mitchell, and their friends, leaving the hall never to return there.

In the following year Ireland's greatest son died, May 15, 1847, at Genoa, on his way to Rome. As he could not reach the cherished goal of his pilgrimage, he willed that his heart should be sent there. It reposes in the Irish Church of St.

Agatha, enshrined in a monument erected by Bianconi, whose daughter afterwards married the Liberator's nephew, Morgan John O'Connell, M.P. The whole nation was plunged in grief. The people forgot their own dire woes and dissensions in the loss of their idolised chief. His remains were brought back to Ireland and interred in Glasnevin, amid such an outburst of national mourning as no crowned monarch's death ever received. For a short interval the Young Ireland Party fell into disfavour. They were blamed for hastening the death of the Liberator. William Smith O'Brien was forbidden to attend his funeral; and when, many months later on, some of his enthusiastic admirers invited him and Mitchell to a banquet in Limerick, the house in which it was given was assailed by a furious mob, and they narrowly escaped with their lives. But this did not last long. The agony of the ever-increasing famine drove the nation mad. Mitchell started the *United Irishman* expressly for the purpose of preparing the people for insurrection, and soon got himself transported for life. This severe sentence did not deter his associates. It only stung them to renewed exertions. The "promise for me, Mitchell," shouted out in the face of the judge to Mitchell's appeal from the dock to continue the organisation, was caught up with desperate enthusiasm. Clubs were formed in all the leading centres. Guns were procured in spite of the Arms Act, and pikes were manufactured as fast as smiths and carpenters could be got to incur the dangerous risk.

William Smith O'Brien became the acknowledged leader of the revolutionary movement. His worst foes could not deny him the merit of a high-souled patriotism, and a courage worthy of the best days of the princely house from which he was descended. He shirked no danger. He boldly faced almost certain defeat and death in the desperate effort to lift up fallen, starving Ireland. His career was affectionately and with feelings of pride watched from his native county. It used to be whispered about that he paid it occasional stolen visits to meet local leaders, and give them his instructions. It need hardly be added that Government spies were at all times on his track and on the track of all the prominent leaders, and that the movement was allowed to proceed only to entrap as many as possible, and then pounce on it with the more crushing effect.

The French Revolution of '48 gave an impetus to the Irish Confederation. Smith O'Brien boldly proposed a resolution congratulating the French people, and went over openly with Meagher to present an Address to Lamartine, the President of the newly-formed Government in Paris. When returning through London, he found Parliament busily rushing on one of those numerous Coercion Acts with which mainly England governed Ireland since the Union. Some idea of his strength of character may be formed from the fact of his presenting himself in the House, and claiming, amid the yells of the infuriated Assembly, the right of the people of Ireland to arm in the defence of liberty. His action presented a strong contrast to that of O'Gorman Mahon, who was then member for Ennis, and who voted generally with the Government. His brother, Sir Lucius O'Brien, and William N. MacNamara, who were the county members, were, it need hardly be said, on the side of "law and order."

The movement against such odds was doomed to disastrous failure. At the right moment it was brought to a head and easily crushed. O'Brien courted death at Ballingarry. He went up to the very guns of the besieged police, inviting them vainly to surrender. In the dock he displayed the same fearlessness. While the mock trial was proceeding towards the sentence to be "hanged, drawn, and quartered," he was writing on slips of paper, and distributing to friends in Court, Pope's stirring lines—

> "Whether on the scaffold high
> Or in the battle's van,
> The noblest place for man to die
> Is where he dies for man."

The sentence was commuted into transportation for life; but, after many years of bitter exile, he was allowed to return and lay his bones in the land of his love.

His last public act was a visit to Carrigaholt, where the present writer was then officiating. He brought with him a valuable gift of Irish books as premiums for the boys who had been studying the old tongue. He spent the evening in the hospitable residence of one of his greatest friends, Father Meehan, the parish priest; and, in response to a popular welcome organised by the people, made his last speech in view of the castle where another O'Brien lived who fought and lost for Ireland. Within a few months he died at Bangor, in Wales, where he was staying in the vain hope of recovering his health.

He too fought and lost for Ireland, but it was not for want of courage and perseverance. The fine statue near O'Connell's Bridge in Dublin will keep his memory alive in the heart of the nation. In his own native Clare, and among the people of his race all the world over, his name will ever be a "household word."

After the collapse of the insurrection, O'Gorman, O'Donnell, and Doyle fled to Clare. The former had many relatives there, and all three had stout friends in every corner of the county, willing to face the risk of sheltering them and helping them to escape. It involved in the eye of English law the guilt of High Treason, as the writer was solemnly warned of from the bench when he and others were engaged in '67 in similar wicked practices. With great difficulty they were put safely on board a ship at Carrigaholt. They were thrown almost into despair at the last moment, when the captain, who had undertaken to carry them out of the country for a large sum of money, refused to receive them on board until the notes they offered him would be converted into gold. The local authorities had some reason to suspect that they were in the neighbourhood, and a sharp look-out was kept; but their friends were still more on the alert. The coin was procured, and they sailed away to liberty. Of those most active in effecting their escape, two are now dead—Father Meehan and Father Moran. Two others still live, Garrett Doherty and Dick Brew, in whose premises they were concealed, while the police and soldiers were scouring the country round. Of the three fugitives, two, O'Donnell and Doyle, returned, when matters cooled down, to Limerick, where they had large practice as solicitors, and were held in high esteem while they lived. O'Gorman, for whose capture a reward of £300 had been offered, still lives and does honour to his country in one of the highest legal positions in New York.

Immediately after the famine, while the people were yet in the depths of poverty and despondency, an attempt at proselytism on a large scale was made in the parish of Carrigaholt. Being almost an island, and up to that time badly provided with schools, it was regarded by those who delight in tempting the starving poor as a suitable field for operation. An agent, who ruled with despotic sway over the greater part of the parish, actively supported as well by the Kildare Street Society, as by the landlord, his father-in-law, set himself with vigour to the work of Protestantising the peninsula. Schools were rapidly built at different points, a staff of parsons, Scripture readers, and teachers provided, and his own brother, at a good salary, planted down as resident superintendent of the mission. Some progress was made for awhile among the very poor and the small farmers, who, being tenants-at-will, were at the mercy of landlord and agent. The new parish priest, Father Meehan, who succeeded the cholera-stricken Father Duggan, devoted all his great energy and zeal to the task of counteracting the efforts of the proselytisers. The struggle was maintained with great vigour, and bitterness too, on both sides for about ten years. When Father Meehan could not get a site on which to build a chapel in the most remote and populous part of the parish, he contrived to get possession of a house from an emigrant, converting it, poor and despicable as it was, into what he called St. Patrick's Church. Out of this he was evicted as soon as the law could be put in force. In his extremity the thought occurred to him of building a timber, movable hut, fixing in it an altar, and placing it in an open space on the sea-shore. This he called "The Ark," and round it the people for some years flocked in all weather to hear mass and receive instruction. Dr. Cahill, the eminent preacher and lecturer, while staying at Kilkee, heard of this novel method of carrying on church work. He went to the "Ark," preached from it, and began at once to call public attention through the press to the conduct of the proselytisers in West Clare. The agent was compelled by the strong feeling aroused to give a site, upon which soon after Father Meehan was able, with the contributions that came in from generous sympathisers, to erect a handsome Gothic church, within which the "Ark" is preserved. This was practically the end of proselytism in the district. It was carried on in a dying condition for some years longer. Those who had been committed to it left as quickly as they could for America, bringing certificates, in many instances, that they had been received back into the Church. At the present time one individual is the outcome in full of the prolonged and costly undertaking.

In other parts of the country, at Ruan, Tulla, and Newmarket, similar attempts were made, but on a much smaller scale. The will was there, but public opinion was too strong for those who took advantage of dire distress to traffic in human souls. Giving employment was the specious pretext used, but the object was soon made manifest, and the end was soon reached.

In the last chapter some account was given of the progress of education in the county during the earlier years of the present century. It has ever since been steadily advancing. About the middle of this century the Christian Brothers took up positions in Ennis and Ennistymon. The Sisters of Mercy, in an ever-increasing body, took charge of the education of girls. A very efficient classical school for intern and extern pupils was established in Ennis by Mr. Fitzimon and Mr. Power. This became at once an important centre for education, to which flocked not only the youths of the county preparing for the various professions, but those of the neighbouring counties—Kerry, Limerick, Tipperary, and Galway. In course of time it merged into a Diocesan College, with the present Bishop of Killaloe, Dr. M'Redmond, and the late Bishop of Waterford, Dr. Egan, for its first directors, and holds still in its splendid new buildings the foremost position it took under their able management.

During the third quarter of this century, the political life of Clare, apart from the Fenian movement, of which something will be said, was kept up in a series of exciting election contests, in which, on the Conservative side, Colonel Vandaleur of Kilrush always bore the standard; and on the Liberal and Independent Opposition side at various stages, Cornelius

O'Brien, Sir John Foster Fitzgerald, Lord Francis Conyngham, Francis MacNamara Calcut, Luke White, Charles White, Sir Colman O'Loghlin, and Sir Bryan O'Loghlin. In the borough of Ennis no one but a Liberal offered himself, and it was held all the time by J. D. Fitzgerald, J.C., who defeated O'Gorman Mahon in 1852, and William Stacpoole of Edenvale. The county contest was usually a three-cornered fight. The Conservatives, backed up by the then powerful landlord influence, struggled hard to secure one seat. It was on all occasions a very close run—on one of these the Liberal majority being but one. As might be expected, the Conservative stronghold was in the west of the county, where Colonel Vandaleur, Lord Leaconfield, and the other landlords, with their agents, had practically absolute power over their tenants-at-will, and used it with little scruple. Pressure of a similar kind was put upon voters in the eastern parts, but it was met with more vigour. Popular feeling was more concentrated and stronger. Those of the tenants who voted with their landlords—they were not very many—came to the polling booths at Tulla and Six-Mile Bridge under military protection. At the latter place, in 1852, the soldiers fired upon the people, taking many lives. On the same day at Tulla a greater catastrophe was narrowly escaped. A large crowd, densely packed between the soldiers and the houses on the side of the street, became very excited on the arrival of some protected voters. A local landlord, not popular then nor since, infuriated by the threats and gibes of the crowd, was said to have called, in his capacity of Justice of the Peace, upon the commanding officer to fire upon the people. If he had obeyed the order, every bullet should have told. He exhibited however, great patience, but ordered his men to load. The danger of the situation becoming known within the booth, John O'Brien, R.M., Maurice O'Connell, J.P., and some priests, hastened to the scene, rushed in between the people and the muzzles of the guns, and succeeded in driving back and calming the foolhardy crowd. The Ballot Act and the Household Franchise Act have made such scenes—at least as between Conservatives and Liberals—impossible for evermore in Clare. Both these parties are extinguished. Isaac Butt's

Home Rule movement pushed forward all who had ranged themselves hitherto under the banner of the English Liberal Party into the higher, and for Irishmen, broader platform of Irish nationality. There are no mere Liberals in Clare now; and when the Conservatives were impolitic enough to put forward their strength against the Nationalists at the election of 1885, Lord Inchiquin's son, the grandnephew of William Smith O'Brien, and Carey Reeves, D.L., the most popular Conservative in Clare, polled between them only 538 against over 13,000 given for the Nationalist candidates, J. Jordan and Mr. Cox, both strangers to the people and to the county. The position of parties thus defined remains since, and promises to remain in the future, unchanged.

Soon after the Crimean War, one of the captured Russian guns was sent on to Ennis. It was proposed to fix it as a trophy of English victory on the site of the old court-house.[1] But that too was the spot on which the battle for Catholic Emancipation was fought and won, and that victory deserved to be commemorated in the people's minds far more than the success at the Crimea. An outcry was raised against the planting of the cannon there, and the idea started of raising instead of it a monument to the Liberator. The whole county became enthusiastic over it. Collections were made in every parish, and Michael Considine, the guiding spirit of the congregated trades of Ennis, whose homely eloquence had done much to stir up public spirit in the matter, was deputed by the committee to seek aid from the Irish in England. The execution of the work was committed to Cahill, the sculptor. The material for both column and statue was the fine limestone which abounds in the neighbourhood of Ennis. On the stately column, 74 feet high, he placed a colossal but graceful figure of O'Connell looking over the scene of his triumph, which as a work of art helped him to fame, and of which any city might well be proud. The unveiling of the statue took place on the 3rd of October 1865, in the presence of an immense gathering. To Dr. Power, Bishop of Killaloe,

---

[1] It had been taken down but a few years before, when the present commodious and elegant structure was completed at the east end of the town.

was given the honour of unveiling it. When the splendid figure was exposed to the delighted gaze of the multitude, Sir Colman O'Loghlin, the bosom friend of O'Connell, who was then member for Clare, delivered an eloquent harangue, and concluded it by handing over to Dr. Power and his successors in the See of Killaloe, in the name of the committee, the care of the monument.

There was a rush of prosperity during and after the Crimean War, which had disastrous consequences in Clare. Much of the land of the county had changed hands in the few preceding years. Many of the small and middle farmers had been completely broken down by the famine; and the working of the Encumbered Estates Act in getting rid on frequently unfair terms of needy landowners, introduced a new set of grasping landlords. These looked for the largest interest possible on their outlay. Many of them never saw the county; but whether in the county or out of it, they were able to secure agents, whose interest it was to run up rents in order to secure a good percentage for themselves. The fictitious value given to the land during the foreign war aided them. Competition became keen, old rents on many estates were increased, as there was no security of tenure; and thus burdens were imposed on the people under which they soon began to totter.

The first shock came in '63 and '64. Wet summers had succeeded each other, causing the potato crop to fail. A great scarcity of food ensued, especially in the poorer districts along the coast. Eviction for non-payment of excessive rents, made still more so by the failure of the crops, became frequent; and were it not that public attention was soon called in the press to the impending danger, some of the scenes of '48 and '49 would be, though on a smaller scale, repeated. Local committees for the distribution of charity were formed. The Society of Friends again stepped nobly to the front. They and others took upon themselves the duty of saving the poor from starvation, which should have been the care of the Government.

The failure of the insurrection of '48, followed by the collapse of the Independent Opposition movement, left the county politically in a stagnant condition. But it was not to continue so long. The American War trained to arms very many thousands of Irish emigrants, and when it came to an end, being disbanded the bolder spirits among them began to think of the possibility of rescuing Ireland from the hated yoke of England. The lesson of that war—the lesson so plainly taught, that modern military science leaves hardly any hope for success in an insurrection against a firmly-established government—was lost on their ardent temperaments. The Fenian movement was started on both sides of the Atlantic, and the youth of Clare found themselves among the first in the whirl of the excitement. They foolishly believed the stories told them of the landing and secreting of large consignments of war material to be followed by an invasion of well-trained Irish-American soldiers, they had only to drill privately, and, when the right moment came, fall into the ranks and fight for the old land. The hot blood of a fighting race was aroused at such a prospect, the secrecy of the preparation added a zest to their vivid imaginings, and within a very short time there was hardly a young man in Clare who had not taken the Fenian oath. Casey's spirited ballad, " The Risin' of the Moon," was no mere fancy picture. In very many of the retired and sheltered nooks of Clare, as elsewhere, returned Americans—ay, and even some who had taken Her Majesty's shilling—were busy teaching military exercises. The escape of James Stephens encouraged the movement immensely.

The inevitable end came on the night fixed for the rising, March 5, 1867; bodies of young men in various parts of the county took to the field. They were led to believe that on the following day they would be massed at points of vantage, and provided with the arms supposed to be hidden and at the disposal of the leaders. They were deceived on every side. The hidden war material proved to be a myth; and Corydon, one of the inner circle of five who had control of the whole organisation, being in the pay of the Government, had given due notice of the precise time for the rising. Precautions had been taken everywhere to frustrate it, and the collapse came on the heels of the attempt. Though many hundreds were "out" that night in all parts of Clare, only at one place —the coastguard station near Kilbaka, in the remote west— did any collision take place. It was not much. One Fenian and one of the coastguards were wounded rather badly. The Fenian could not escape, and was arrested, tried by Judge Keogh, and sentenced to ten years' penal servitude. The others who were known to be engaged in the attack were, after many hair-breadth escapes and much worrying of the district, got out of the country. So ended there, and wherever else such attempts were made, what was regarded as a very formidable organisation.

The break-up of Fenianism produced a crop of informers. The Habeas Corpus Act being suspended, the jails were soon filled, and it was found easy to excite suspicion of each other among the prisoners. Clare was, however, remarkably steadfast in this respect. Only two persons — and these of indifferent character — could be got to turn upon their comrades. In the western district, where the trouble was greatest, not even one could be induced to give information of any kind. The writer knew many poor persons who had it in their power to secure money by telling privately where the fugitives were being sheltered, and who scorned to do so. Instead of this, they helped them in every way to escape; and at no small risk to themselves, for they also had been warned from the bench at Kilrush, on the occasion of one of the trials, that they and all such evil-doers as would give them aid or countenance would be as guilty in the eye of the law as the persons who actually rose up in arms.

The events in the county still to be recorded are of such recent date that a bare recital will be the most appropriate. These late years were indeed eventful in giving much food for angry controversy, the end of which is not yet reached.

Following closely upon the failure of the Fenian movement, though not of course as a result from it, came a rush of prosperity over the whole country. Prices for cattle and butter ran very high, and Clare being for far the greater part a pastoral county, shared largely in the up-rise. There was, however, general uneasiness, owing to the very insecure position of nearly all the tenants. There had been much inadequate legislation on the subject, but no real relief of the tension. A combined effort began in the country to press for fixity of tenure at fair rents and freedom of sale, and in Clare a very influential Farmers' Club was established in 1877, holding its monthly meetings in Ennis, but with members in all parts of the county. It organised in the same year a great public meeting on the fair-green of Clonroad, at which resolutions calling for the above-named changes in the Land Laws were unanimously passed.

The broader question of Home Rule was also being energetically pressed to the front by Isaac Butt. He had acquired great popularity by his, in some instances, unpaid defence of Fenian prisoners. The appeal for amnesty, following the noble example set by the United States, and in favour of which, among other places, an enthusiastic meeting was held in Kilrush presided over by Dr. Dinan, P.P., V.G., had been only partially heard, but the spirit of the country was rising. Sir Colman O'Loghlin and Lord Francis Conyngham were triumphantly returned for Clare as Home Rulers in 1875, and henceforward the cry for Home Rule and a radical readjustment of the Land Laws gained day by day in volume. Mr. Parnell, the very personification of persistent determination, stepping out of the landlord ranks, took the guidance of the movement out of the feeble, failing hands of Isaac Butt; and then in good truth history of a new and startling kind began to be made.

Michael Davitt raised the cry of "The Land for the People." After some hesitation it was adopted by Mr. Parnell. The "Land League" was formed, into which the Clare Farmers' Club soon merged; its two first presidents—the present writer and Father Matt. Kenny of Scariff—having agreed, at Mr. Parnell's call, to act on the originating committee. It spread rapidly. The League being, unlike Fenianism, an organisation within the law, soon counted within its ranks young and old, almost without an exception, among the people of the county. Branches were formed in every parish, with usually the priests at the head. Meetings were publicly held, and the whole county was drilled almost into the precision of a regiment.

As if to intensify the growing desire for a fixed settlement of this burning question of the land, the gaunt spectre of hunger once more hovered over the whole country. For the second time within twenty years, I found myself in Clare sitting on relief committees distributing public charity to the labouring, artisan and farming classes; and that in a country as much blessed by Providence with fertility as any other on the face of the earth. It was a humiliating, a sickening spectacle, to witness crowds of decent people [1] clamouring for food on the land which their forefathers owned, but which England took from them and handed over to the exacting, spendthrift, and hostile landocracy, of which the world has been hearing so much lately in the Land Courts. With this terrible strain, and the shame of it upon them, the people braced themselves up for a final struggle with landlordism. The issue is now well known. Mr. Parnell's "boycotting" speech at Ennis, followed by another at Maryborough, in which he advocated the policy of gauging the value of Mr. Gladstone's Land Act by submitting only slightly over-rented farms, in the first instance, to the Land Courts as test cases, led to his arrest and imprisonment on the 14th of October 1882. With him were imprisoned, as suspects under Forster's Act, many of the able body of men who were allied with him in and out of Parliament. Then came the "No Rent Manifesto," followed by a condition of things all over the country little short of civil war.

Soon after his release, the circumstances of which, and the tragic accompaniment of the Phœnix Park murders, are so well known as to need no recounting here, Mr. Parnell fulfilled the promise he made the writer, of addressing a

---

[1] As I write, the Relief Committee book of the parish of Miltown-Malbay, A.D. 1880, is before me. I take one extract as a sample: "Feb. 13. Ticket orders for bread-stuffs were filled for 316 applicants, numbering 1261 individuals, at an expenditure of £42, 12s. 6d., averaging 8d. per head per week." The whole population was then under 5000. Very inadequate contributions came from local landowners. Mrs. Morony of Miltown House offered £10 from a rental of over £2000, but on condition of getting £10 worth of broken stones. Major George Studdert and Captain Ellis represented by their contributions and exertions the best side of the landowners' class.

meeting at Milltown-Malbay. The town could not hold the multitudes who assembled, and the meeting was held on the lawn before the Parochial House.[1] Every parish in the county was well represented there on that memorable 26th of January 1884. He proceeded amid great enthusiasm, before speaking, to turn the first sod of the railway which we had only just secured after a long struggle. The day having been very fine for such a period of the year, contributed much to the success of the meeting. With its numerous bands, and still more numerous banners swaying under the Atlantic breezes, the immense gathering presented certainly a splendid spectacle, second only to that of Ballycoree in O'Connell's time. As conciliation had become the policy of the Government, the speeches delivered were moderate but firm in tone. The greatest regularity prevailed. We undertook to preserve order, if police were not intruded on the meeting. The condition was complied with, and neither hitch nor accident nor disturbance of any kind marred the proceedings. Intense satisfaction was felt by all present, as the old county had clearly scored one of its red-letter days. This was the only county meeting addressed by Mr. Parnell after his imprisonment; and doubtless it had no little to say to that dogged "right or wrong" spirit with which so many clung to him in after days.

The suppression by a Tory Government of the National League, which had succeeded the Land League, brought much trouble into Clare. It was the only county in Ireland over all of which the new coercion code of Lord Salisbury and his nephew—Mr. Balfour, the Chief Secretary—had full swing. All the same, the various branches of the League continued holding their now *illegal* meetings privately; and when Mr. Balfour boasted in Parliament that, under his rule, the League was a "thing of the past," at the call of the Irish Parliamentary Party, open assemblies were held simultaneously on the 8th of April 1888, at, among other places in the proclaimed counties, Ennis, Kilrush, and Milltown-Malbay. Those who attempted to speak, priests and members of Parliament, fully expected arrest and prosecution; but beyond being

[1] Built in 1876–77, while the writer had charge of the parish.

dispersed at the point of the bayonet, little else followed, except at Ennis, where a riot was forced on and a few received terms of imprisonment.

The places in Clare most harried under the coercion *régime* were Bodyke and Milltown-Malbay. Owing to evictions for the non-payment of rents, declared afterwards in the Land Courts to be grossly unfair, a fierce conflict was carried on in both places. At Bodyke, after an interchange of shots between the police and the people, and an exciting series of evictions from barricaded and well-defended houses, a fair settlement was arrived at. The struggle at Milltown-Malbay was kept up all along, owing to the obstinacy of one individual, backed up as a matter of course by the authorities, and led to the imprisonment at various periods of many of the most inoffensive and respectable people of the parish. When it was in some degree dying out, the agent on the Carroll property renewed it by letting part of an evicted and highly rack-rented farm. This brought on more excitement, more prosecutions, and more imprisonments. The elements of the long-continued strife, though somewhat subdued, are there still.

This history of Clare comes now to an end. It shall not deal with the deplorable division caused in the National ranks by the unhappy fall of Mr. Parnell. That is for wider ground than is taken up here, and may well be reserved for a calmer atmosphere. While the last lines are being written, Mr. Gladstone is for the second time energetically pressing through Parliament a Home Rule Bill which in substance meets with the approval of all Irish Nationalists. If it gives to Ireland, as it must give sooner or later, self-government, the writer fondly hopes that whoever may in the future take up the thread of Clare narrative will find in it a subject more encouraging and more inspiring than fell to his lot.

APPENDIX I.

I. Sir J. Perrott's Tripartite Deed—II. Grant to T. O'Brien as Seneschal of Burren—III. King James I.'s Letter to Sir D. O'Brien of Dough—IV. O'Loughlin's Transfer—V. O'Conor's Deed.

I°. *This Indenture Tripartite*, made betwixt the Right Honourable Sir John Perrott, Knight, Lord Deputy Generall of Ireland, for and in behalfe of the Queen's Most Excellent Majestie, of the one parte, and the Lords, spirituall and temporall, Chieftanios, freeholders and ffarmers and inhabitants of lands or holdings in parte or parcell, of the Province of Connaught called Thomond, that is to witt, Donnogh Earl of Thomond, and Morrogh Lord Barron of Inchiquine, the Rev. Fathers in God Mauritius, Bisshopp of Killalow, Daniell Ellecte, Bisshop of Killfinnoragh, Donogh O'Horane, Deane of Killalow, Daniel Shennaghe, Deane of Killfinorogh, Dennis, Archdeacon of the same, Sir Edward Waterhouse, of Downassy, Knight, Sir Terlagh O'Brien, of Ennistyman, Knight, John McNemara, of Cnappogue, otherwise called McNemara, of West Clancullane, Daniell Reagh McNemarra, of Carrowlagh, otherwise called McNemarra, of East Cloncollan, Teige McMahon, of Clonaddorala, otherwise called McMahon, of East Corconwaskine, Terlagh McMahon, of Moyartie, chiefe of his name in West Corcovaskin, Monertagh O'Brien, of Dromaleyne, Gent., Mahonne O'Brien, of Clonduane, Diony O'Laughline, of the Gragans, otherwise called O'Laughline, Rosse O'Laughline, of Glancollumkyle, Tanist to the same O'Laughline, Mahon and Dermot O'Dea, of Tullaghdea, chief of their names, Connor McGilreooghe, of Cragbreane, chief of his name, Terlagh McTeige O'Brien, of Beallacorege, gente, *Luke Brady, sonn and heir of the late Bisshopp of Meath*, Edward White, of the Crattelagh, gente, Geo. Cusake, of Dromoylin, gente, Boetius Clanchy, of Knockffynne, gente, John McNemarra, of the Moetullen, gente, Henery O'Grady, of the Iland of Inchecronan, gente, Donogh McClancy, of the Urlion, chief of his name, Donogh Garragh O'Brien, of Ballecessye, gente, Connor O'Brien, of Curharcorcal, gente, and George Ffanninge, of Lymericke, merchant, of the other parte : *Witnesseth* that where the said whole countrey or territorie of Thomond is devided into nine principall Baronies, that is to say—

1. The Barony of Tullaghynaspyll;
2. The Barony of Dengynvyggon;
3. The Barony of Clonraude, "otherwise called" the Islands;
4. The Barony of Clunderala, "otherwise called" East Corcawaskine;
5. The Barony of Moarte, "otherwise called" West Corcowaskine;
6. The Barony of Ibrackane;
7. The Barony of Corcumrow, otherwise called Doughycomogher;
8. The Barony of Gragans, otherwise called Borren;
9. And the Barony of Tullaghydae; which containe in themselves, as well by antient division as by later inquisicon and presentment hereunto annexed, the number of "one thousand two hundred fifty-nine quarters and a halfe and one-third part of land, estimating every quarter with his pasture, meaddow, woode, and bogge of att a hundred and twenty acres, as by a more particular layeing downe of ye same in manner and forme following it may appear:

1°. In the Barony of (*Tullaghypyll*) there is a quantity of land called *Tuomore*, consisting of thirty-nine quarters. Also *Tullæ*, consisting of twelve quarters, belonging to Her Majestie, as in right of the Abbay of Tullæ. Of *Tullaghline*, consisting of thirteen quarters. Also *Tæronye*, consisting of twenty-one quarters. Also *Termonigrady*, consisting of eighteen quarters, belonging to the Queen's Majestie, as in right of the spiritual living of Tomgrenny. Alsoe *Moynose*, consisting of four quarters, belonging to the Queen's Majestie, as in right of the spiritual living of Maynooe aforesaid. Alsoe *Tuogonnill*, consisting of fourteen quarters. Alsoe *Trog*, Killalow, consisting of twenty-eight quarters, whereof belongeth to the *Bisshopricke of Killalow* five quarters. Alsoe *Annaghmore* and *Annaghbegg*, consisting of nine quarters. Alsoe *Tuoglanny*, consisting of twelve quarters. Also *Tuoghiwine*, consisting of fifteen quarters. Alsoe *Toanohowne*, consisting of sixteen quarters. Alsoe *Togherishart*, consisting of seaven quarters. Alsoe *Kyllaclownell*, consisting of forty-four quarters, whereof lyeth in this Barony twenty-two quarters, and in the Barony of Dengynnyviggon other twenty-two quarters, which in ye whole within this Baronie of Tullaghynespeill cometh to *Tuo hundred* twenty-eight quarters.

2°. In the Barony of *Denginyviggon* there is a quantity of land called ye *Tou-Cloncollen-Woghtraghe*, consisting of forty-six quarters. Alsoe *Touenevercone*, consisting of forty quarters. Alsoe *Tollwoghtrugh-Traderee*, consisting of thirty-three quarters, whereof one quarter beareth cheefry to the Byshoprick of Killalow. Also *Tuovannagh-Tradry*, consisting of thirty-nine quarters and a half, whereof of six quarters beareth cheefry to the Bishopricke of Killalow, *Tooightraygh-Tradry*, consisting of thirty-eight quarters, whereof

APPENDIX I. 379

two quarters beareth cheefry to the Bisshopricke of Killalow. Allsoe *Tulluomarrod*, consisting of forty-nine quarters. Alsoe *Torrespard*, consisting of seven quarters. Alsoe *Kynnadownoll*, alias *Killanadownell*, consisting of forty-four quarters, whereof belongeth to this barrony twenty-two quarters as aforesaid, which in the whole within that Baronie cometh to *two hundred seventy-four quarters and a half.*

3°. In the Barony of *Clonraude*, otherwise called the Ilands, there is a quantity of lands called *Coggryanke*, consisting of twenty-three quarters. Alsoe *Icormuck*, consisting of forty-one quarters. Alsoe *Clonranch*, consisting of twelve quarters. Alsoe Killone, *Ballyruthclæ*, consisting of three quarters, belonging to the Queen's Majestie in right of ye Abby of Killoone. Alsoe *Clanchonsodyne*, consisting of four quarters. Alsoe *Belacoryge*, consisting of two quarters. Alsoe *Innisdadroon-Couppal* of one quarter. Alsoe of *Dromiline*, consisting of seaven quarters, belonging to the Bishoprick of Killalow. Alsoe the Abbay of Clare, consisting of fifteen quarters, belonging to the Queen's Majestie as in right of said Abbay. Alsoe *Tubermaley*, consisting of one quarter. Alsoe *Ballynicoody*, consisting of three quarters. Alsoe *Killyglasse*, consisting of two quarters. Alsoe *Knockneballymock*, consisting of one quarter. Alsoe *Illannagananagh*, consisting of two quarters, which in the whole within that Barony cometh to one hundred and seaveenteene quarters.

CLONDERLAW.

4°. In the Barronie of *Clonedderalae*, otherwise called East Corcowaskine, there is a quantity of land called *Tramolke*, consisting of fourteen quarters, whereof one quarter beareth cheefry to the Bishopricke of Killalowe. Alsoe Tooencfyorny, consisting of thirteen quarters, whereof one quarter beareth cheefery to the Bishop of Killalowe. Alsoe Toeaallae, consisting of thirteen quarters *Di*, whereof two quarters *Di* beareth cheefry to the Bishopricke of Killalowe. Alsoe Tuonekelly, consisting of thirteen quarters, whereof five quarters beareth cheefry to the said Bishopricke. Alsoe Tocœagneagh, consisting of eleven quarters, whereof three quarters beareth cheefry to the said Bishopricke of Killaloe, which in the whole within the Barony cometh to three score five quarters.

MOYARTIE.

5°. In ye Baronie of *Moyartie*, otherwise called *West Corkowaskine*, there is a quantity of land called *Aghamoanagh*, consisting of twenty-six quarters, whereof fourteen quarters beareth cheefry to *the Bishopricke of Killalow*. Also the west side of the said Barony, consisting of forty-one quarters, whereof twenty-three beareth cheefry to the said Bishoprick of Killalow, which in the whole within that Barony cometh to sixty-seven quarters.

IBRACKANE.

6°. In the Barony of Ibrackane there is contained *sixty quarters*, which the said Earl of Thomond challengeth wholly and freely to himselfe; alsoe in *Penle Mullou Killarnane* and in *Enlagh* one quarter; alsoe Cloghoane and Dremardlough, consisting of two quarters challenged by the said Earle to his household officers, which in the whole within that Barony cometh to sixty-three quarters.

CORCOMROE.

7°. In the Barony of Corcomroe, otherwise called *Doughiconnoghr*, there is a quantity of land called *Tollwoughter-fflahertie*, consisting of forty quarters, whereof belongeth to ye Bisshopricke of Killfynnoragh two quarters, do. to the Deanery of the same one quarter, and unto the Queen's Majesty as in right of the Abbay of Killoone one quarter; also *Toowoughter-She*, consisting of forty-five quarters, whereof belongeth in right of the Abbay of Killsonnagh five quarters, and to ye Bishopricke of Kilfynnoragh seven quarters; also *Tooraine*, consisting of thirty quarters, whereof belongeth to the Bishopricke of Kilfinnoragh seven quarters; alsoe *Quoilea*, consisting of twenty-six quarters, whereof belongeth to the said bishopricke half a quarter, which in the whole within that Barony cometh to one hundred and forty-one quarters.

GRAGANES.

8°. In the Barony of *Graganes*, otherwise called *Borren*, there is a quantity of land called *Toofflanneth*, consisting of twenty-five quarters, whereof belongeth to the Bishopricke of *Killfynnoragh* two quarters and two-third parts of a quarter; also *Toonagh*, consisting of thirty-seven quarters and one-third part, whereof belongeth to the said Bishopricke of Kyllfynnoragh six quarters and one-third part, and to the Bishopricke of Killalow two quarters one-third part; also *Moynterargagh*, consisting of twelve quarters one-half part, whereof belongeth to the Bishopricke of Killfynnoragh one quarter; also *Glannomannagh*, consisting of twenty-one quarters and two-third parts, whereof belongeth to the Queen's Majestie as in right of the Abbay of Corcomroe ten quarters and two-thirds, and to the Bishopricke of Killfynnoragh two quarters and two-third parts; also Gloight-Donough-O'Loghline, consisting of eight quarters, whereof belongeth to the Bishopricke of Killfynnoragh one quarter one-third part; also Gloight-Jerroll, consisting of nine quarters one-third part, whereof belongeth to the Bishopricke of Killfynnoragh one quarter and a third part; also the Towne of the Gragannes, consisting of two quarters two-third part; also Muckenish, two-third parts; also *Carricogane*, consisting of one quarter one-third part; also the island called Aghnis, consisting of one quarter one-third part, which in the whole within that Barony cometh to one hundred and twenty-seven quarters and one-third part.

TULLAGHADEA.

9°. In the Barony of Tullaghadae there is a quantity of land called *Cloonofarrane*, consisting of nineteen quarters, whereof belongeth to the Bishopricke of Killalow four quarters; also *Too Inchiguine*, consisting of seven quarters; also *Moynee*, consisting of four quarters; also *Toenovicke*, consisting of fifteen quarters; also *Toevalaryne*, consisting of fourteen quarters, whereof belongeth to the Bishopricke of Killalow four quarters; also *Toekmalwoyre*, consisting of seventeen quarters, whereof belongeth to the Bishopricke of Killalow four quarters; also the *Dyserte*, consisting of four quarters, belonging to the Bishopricke of Killalow; also *Killfynnan Kilceoriske*, consisting of two quarters, belonging to the Bishopricke of Killalow; also *Magheryfargagh*, consisting of three score and twelve quarters, whereof belongeth to the Bishoppricke of Killalow one quarter; also *Tullaghcomone*, consisting of two quarters; alsoe *Killowlaghy*, consisting of thirty-two quarters; also *Aghryme*, consisting of one quarter, which in the whole within that Barony cometh to one hundred three score and seventeen quarters. All which being drawn into one total cometh to the aforesaid number of one thousand two hundred fifty-nine quarters and a half and one-third part, whereof belongeth unto Her Majestie three score and eight quarters two-third parts, and to the aforesaid Lords Spiritual one hundred twenty-seven quarters.

The said lords, chieftenios, gents, freeholders, and ffarmers, acknowledging the *manyfould benefitts and easements* which they find in possessing of their lands and goods, since the peaceable government of the said Lord Deputy, and the just dealinge of Sir Richard Binghame, Knight, their chief officer, as well against comon malefactors and spoyllards, also against *the unmeasurable cesses and oppresssions of all sorts of men of war heretofore laid upon them*, 𝔥𝔞𝔟𝔢 in consideration thereof, and for that alsoe, the said Right Honourable the Lord Deputie doth promise, covenant, and grant to and with the said lords, chieftenios, gents, freeholders, and inhabitants of the said County of Thomond, for and in the behalfe of the Queen's Most Excellent Majestie, that they and every of them, their heirs, successors, and assigns, for their lands within the said County of Thomond, shall from and after the date hereof be freely and *wholy discharged, acquitted, and exonerated for ever of and from all manner* of customs, taxes, charges, exactions, cuttings, impositions, purveying cuttings, findings, or boarding of souldiers, and *all other burdens whatsoever other than the rents, reservations, and charges hereafter in this indenture specified, and to be enacted by Parliament*, willingly and thankfully for them, their heirs, successors, assigns, given and granted, like as hereby they do give and grant to the said Right Honourable the Lord Deputy, and his heirs, to the use and behooffe of the Queen's Most Excellent Majestie, her heirs and successors for ever, *one yearly rent charge of ten shillings of good and lawful money of England, going out of every quarter of one thousand fourscore and seventeen quarters* of the aforesaid number of one thousand two hundred and fifty-nine quarters D, and one-third part of land, within the whole, amounteth yearly to the sum five hundred forty-three pounds tenn shillings sterling, payable at the feasts of St. Michael the Archangell and Easter, by even portions; the first payment to begin at the feast of St. Michael the Archangell next ensuing the date hereof, and so yearly for ever at the severall feasts aforesaid, at Her Highness's Exchequer, within the same realm of Ireland, or to the hands of ye Treasurer or General Receiver of the said realme for the time being. And for the lacke of money to be paid into the Exchequer as aforesaid, the same Treasurer or General Receiver to receive kyne to the value of the said rent, or soe much thereof as shall remain unpaid, att ye rate of thirteen shillings four pence sterling for every good and lawful beof. 𝕬𝖓𝖉 iff it fortune the said rent of five hundred forty-three pounds tenn shillings sterling to be behind and unpaide in part, or in all, in manner and form aforesaid, that then it shall be lawfull unto the said Right Honourable the Lord Deputie or other governor or governors of this realm, for the time being, or to the Treasurer or General Receiver for the time being, to enter and distrain in all and singular the lands, tenements, and hereditaments of the said one thousand four score and seaven quarters soe being in arrear, and the distress taken, to detain and keep until the said yearly rent as aforesaid be fully and wholly satisfied and paid. 𝔓𝔯𝔬𝔳𝔦𝔡𝔢𝔡 always that if it fortune any part of the quarters subject to this composition to be so *wast as that it beareth neither horne nor corne*, that the same be not laid upon the rest that is inhabited, till the lands so wast be inhabited as aforesaid.

And further, the persons above named, for them, their heirs, successors, and assigns, doe covenant, promise, and grant to and with the said Right Honourable the Lord Deputy and his heirs for and in the behalf of the Queen's Most Excellent Majestie, her heirs and successors, *not only to answer and beare yearly for ever to all hostings, rades, and journys* within the said Province of Conaught *and Thomond, whereas* and ( ) at what time they shall be thereunto commanded by the Lord Deputy, or other governor or governors of this realme, or by the chiefe officer of the said province, *forty good able horsemen and two hundred footmen, well armed, upon their owne proper costs and charges, over and besides the rent aforesaid* (the lands assigned by this indenture as domains to the mannors and houses of the late Earl of Thomond, the Barron of Inchiquine, and the Bisshopps of Killalow and Killfynnoragh, always excepted); but *also to answer and beare all general hostings* proclaimed in this realme, fifteen good and able horsemen and fiftie footmen, well armed and furnished with carriage and victualls upon their own proper costs and charges, during the time of the said hostings, if the

APPENDIX I.

Lord Deputy or other governor of this realm, for the time being, doe require the same, *securing* and *reserving always* this priviledge and favour of Her Majesties grace to the said Earl of Thomond, the Lord Barron of Inchiquine, and the Bishops of Killalow and Kilfynnoragh, that they shall in no other sort or manner answer or beare to this general hosting then as their peers of English—earles, barrons, and bishops doth or ought to doe. **And** *further, it is condescended (sic), concluded, and agreed* as well by the said Right Honble. the Lord Deputy for and in the behalf of the Queene's Most Excellent Majestie, and also by the said Donough Earl of Thomond, Murrough Baron of Inchiquin, Sir Tyrrolagh O'Brien, Knight, John Macnemarra, Daniel Roough McNemarra, Teige McMahoune, Tyrlagh McMahoune, Bryan (or Owen) Laughline, Rosse O'Laughline, Mahoune O'Dae, Dermott O'Dae, and Conor McGillreowgh, *and others of the Irishry above named*, in manner and forme following, (viz.) that *the names, stiles, and titles of captaines ships, Tanish ships, and all other Irish authorities and jurisdictions heretofore used by the said chieftaines and gentlemen, together with all ellection and customary division of lands, occasioning great strife and contention amongst* them, shall from henceforth be utterly *abolished, extinct, renounced*, put back within the said county of Thomond *for ever*. In consideration whereof, and for that Her Majestie doth graciously mind the benefit and advancement of every good subject according to his degree, *by reduceing of their uncertain and unlawful manner of takeing from others to a certain and more beneficial state of liveing for them and their heirs than their said pretended titles and claimes did or could hitherto afford them*. **The** said Right Honble. Lord Deputy for and in behalfe of the Queen's Most Excellent Majestie, and also the aforesaid lords, chieftains, gents, and freeholders, on the behalfe of themselves and the rest of the inhabitants of the said countrey, doth covenant, promise, and agree to and with the said Donogh, Earle of Thomond, **That** where the Barony of Ibrickane consisteth of three-quarters of land fully exonerated and discharged, the said Donogh, Earl of Thomond, shall have, hold, possess, and enjoy to him and to the heirs males of the body of his grandfather Donough O'Brien, late Lord Barron of Ibrickane, the said three score and three-quarters of *land freely exonerated and discharged from the said composition of five hundred and forty-three pounds ten shillings sterling, as a domain to his castles of Ibraccane, Cahirnishe, and Downorgan, with all the goods and chattels of persons* attainted of felony that shall happen or chance to dwell or inhabit within the aforesaid three score and of land, *all other casualties* and amerciaments that shall grow from time to time within the same; and whereas the Barrony of *Clonrande* consisteth of one hundred and seaventeen quarters of land, whereof thare is of abbey land eighteen quarters, and belonging to the Bisshoprick of Killalow seaven quarters, and soe remaineth three score and twelve quarters. **It is** likewise agreed that the said earle shall have, hold, possess, enjoy to him and his heirs for ever as aforesaid, *twelve quarters* of the said remainder as a *domayne* to his mannor of CLONRANDE, and one quarter to his *Castle of Clare*, freely exonerated and discharged of and from the said composition, and alsoe out of every quarter of the residue of the said quarters, being three score and nineteen five shillings sterling, amounting by the year to *nyneteen pounds* 15s. ½d. *sterling, in full recompense of all duties, exactions, and spendings by him claymed* upon the ffreeholders of the same note, charging the portion of the wast land upon the inhabitted; and that they and every of them according to his estate, their heirs and assigns, shall hold the said three score and nineteen quarters of the said earle and the heirs males of his grandfather as aforesaid *by knight's service; that is to say, by the fortieth part of a knight fee (?) and the rent aforesaid as of his* mannor of Clonronde, and *shall doe suite to his Courte Barron and Courte Leete of the said mannor,* together with all the goods and chattles of persons attainted of felonie that shall happen or chance to dwell and inhabitt within the aforesaid quarters of land assigned to him as well in *domayne as in services,* and all other casual ammercements that shall grow from time to time within the said townlands.

𝔄𝔫𝔡 whereas the Barrony of Dongynnyviggoon consisteth of 274 quarters, di., whereof belongeth to the Bisshoppricke of Rallatnoe (sic, quere *Killaloe*), nine quarters, and allowed to MCNEMARRAS, and ssone by way of freedome six quarters, and nine quarters in controversie betwixt the Barron of Inchiquine and Sir Tirlagh O'Briene, and soe remaineth two hundred and fiftie quarters di. It is farther covenanted, promised, granted, and agreed by the said Right Honourable the Lord Deputie for and in the behalfe of the Queen's Most Excellent Majestie, and the aforesaid Lord Chieftains, gents, and freeholders on the behalfe of themselves and the rest of the inhabitants of the County of Thomond, that for the better support or care of the state and dignitie of the said Earle, he shall have to him and his heirs as aforesaid *six quarters* of the aforesaid 250 quarters di. as a domain *to his Castle of Bunratty, freely exonerated and discharged of the said composition.* And one yearly rent charge of 5s. sterling goeing out of the residue of the said quarters, being 244 quarters di. to him and his heirs as aforesaid, amounting by the yeare to 62l. 2s. 6d. sterling, not charging the portion of the wast land upon the inhabitted. *In full recompense of all duties, exactions, and spendings by him claymed upon the freeholders of the same,* and that they and every of them, their heirs, and assigns, according to his rate, shall hold the same of the said Earle, and the heirs males of his grandfather, *by Knight's service,* that is to say, by the 40th part of a Knight's fee, and the rent aforesaid, as of his Castle of Bunratty, and shall alsoe doe suite to his Court Barron and Courtleete of his said Castle, together with all the goods and chattles of persons attainted of felony that shall happen or chance to dwell and inhabit within the aforesaid quarter of land assigned to him, as well in domayne as in services, and all other casualties and amerciaments that shall grow from time to time within the same.

And whereas the Barrony of Tullaghynaspyll consisteth of 228 quarters, whereof belongeth to the spiritual living of Tomgeny, Tullagh, and Moynooe, thirty-four quarters, to the Bishoprick of Killalow, five quarters, to ye Barron of Inchiquine, eighteen quarters, and to *McNemarra Rough*, as a freedome allowed him by this indenture, six quarters, to *Sir Edward Waterhouse*, Knight, nine quarters, whereof allowed to him as a free domaine to his Castle of Downasse, eight quarters, soe remaineth 156 quarters. It is upon like consideration, granted, covenanted, and agreed, as well by the said Right Honourable the Lord Deputy as the said Lords Chieftains, gents, freeholders, and the rest above-named, that the said Earle shall have to him and his heirs, masles as aforesaid, one yearly rent charge *of 5s. sterling, goeing out of every quarter of the said remaine of one hundred fifty-six quarters*, amounting by the yeare to 39*l.* sterling (not charging the portion of the wast land upon the inhabitted) *in full recompense of all his duties, exactions, and spending by him, claymed upon the freeholders and inhabitants* of the said Barrony, and that they and every of them (according to his rate), their heirs and assigns, shall hold the same of the Queen's Majestie, his heirs and successors, by Knight service, that is to say, by the 40th part of a Knight's fee, as of Her Majestie, or mannour of Innyshe, in the County Clare, with the *moyety* or *half fondeale* (sic) of all the goods and chattles of persons attainted of felonie that shall happen or chance to dwell and inhabitt within the aforesaid, 156 quarters of land, and all other casualties (&c., vide supra).

And whereas the Baronie of Clonderrealae consisteth of sixty-five quarters, whereof belongeth to the Bishop of Killalow 14 quarters, and to McMahowne, as a freedom allowed to his house of Clonedarralea and Dongen, 6 quarters, and so remaineth 45 quarters. It is upon like consideration granted, &c., that the Earle shall have to him and his heirs as aforesaid one yearly rent-charge of 5*s.* sterling gooing out of every quarter of said 45, amounting by year to 11*l.* 5*s.*, &c., by 40 parts of a Knight's fee, as of her house or mannor of Innyshe, in the County of Clare, with the moyetie or halfendall of all the goods and chattles, of possessions, &c. (as above).

Moyartie, 67 quarters.

Bishoprick Killaloe . 37
Turlough McMahonne, as a free domain to his house of Moyartie and Dounehoissie.
    Quarters . 6
                               —43
And so remaineth . . —24 quarters.
It is upon like consideration, &c., 5*s.* a quarter, or 6*l.*

The Baronie of Gragganes consisteth of quarters 127⅓

Bishoprick of Kyllfennoragh in chiefery,	Qrs. 10⅔
In domaine to his house in Kyllfynnoragh and Killashykll mannor,	4
Bishop Killalow in chiefry,	2⅔
To O'Laughline as a free domain to his houses of the Gragranes and Glancollowkylly,	6

———23⅓

And soe remaineth ———104

To said Earle 5s. a year, or 26l., and the rest as above.

Barrony of Tullaghada, quarters 177
Bishoprick Killalow, ... 19

156 (8)

The Lord Barron of *Inchiquine,* for ye better supportacon of his name and dignity, shall hold, possess, and enjoy to him and his heirs male of the body of his great grandfather Morrough O'Brien 6 quarters, as a domain to his Manor of Inchiquine, freely exonerated, &c., and discharged of and from this composition and all other rents and demands of the Earle of Thomond; and the said Lord Barron shall *have* also to him and his heirs males as aforesaid one yearly rent-charge of 5s. sterling, gooening out of every quarter of the residue, or 38l. sterling per annum (conditions of duty and obligation mutually as above, but to Lord Barron of Inchiquine); alsoe said Lord Barron shall have, hold seven quarters of his own land in Barony of Tullaghynaspyll freely discharged of this composition.

And further, Lord Bisshop of Killalow and his successors shall have 5 quarters of land as a domain to his house or manor of Killalow freely exonerated and discharged of this composition, with all the goods and chattles of persons attainted of felonie and all other casualties and amerciaments growing of the inhabitants dwelling within the said 5 quarters from time to time; and that allsoe the Lord Bishop of Kilfynnoragh and his successors *like freedom* in 4 quarters as a domain adjoining to his houses of Killfynnoragh and Killaspicklomann, in Barony of Corcomroe.

And further, with *the said Tirlogh O'Briene,* Knight, that where the Barronie of Corcamroe consisteth of 147 quarters, whereof belongeth to the Queen 6 quarters, to Bishop Killfynoragh 17, *to Dean* 1 *quarter,* 3 *quarters di. allowed to Boetius Clanchye as a free* domain to his house or castle of *Knockfine*, and soe remaineth 114 quarters, that the said Turlogh O'Briene, for the better maintenance of said degree, whereunto it hath pleased the Queen's Majestie to call him, shall possess and enjoy to him and his heirs 14 quarters *of the aforesaid as a domain to his house of Douoghyconnogher, Innyshtynnan*, and *Ballynelackney*, within the said Barronie, freely exonerated and discharged of and from this composition, and of and from all other rents and *demands of the Earle of Thomond* and his heirs. And that the said Sir Tirlough shall have to him and his heirs one yearly rent-charge of 5s. sterling, gooing out of every quarter of the aforesaid 100 quarters, amounting by year to 25l., not charging the portion of the wast land upon the inhabitants *in full recompense of all duties, exactions, and spending claymed*, as well by him as by the Earle of Thomond, upon the freeholders of the said Barrony, and that they and every of them according to his rate, their heirs and assigns, shall hold the same of the same (said Sir Tirlough and his heirs) for ever as of his castle or mannor of Doughhyconougher, in the Barrony aforesaid, by Knight's service, viz., by the 40th part of a Knight's fee, and the rent aforesaid, and shall alsoe doe suit to the Court Barron and Leete of the said castle or manor of *Doughyconnougher*, with all the goods, &c., &c., *within said* 14 *quarters assigned as* domain, with the moyetie or *halfendall of like royaltie* growing from time to time within the said 100 quarters of land assigned to him in service. 𝔄𝔫𝔡 it is likewise covenanted, granted, &c., &c., with *Shane McNemarra*, otherwise called *McNemarra Sinne*, that for his better maintenance of living he shall hold, &c. . . . . for his heirs and assigns for ever, for the castle (?) of *Cnappocke*, in the Barrony of Dongynnyviggoon, with four quarters of land with their appurtenances belonging to the same, and two quarters of land with their appurtenances in the *town of Dangen*, freely exonerated and discharged of and from this composition of and from all other rents or demands of the Earle of Thomond and his heirs, together with all the goods and chattles of persons attained, &c., &c. . . . . and shall also hold and possess 19 quarters of land, with their appurtenances, belonging to the same, whereof he is now to be seized as his inheritance, the same to be holden of Her Majestie, &c., by Knight's service, viz., by the twentieth (sic) part of a Knight's fee, as of her house or mannor of Innysh. And that after the decease of the said Shane McNemarra, all such rents, duties, and customs as are challenged to be belonging to the name of McNemarra Sissine shall (in consideration that the same is nott extorted and—) be henceforth utterly determined and extinct for ever.

𝔄𝔫𝔡 it is likewise covenanted, granted, promised, and agreed as aforesaid, to and with *Daniell Roogh McNemarra*, otherwise McNemarra Roogh, that for his better maintenance of living, he shall have, hold, possess, and enjoy to him, his heirs, and for ever, the castle of *Garruaroghe, in the Barony of Tullaghnaspyll*, with four quarters of land with their appurtenances belonging to the same. And two quarters of land with their appurtenances belonging to the town of Dongen, wholly exonerated and from composition, &c., to Earle of Thomond, &c., and shall alsoe have 11 quarters of land, whereof he is said to be now seized, as his inheritance in the Barrony of Tullaghynaspyll, the same to be holden of Her Majestie by Knight's service, viz., one-twentieth part of a Knight's fee, as of her Majestie's house or manor of Innyshe. And that after the decease of the said Danl. Roogh McNemarra all such rents, duties, and customs as are claymed to be belonging to the name of McNemarra Roogh, in consideration that the same is but extorted, shall be henceforth extinguished and determined for ever.

And it is likewise covenanted to and with *Tiege McMahowne*, otherwise called McMahowne, that for his better maintenance of living, his heirs, &c., shall have, hold, &c., for ever the *Castle of Clonderlaw*, in the Barony of Clonedderlaw, with three quarters of land with their appurtenances freely belonging to the same, and to his Castle of Dongen, three quarters, &c., each one rated, &c., and shall also enjoy eleven quarters on Knight's service; and that after decease of said Teige McMahone all such rents, duties, and *customs as are challenged to be belonging to the name of McMahowne*, shall, in consideration that the same is butt extorted, be extinguished, &c., &c.

And it is likewise, &c., that the *said Tirlagh McMahowne* shall hold the towne of *Moyartie* with two quarters, and the Castle of *Downobegg* with four quarters, also four quarters.

And it is likewise covenanted, &c., with Owen O'Laughline, otherwise called O'Laughline, that for his better maintenance, &c., and shall hold, &c., the *Castle of the Graganes* and the Castle of Glancollidkylle, with two quarters of land discharged from demands of Earl of Thomond or Tirlagh O'Briene, their heirs, &c., to be holden by Knight's fee, and that after decease of, &c., as above.

Also it is likewise, &c., with *Mahowne O'Briene of Clonduane* (?) . . . . . said Castle of Clonduane, ... with six quarters freely exonerated from composition, rents, claims, demands of Earl of Thomond and the Lord Barron of Inchiquine, on Knight's service, &c. . . . . (*N.B.*—No reservation of life use, as supra.)

And it is condescended, granted, &c., for better inhabiting of *Sir Edward Waterhouse, Knight, to inhabit the lands which he has purchased in the said County of Thomond, bordering upon ill neighbours,* that he shall have, hold, possess, &c., to him, and heirs, and assigns, the Castle of *Downassye, otherwise called Annaghmore, in the Barrony of Tullaghnaspyll,* which and with eight quarters of land, with their appurtenances, &c. The same to be holden in soccage, according to the tenure and purport of Her Majesties' letters, bearing date xxviii.th Augusti, in the xxviii.th yeare of Her Majesty's reign, discharged from all manner of services, other than are mentioned in the letters patents.

And that *Doctor James Neylaine, in respect of his assistance and good inclynation towards the State*, whereof he hath good testimony, under the hands of many governours of this realme, shall have, hold, &c., to him, his heirs, and assigns, the Castles of *Ballaly, Ballyvickahill, and Ballycowrie,* with 240 acres of land to them belonging, freely *acquitted, exonerated, &c., from composition,* rents, demands, &c., of the Earl of Thomond, McNemarra, or any other, for him and heirs for ever, to be holden by knight's service,—viz., one-fortieth part of a knight's ffee, as of her said house and manor of Innigshe.

And that *Boetius Clancy, of Knocfynne, gent.,* in regard of his birth, learning, and good bringing upp, shall have, hold, possess, and enjoy, to him, his heirs, and assigns, the said Castle of Knockfynne, with three-quarters and a half of land, with their appurtenances, freely acquitted, exonerated, and discharged of and from this composition, and from all rents and demands of Sir Torlagh O'Briene, or any other, their heirs and assigns, together with all the goods, &c.
. . . . . Alsoe *Edward White,* Clarke of the Councill, in the said Province of Conaght, shall, in consideration of his service, have, hold, possess, and enjoy to him and his heirs, *the Castle of Crattalagh,* with three-quarters of land lying in the said *Crattagh Kuyrenboy, Portreyne, and Clansynshon,* freely exonerated, &c., also of all duties, &c., from McNemarra, or other, to be holden of the Queen's Majesty, by Knight's service—viz., 40 part, &c.

And that alsoe George Cusacke of *Dromolyne,* in the Barrony of Danginnyviggoon, gent., shall, for his better encouragement to inhabit the west land by him purchased in the said county, have, hold, possess, enjoy to him and his heirs, the said Dromolyne, with four quarters of land belonging to the same, freely exonerated and discharged, &c., by Knight's service.

And the said Lords and Temporal and chieftains, gents, freeholders, farmers, and inhabitants, for them and either of them, their heirs, successors and assigns, have and by these presents doe give full power, consent, and assent that the present deed indented   in Court of Chancery   there to   of record for ever.

In Witness whereof each of the aforesaid parties have hereunto putt their seales and subscribed the seaventeenth day of August Anno Domini 1585, in the seaventeenth year of the reigne of our Soveraigne Lady Lady Elizabeth, Queen of England, France, and Ireland, Defender of the Faith.

        Do. Thomond.
        Mauriti Laoon.
        Donaldi Syne (Brien) ?
        Dame Marie M. G. Garrett Inchiquine
          for the young Barron her Sonne.

Therlagh O'Briene.
1. Meriortagh O'Briene (mark, M. B.).
2. McNemarra Roogh (mark, D.).
3. Teige McMahowne (T. M.).
   Tirlagh McMahowne.
4. Mahowne O'Dia (is marke D).
5. Mahowne O'Briens (M. V.).
6. Owen O'Loghlins (marke D.).
7. Rosse O'Loghlins (marke T. S.).
   Edward White.
   Geo. Cusacke.
   James Nelleyne.
   Boetius Clanchy.
8. Connor McGilreaghs (marke D.).
9. Donogh Glanckoigh (is marke W.).
10. Conor O'Brienes (marke, G. O.).
    George Ffeminge.

Whereas humble suite is made unto us by the three daughters and co-heirs of Thady McMurrough O'Brien, of Ballingown, Tirlagh McTeige O'Brien, of *Boolacorige*, Murrough McConnor O'Brien, of *Cahirmonan*, and Moriatagh McConor O'Brien of Drumleyne, to grant unto them certaine quarters of land free of Her Majesty's composition in respect of their birth and dignitie, viz., the Castle of Ballycarre and two quarters of land thereunto belonging, to Onora Ny Brien; the Castle of Tullamore and four quarters of land with their appurtenances, to Slany ny Brien and Ony ny Brien; the Castell of Bealytige (?) with three quarters . . . . (lacuna) Inyshelane adjoining to . . . . (lacuna) . . . . . the first part at Inyshoviccony . . . . . . to Conor O'Brien, Caharnonane with three quarters of land and appurtenances, viz., the quarters of Cahernonanmore, the quarter of Carroowgane, Curragh-fflaherty, the quarter of Ballypadine to Morortagh O'Conor O'Brien of Dromlyne, the quarter of the Castle of Dromlyne, the quarter of Clensoghine, adjoining to the same, and the quarter of *Manish Begg*, belonging to the house of Manisbegg, although we cannot grant the same, without breaking the Order of Her Majesties composition, yet we think reasonable that the same be granted unto them by Letters Pattents from Her Majestie iff soe itt shall stand with the pleasure of the Right Honble.

2603.

II°. Grant unto our well-beloved Tireleigh O'Brien, Esq., son of Sir D. O'B., Knight, the office of seneschall of the two Baronies of Corkamrowe and Burren, in Co. Clare, province of Munster, to enjoy the said office, with profits, &c., during so long time as he shall, will, and uprightly behave himself in the exercise of the said office. And further, we give full power and authority to the said

Sir T. O'B. to call together and assemble all freeholders, farmers, and all other the inhabitants being abiding and dwelling within the said baronies, of what profession, nation, degree, or condition . . . to charge and command to do what shall be for the defence of the two baronies, the public wealth of the inhabitants of the same, or punishments of malefactors.

Sir T. is to prosecute, invade, chase away, banish, withstand, punish, correct by all manner of ways and means, all malefactors, their servants, followers, adherents, which are or shall be malefactors, rebels, vaccabounds (sic) *rimnors, Irish harpers, idell men and women*, and all such unprofitable members whatsoever, &c. All to assist.

Letters to be made patents, &c. 13 March, 1575.

III°. King James's letter to Daniel O'Brien, son of Sir Turlough O'Brien.

Whereas, at the humble suit of the inhabitants of the province of Connaught and county of Clare, we signified our pleasure to be to accept a surrender of them of all such lands as they respectively should be found to be seized and possessed of, and by one or more grants under the great seal of that of our realm to grant the same unto them, their heirs and assignes, or such person or persons, his or their heirs and assignes, as they shall nominate and appoint as of our Castle of Athlone by . . . services.

We are informed by the humble suit of our faithful subject, Daniel O'Brien, of Dowagh Iconogher, in our said county of Clare, Esqre., son and heir-apparent unto Sir Turlough O'Brien, Knight, that by the indentures of composition made in the seven and twentieth year of our late sister Queen Elizabeth, it was, amongst other things, agreed that all the lands in the Barony of Corkamrowe, in our said county of Clare (except the lands of the Bishop of Kilfenora and some other few parcels in the said indentures mentioned), should be hould of the said Sir Turlough, his heirs, by certain services and yearly rents, with services and rents . . . surrenders unto us by force of our foresaid warrant and letters patents thereupon to be made, our said subject, Daniel O'Brien, unto whom his said father conveyed the premises, is in danger to lose if we out of our princely bounty prevent not the same.

And therefore hath humbly besought us to be graciously pleased to grant that in all grants from us to be made by force of our said warrant of and lands, tenements, or hereditaments within the said Barony of Corkamrowe, the immediate tenure be reserved to be holden of the said Daniel, his heirs and assignes, by the services and yearly rents mentioned by the said indentures unto his said father, to whose humble suit we have condescended. Wherefore we will and authorize you to provide and take order that in all grants to be passed from us of any lands, tenements, or hereditaments, within the said barony, by force of our said warrant, to any person or persons other than the said D. O'Brien, the immediate tenure be reserved unto the said Daniel, &c., by the services and yearly rents mentioned for his father by the said indentures.

And that the immediate (right) be reserved unto us, our heirs and successors, in such manner as in our former warrant is expressed.

And we are further pleased, and so do will and authorize, to cause to be passed by grant from us under the great seal of that realm unto the said Daniel, &c., all such courts, liberties, privileges, jurisdictions within the said barony, as in and by the said indentures we mentioned for his said father, with such other liberties, privileges, and immunities as to you shall be thought fit. And these our letters shall be as well to your own deputy and chancellor there now being as to any other, &c., hereafter given under our signet at our palace at Westminster, the four and twentieth day of December, in the 19th year of our reign of England, France, and Ireland, and of Scotland the five and fiftieth, &c., &c.

To the Lord Viscount Grandison,
    our Deputy, &c., &c.   30 Nov., 1621.

IV°. Copy of an Irish writing which the slucht or descendants of Muilleaghin O'Loughlin past to Conor O'Brien, the original remaining with Boetius MacClancy, of Knockfyn. 9th June, 1590.

Be it known to all men who read or hear writing that we are now in existance of the descendents of Malleikey O'Loughlin, of Ballyvaughan, i.e., Trial, the son of Ross, and Donogh the son of Brien, and Lucius the son of Mahon, of Ballyayvola, in the agrement that passed between Connor the son of Turlough O'Brien, the great grandfather of the present Earl and our progenitors, to be from ourselves unto you Donogh O'Brien, and in concordance with that here we sign these in presence of those people who will be as witness to this instrument, and this is the agreement.

All those the descendents of Mallakey and of Ballyvaughan and of Binnrow, and all their hereditary estates to be made over all conferred by us and our heirs on Connor O'Brien and his heirs after him, and that we and they are bound not to sell or mortgage any castle or estate but by and with the consent of Connor or his heirs after him, and that said Connor or his heirs are the true heirs of Mallakey. And we further bind ourselves to be at his will, and our dependants also to be at the will, of Connor O'Brien and his heirs after him.

Furthermore, I, the Earl of Thomond, acknowledge on my honour that I promised whatever part of the estates or castles belonging to these people that came to perfection that I will leave it to the arbitration of Boetious MacClanchey, John Tirney, and Eugene O'Daly to be from the Earl unto them, and we will not put any of the lands that Boetious MacClanchey holds in this agreement, anno x.p. 1590. This 9th day of June, at Knockfinn, we gave our consent to this writing, and signed it in concordance with the old agreement, and the heirs of those people to be bound for ever one to the other.

I, Gilbert Dovoren, wrote this copy.

Donogh Thomond.

Donogh O'Loughlin copia vera ex lbs.

Bat Clancy Nial O'Loughlin, written deade, was written, read, and published.

John Tierney.
Eugene O'Daly.

O'Conor's Deed.

V°. Omnibus Christi fidelibus ad quos per præsens scriptum pervenerit. Salutem. Sciatis, nos Teige McPhelim O'Conor, de Killeylagh, gent.; Cahil McMahown O'Conor, de Cahirmenaubeg.

Donell Mc—— O'Conor, de Fantii, gent.; Conor McOwen O'Conor, de Ballyhea, gent.; Conor MacConor O'Conor, de Innisdyman, gent.; Bryen Mohoone O'Conor, de Liskannor, gent.; Brian McCahil O'Conor, de Down-na-goarr, gent.; Donell McTeige O'Conor, de Glan, gent.; Edmund Altie McRory O'Conor, de Ballygrical, gent.; et Brian McConor O'Conor, de Innishdyman, gent.

Remisisse, relaxasse, et o͞io de nobis et hereditibus nris. imppetund Terrentio al Therrallay O'Briean, de Innishdyman, in Co. Clare. Armigero totum jus nostrum, titulum et clameum quod habemus, vel aliqus nostrum habet, vel habere in futuro poterimus, de et in omnibus terris et tenementis et heriditamentis.

Dough alias Dough I. Conor, Innisdyman, LisCannor, Dunebal Jehearie Dunnagoar. Tulla, Innishovehause et Ballagh in Corckomoroe, alias Barronia de Dough in al. Terralagh, heredibus et assignatis suis imppetum. ad proprium usum dic Ter. also Tarralagh et hered. su. aliquid jus, Titulum vel Clameum in premissis habere poterimus. In cujus rei testimonium nostra signa, et nostra manualia apposuimus.

Datum apud. Ballyvehane vicessimo secundo die men Januar, 1582, ad reg. dnœ. nos Elizabethæ Ang. Fran. et Hib. Reginæ fidei defensoris. Anno vicessimo quinto.

(The signs are in Irish character.)

Witnesses,

Boetius Clancy.
Dionys. Hellanus.

James Coyne.

APPENDIX II.

THE CASTLES OF THE COUNTY OF CLARE.

This return of Clare castles for the year 1584 is preserved in a Trinity College manuscript. The writer tries in the text—Chapter XVII.—to unriddle the barbarous English rendering of the Irish names.

BARONY OF TALLAGHNANASPULL.

Containing McNamara's County, alias Mortimer's County, by east the Baron of Inchiquin and Donald Reagh McNamara, chiefs in same.

Gentlemen.	Castles.	
Donald Reagh McNamara	Tullagh	1
Edmond O'Grady	Toymegrane	2
Ditto	Maynoe	3
Donough and Rory McNamara	Ffortingaroingnagh	4
Donald Reagh McNamara	Flychlenearly	5
Rory McNamara's son's	Island Caher	6
Donough McNamara	Killalowe	7
Moriertagh Custos	O'Brien's Bridge	8
Baron of Inchiquin	Castlelough	9
Shane na Gettagh	Dunasse	10
Donnell Roe	Cuttislough	11
Teige oge McCommea	Neadenmorry	12
Turlough MacDonnellroe	Glanomra	13
Donnell Reagh MacNamara	Scartcashel	14
Sivda, MacRory	Moynetallown	15
Turlough O'Brien	Gleanmadow	16
Flan McNamara's son	Moynogeanagh	17
Donnell Reagh McNamara	Tyrowannin	18
Shane MacMahon	Enagh O'Floyn	19
Shane MacDonnell	Beallacuttin	20
Brian MacDonnell	Beallacarilly	21
Comea McMahon	Beallamhullin	22
Earl of Thomond	Castelcattagh	23
Donough McConoher	Abereynagh	24
Fynin McLoughlin	Rosroe	25
Teige Oultagh	Ballymogashill	26
Corney McShane, reagh	Quaromoyre	27
Same	Callane	28
Rory McMahowne	Kilkishen	29
Same	Lisoffin	30
Same	Lismeehan	31

APPENDIX II.

BARONY OF TALLAGHNANASPULL—*continued.*

Gentlemen.	Castles.	
Turlough O'Brien	Fomerla	32
Same	Tyreadagh	33
Shane McNamara	Cappagh	34
Edmd. O'Grady	Skariff	35
Same	Truagh	36
Rory Meal Macffynin	Beallagh	37

DANGAN WEST.

MacNamara's County.   Shane McNamara chief in same.

Shane McNamara	Dangan	38
Turlogh O'Brien	Cnoppogue	39
Shane McNamara	Dangenbrack	40
Donogh McMorough	Quinchy	41
Donogh MacMahowe	Dromollyn (Dromline)	42
William Nellaw	Ballyhanneen	43
Brune O'Brien	Castleton nemanagh	44
James Nellan	Ballycasheen	45
Same	Ballyally	46
Donoghue MacClanchy	Ballycashell	47
Donogh O'Brien	Mughaue	48
		49
		50
		51
		52
Earl of Thomond	Rossmanaher	53
Fineen MacLoughlin	Seywarro	54
Donel MacTeige	Crattelaghmore	55
Shane McNamara	Crattalaghmall	56
Earl of Thomond	Bunratty	57
Same	Cloynemonegh	58
Donel MacNamara	Crattalagh Keal	59
Moriartagh O'Brien	Drumline	60
Donogh MacClanchy	Clonloghan	61
Teige MacClanchy	Ballynaclogh (Stone Hall)	62
Moriartagh MacClanchy	Nurlin	63
Brian na Fforiry	Flynish	64
Mac Enery Trony	Ballincraige	65
Donogh O'Brien	Rachavollayne	66
Teige MacMorrough	Ballyconilly	67
Donogh O'Grady	Cloyne	68
Shane MacMahowne	Corbally	69
Donogh MacClanchy	Bodevoher	70

CLOYNDERLAW.

Containing East Corkevaskin.   Teige McMahowne chief in same.

Teige MacMahowne	Dangan Moyburke	71
Same	Clonytheralaw	72
Same	Caheracon	73
Same	Bally MacColman	74
Same	Derrycrossan	75
Teige MacConor O'Brien	Carroobrighane	76
Teige MacMoriertagh Cam	Donogrogue	77

MOYARTA.

Containing West Corkevaskin. Turlogh MacMahowne chief in same.

Gentlemen.	Castles.	
Charles Cahane (by inheritance called a Corboe)	Inish Catha	78
James Cahane	Ballykette	79
Turlough MacMahowne	Carrigahowly	80
Same	Moyarta	81
Same	Dunlecky	82
Sir Donnell O'Brien, Knt.	Dunmore	83
Same	Dunbeg	84

TUAGH MORE Y CONOR.

Containing Corkemroe. Sir Donel O'Brien, Knt., chief in same.

Sir Donel O'Brien	Inisdyman	85
Same	Glan	86
Same	Ballhanire	87
Teige MacMorroh	Tullowmore	88
Same	Ffante	89
Same	Ballingowne	90
Teige MacMorrogh	Inchonea	91
Same	Ballyshanny	92
Same	Raveen	93
Sir Donell O'Brien	Beancorroe	94
Teige MacMorrough	Cahirnimane	95
Sir Donell O'Brien	Tullagh	96
Teige MacMorrough	Legmeneagh	97
Sir Donnell O'Brien	Dinnegoir	98
Teige MacMorrogh	Sunny c Phelim	99
Conor MacClanchy	Tuomullen	100
Teige MacMorrogh	Ballanclacken	101
Same	Beallagh	102
Same	Lockbulligan	103
Same	Kylemna	104
Sir Donel O'Brien	Duagh	105
Sir Donel O'Brien	Lis Cannor	106

GREGANS (Burren Barony).

O'Loughlen	Caherclogan	107
Same	Lysegleeson	108
Same	Cahirenally	119
Same	Ballymonoghan	110
Same	Meghanos	111
Same	Glensteed	112
Same	Gregans	113
Same	Glaninagh	114
Same	Ballyvaughan	115
Same	Shanmokeas	116
Same	Nacknasse	117
Same	Kynvarra	118
Same	Turlough	119
Same	Glancollymkilly	120

APPENDIX II.

GREGANS (Burren Barony)—*continued.*

Gentlemen.	Castles.	
Same	Neassalee	121
Same	Castleton	122
Same	Creaghwell	123
Same	Rughaine	124

TULLAGH O'DEA.
Sir Donel O'Brien, Knt., chief in same.

Gentlemen.	Castles.	
Baron of Inchiquin	Inchiquin	125
Mahon MacBrien O'Brien	Tiremacbryne	126
Same	Ballycottry	127
Same	Carrowduff	128
Teige MacMorrogh	Bohinim	129
Moriertagh Gorr	Cahercorcraine	130
Moriertagh, Garr	Rath	131
Sir Donel O'Brien	Killinbuoy	132
Teige Mac MacMorrogh	Drominglass	133
Mahowne O'Dea	Bealnalicke; Magowna	134
O'Griffie	Ballygriffll	135
Donogh Duff MacConsadine	Ballyharahan (Port)	136
Earl of Thomond	Mœthrie	137
Baron of Inchiquin	Derryowen	138
Mahon O'Brien	Clonowyne	139
Dermot O'Brien	Cloynshelhearne	140
Same	Owarronnaguille	141
Owen MacSwyne	Doonmulvihill	142
Same	Carriganooher	143
Same	Bealnafireamadronayn	144
Donel Meal O'Dea	Desert	145
Mahon (the Baron's Son)	Kilkeedy	146

CLONRAWDE.
Earl of Thomond chief in same.

Gentlemen.	Castles.	
Earl of Thomond	Clonrawde	147
Same	Clare	148
Same	Inish	149
Baron of Inchiquin	Killone	150
Same	Ballymacooda	151
Conogher MacClanchy	Enerishy	152
Brian Duff	Shalen	153
Teige MacMorrough	Maghowny	154
Teige MacConor O'Brien	Inishacivahny	155
Same	Inishdagrome	156
Same	Inishnawar	157
MacGillereagh	Crag Brien	158
Same	Tyrmiclane	159
MacCraith	Island Magrath	160
Teige MacConor	Belacorick	161
Baron of Ibrickan (eldest son of the Earl of Thomond)	Moyobreacain	162
Earl of Thomond	Caherrush	163
Tiege MacConoher	Tromra	164
Teige MacMorrogh	Donogan	165

ABBIES.[1]

		Possessed by	
Clare	. . .	Sir Donel and Tiege Mac-Connor his Son . . .	1
Inish	. . . . .	James Nellan	2
St. John's Nunnery (Killone)	.	Baron of Inchiquin . . .	3
Corcomroe	. . . .	Same	4
Island Chanons	. . .	Earl of Thomond . . .	5
Kiltena	. . . . .	Same	6
Quinchy	. . . . .	Friers	7
Inchcronan	. . . .	Same	8

ROUND TOWERS IN KILLALOE DIOCESE.

Cloigtheach Round Tower, par of Kilnaboy, Bar of Inchiquin.
,, ,, par of Dysert ,, No. 24.
,, ,, par of Drumcliffe, Bar Islands, No. 33.
,, ,, par of Inniscattery.
,, ,, par of Inniscaltra.
,, ,, par of Roscrea.

ANCIENT CROSSES IN CLARE.

St. Flannan's, Killaloe, Barony of Tulla, Lower.
St. Tola's Cross, Dysert, Barony of Inchiquin.
Knockannacrusha Cross, Dysert, Barony of Inchiquin.
Inneenboy Cross, Kilnaboy ,,
Kilfenora Cross, in Corcomroe.
Noughaval Cross, in Burren.
Termon Cross, in Burren, Parish of Carran.

[1] *History of the Diocese of Killaloe.* Canon Dwyer.

www.ingramcontent.com/pod-product-compliance
Lightning Source LLC
Chambersburg PA
CBHW020100020526
44112CB00032B/627